A Special Issue of
Visual Cognition

Mechanisms of Visual Attention
A Cognitive Neuroscience Perspective

Edited by

Werner X. Schneider

Ludwig-Maximilians-Universität, München, Germany

Sabine Maasen

Max-Plank-Institute for Psychological Research, München, Germany

Routledge
Taylor & Francis Group
LONDON AND NEW YORK

First published 1998 by Psychology Press Ltd

Published 2018 by Routledge
2 Park Square, Milton Park, Abingdon, Oxon OX14 4RN
52 Vanderbilt Avenue, New York, NY 10017

First issued in paperback 2018

Routledge is an imprint of the Taylor & Francis Group, an informa business

Subject Index compiled by Christine Boylan
Cover design by Joyce Chester
Typeset by Quorum Technical Services Ltd., Cheltenham, UK

ISBN 13: 978-1-138-87734-4 (pbk)
ISBN 13: 978-0-86377-981-7 (hbk)

MIX
Paper from responsible sources
FSC™ C013985
www.fsc.org

Printed in the United Kingdom
by Henry Ling Limited

Contents

VISUAL COGNITION, 1998, 5 (1/2), 1–8

An Introduction to "Mechanisms of Visual Attention: A Cognitive Neuroscience Perspective"

Werner X. Schneider
Department of Experimental Psychology, Ludwig-Maximilians-University, Munich, Germany

There is a growing consensus that the computation of the "internal visual world" does not occur in a purely automatic and obligatory way. Humans process part of the available visual information with priority dependent either on the current task (intention) or the structure of the stimulation. This assignment of priority in visual processing is usually termed "visual attention". Most of what we currently know about visual attention is based on behavioural studies in humans. Such experimental paradigms as "spatial pre-cueing" (e.g. Posner & Petersen, 1990), "visual search" (e.g. Wolfe, 1994), "partial report" (e.g. van der Heijden, 1992), "flanker interference" (e.g. Eriksen, 1995) and "negative priming" (e.g. Fox, 1995) have been developed in the tradition of experimental psychology over the last decades. During the past few years, an increasing number of neuropsychological and neuroscience studies on visual attention have extended the database. Neuropsychological experiments with brain-damaged patients and animals have attempted to identify the role of different brain areas for the control of visual processing priority (for overviews, see Driver & Mattingley, 1995; Duncan, Humphreys, Ward, & Shapiro, 1997; Humphreys & Bruce, 1989; Posner & Petersen, 1990); the dependent variables in the main have been behavioural measures, such as reaction time and accuracy. In the neurosciences, the effects of visual attention have been measured in modulations of brain activity. At the level of individual neurons, single-unit recordings have revealed firing rate changes of attentional manipulations (for overviews, see Desimone & Duncan, 1995; Duncan et al., 1997). Event-related potentials (ERP) derived from very large populations of neurons have provided insights

Requests for reprints should be addressed to Werner X. Schneider, Department of Experimental Psychology, Ludwig-Maximilians-University, Leopoldstr. 13, 80802 Munich, Germany. E-mail: wxs@mip.paed.uni.muenchen.de

I would like to thank Heiner Deubel, Martin Eimer and especially Martin Fischer for constructive comments on an earlier draft of the manuscript.

into the temporal structure of prioritized processing (for overviews, see Eimer, this issue; Hillyard, Mangun, Woldorff, & Luck, 1995). Information about the brain site of attention-dependent neural activity modulations has been gained by functional brain imaging methods such as PET and fMRI (e.g. Corbetta, Shulman, Miezin, & Petersen, 1995; Posner & Raichle, 1994).

In summary, our scientific knowledge about visual attention has increased considerably in the last decades and now consists of behavioural as well as neurobiological findings. However, there is still not much consensus about the mechanisms that underlie the data from experiments on attention. The critical issues include: Where within the processing system does priority assignment and selection occur ("early" and/or "late")? How is selection realized? Is it space- and/or object-based? How is visual attention controlled? (For overviews, see Allport, 1989, 1993; Johnston & Dark, 1986; Schneider, 1993.) Furthermore, the assumption of a single selection mechanism has recently been challenged (see Allport, 1989, 1993). It cannot be taken for granted that the behavioural measures of "visual attention" in different experimental paradigms, such as spatial pre-cueing, partial report and negative priming, and in neuropsychological "attention disorders" (such as different versions of neglect) refer to the same mechanism. Simply using the same term, namely "visual attention", does not verify the assumption of a single selection mechanism.

Depending on the answers to the above questions, different and partly incompatible theories of visual attention have been postulated over the last 20 years (see Bundesen, 1990; Duncan & Humphreys, 1989; LaBerge & Brown, 1989; Posner & Petersen, 1990; Treisman, 1988; Treisman & Gelade, 1980; van der Heijden, 1992; Wolfe, 1994; for overviews, see Allport, 1989, 1993; Schneider, 1993). Fortunately, the recent inclusion of neurobiological data on attentional effects and on the architecture of the visual system has helped to constrain this theorizing. Based in part on these additional neurobiological constraints and on new behavioural data, a move to a consensus on the central issues has taken place. One example of such convergence is the assumption that at least one attentional mechanism in vision is space-based (see Bundesen, this issue; Humphreys & Heinke, this issue; LaBerge & Brown, 1989; Logan, 1996; Olshausen, Andersen, & VanEssen, 1993; Schneider, 1993; van der Heijden, 1992; Wolfe, 1994).

This approach to explicitly relate data and theories from cognitive psychology and neuroscience in an attempt to understand classical "cognitive" domains such as visual attention has been labelled "cognitive neuroscience" (for overviews, see Gazzaniga, 1995; Humphreys & Bruce, 1989; Kosslyn & Koenig, 1992; Posner & Raichle, 1994). As noted above, an advantage of this approach is that information about the architecture of the visual system and about the effects of visual attention manipulations at the level of brain activity (single cells, activation of whole brain areas) provide additional constraints for resolving debated issues on the nature of visual attentional mechanisms.

A second promising prospective to tackle these issues is to ask what kinds of functions visual attention processes might serve. Usually, empirical research focuses on certain experimental paradigms, such as visual search or spatial pre-cueing, but does not consider the possible functions of attention (for discussions of this issue, see Allport, 1987; Neumann, 1987; Prinz, 1983; Schneider, 1993). However, it is reasonable to assume that attentional mechanisms have evolved to fulfil certain basic functions. "Selection-for-action" (e.g. Allport, 1987) and "selection-for-object-recognition" (e.g. LaBerge & Brown, 1989) are examples of such basic functions. Given several candidate functions, further questions about the attentional mechanisms arise. Are the suggested underlying mechanisms for different functional domains (e.g. spatial–motor action, object recognition) identical or different? If they are different, are they coupled or independent? Attempts to answer these questions (e.g. Deubel, Schneider, & Paprotta, this issue) might generate new and productive constraints for conceptualizing attentional mechanisms.

With these two perspectives in mind, namely the cognitive neuroscience approach and an emphasis on attentional functions, Sabine Maasen and I organized a symposium on visual attention mechanisms in Holzhausen, Germany. Consequently, we invited neural network and mathematical modellers, as well as experimentalists using not just behavioural but also neuropsychological methods and neuroscience methods, to attend. Furthermore, researchers focusing either on mechanisms in different functional domains (e.g. selection-for-action, selection-for-object-recognition) or on certain aspects of these putative mechanisms (e.g. control) were invited.

The papers in this special issue are based on the invited talks at the symposium. The structure of the issue consists of four sections on visual attention mechanisms. The first three section reflect different functional domains of attentional mechanisms, whereas the fourth section deals with issues of mechanisms beyond individual functions.

The first section is entitled "Visual attention mechanisms for shape-based object recognition" and contains papers by Humphreys and Heinke and by Hummel and Stankiewicz. Humphreys and Heinke present a neural network (connectionist) model of a visuospatial attention mechanism, called the Selective Attention for Identification Model (SAIM). The function of the suggested attentional mechanism is to allow translation-invariant shape-based object recognition. One goal of SAIM is to explain neuropsychological data on different versions of attentional disorders, that is, "space- and object-based" neglect. By lesioning different parts of network modules, the simulations show how these attentional disorders can arise.

Hummel and Stankiewicz introduce a neural network model that is based on the assumption that shape-based object recognition works by relying on structural descriptions of parts and their spatial relationships. An attentional process is introduced that is different from the spatial attention window proposed by

Humphreys and others. Its function is to mediate part-based recognition at the class- and instance-level. The network simulations show, for instance, that reduced "attention" still leads to class-level recognition but not to instance-level recognition.

The second section is entitled "Visual attention mechanisms for perception and for the control of spatial-motor actions" and contains papers by Deubel, Schneider and Paprotta and by Craighero, Fadiga, Rizzolatti and Umiltà. The paper by Deubel et al. investigated if and how the selective programming of a reaching movement to an object in space (selection-for-action) and the selective perceptual processing of an object (selection-for-object-recognition) are coupled. The experimental paradigm required subjects to recognize a discrimination target among distractors while simultaneously preparing a movement to a reaching target. Their results show that discrimination performance is best by far when the discrimination target and the movement target refer to the same object in space. The results indicate a coupling of visual attention functions by one common mechanism. It may be the same kind of mechanism Humphreys and Heinke have proposed for solving the problem of translation-invariant object recognition.

Craighero et al. investigated whether perceptual processing of an object influences motor programming, or, in terms used by the authors, whether "visuomotor priming" occurs. In two experiments, subjects had to grasp an oriented bar. Before a "go" signal allowed this motor action, a visual prime stimulus was presented. The orientation of the prime was either congruent or incongruent with the orientation of the to-be-grasped bar. Craighero et al. found a priming effect, that is, grasping initiation time was shorter in the congruent that in the incongruent condition. The authors discuss their results in terms of the "premotor theory of attention", which claims that a spatial attention mechanisms is controlled by brain areas responsible for motor programming of saccadic eye movements and arm movements.

The third section is entitled "Visual attention mechanisms for the construction (binding) of integrated internal objects". It contains papers by Irwin and Gordon, by Wojciulik and Kanwisher and by Hommel. Irwin and Gordon present experimental data on how the selective construction (priority assignment) of visual object representations might work across saccadic eye movements. Two experiments show first that a limited number of objects are stored in "transsaccadic memory"—the site of the visual representation of the world across saccadic eye movements—and, second, that a spatial attention mechanism determines the content of this memory. Only attended objects can be represented in transsaccadic memory. Furthermore, a neurocognitive attentional mechanism is suggested that is assumed to regulate access to transsaccadic memory and the setting up of integrated object representations. This mechanism might also be used for selection-for-object recognition and for selection-for-spatial-motor-action.

The paper by Woljciulik and Kanwisher presents the results of a neuropsychological study of the role of the parietal lobe in the selective binding of individual features into representations of an integrated object. The abilities of the patient RM (who suffered bilateral parieto-occipital damage) for implicit and explicit feature binding were investigated in two experiments using a Stroop task. The result show a dissociation between both forms of binding; that is, no explicit but implicit binding. This hints at the possibility that the parietal lobe might be necessary for explicit but not for implicit binding. These results represent a real challenge for any neurocognitive theory of visual attention mechanisms (e.g. Duncan, 1996; LaBerge, 1995; Schneider, 1995).

The paper by Hommel also suggests a role for attention in binding visual features into integrated object configurations, called "object files" by Kahneman, Treisman and Gibbs (1992). Three experiments focus on whether action-related information is part of these object files. Compatible with Hommel's expectation, his results show that response features (spatial patterns for keypress) are also part of the internal object configuration—the term "event file" is suggested for this structure. Hommel concludes that the binding function of attention not only consists of setting up visual perceptual representations of objects, but also includes action- or response-related representations within the same object representations.

The fourth section is entitled "Visual attentional mechanisms beyond individual functions" and contains papers by Hahn and Kramer, by Eimer and by Bundesen. Hahn and Kramer ask whether the often suggested visuospatial attention mechanism can simultaneously be allocated to several locations in space. Five reaction time experiments are reported that required same–different matching with target letters embedded among distractor letters. The results of these experiment are hard to reconcile with the claim that "attentional resources" can only be allocated contiguously in space and they can be taken as evidence for the ability to "split attention" among several locations. In the discussion, these data are related to a neurocognitive model of attention by LaBerge (1995).

The paper by Eimer reviews a number of experiments that measured attentional effects in form of event-related brain potentials (ERPs). Distinct ERP components (P1, N1, Nd1, N2pc) are described which were noted in different attentional tasks, such as sustained and transient spatial pre-cueing. The author argues that these distinct ERP components can be localized in different parts of the brain and may in part reflect distinct attentional mechanisms. How the underlying mechanisms of these effects might be conceptualized is also discussed in terms of the neuroanatomically based model of LaBerge (1995).

The final paper, by Bundesen, presents a mathematical theory of attentional mechanisms with a large explanatory range. The development of the theory from a simple choice and race model towards a computational Theory of Visual Attention (TVA) is outlined. The TVA assumes two attentional mechanisms, called "filtering" and "pigeonholing", that together determine the final result of prioritization in vision. Very recent extensions of the TVA by Logan (1996), which allow the integration of perceptual grouping effects on visual selection efficiency, are also described. Finally, by localizing some of TVA's basic components in different parts of the brain, neuropsychological data on neglect are explained.

The symposium took place in Holzhausen near Munich between 3 and 5 August 1996. The following researchers participated as invited speakers and/or discussants: Alan Allport, Claus Bundesen, Leonardo Chelazzi, Heiner Deubel, Martin Eimer, Bernhard Hommel, John Hummel, Glyn Humphreys, Dave Irwin, Gordon Logan, Wolfgang Prinz, Werner Schneider, Carlo Umiltà and Ewa Wojciulik. Art Kramer was also invited to give a talk but could not attend; however, he and his colleague Sowon Hahn presented an exciting paper. Furthermore, the following were guests at the symposium: Bruce Bridgeman, Dietmar Heinke, Don MacKay, Lex van der Heijden and Rainer Wolff. All of these people made the symposium a very stimulating and productive enterprise. However, two individuals require a special mention. First, Wolfgang Prinz can be considered the father of this project: He explicitly encouraged us to organize the symposium. Also, he made available money from the Max-Planck Society to finance the whole project. The other person without whom the symposium would not have been possible is Sabine Maasen. She managed all the financial and practical aspects, including finding the venue, and helped to create a very lively and productive atmosphere that shaped the overall symposium. Moreover, Sabine did an excellent job as co-editor of this special issue.

Review procedures and reviewers

All contributions to this special issue were reviewed by two or three reviewers. For each paper, one of the reviewers was a symposium participant, while the other one or two were not. All reviewers, except those for the paper by Deubel, Schneider and Paprotta, were selected by myself; Dave Irwin selected the reviewers for the paper by Deubel et al. The reviewers are listed below in alphabetical order; the reviewers chosen by Dave Irwin are not listed because they are not known to the editors (WXS, SM). Overall, this special issue owes much to the comments and recommendations of all the reviewers.

Alan Allport, University of Oxford, UK
Claus Bundesen, University of Copenhagen, Denmark
Leonardo Chelazzi, University of Verona, Italy
Heiner Deubel, Ludwig-Maximilians-University, Munich, Germany
Martin Eimer, Ludwig-Maximilians-University, Munich, Germany
Martin Fischer, Ludwig-Maximilians-University, Munich, Germany
John Henderson, Michigan State University, USA

Bernhard Hommel, Max-Planck-Institute for Psychological Research, Munich, Germany
John Hummel, University of California, Los Angeles, USA
Glyn Humphreys, University of Birmingham, UK
Dave Irwin, University of Illinois, Champaign, USA
Sten F. Larsen, University of Aarhus, Denmark
Kevin O'Regan, CNRS, Paris, France
Bruno Olshausen, University of California, Davis, USA
Hal Pashler, University of California, San Diego, USA
Wolfgang Prinz, Max-Planck-Institute for Psychological Research, Munich, Germany
Carlo Umiltà, University of Padova, Italy
Lex van der Heijden, University of Leiden, The Netherlands
Dirk Vorberg, Technische Universität Braunschweig, Germany
Ewa Wojciulik, Harvard University, Cambridge, MA, USA
Josef Zihl, Max-Planck-Institute for Psychiatry, Munich, Germany

REFERENCES

Allport, D.A. (1987). Selection for action: Some behavioral and neurophysiological considerations of attention and action. In H. Heuer & A.F. Sanders (Eds), *Perspectives on perception and action* (pp. 395–419). Hillsdale, NJ: Lawrence Erlbaum Associates Inc.

Allport, D.A. (1989). Visual attention. In M.I. Posner (Ed.), *Foundations of cognitive science* (pp. 631–682). Cambridge, MA: MIT Press.

Allport, D.A. (1993). Attention and control. Have we been asking the wrong questions? A critical review of twenty-five years. In D.E. Meyer & S. Kornblum (Eds), *Attention and performance XIV: Synergies in experimental psychology, artificial intelligence, and cognitive neuroscience* (pp. 183–218). Cambridge, MA: MIT Press.

Bundesen, C. (1990). A theory of visual attention. *Psychological Review, 97*, 523–547.

Corbetta, M., Shulman, G.L., Miezin, F.M., & Petersen, S.E. (1995). Superior parietal cortex activation during spatial attention shifts and visual feature conjunction. *Science, 270*, 802–805.

Desimone, R., & Duncan, J. (1995). Neural mechanisms of selective visual attention. *Annual Review of Neuroscience, 18*, 193–222.

Driver, J., & Mattingley, J.B. (1995). Selective attention in humans: Normality and pathology. *Current Opinion in Neurobiology, 5*, 191–197.

Duncan, J. (1996). Cooperating brain systems in selective perception and action. In T. Inui & J.L. McClelland (Eds), *Attention and performance XVI: Information integration in perception and communication* (pp. 549–578). Cambridge, MA: MIT Press.

Duncan, J., & Humphreys, G.W. (1989). Visual search and stimulus similarity. *Psychological Review, 96*, 433-458.

Duncan, J., Humphreys, G.W., & Ward, R. (1997). Competitive brain activity in visual attention. *Current Opinion in Neurobiology, 7*, 255–261.

Egeth, H.E. (1977). Attention and preattention. In G.H. Bower (Ed.), *The psychology of learning and motivation* (Vol. 7, pp. 277–320). New York: Academic Press.

Eriksen, C.W. (1995). The flankers task and response competition: A useful tool for investigating a variety of cognitive problems. *Visual Cognition, 2*, 101–118.

Fox, E., (1995). Negative priming from ignored distractors in visual selection: A review. *Psychonomic Bulletin and Review, 2*, 145–173.

Gazzaniga, M.S. (1995). *The cognitive neurosciences.* Cambridge, MA: MIT Press.

Hillyard, S.A., Mangun, G.R., Woldorff, M.G., & Luck, S.J. (1995). Neural systems mediating selective attention. In M.S. Gazzaniga (Ed.). *The cognitive neurosciences.* Cambridge, MA: MIT Press.

Humphreys, G.W., & Bruce, V. (1989). *Visual cognition.* Hove: Lawrence Erlbaum Associates Ltd.

Johnston, W.A., & Dark, V.J. (1986). Selective attention. *Annual Review of Psychology, 37*, 43–75.

Kahneman, D., Treisman, A.M., & Gibbs, B.J. (1992). The reviewing of object files: Object-specific integration of information. *Cognitive Psychology, 24*, 175–219.

Kosslyn, S.M., & Koenig, O. (1992). *Wet mind: The new cognitive neuroscience.* New York: The Free Press.

LaBerge, D. (1995). *Attentional processing.* Cambridge, MA: Harvard University Press.

LaBerge, D., Brown, V. (1989). Theory of attentional operations in shape identification. *Psychological Review, 96*, 101–124.

Logan, G.D. (1996). The CODE theory of visual attention: An integration of space-based and object-based attention. *Psychological Review, 103*, 603–649.

Neumann, O. (1987). Beyond capacity: A functional view of attention. In H. Heuer & A.F. Sanders (Eds), *Perspectives on perception and action* (pp. 361–394). Hillsdale, NJ: Lawrence Erlbaum Associates Inc.

Olshausen, B.A., Anderson, C.H., & Van Essen, D.C. (1993). A neurobiological model of visual attention and invariant pattern recognition based on dynamic routing of information. *The Journal of Neuroscience, 13*, 4700–4719.

Posner, M.I., & Petersen, S.E. (1990). The attention system of the human brain. *Annual Review of Neuroscience, 13*, 25–42.

Posner, M.I., & Raichle, M.E. (1994). *Images of mind.* New York: Scientific American Library.

Prinz, W. (1983). *Wahrnehmung und Tätigkeitssteuerung.* Berlin: Springer-Verlag.

Schneider, W.X. (1993). Space-based visual attention models and object selection: Constraints, problems, and possible solutions. *Psychological Research, 56*, 35–43.

Schneider, W.X. (1995). VAM: A neuro-cognitive model for visual attention control of segmentation, object recognition, and space-based motor action. *Visual Cognition, 2*, 331–375.

Treisman, A. (1988). Features and objects: The fourteenth Bartlett memorial lecture. *Quarterly Journal of Experimental Psychology, 40*, 201–237.

Treisman, A., & Gelade, G. (1980). A feature-integration theory of attention. *Cognitive Psychology, 12*, 97–136.

Van der Heijden, A.H. (1992). *Selective attention in vision.* London: Routledge.

Wolfe, J.M. (1994). Guided search 2.0: A revised model of visual search. *Psychonomic Bulletin and Review, 1*, 202–238.

VISUAL COGNITION, 1998, *5* (1/2), 9–47

Spatial Representation and Selection in the Brain: Neuropsychological and Computational Constraints

Glyn W. Humphreys

Cognitive Science Research Centre, University of Birmingham, Birmingham, UK

Dietmar Heinke

Division of Neuroinformatiks, Technical University of Illmenau, Illmenau, Germany

We report joint neuropsychological and computational research into the nature of spatial representation and visual selection in the brain. In the first part of the paper, we discuss patterns of double dissociation between the performance of patients with selective brain lesions, suggesting the existence of independent forms of spatial representation in vision. In the second part we report the effects of simulating lesions in a computational model of translation-invariant object recognition. In the model, objects compete to achieve a mapping from retinal input to a translation-invariant "focus of attention". Spatially selective lesions affect either the mapping from one side of retinal input or the mapping to one side of the attentional window, so generating different disorders of spatial representation and attention. We propose that forms of selection in vision, and different forms of spatial mapping, can emerge as a consequence of the need to achieve viewpoint-independent object recognition. Neuropsychological deficits typically attributed to disorders of visual attention or to particular spatial representations can arise out of damage to different parts of a visual system designed for object recognition.

INTRODUCTION

The aim of this paper is to review the relations between spatial representation and attention in the brain, using evidence from both cognitive neuropsychology and computational modelling. In using evidence from both neuropsychology

---

Requests for reprints should be addressed to Glyn W. Humphreys, Cognitive Science Research Centre, School of Psychology, University of Birmingham, Birmingham B15 2TT, UK.

This work was supported by a grant from the DAAD (Germany) to D.H., and by grants from the MRC and the BBSRC (UK) to G.W.H. We thank all the patients involved for taking part in the project and the Visual Cognition Group at Birmingham University for their comments.

---

and modelling research, we hope to demonstrate how traditionally different disciplines can converge to provide deeper understanding of the processes mediating visual cognition, and how they can lead to the generation of new testable hypotheses. First, we review the neuropsychological evidence, summarizing some recent data from our laboratory on dissociations between different forms of visual neglect. Subsequently, we summarize recent computational studies that demonstrate how different forms of spatial representation, and forms of spatial selection, can emerge from the need to achieve viewpoint-independent object recognition.

SPATIAL REPRESENTATION IN THE BRAIN

Neurophysiological and neuropsychological research converges in demonstrating that there is no simple Cartesian representation of space in the brain. Single-cell studies in the monkey, for example, reveal that there are multiple areas in the cortex that are specialized to process visual signals (see, e.g. Desimone, 1992; Desimone & Ungerleider, 1989). Many of these areas have their own spatial maps and within these maps activity may be determined by the positions of stimuli on the retina. In some cortical regions, however, the position of the stimulus with regard to the animal's head or body is important (Andersen, 1988; Graziano & Gross, 1993). In yet other areas, cells respond in a more view-invariant way, having large receptive fields that span wide areas on the retina or receptive fields that are tuned to the location of a feature within an object (Olson & Gettner, 1995).

These different spatial tunings of cells probably reflect the differing computational needs for efficient object recognition and for efficient action. Ungerleider and Mishkin (1982) first argued for a separation between two broad visual streams within the cortex, one ventral stream from the occipital to the temporal lobes, and one dorsal stream from the occipital to the parietal lobes. They proposed that the ventral stream mediates pattern recognition and the dorsal stream mediates the coding of spatial location. For example, it can be argued that object recognition needs to operate in a way that is relatively robust to changes in viewpoint, of either the object or the observer, so that the same memory representation can be accessed by an object irrespective of the viewing position (e.g. Marr, 1982; but see Tarr, 1995). It follows that the ventral stream of visual processing, concerned with object recognition, may utilize forms of viewpoint-independent coding. Consistent with this, cells in the temporal cortex tend to have large receptive fields and to be relatively indifferent to the positions of objects in the visual field (Desimone, Albright, Gross, & Bruce, 1984; Gross, Rocha-Miranda, & Bender, 1972). Within the parietal lobe, cells typically remain tuned either to the retinal position of stimuli or to the positions of stimuli with regard to body or head coordinates, and their activation is linked to actions being directed to the objects in space (Andersen, 1988; Goldberg &

Segraves, 1987; Sakata, Shibutani, Kawano, & Harrington, 1985). These latter results mesh with the idea that the dorsal visual stream is concerned with encoding space for action (Milner & Goodale, 1995).

Neuropsychological research, operating at a more macroscopic level than single-cell analyses, also indicates that space is not coded in a unitary way in human vision. Following damage to the parietal lobe, patients can have spatially related problems in responding to stimuli, as in the syndrome of unilateral visual neglect (Critchley, 1953; de Renzi, 1982). In some cases, patients have deficits in responding to stimuli presented on one side of space near to their body but not to stimuli presented at more distant spatial locations (even if the visual angles of the stimuli are held constant; e.g. Halligan & Marshall, 1991); in other cases, patients are impaired when stimuli are presented in far but not near space (Cowey, Small, & Ellis, 1994). This double dissociation between the two forms of spatial deficit in the patients suggests either a differentiation between representations of space near to or far from the body, or a differentiation according to the actions typically linked to objects near to or far from the body.

Other patients, however, demonstrate a form of neglect that seems relatively independent of the spatial position of the object on the retina or relative to the viewer's body. Driver and Halligan (1991) reported a case in which the left part of an object was neglected even when the object was rotated so that its left part fell in the patient's right visual field. Young, Hellawell and Welch (1992) documented a patient who had left neglect of faces even when the stimuli were presented in the right visual field (see also Young, Newcombe, & Ellis, 1991, for similar evidence with words). Interestingly, Young and co-workers' patient did not show left neglect when presented with two left sides of faces placed alongside one another. Young et al. suggested that neglect was apparent only when the parts of the object (the two halves of the face) configured to form a "good" perceptual object (e.g. having closure). Caramazza and Hillis (1990) even reported a patient who not only showed neglect when reading the right-hand ends of words and nonwords when the letter strings were written left-to-right, but also when the strings were mirror reversed, so the right-end letters then fell on the left side of space in viewer-centred terms (see Hillis & Caramazza, 1995, for further evidence on these lines). They argued that neglect can reflect damage to different forms of spatial representation, some of which are coded in retinal coordinates and some in coordinate systems centred on the object. In the latter case, there will be neglect of one side of an object irrespective of the object's location with respect to the viewer. Somewhat similar evidence has been reported by Behrmann and Tipper (1994; Tipper & Behrmann, 1996). They had patients detect a target presented on the left or right side of an object, and the object rotated slowly through 180°. They found that slowed detection to left-side targets shifted to slowed detection of right-side targets as the object rotated, so that the original left part appeared on the right side. This effect only occurred when the two parts were connected by a bar, so that the parts grouped to form a single object. Thus, in this case, neglect seemed tied to the original coding of the part within a frame of reference based on the object; relative to the frame of the object, the part maintained its position on the left or right as the object was rotated in the field. Note, however, that in all of these instances neglect has been associated with damage to the dorsal rather than the ventral visual stream (e.g. damage to frontal and parietal areas), precluding any direct link between object- and viewer-centred forms of neglect and information processing within the ventral and dorsal visual streams.

SPACE WITHIN VERSUS BETWEEN PERCEPTUAL OBJECTS

One other distinction between different spatial codes within the brain, based on evidence from patients with unilateral neglect, has been made by Humphreys and Riddoch (1994, 1995; Riddoch et al., 1995a,b). Humphreys and Riddoch reported two patients, both of whom showed neglect of either the right or left sides of space, according to the kind of task being performed. Patient JR, for instance, was presented with an A4 page with words and nonwords printed at random spatial positions. He made omission errors where he failed to make any response to some of the stimuli down the right side of the page, but also "left neglect" errors when reading individual stimuli (e.g. pitch → bitch); the left neglect errors occurred irrespective of the positions of the words on the page. The same pattern of performance was observed when JR was asked to name pictures or to bisect lines on a page (i.e. there were right-side omissions of whole stimuli plus left neglect errors on individual stimuli, where he based his naming response on only the right-side features of objects or where he was biased to the right in bisection). Humphreys and Riddoch (1994, 1995) suggested that JR manifested left-side neglect of individual objects but right-side neglect when he attempted to process multiple objects. The different effects did not simply reflect the spatial area where stimuli fell. When presented with individual large words whose letters now fell on the right of the page where he had previously made omission errors, JR still made left-side neglect errors. Perhaps most tellingly, when asked to read aloud the letters rather than to read the whole word, he then made right-side omission errors and read the left-hand letters correctly! Thus the two patterns of neglect could occur with exactly the same stimulus, and a determining factor in whether neglect was expressed on the right or left side of space was the task. When asked to encode the whole stimulus for the response (e.g. in whole-word reading), neglect was expressed on the left; when the parts of this whole were represented as objects for individual responses in their own right ("read aloud the letters"), neglect was expressed on the right. The two forms of neglect shown by JR probably reflected the fact that he suffered bilateral brain lesions, to the right fronto-parietal region and the left occipito-parietal regions respectively (there was, in addition, a lesion to the right cerebellum). Humphreys and Riddoch proposed that the two forms of neglect revealed the existence of two separable internal representations of space: a within-object spatial representation, in which the parts were encoded relative to a whole; and a between-object spatial representation, in which the parts were coded as independent perceptual objects. JR showed left neglect within perceptual objects, but right neglect between perceptual objects.

This distinction, between within- and between-object spatial codes, can be used to account for the pattern of neglect reported by Young et al. (1992). Note that Young and co-workers' patient showed left neglect when parts configured to form faces but not when they did not, and this occurred irrespective of the positions of the parts in the field. In our terms, there was left neglect within perceptual objects (see also Walker, 1995; Walker, Findlay, Young, & Lincoln, 1996; Young et al., 1991).

BEYOND SINGLE CASES: DISSOCIATING WITHIN- AND BETWEEN-OBJECT REPRESENTATIONS ACROSS PATIENTS

The individual case studies of patients showing neglect either within or between perceptual objects have suggested the existence of different forms of spatial representation, but they are limited if we want to know about the sites in the brain where these representations are localized; to make inferences about brain localization, it is more reliable to make deductions from groups of patients where a common lesion site can be analysed. Humphreys, Riddoch and Romani (submitted) attempted to do this. They evaluated a group of five patients, all of whom showed left neglect in standard clinical tasks such as drawing from memory. In the full study, the patients were asked to carry out a series of four additional tasks, which were chosen to contrast spatial representations within and between objects. Here we report the results of the tasks examined.

Chimeric faces

There were two conditions. In one, the patients were presented with a single "object", which was either a photograph of a normal whole face or a chimeric made by combining the right and left halves of male and female faces. The task was to decide whether either a whole male or whole female face was present, or whether a chimeric male/female face was present. In the second condition, the patients were presented with two whole faces, one on the left and one on the right of the patient's midline. At the start of each trial the patient looked away and either one or both faces were replaced by the addition of one or two new faces placed on either the left, the right or on both piles. The task was to decide on each trial how many new faces there were, one or two, whether the new faces were male or female. Presentation times were unlimited. Example stimuli are given in Figure 1.

If patients have difficulty in encoding the left side of individual objects, then they may have difficulty in the chimeric face test, since it requires discriminating both sides of each individual face. However, the patients may perform the task with two faces relatively well if they are able to make discriminations based on the right side of each face. In contrast, if patients manifest neglect only within a spatial representation in which the relations between independent objects are coded, then they may show neglect of the left of two separate faces (e.g. failing to notice a new face in the left pile, in condition 2). If there is no neglect of space within perceptual objects, neglect may not be shown in tasks requiring discrimination of the left and right sides of a single chimeric face (in condition 1 here).

Detecting a Missing Element in Brackets

Patients were presented with rectangles composed of bracket elements (at the corners of the rectangles). The task was to decide whether all the elements present were full brackets or whether one of the brackets had a missing element (i.e. whether it was a single line). In the *single-object* condition, there was a maximum of four brackets present, and they configured to form a rectangle either on the left or the right side of fixation, or a rectangle that fell across fixation. The target, when present, could fall on the left or right of the single object. In the *two-object* condition, there was a maximum of eight bracket elements, which configured to form two rectangles, one either side of fixation. The target could appear on the left or right of either the left or right object. To prevent eye movements, the stimuli were presented on a computer screen (of an Apple Macintosh) for 200 msec and followed by a pattern mask. In the two-object condition, each rectangle covered a visual angle of 1°, and they were separated by an angle of 1° (0.5° either side of fixation). In the single-object condition, the rectangle always covered 1° of visual angle, including when it fell across fixation (when the brackets were the inside elements from the rectangles in the two-object condition, but rotated to face one another). Example stimuli are given in Figure 2.

Neglect within an object should be manifest in terms of poor detection of targets on the affected side of single objects and on the affected side of each of the two objects in the two-object condition. Within-object neglect may also occur irrespective of the location of the object in the visual field (e.g. patients may miss a target on the left-side of an object, even if the object is presented in the right visual field). Neglect between objects should lead to deficits only when there are two objects present, and performance should be relatively good when a single object is present, even when if falls on the affected side relative to fixation. When two objects are present, patients may, for example, miss

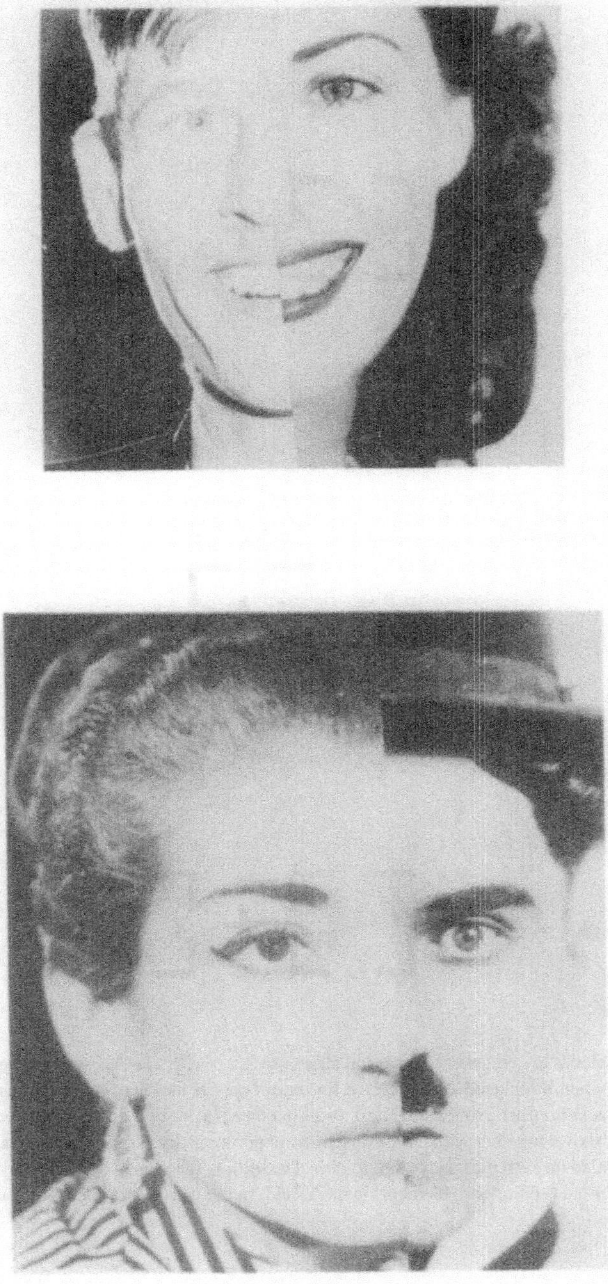

FIG. 1. Examples of chimeric faces

(a)

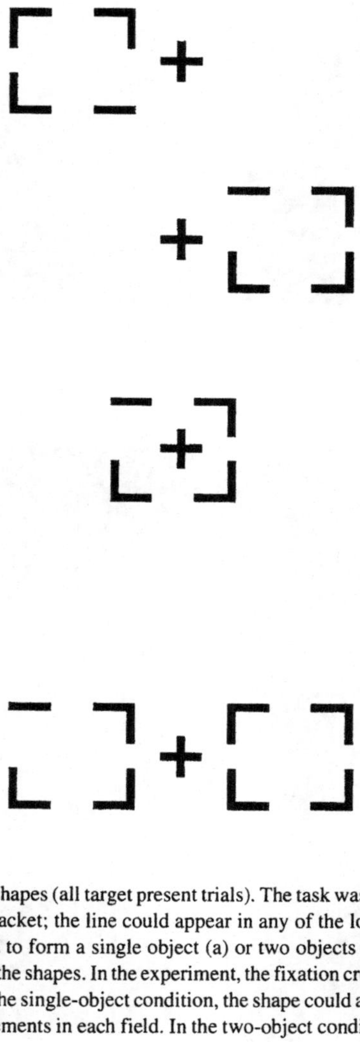

(b)

FIG. 2. Examples of the "bracket" shapes (all target present trials). The task was to detect the presence of a single line when it replaced a bracket; the line could appear in any of the locations occupied by a bracket. The brackets either grouped to form a single object (a) or two objects (b). For reference, the fixation cross is shown together with the shapes. In the experiment, the fixation cross disappeared before the shapes appeared on each trial. In the single-object condition, the shape could appear in the left visual field, the right visual field or with elements in each field. In the two-object condition, one object fell in each visual field.

targets in the left one. It may then make little difference whether the target is on the left or right side of the neglected object.

Patients

Data were collected from five patients (see Table 1 for lesion and clinical details). All patients manifested neglect on drawing tasks (copying and drawing from memory), in which they missed parts selectively on one side of an object. Four patients (PB, AM, SM and GW) showed left-neglect; the fifth, MH, showed right-neglect (see Table 1). The data from the patients were compared with those from a set of 10 age-matched control subjects, all of whom showed ceiling-level performance on each test.

Empirical data

The five patients clustered into two distinct groups across the two tests. Three (PB, AM and GW) showed neglect of the left sides of single objects, but showed little effect of whether the object was the left or right member of a pair of objects. That is, they showed neglect within- but not between objects. The other two patients, SM and MH, showed no neglect when they were presented with single objects for a response, even when it was presented on the affected side relative to fixation. However, they neglected respectively the left (SM) or the right member (MH) of a two-object pair. In all cases, the spatially selective errors made by the patients fell more than four standard deviations away from the

TABLE 1
Clinical Details of the Patients

Patient	*Sex*	*Aetiology*	*Age (years)*	*Site of Lesion*	*Clinical Symptom*
PB	F	Stroke	58	Right inferior and superior frontal gyri; superior temporal gyrus; inferior parietal lobe	Neglect on drawing
AM	M	Stroke	62	Right inferior and middle frontal gyri; superior temporal gyrus; post- and pre-central gyri	Neglect on drawing
GW	F	Stroke	70	Right inferior frontal gyrus; superior and middle temporal gyri; head of caudate; internal capsule and lentiform nucleus	Neglect on drawing
MH	M	Anoxia	45	Bilateral lentiform nuclei; left posterior parietal	Neglect on bisection
SM	F	Stroke	69	Right middle and superior frontal gyri; pre-central gyrus; inferior parietal; left angular gyrus and parieto-occipital sulcus	Neglect on drawing

mean number of errors made by the controls, and represented a significant deficit.

Tables 2 and 3 show the data from the chimeric face task and the "brackets" task. In the chimeric face task, PB, AM and GW made errors when presented with single chimeric faces. These errors always involved them failing to detect the presence of a chimeric face and giving instead the sex of the face on the right side of the chimeric. However, when presented with pairs of faces, the patients were nearly always able to detect the co-occurrence of male and female faces (in the left and right piles), presumably using information from the right side of each face. In contrast, SM and MH both showed deficits in the two-face condition and not with chimeric faces. In the two-face condition, SM failed to notice the occurrence of a new face in the left pile, and MH the occurrence of a new face in the right pile, on a significant proportion of trials. Yet both patients performed at ceiling with chimeric faces, being able to discriminate both the presence of the chimeric and the sex of each half face. The good performance on the chimeric face test is quite striking, given the severity of the clinical pattern of neglect shown by at least SM (see Figure 3). Previously, tests with chimeric faces have been thought to provide a sensitive measure of unilateral neglect (Mattingley, Bradshaw, Phillips, & Bradshaw, 1993). Our data suggest that such tests do provide a sensitive measure of neglect within visual objects, but not of neglect between objects. A patient with severe neglect between objects but no neglect within objects will not necessarily be impaired on this test.

A similar pattern of dissociation occurred in the brackets task. In Table 3 the data are presented as a function of the position of the target, on target-present trials. All the patients performed at ceiling level on target-absent trials. In the single-object condition, SM and MH made no errors, and detected targets that

TABLE 2
Scores (out of 20) on Male–Female Face Trials in the Chimeric and Two-face Gender Discrimination Task[a]

		Two Faces	
Patient	*Chimeric*	*Left Face*	*Right Face*
PB	13[b]	17	20
AM	13[b]	20	20
GW	14[b]	20	20
MH	20	20	14
SM	20	8	20

[a]In each case there were a further 10 trials with male–female and 10 with female–female faces.

[b]All responses were to the right side chimeric.

TABLE 3
Scores (out of 12, on Present Trials Only) with the Bracket Stimuli[a]

			Two Objects			
	Single Object		*Left Object*		*Right Object*	
Patient	*Target Left*	*Target Right*	*Target Left*	*Target Right*	*Target Left*	*Target Right*
PB	6	12	4	11	10	12
AM	8	12	7	11	8	12
GW	8	12	5	12	8	12
MH	12	12	12	12	8	7
SM	12	12	0	1	10	12

[a]There were 24 absent trials in the single- and two-object conditions, on which all patients performed at ceiling.

occurred on both the left and right of the objects, and when targets appeared in the left as well as the right visual fields. However, these two patients made errors in the two-object condition. SM made hardly any detections of targets presented in the left object; MH made errors only to targets presented in the right object in a pair. The errors made by both patients in the two-object condition occurred irrespective of whether the targets fell on the right or left

Coliria is an imaginary country located on an imaginary continent. Here is its *tescription*. Coliria is a small country. It is about one fifth the size of Texas, but it has a much higher population density. It has about tem million people. One side of Coliria *bordern* on the ocean. The coast is lined by long, white sand beaches and it is very 'touristy'. This part of the country, in fact, *fhrives* mainly on tourism and fishing and it is very prosperous. Villages of various sizes are found at regular intervals all along the coast.

The inland part of the country is not very populated. It is flat and very dry. Because there is not enough water, the land is not cultivated. It is covered by grass, bushes and, occasionally, rare groups of trees. People in this area live mainly by raising cows. *theep* and goats, and by hunting deer and antelope. In the summer, the whether is terribly hot and it is *difficulp* to work outside during the day.

FIG. 3. Example of clinical neglect in patient SM. The task was to detect the presence of spelling errors in the text. The spelling errors (here marked in italics) fell at either the beginning or ends of words, or on the left or right side of the text. SM showed marked neglect of the passage, barely detecting any errors apart from those falling in the right-most columns. Interestingly, and consistent with the other data reported here, she was able to detect spelling errors irrespective of whether they fell at the left or right sides of individual words.

sides of the neglected object. The other three patients, PB, AM and GW, showed a different pattern of performance. These patients all made errors in the single-object condition, when they failed to detect targets present on the left side of the object. In the two-object condition, the patients tended to make errors to targets on the left of each object, and this held even when the target was in the right visual field (i.e. errors were to targets on the left of the right object in the pair). Indeed, each patient made a significant number of misses of targets on the left side of right field objects, but not to targets on the right side of left field objects, when compared to the control subjects (who showed errorless performance). Thus for PB, AM, and GW, performance was determined by the position of the target within each object rather than by the position of the target in the visual field.

Table 4 gives a summary of the patterns of spatially selective deficit across each task, for each patient. This illustrates that SM and MH showed neglect in the conditions in which they had to discriminate stimuli in the left- or right-hand member of a pair of objects respectively (in the between-object conditions). However, neither patient showed neglect when required to discriminate both sides of single objects (single chimeric faces or single rectangles). PB, AM and GW had the opposite pattern of impairment. These patients all presented with left neglect when required to discriminate the left sides of single objects (in the within-object conditions), but they did not manifest neglect of the left member of a pair of objects (when discriminations could be based on the right side of the left object). There is thus a clear pattern of double dissociation across the patients; three patients show a lateralized deficit with single objects, two show a lateralized deficit only with multiple objects present. We suggest that these dissociations reflect the different representations mediating task performance. PB, AM and GW have impaired representations of space within perceptual

TABLE 4
Summary of Whether the Patients Showed a Spatially Selective and Abnormal Pattern of Performance Across Four Tasks Requiring Responses to Either Individual Perceptual Objects or to Separate Percpeptual Objects

	Within-object Tasks		*Between-object Tasks*	
	Chimeric Faces	*Brackets*	*Two Faces*	*Brackets*
PB	+	+	–	–
AM	+	+	–	–
GW	+	+	–	–
MH	–	–	+	+
SM	–	–	+	+

Note: "+" indicates the presence of a spatial deficit; "–" indicates the absence of a spatial deficit.

objects but can encode and attend to the presence of independent objects. In contrast, SM and MH have impairments in using a representation in which the spatial relations between separate perceptual objects are coded, but they do not have impaired representations of space within perceptual objects. It is possible that SM and MH have particular difficulty in disengaging attention from an ipsilesional object, to respond to a contralesional item, when there are multiple items present. Irrespective of this, the data suggest that the underlying representation upon which any problem with attentional disengagement is expressed is one in which visual elements are coded independently and demand separate actions.

This double dissociation between the two sets of patients is consistent with the existence of at least two separate forms of spatial representation in the brain — within- and between object spatial representations (see Humphreys & Riddoch, 1994, 1995).

FUNCTIONAL LOCALIZATION OF WITHIN- AND BETWEEN-OBJECT SPATIAL REPRESENTATIONS

The group of patients studies by Humphreys et al. (submitted) is the largest yet to demonstrate the distinction between within- and between-object spatial representations across a range of tasks. With clusters of patients manifesting the same underlying impairment, it becomes possible to assess the critical site of lesions, by examining the common areas of damage. In this analysis, we compared the lesions in PB, AM and GW, plus also the apparently critical right hemisphere lesion in patient JR (Humphreys & Riddoch, 1994, 1995), which led to left-neglect within perceptual objects in these patients. The common lesion area for these patients was in the inferior frontal lobe, Brodmann area 44, though in some cases the lesions were quite large and affected widespread areas in the right hemisphere (particularly in PB).

The patients we have documented as showing neglect between perceptual objects—all had some degree of bilateral damage. In JR, in addition to the right fronto-parietal lesion noted above, there was damage to the left occipito-parietal region and the right cerebellum (see Humphreys & Riddoch, 1994, 1995). We attribute his right-side neglect between perceptual objects to the left occipito-parietal lesion. MH had bilateral damage to subcortical structures (the lentiform nucleus), along with some damage to the left posterior parietal region overlapping the areas affected in JR. SM had damage to the right fronto-parietal region, along with increased signal in a more posterior area in the right inferior parietal lobe analogous to an area in the left hemisphere damaged in JR and MH. It may be that this posterior parietal region is involved in encoding the spatial representations between perceptual objects or in shifting attention between representations of separate objects, leading to right-side neglect in JR and MH (due to the left hemisphere lesion) and left-side neglect in SM (due to the right hemisphere lesion). However, SM also had quite widespread damage to her left parietal lobe, and it remains feasible that this played some role in her neglect. For example, one possibility is that the left parietal lesion generates a deficit in shifting attention between objects and normally this would be expressed in terms of there being an impairment in responding to stimuli on the right side of a multi-object display (cf. JR and MH). For SM, though, the presence of a right-hemisphere lesion leads to poor encoding of information on the left side of visual space which, coupled with a deficit in shifting attention between objects, biases her to attend to the right members of multi-object displays and them to show impairments in shifting attention subsequently to new objects. On this account, there are essentially two problems, one in encoding visual information and one in shifting attention between objects. In patients with a unilateral lesion to the left parietal lobe, these two problems may combine; problems in shifting attention between objects will co-occur with relatively poorer coding of visual information on the right side of space. As a result of this, there is right-side neglect between perceptual objects. In a patient such as SM, the encoding bias may favour right-side stimuli, generating left-side neglect between perceptual objects. The argument, for the left parietal lobe being important in shifts of attention between separate objects, accords with other recent neuropsychological data. For example, Egly, Driver and Rafal (1994) found that patients with left parietal lesions were impaired at shifting attention from a validly cued object to a target location within another object. Buck et al. (in press) have reported similar problems in shifting attention between objects associated with decreased activation in the left parietal region of Alzheimer patients. Whichever account we hold for SM (whether we believe the left or right parietal lesion crucial), the data implicate the posterior parietal lobe in the encoding and shifting of attention between separate perceptual objects.

Few previous cases have been reported in which neglect has been clearly demonstrated as being selectively between and not within perceptual objects, making it difficult to make comparisons with the present lesion data. In prior cases of within-object neglect, lesions have either not been reported in detail (Young et al., 1991) or reported as residing solely in the parietal lobe (Caramazza & Hillis, 1990; Tipper & Behrmann, 1996), the parieto-temporal or the temporo-frontal regions (Tipper & Behrmann, 1996; Walker et al., 1996). However, there are problems with such analyses: For example, the scans were either not reported or not compared across patients. Also, in some of these cases, it is not clear whether processes of mental rotation were required by the tasks (e.g. to identify rotated stimuli or to track stimuli as they rotated)—such processes may depend on activity in the parietal lobe (Farah & Hammond, 1988; Ratcliff, 1979). In the tasks we have used (e.g. requiring the identification of upright faces and shapes), it seems unlikely that mental rotation played much of a part, and we suggest that we are witnessing a relatively pure deficit in within-object spatial coding in our patients. The involvement of the inferior frontal lobe in within-object neglect may be due to this area receiving projections from both object- and space-based processing routes (in the ventral and dorsal streams respectively), enabling explicit coding to take place of the spatial relations between the parts of objects. We return to this point in the General Discussion.

SPATIAL REPRESENTATION AND ATTENTION: A COMPUTATIONAL APPROACH

The neuropsychological evidence we have reviewed is consistent with there being different forms of spatial representations in the brain, and with the argument that these representations can be damaged in such a way as to produce unilateral impairments, affecting one side of the space more than the other. These different spatial representations are likely also to mediate different visual behaviours. For example, within-object spatial representations may be necessary to identify objects, since the spatial relations between the parts of objects can determine their identity (see Biederman, 1987); between-object spatial representations may be useful for guiding actions to or between objects in space (e.g. when we navigate between obstacles) (see Riddoch et al., 1995a,b). Different spatial representations may arise out of the need for behaviour to be controlled by contrasting forms of information.

One approach to understanding why different spatial representations mediate visual cognition, and the role that the different representations may play with respect to one another, is to simulate the proposed behaviours in computational models; within such models, the functional role of the different representations can be clarified relative to the operation of the rest of the processing system. We illustrate this point with reference to the Selective Attention for Identification Model (SAIM), proposed by Heinke and Humphreys (in prep.). The primary aim of SAIM is to achieve translation-invariant object recognition. It does this by mapping input from locations on a retina through to a smaller "attentional" window, the focus of attention (FOA), with activation within the FOA providing the input to an object recognition system (see Olshausen, Andersen, & Van Essen, 1993, 1995; Postma, 1994). Since the same units in the FOA are activated irrespective of the location of stimuli on the retina, recognition can be translation-invariant.

However, such an approach to translation-invariant object recognition encounters problems when there are multiple objects in the visual field. For example, if features of each object are mapped concurrently into the FOA, then the FOA will provide ambiguous input into the object recognition system, making recognition inefficient. To generate efficient object recognition, only one of the objects present should be mapped into the FOA at a time. Thus, the need to achieve translation-invariant recognition may force the system to implement a form of visual selection for identification. SAIM embodies this process of selection for identification by means of the constraints that govern how information on the retina is mapped into the FOA.

The architecture of SAIM is illustrated in Figure 4. The mapping of input from the retina through to the FOA is mediated by two networks, the "contents" and the "selection" networks. The contents network contains "sigma-pi" units (Rumelhart, Hinton, & McClelland, 1986) that determine the activation values assigned to units in the FOA by combining multiplicatively activation in retinal units with that in units in the selection network. There is one unit in the contents network for every unit in the FOA. The selection network is considerably larger and it determines which retinal units have their activation values mapped through to the FOA (via the contents network). Within the selection network

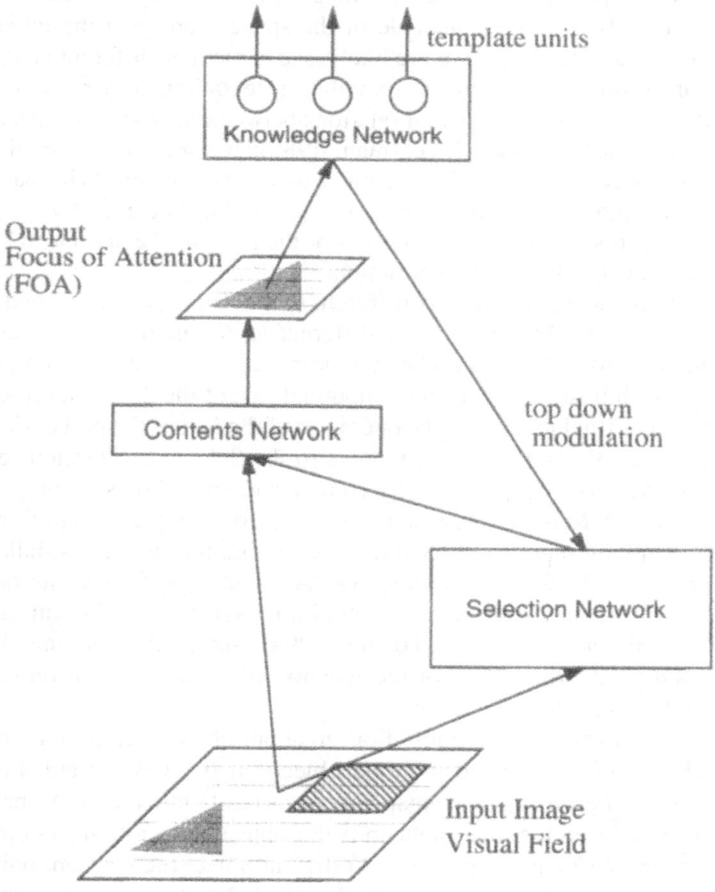

FIG. 4. The architecture of SAIM.

there are separate "control layers" of units, and units in each control layer are activated by input from specific retinal locations. For each retinal location there are as many control layers in the network as there are units in the focus of attention (one layer for each mapping), with these multiple control layers being needed to represent all possible mappings from each retinal location into each location in the FOA. This is computationally expensive and, in a system that is biologically more realistic, problems connected to the large numbers of units required may be rendered more manageable by using multi-scale representations (Olshausen et al., 1995). However, in the present simulations, we maintained local one-to-one mappings from retinal units to units in the selection network and the FOA, to facilitate the analysis of network performance.

Which retinal units come to be mapped through to the FOA is determined by a process of mutual constraint satisfaction between units in the selection network, and mutual constraint satisfaction is in turn achieved by the network embodying certain constraints in its pattern of inter-connectivity. In particular:

1. Only one location in each control layer can be maximally active, and active units inhibit other units in the same control layer in a "winner takes all" fashion, so that (ultimately) each unit in the FOA is controlled by one unit in a control layer. Activation in each control layer is mapped through to the content unit that gates access to one unit in the FOA, so there is competition between units within a control layer to govern this mapping.
2. There is inhibition across control layers between units that encode the same location on the retina.
3. Neighbourhood relations between active retinal locations are preserved by a Gaussian spread of activation from each unit in a control layer to units in other control layers that represent neighbouring locations. This implements a simple form of perceptual grouping, determined by the proximity of the elements.

Details are given in the Appendix of the activation functions that realize these constraints. Figure 5 illustrates the pattern of inter-connectivity between the units in the selection network, and how these conditions implement constraints (2) and (3).

When successful mapping through the selection network to the FOA takes place, pixels that fall at the centre of gravity in objects tend to be mapped through to the centre of the FOA, since these pixels will be maximally supported by occupied neighbouring locations.

SAIM attempts to map input from any part of its retina onto the FOA, and activation in the FOA is subsequently mapped through to a set of stored representations to achieve pattern recognition. Knowledge about objects is represented by the set of weights connecting locations in the FOA to the templates. Since the mapping for recognition is from a common input (the FOA)

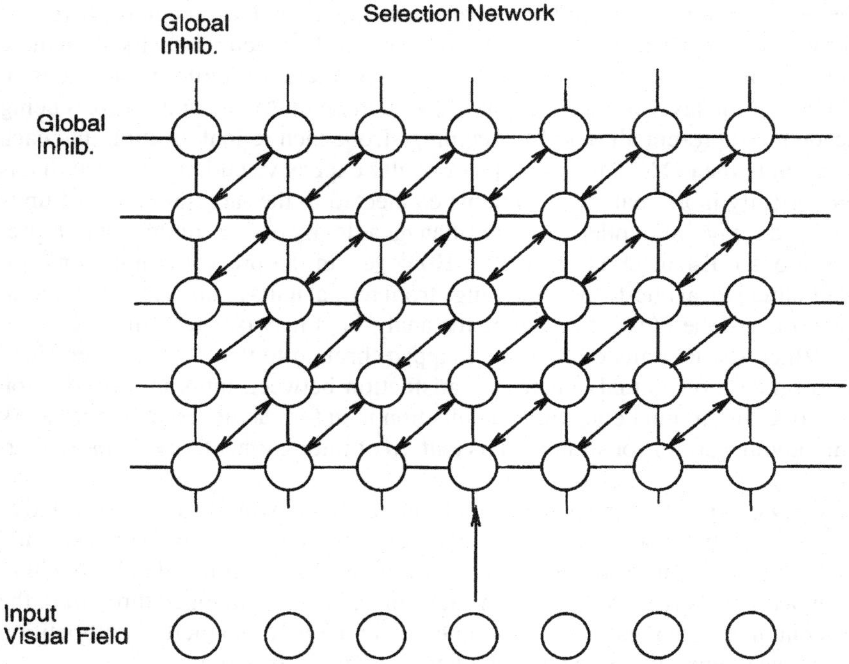

FIG. 5. The topology of the selection network in SAIM. Each row of the network stands for a control layer. The vertical and horizontal connections are inhibitory, and act to prevent (1) more than one connection operating from the visual field to the selection network (vertical connections), and (2) more than one connection operating from the selection network to the FOA (horizontal connections), respectively. The arrows between adjacent units of adjacent layers depict excitatory connections that generate grouping by proximity (local neighbourhood support).

for objects irrespective of their location on the retina, the task of translation-invariant pattern recognition becomes simplified. Note, however, that in achieving a mapping from the retina to the FOA, a form of visual selection is instantiated by the competition within the selection network when units from the same control layer, or from different control layers, attempt to control a common unit in the FOA. When two objects are present, this competition is "won" by the object that creates the strongest activation in the selection network, which is in turn determined by the size of the object; larger objects enjoy more mutual support through proximity grouping. The larger of two objects will tend to be mapped through to the FOA, and its stored representations will be activated prior to those of the smaller object. If the presentation time for the object is limited, only the larger one will be identified.

We have also implemented a version of SAIM in which attention can be switched from a first to a second object in the visual field. This is done by inhibiting the template and locations in the selection network associated with the first identified object, once identification has taken place. This enables activation from an initial "loser" now to win the competition to gain the mapping into the FOA; attention switches from a first to a second object.

BEHAVIOURAL PROPERTIES OF SAIM

Unlesioned

SAIM shows several behavioural properties that simulate human visual performance. For example, there is a time course for mapping input through to the FOA, and for recognition to occur subsequently. The time taken to map a target through to the FOA can be speeded-up by pre-cueing its location (e.g. by presenting an input briefly, for a few iterations, at the location of the following target; the target is "clamped" onto the retina until recognition takes place). Also, mapping into the FOA can be slowed down by presenting the pre-cue at a location other than that of the target (when, with short intervals between the cue and the target, there can be competition between the stimuli for selection) (see Figure 6). This mimics the effects of spatial cueing studied originally by Posner and his colleagues (Posner, 1980). Also, as noted above, when two targets are presented, recognition takes place for only one at a time; all the parts of the object first selected activate stored memory representations together, and the parts of separate objects are selected serially. This mimics human data on the temporal limitations in identifying multiple targets and on the benefits for selecting parts that belong to one rather than two objects (Duncan, 1984).

Lesioned

Of most relevance to the present paper, however, are the results found when the effects of brain lesioning are simulated using SAIM. Different components in SAIM may be thought of as being equivalent to different parts of the primate visual system. For instance, in general terms, those parts of the model concerned with representing and recognizing (matching to stored knowledge) the contents of the retina, may carry out similar functions to the ventral visual system (i.e. the contents and knowledge networks; see Figure 4). Consistent with this, template units in the knowledge network have large receptive fields and are indifferent to effects of lateral translation across the retina, similar to cells in the more anterior parts of the ventral visual system (e.g. the inferior temporal lobe; Gross et al., 1972). In contrast, those parts of the model concerned with mapping the contents of the retina into the correct positions in the FOA may carry out similar spatial coding functions to the dorsal visual system (i.e. the selection network) (cf. Ungerleider & Mishkin, 1982). Dorsal lesions, which lead to problems in spatial representation in primates, may be mimicked by simulating lesions to the selection network in the model. We have "lesioned" SAIM in several ways. For example, we have examined the effects of damag-

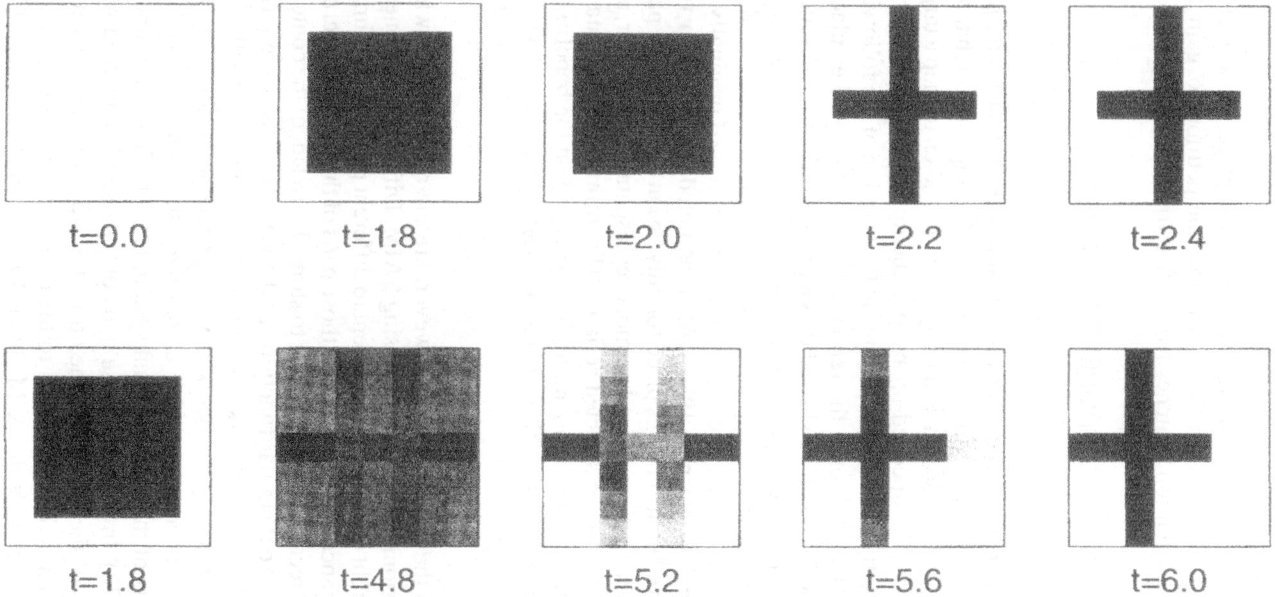

FIG. 6. Performance of the unlesioned model under conditions of spatial cueing. In each window we depict the activation within the FOA, as a function network iterations. The experiment involved first presenting a square at one retinal position for 1.3 cycles, followed by a cross centred either at the same location or at a location on the opposite side of the retina. The top windows show performance when the cue was valid (in the same location as the cross); the bottom windows show performance when the cue was invalid (on the opposite side of the retina to the cross). The model took longer to complete the mapping of the cross into the FOA when the cue was invalid.

ing: (a) input into the selection network from one side of the retina; (b) connections within part of the selection network that receives input from one side of the retina ("vertical lesioning"[1]); (c) connections within the selection network that project out to units on one side of the FOA ("horizontal lesioning"). Figure 7 illustrates the sites of damage in cases (b) and (c).

Examples of the mapping through to the FOA that takes place after lesioning the network are shown in Figures 8 and 9. In these examples, the model was presented with a single cross-stimulus, which would normally (in the unlesioned state) be mapped through so that its centre of gravity is placed at the centre of the FOA. Figure 8 shows the performance of the model after it has sustained a "vertical" lesion affecting input from the left side of its retina, together with damage to the intrinsic connections to and from units in the selection network that receive the damaged retinal projections. In the example, the position of the cross in the visual field is shifted, gradually, from left to right. When the cross is in the far left of the field (far left example), SAIM manifests a form of spatial neglect; only activation from the right-side of the cross is mapped through to the FOA. Underactivity on the (lesioned) left side of the selection network results in activation from just the right side of the cross being projected into the FOA; also, since there is a spread of activation in the selection network to the right but not the left side of the cross, the computed centre of gravity of the cross is shifted and the shape is projected into the left side of the FOA. However, as the cross moves into the centre and right of the visual field, so it falls onto parts of the selection network where the units are unlesioned, and the neglect resolves.

Figure 9 shows the activation values in the FOA of SAIM after a "horizontal" lesion has been applied, which impairs the connections between the units that project to the left side of the FOA. The same pattern of activation in the FOA was found irrespective of the position of the cross in the visual field (i.e. from far left to far right); there was neglect of the left-most pixels in the cross, which were not projected into the FOA. The reasons for the cross being projected too far to the left of the FOA are the same as for the case when a "vertical" lesion was applied; however, since in this instance the units affected were those

[1]The terms "vertical" and "horizontal" lesioning can be understood by reference to Figure 5. The units in vertical columns in the selection network receive input from the visual field, with the columns on the left side of the network receiving input from units on the left of the retina, and those on the right side of the network receiving input from the right side of the retina. A "vertical" lesion, affecting the left-most columns in the network, will selectively affect units that respond specifically to stimuli on the left of the retina. Imagine also that the units in the horizontal layers of the selection network feed activation into the FOA, with the lowest horizontal layers feeding into the left side of the FOA and the uppermost layers feeding into the right side. Now a "horizontal" lesion, affecting the lowest rows in the selection network, will impair the mapping of activation into units on the left side of the FOA.

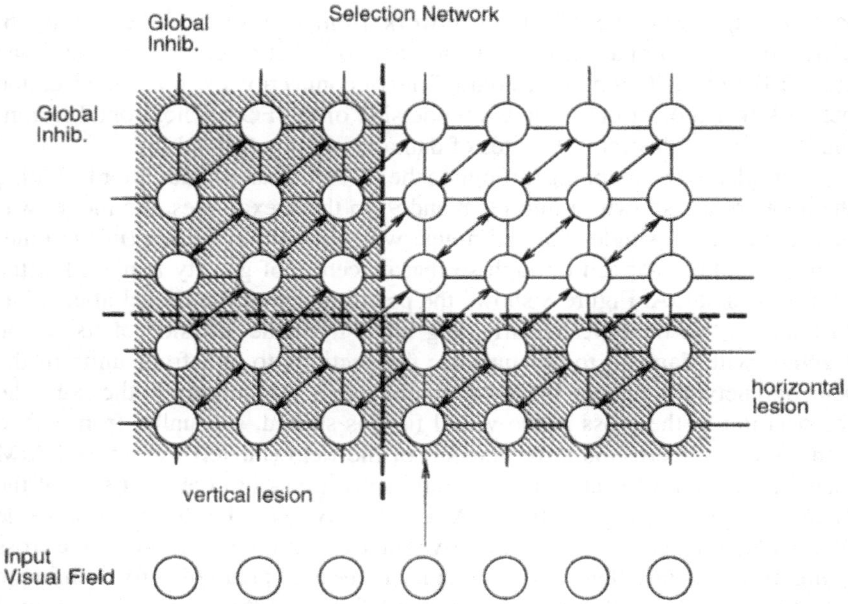

FIG. 7. Lesioning of the selection network. The "vertical" lesion disrupted connections between units connecting to the left side of the retina; the "horizontal" lesion disrupted connections between units connecting to the left side of the FOA.

projecting to one side of the FOA, and these units were involved irrespective of the lateral position of the stimulus on the retina, there was a form of neglect in which the left side of the object was affected consistently across different retinal positions.

These simulations demonstrate that different patterns of neglect can emerge after damage to contrasting sites in the model. Furthermore, SAIM manifests a form of neglect that is independent of the lateral position of the object even though the model does not employ any form of object-centred representation for recognition, in the sense that no representation is formed using a coordinate system centred on the object (cf. Caramazza & Hillis, 1990; Marr & Nishihara, 1978). Neglect independent of lateral position occurs in SAIM when there is disruption to the mappings into one side of the FOA, but the FOA itself remains coded in retinal coordinates. This is not to state that forms of object-centred neglect may not occur, in which neglect is linked to spatial coordinates defined relative to a property of the object (though see also Buxbaum, Coslett, Montgomery, & Farah, 1996, for evidence that apparent object-centred neglect may be linked to a mental rotation strategy). However, the model does show that neglect that is simply independent of the lateral position of the stimulus may be distinguishable from true object-centred neglect, and that the former

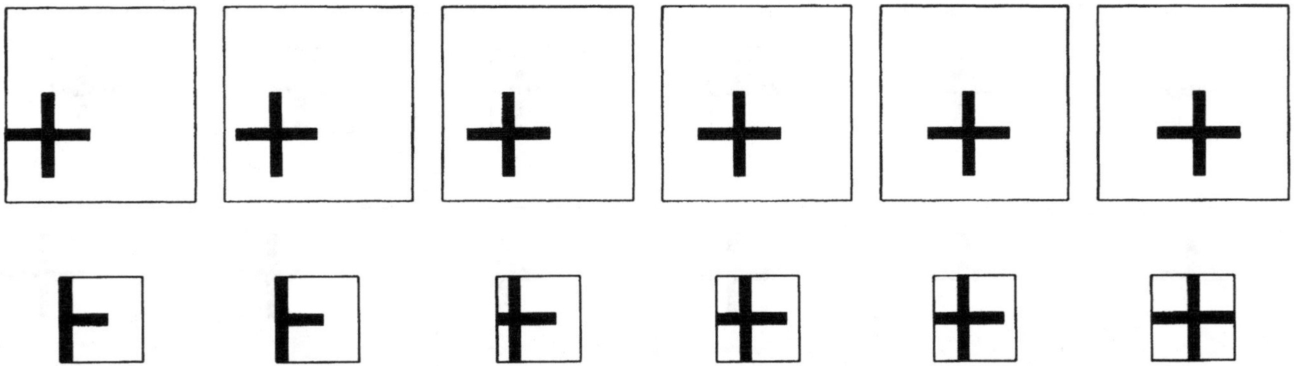

FIG. 8. The mapping of activity through to the FOA after a "vertical" lesion. The top windows illustrate the positions of the cross as it is moved from the left to the right side of the retina. The bottom windows show activity in the FOA for each spatial position. When the cross is in the left visual field there is pronounced neglect of the left arm of the cross, which resolves as the cross is moved to the right side of the field.

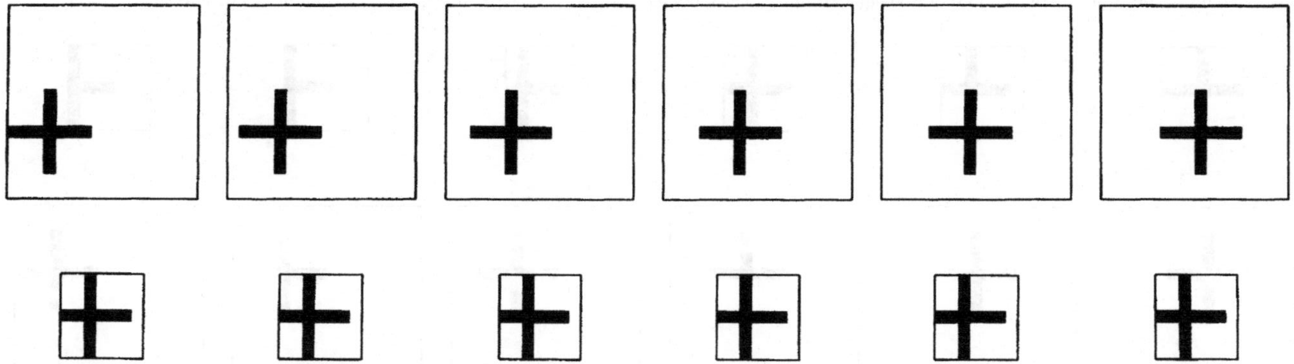

FIG. 9. The mapping of activity to the FOA after a "horizontal" lesion. In this case, there is neglect of the left arm of the cross (a failure to represent the left-most pixels in the FOA) even when the cross appears in the right visual field.

type of neglect should not be taken to imply the existence of object-centred representations.

ATTENTION AND REPRESENTATION

Theoretical interpretations of unilateral neglect typically make a contrast between "attentional" and "representational" accounts of the syndrome (see Bisiach & Luzzatti, 1978; Riddoch & Humphreys, 1987, 1994). Within an attentional account, neglect is attributed to a deficit in orienting visual attention to the affected side of space. Within a representational account, neglect is attributed to the impairment of one side of a particular spatial representation. Two pieces of evidence often marshalled in favour of the attentional account are the effects of spatial cueing on neglect and the phenomenon of extinction. The effects of spatial cueing on neglect are asymmetrical; the detection of stimuli on the neglected side can be improved when the patient is cued to attend to that side, but detection can be severely disrupted when attention is cued to the opposite side (Posner, Walker, Friedrich, & Rafal, 1984). In the phenomenon of extinction, a patient may be able to detect a single stimulus shown on the affected side, but fails to detect the same stimulus when another (competing) stimulus is shown simultaneously on the affected side (Karnath, 1988). In both instances, the degree of impairment varies under conditions that place the stimulus on the affected side under competition for detection with a stimulus on the unaffected side, consistent with the stimulus on the affected side only weakly attracting attention.

Interestingly, SAIM, when lesioned, manifests both asymmetrical cueing effects and the phenomenon of extinction. For example, if a spatial pre-cue is provided by activating pixels briefly on the affected or unaffected side of space prior to the presentation of a target on the affected side, then the mapping of the target into the FOA is improved when the cue is on the same side but it is markedly disrupted when the cue is presented on the unaffected side (see Figure 10). Similarly, a single stimulus presented on the affected side may be mapped into the FOA, but it may fail to be mapped into the FOA when a second stimulus is presented on the unaffected side (Figure 11). If the stimuli are presented for a brief duration to the model, then the affected stimulus will not be mapped into the FOA at all. This mimics the phenomenon of extinction.

SAIM generates both asymmetrical cueing effects and extinction, even though it has no explicit mechanism of visual attention. In the model, the cueing and extinction effects emerge because there is competition between stimuli to "win" the mapping from the selection network to the FOA, and this competition is unbalanced when the model is spatially lesioned. In this respect, SAIM performs similarly to other recent models of visual attention in which the effects of spatially cueing in neglect are captured by unbalancing competitive interactions between units on the left and right sides of space (Cohen, Romero,

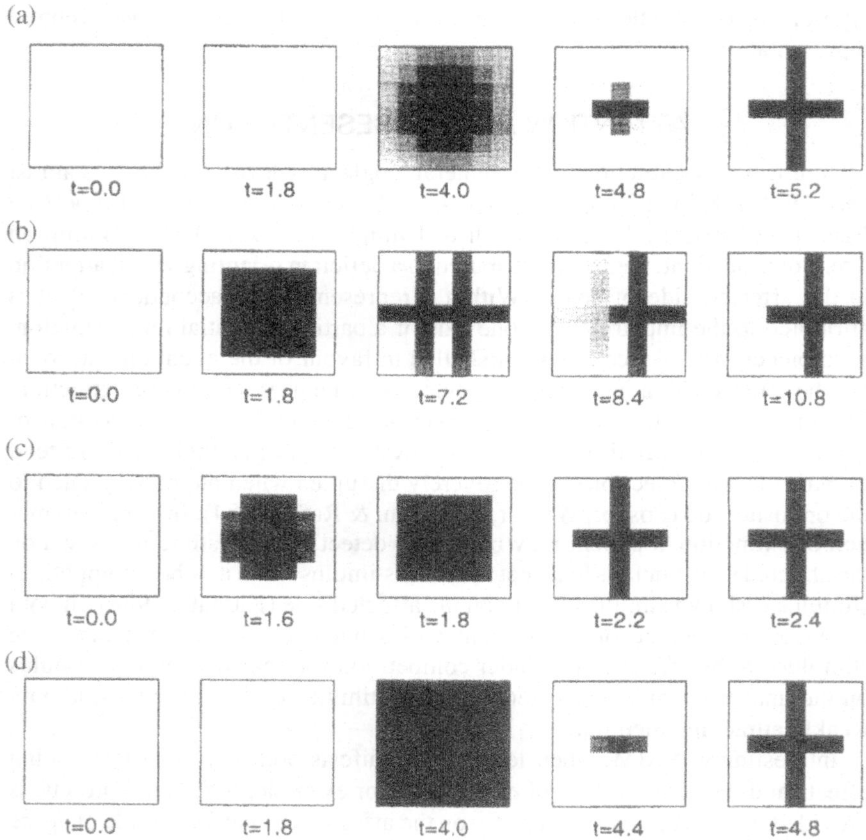

FIG. 10. Performance of the lesioned model under conditions of spatial cueing (with a "vertical" lesion). The presentation conditions were the same as for the cueing experiment with the unlesioned model (Figure 6). (a) Performance with a valid cue and the target in the impaired field; (b) performance with an invalid cue and the target in the impaired field; (c) a valid cue and the target in the unimpaired field; (d) an invalid cue and the target in the unimpaired field. The model shows a large effect of invalid cueing, particularly when the target is in the impaired visual field (note that the cross used was smaller than that in Figures 8 and 9, and so showed less neglect).

Servan-Schreiber, & Farah, 1994; Humphreys, Olson, Romani, & Riddoch, 1996). However, in SAIM, "attentional" operations are implemented through interactions within a spatial mapping process and not within a specific mechanism of visual attention; thus, in SAIM, the attentional and representational accounts of neglect converge.

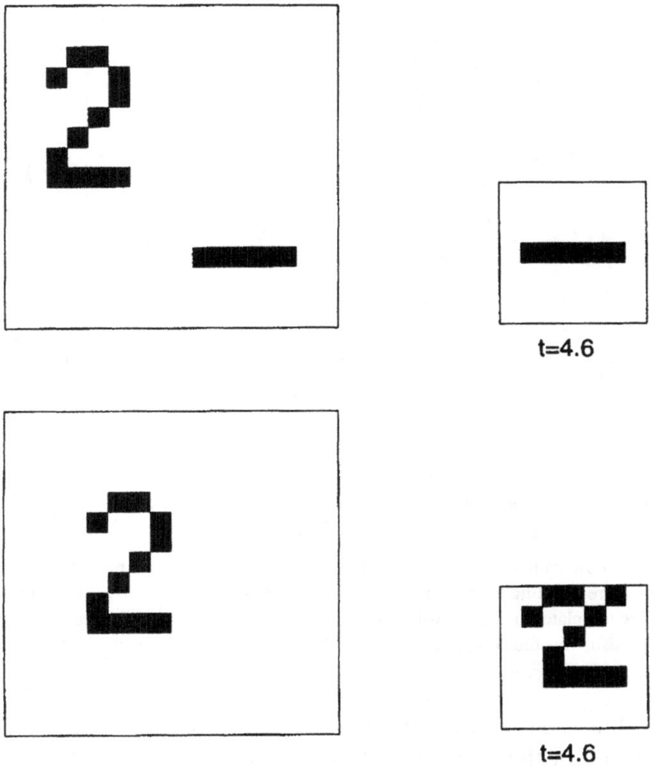

FIG. 11. "Extinction" in the model after a "vertical" lesion. With two stimuli in the visual field (a bar in the unimpaired field and a "2" in the impaired field), the bar is preferentially mapped into the FOA (even though it is the smaller stimulus and would normally be mapped into the FOA second). When just the "2" is present (still in the impaired field), it is mapped into the FOA within the same time period (though here with some degree of spatial distortion).

DISENGAGING ATTENTION FROM OBJECTS

So far we have dealt with how one of two objects, or the parts of a single object, are initially mapped through to the FOA in SAIM. In the full version of the model, however, activity in the FOA is subsequently mapped through to a set of "template" units, to simulate object recognition. After recognition has taken place, inhibition is applied to locations in the selection network that match attended locations (in the FOA). This removes the object first identified, and allows other objects in the visual field to be selected for identification; attention is "switched" from one object to another. An example of SAIM switching attention is shown in Figure 12. The model was presented with an arrow

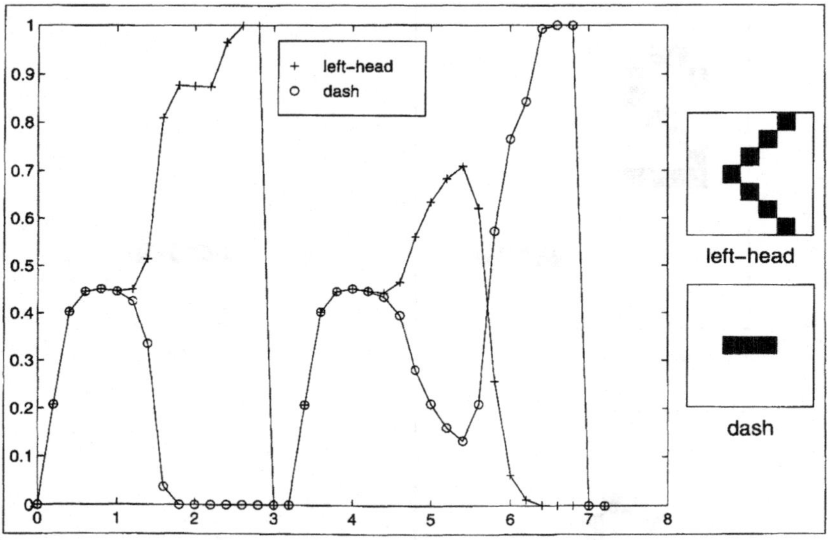

FIG. 12. Attention-switching in the unlesioned version of SAIM. Here we plot the activation values in template units corresponding to an arrow head (<) and a bar (–). The arrowhead was presented to the left of the bar. The template for the arrowhead first reaches threshold (and is then re-set); as processing continues, so the dash wins the competition for the FOA and its template reaches threshold.

stimulus, <–, but had two templates (for < and for –). Figure 12 illustrates the activation values in the two template units as a function of the number of network iterations after the onset of the stimulus. Initially, there is activation of both templates; however, over time, the template for the arrowhead becomes dominant (since there are more input pixels supporting that stimulus, so that it wins the competition to map through to the FOA). When the arrowhead template activation value reaches 1.0, identification is deemed to have taken place and associated locations in the selection network are inhibited. This enables activation from the dash stimulus (–) to become dominant and, subsequently, for its template to reach threshold.

In Figure 13, we show the performance of the model after we implemented a "horizontal" lesion that was sufficient to distort the mapping from the selection network to the left side of the FOA but not so severe as to prevent the stimulus being identified (this might happen if there were severe neglect of the individual stimulus). The results contrast with those in the unlesioned model (Figure 12) in two ways. First, the initial template that becomes activated is the one corresponding to the dash (in the right field) not the arrowhead (in the left field), even though the arrowhead is the larger of the two stimuli and would normally be identified first. There is thus a spatial bias in selection. Second, SAIM fails to inhibit successfully those locations in the selection network

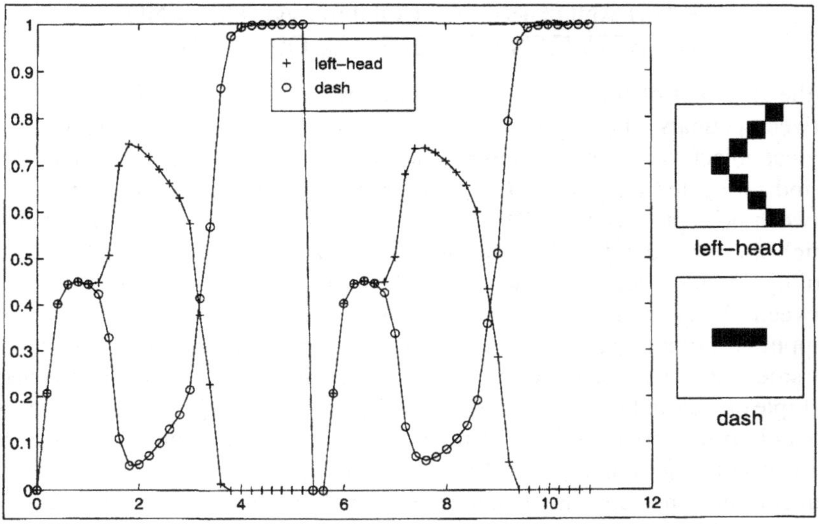

FIG. 13. A disengagement deficit. SAIM was given a "horizontal" lesion insufficient to produce neglect of individual stimuli. Activation values in the template unites are plotted for the arrowhead and bar stimuli (as in Figure 12). The template for the bar now reaches its threshold first (unlike in Figure 12) and is re-set. However, due to the bar being displaced within the FOA, it is not properly inhibited within the selection network and continues to compete for selection with the arrowhead as processing continues. SAIM then fails to "disengage" attention from the first object to the second.

linked to the dash, even when the template ifself is re-set to zero after identification takes place (see Figure 13). This problem in inhibiting previously identified stimuli occurs because there is some distortion in the spatial mapping of stimuli from locations activated in the selection network to locations in the FOA (as we have shown above, a severe distortion in this mapping process can lead to the neglect of individual stimuli). Thus inhibition is not necessarily applied to the locations in the selection network activated by the input, enabling that input again to compete for attention. This generates a problem in disengaging attention from the right-most object, and neglect of the left-most of two objects. Note that a behavioural problem in disengaging attention is produced here even though there is no impairment to the processes that bring about attention disengagement in the model—there is no lesion affecting the inhibition of any template following its activation, and no impairment affecting how inhibition is applied to the associated units in the selection network. All the network's problems reflect the impaired initial mapping into the FOA. The simulation shows that a behavioural problem in disengaging attention does not necessarily reflect an impaired "disengagement mechanism" (see also Cohen et al. 1994; Humprhreys et al., 1996).

SAIM AND SPATIAL CODING WITHIN AND BETWEEN PERCEPTUAL OBJECTS

In the first part of this paper, we reported evidence of a double dissociation between patients who neglect one side of individual objects and patients who neglect objects on one side of multi-object displays, and we interpreted the data as indicating the existence of separate representations of space within and between perceptual objects. The simulations with SAIM illustrate one way in which these different representations may relate to one another. In SAIM, activity in the selection network can be thought to implement a form of between-object spatial coding, in which separate objects compete to win the mapping for object recognition. A lesion that affects the mapping of input *into* one side of the selection network will bias the competition for selection between multiple objects to favour those falling on the unaffected side. However, objects that fall on the unaffected side can be fully represented within the FOA. The FOA, in contrast, implements a form of within-object spatial coding, in which elements are considered as parts of a common object by the recognition system. Neglect within perceptual objects arises if a lesion disrupts those outputs from the selection network that map into lateral parts of the FOA. In addition to the above, there can be problems in disengaging attention from an object first attended, if that object is not mapped correctly into the FOA (if the object is neglected or, indeed, if there is some other form of spatial distortion). In SAIM, a disengagement problem can emerge following both types of lesions — those affecting between-object competition between inputs and those affecting the mapping of parts within objects in the FOA, since both lesions can produce spatial distortions and neglect in the FOA. The magnitude of the disengagement problem will increase as a function of the degree of distortion present in the FOA. Interestingly, this predicts that there can be patterns of association as well as dissociation between the different forms of neglect. In patients with relatively mild neglect within objects, there may be relatively little problem in disengaging attention between objects, since the spatial distortion will be relatively slight. However, in more severe cases, disengagement problems will emerge because spatial distortions are introduced. In the latter cases, there will be neglect not only within but also between separate objects. In contrast to this, it should be possible to have severe neglect between objects but still to show intact processing of both sides of items in the unaffected field.

One other point to note is that, in SAIM, both within- and between-object spatial representations are coded retinotopically. Thus the nature of the coordinate system involved does not differentiate the two forms of representation, rather the representations are differentiated by the relationship between their elements; elements in separate objects compete for selection, whereas those in within-object spatial representations cooperate in visual object recognition. In SAIM, within-object spatial representations are outcomes of the competition between separate perceptual objects to achieve translation-independent object recognition. This order of spatial coding suggested by SAIM is also consistent with patients with neglect between perceptual objects having more posterior lesions than those showing neglect within objects (see above), a point we return to below.

We should also note that, because SAIM uses view-dependent coding of parts within objects, it does not provide a ready account of those additional neglect patients whose deficit seems to remain on one side of the object even when the object is rotated so that the affected part falls on the ipsilesional side of viewed space (cf. Caramazza & Hillis, 1990; Tipper & Behrmann, 1996). However, it may be that forms of mental rotation are involved in such cases (Buxbaum et al., 1996), so that, essentially the input is re-mapped; one effect of this may be that stimuli on the right side of the retina now fall on the left of the internal spatial representation, and this representation serves as input to the recognition system in the normal way. It is also possible that forms of rotation may be simulated by SAIM if top-down activation is allowed to play a substantial role in the selection network. This topic awaits future research.

CONCLUSIONS

We have summarized two lines of research showing:

1. A double dissociation between patients who manifest neglect within individual perceptual objects, and patients who show neglect between separate perceptual objects.
2. That the two forms of neglect are associated with contrasting lesion sites in patients, possibly in the inferior frontal and posterior parietal lobes for within- and between-object neglect respectively.
3. That different patterns of spatial representation can emerge in a computational model, SAIM, in which translation-invariant object recognition is achieved through a process of selective mapping into a single focus of attention (FOA). In the model, a form of between-object coding operates in a selection network, where there is competition to win the mapping into the FOA; in contrast, a form of within-object coding operates within the FOA.
4. Different forms of "neglect" can be shown by the model after spatially selective lesioning of either (a) units in the selection network receiving input from one side of the visual field, or (b) units projecting from the selection network to one side of the FOA. In addition, spatially selective lesioning can lead to the model having problems in "disengaging" attention when there are multiple objects present.

The present neuropsychological studies of patients with neglect reaffirm the existence of distinct forms of spatial representation in human vision. The computational work suggests possible roles of these representations in behaviour. In SAIM, between-object spatial coding is used to select between stimuli for object identification; within-object spatial coding is used to achieve identification that is independent of the lateral positions of objects. After lesioning, the forms of neglect manifested by the model reflect the contrasting computational roles of the two types of representation; neglect is based on either the relative spatial positions of separate objects (between-object neglect) or on the relative positions of parts in an object, irrespective of the lateral position of the object in the field (within-object neglect). The model also collapses the distinction between "attentional" and "representational" accounts of neglect, since "attentional" operations in the model emerge from competition within the network to achieve appropriate mappings for translation-invariant identification; the different forms of spatial representation reflect the constraints of this mapping process.

We have also summarized evidence on the functional localization of within-object spatial coding in the brain, based on the common lesion site across the patients. In our cases, the common lesion sites lies in the inferior frontal lobe, a site recently implicated in neglect by other investigators (Hussain & Kennard, 1996). However, the apparent location of within-object spatial representations, in the inferior frontal lobe, is somewhat difficult to reconcile with our current understanding of the brain areas mediating object recognition. Usually it is assumed that on-line object recognition takes place within the temporal lobes (Desimone & Ungerleider, 1989; for recent evidence from PET studies with humans, see Martin, Wiggs, Ungerleider, & Haxby, 1996; Price et al., 1996), and so object recognition should be achieved prior to there being activation of more anterior inferior frontal lobe areas. From this, we might conclude that the within-object spatial codes held in frontal areas are not directly involved in on-line object recognition. It would also follow that the within-object codes constructed in SAIM's FOA are not the same as the codes that are impaired in the patients, because in SAIM translation-invariant coding takes place on-line in object recognition. Against this account, though is that the present patients with within-object neglect did have problems in on-line object recognition; for instance, they misidentified chimeric faces.

A second possibility is that the deficit in within-object spatial coding we observed in the patients does indeed reflect a representation similar to that used by SAIM, but this form of coding (in the inferior frontal lobe) is part of a secondary route for object recognition. The more direct route for object recognition may involve viewpoint-dependent critical parts encoded in the temporal lobe (Logothetis & Pauls, 1995; Logothetis, Pauls & Poggio, 1995; Tarr, 1995). Within-object spatial coding, of the type we have examined in SAIM, may be necessary only when the spatial relations between the parts of objects must be used for object identification, or when attention must be focused on one of many objects present (to avoid competition from multiple parts in different objects).

It is also possible that within-object coding, in the inferior frontal lobe, is used in a top-down manner to help "tie together" visual features encoded within the temporal lobe. These proposals can be evaluated by future research that addresses the nature of within-object neglect in patients in more detail. For example, is within-object neglect apparent mainly when the spatial relations between the parts of objects have to be encoded? Do such patients show little neglect when objects can be identified from individual distinctive features, even if such features fall on the affected side of the object? These speculations go beyond the current research. What is important, however, is that further questions concerning the nature of within-object neglect are generated here from the interaction between neuropsychological research and computational modelling. In this respect, the modelling research can be shown not only to capture known patterns of neglect, but also to generate new hypotheses.

REFERENCES

Andersen, R.A. (1988). Visual and visual-motor functions of the posterior parietal cortex. In P. Rakic & W. Singer (Eds), *Neurobiology of neocortex.* London: Wiley.

Behrmann, M., & Tipper, S.P. (1994). Object-based visual attention: Evidence from unilateral neglect. In C. Umiltà & M. Moscovitch (Eds), *Attention and performance XV.* Cambridge, MA: MIT Press.

Biederman, I. (1987). Recognition-by-components: A theory of human image understanding. *Psychological Review, 94,* 115–147.

Bisiach, E., & Luzzatti, C. (1978). Unilateral neglect of representational space. *Cortex, 14,* 129–13.

Buck, B., et al. (in press). Spatial- and object-based attentional deficits in Alzheimer's disease: Relationship to HMPAO SPECT measures of parietal perfusion. *Brain.*

Buxbaum, L.J., Coslett, H.B., Montgomery, M.W., & Farah, M.J. (1996). Mental rotation may underlie apparent object-based neglect. *Neuropsychologia, 14,* 113–126.

Caramazza, A. & Hillis, A.E. (1990). Levels of representation, co-ordinate frames and unilateral neglect. *Cognitive Neuropsychology, 7,* 391–445.

Cohen, J.D., Romero, R.D., Servan-Schreiber, D., & Farah, M.J. (1994). Mechanisms of spatial attention: The relation of macrostructure to microstructure in parietal neglect. *Journal of Cognitive Neuroscience, 6,* 377–387.

Critchley, M. (1953). *The parietal lobes.* London: Hafner Press.

De Renzi, E. (1982). *Disorders of spatial exploration and cognition.* London: Wiley.

Desimone, R. (1992). Neural circuits for visual attention in the primate brain. In G.A. Carpenter & S. Grossberg (Eds), *Neural networks for vision and image processing.* Cambridge, MA: MIT Press.

Desimone, R., & Ungerleider, L.G. (1989). Neural mechanisms of visual processing in monkeys. In F. Boller & J. Grafman (Eds), *Handbook of neuropsychology,* Vol. II. Amsterdam: Elsevier.

Desimone, R., Albright, T.D., Gross, C.G., & Bruce, C. (1984). Stimulus selective properties of inferior temporal neurons in the macaque. *Journal of Neuroscience, 4,* 2051–2062.

Driver, J., & Halligan, P.W. (1991). Can visual neglect operate in object-centred co-ordinates? An affirmative single-case study. *Cognitive Neuropsychology, 8,* 475–496.

Duncan, J. (1984). Selective attention and the organisation of visual information. *Journal of Experimental Psychology: General, 113,* 501–517.

Egly, R., Driver, J., & Rafal, R.D. (1994). Shifting visual attention between objects and locations: Evidence from normal and parietal lesion subjects. *Journal of Experimental Psychology: General, 123,* 161–177.

Farah, M.J., & Hammond, K.L. (1988). Mental rotation and orientation-invariant object recognition: Dissociable processes. *Cognition, 29,* 29–46.

Goldberg, M.E., & Segraves, M.A. (1987). Visuospatial and motor attention in the monkey. *Neuropsychologia, 25,*107–118.

Graziano, M.S.A., & Gross, C.G. (1993). A bimodal map of space: Somatosensory receptive fields in the macaque putamen with corresponding visual receptive fields. *Experimental Brain Research, 97,* 96–109.

Gross, C.G., Rocha-Miranda, C.E., & Bender, D.B. (1972). Visual properties of neurons in inferotemporal cortex of the macaque. *Journal of Neuropsychology, 35, 96–111.*

Halligan, P.W., & Marshall, J.C. (1991) Left neglect for near but not far space in man. *Nature, 350,* 498–500.

Heinke, D., & Humphreys, G.W. (in prep.). SAIM: A connectionist model of selection for identification, in normality and pathology.

Hillis, A.E., & Caramazza, A. (1995). A framework for interpreting distinct patterns of hemispatial neglect. *Neurocase, 1,* 189–207.

Hopfield, J. (1984). Neurons with graded response have collective computational properties like thos of two-state neurons. *Proceedings of the National Academy of Science, 81,* 3088–3092.

Humphreys, G.W., & Riddoch, M.J. (1994). Attention to within-object and between-object spatial representations: Multiple loci for visual selection. *Cognitive Neuropsychology, 11,* 207–241.

Humphreys, G.W., & Riddoch, M.J. (1995). Separate coding of space within and between perceptual objects: Evidence from unilateral visual neglect. *Cognitive Neuropsychology, 12,* 283–311.

Humphreys, G.W., Olson, A., Romani, C., & Riddoch, M.J. (1996). Competitive mechanisms of selection by space and object: A neuropsychological approach. In A.F. Kramer, M.G.H. Coles, & G.D. Logan (Eds), *Converging operations in the study of visual selective attention.* Washington, DC: American Psychological Association.

Humphreys, G.W., Riddoch, M.J., Romani, C. (submitted). The representation of space within and between perceptual objects: A dissociative and neuroanatomical approach. *Brain.*

Hussain, M., & Kennard, C.J. (1996). Visual neglect associated with frontal lobe infarction. *Journal of Neurology, 243,* 652–657.

Karnath, H.O. (1988). Deficits of attention in acute and recovered visual hemi-neglect. *Neuropsychologia, 26,* 27–43.

Logothetis, N.K., & Pauls, J. (1995). Psychophysical and physiological evidence for viewer-centred object representations in the primate. *Cerebral Cortex, 3,* 270–288.

Logothetis, N.K., Pauls, J. & Poggio, T. (1995). Shape representation in the inferior temporal cortex of monkeys. *Current Biology, 5,* 552–563.

Marr, D. (1982). *Vision.* San Francisco, CA: W.H. Freeman.

Marr, D., & Nishihara, H.K. (1978). Representation and recognition of the spatial organisation of three-dimensional shapes. *Proceedings of the Royal Society, B200,* 269–294.

Martin, A., Wiggs, C.L., Ungerleider, L.G., & Haxby, J.V. (1996). Neural correlates of category-specific knowledge. *Nature, 379,* 949–652.

Mattingley, J.B., Bradshaw, J.L., Phillips, J.G., & Bradshaw, J.A. (1993). Reversed perceptual asymmetry for faces in left unilateral neglect. *Brain and Cognition, 23,* 145–165.

Milner, D.A., & Goodale, M.A. (1995). *The visual brain in action.* Oxford: Oxford University Press.

Mjolsness, E., & Garrett, C. (1990). Algebraic transformations of objective functions. *Neural Networks, 3,* 651–669.

Olshausen, B.A., Andersen, C.H., & Van Essen, D.C. (1993). A neurobiological model of visual attention and invariant pattern recognition based on dynamic routing of information. *Journal of Neuroscience, 13,* 4700–4719.

Olshausen, B.A., Andersen, C.H., & Van Essen, D.C. (1995). A multiscale dynamic routing circuit for forming size- and position-invariant object representations. *Journal of Computational Neuroscience, 2.* 45–62.

Olson, C.R., & Gettner, S.N. (1995). Object-centred direction selectivity in the macaque supplementary eye field. *Science, 269,* 985–988.

Posner, M.I. (1980). Orienting of attention. *Quarterly Journal of Experimental Psychology, 32,* 3–25.

Posner, M.I. Walker, J.A., Friedrich, F.J., & Rafal, R.D. (1984). Effects of parietal lobe injury on covert orienting of visual attention. *Journal of Neuroscience, 4,* 1863–1874.

Postma, E.O. (1994). *SCAN: A neural model of covert attention.* PhD thesis, Computer Science Department, University of Limburg, Maastricht, The Netherlands.

Price, C.J., et al. (1996). The neural pathways sustaining object and colour naming. *Proceedings of the Royal Society, B263,* 1501–1507.

Ratcliff, G. (1979). Spatial thought, mental rotation and the right cerebral hemisphere. *Neuropsychologia, 17,* 48–54.

Riddoch, M.J., & Humphreys, G.W. (1987). Perceptual and action systems in unilateral visual neglect. In M. Jeannerod (Ed.), *Neurophysiological and neuropsychological aspects of spatial neglect.* Amsterdam: Elsevier.

Riddoch, M.J., & Humphreys, G.W. (1994). Towards an understanding of neglect. In M.J. Riddoch & G.W. Humphreys (Eds), *Cognitive neuropsychology and cognitive rehabilitation.* Hove: Lawrence Erlbaum Associates Ltd.

Riddoch, M.J., Humphreys, G.W., Luckhurst, L., Burroughs, E. & Bateman, A. (1995a). "Paradoxical neglect": Spatial representations, hemispher-specific activation and spatial cueing. *Cognitive Neuropsychology, 12,* 569–604.

Riddoch, M.J., Humphreys, G.W., Burroughs, E., Luckhurst, L., Bateman, A., & Hill, S. (1995b). Cueing in a case of neglect: Modality and automaticity effects. *Cognitive Neuropsychology, 12,* 605–622.

Rumelhart, D.E., Hinton, G.E., & McClelland, J.L. (1986). A general framework for parallel distributed processing. In D.E. Rumelhart, J.L. McClelland, & the PDP Research Group (Eds), *Parallel distributed processing: Explorations in the microstructure of cognition,* Vol. 1 Cambridge, MA: MIT Press.

Sakata, H., Shibutani, H., Kawano, K., & Harrington, T. (1985). Neural mechanisms of space vision in the parietal association cortex of the monkey. *Vision Research, 25,* 453–464.

Tarr, M. (1995). Rotating objects to recognize them: A case study on the role of viewpoint dependency in the recognition of three-dimensional objects. *Psychological Bulletin and Review, 2,* 55–82.

Tipper, S.P. & Behrmann, M. (1996). Object-centred not scene-based visual neglect. *Journal of Experimental Psychology: Human Perception and Performance, 22,* 1261–1278.

Ungerleider, L.G., & Mishkin, M. (1982). Two cortical visual systems. In J. Ingle, M.A. Goodale, & R.J.W. Mansfield (Eds), *Analysis of visual behavior.* Cambridge, MA: MIT Press.

Walker, R. (1995). Spatial and object-based neglect. *Neurocase, 1,* 371–383.

Walker, R., Findlay, J.M., Young, A.W., & Lincoln, N. (1996). Saccadic eye movements in object-based neglect. *Cognitive Neuropsychology, 13,* 569–615.

Young, A.W., Newcombe, F., & Ellis, A.W. (1991). Different impairments contribute to neglect dyslexia. *Cognitive Neuropsychology, 8,* 177–191.

Young, A.W., Hellawell, D.J., & Welch, J. (1992). Neglect and visual recognition. *Brain, 112, 51–71.*

APPENDIX

This appendix gives a brief overview on the mathematical foundation of SAIM. For a complete introduction, see Heinke and Humphreys (in prep.).

Contents Network

The contents network contains "sigma-pi" units (Rumelhart et al., 1986) that determine the activation values assigned to units in the FOA by combining multiplicatively activation in units in the visual field with that in units in the selection network:

$$y_{ij}^{FOA} = \sum_{k=1}^{N} \sum_{l=1}^{N} y_{kl}^{VF} \cdot y_{ikjl} \tag{1}$$

Here y_{ij}^{FOA} is the activation of units in the FOA, y_{kl}^{VF} the activation of units in the visual field, and y_{ikjl} the activation of units in the selection network. N is the size of the visual field.

The functioning of the contents network becomes clear in the following example. If we assume that only one unit of the selection network has the value 1 and all other units are 0, then the sigma-pi unit puts the value of the corresponding visual field unit through to the corresponding location in the FOA. This mapping can be achieved for every unit in the visual field and requires that the appropriate unit in the selection network is active. In this way, the contents network enables a translation-invariant representation of the contents of the visual field.

Selection Network

The selection network (y_{ikjl}) is considerably larger than the contents network and it determines which retinal units have their activation values mapped through to the FOA (via the contents network), as discussed in the previous section. Within the selection network are separate "control layers" of units, and the units in each control layer are activated by input from specific retinal locations. The indices k and l of y_{ikjl} refer to retinal locations. Each control layer controls one unit in the contents network. The indices i and j refer to the different control layers and the corresponding locations in the FOA. Figure 5 explains how the control layers control the mapping of the contents network.

Which retinal units come to be mapped through to the FOA is determined by mutual constraint satisfaction between units in the selection network, and mutual constraint satisfaction is in turn achieved by the network embodying certain relationships in its pattern of interconnectivity. This approach is reformulated in terms of the minimization of an energy function using a gradient descent method. This kind of approach was first introduced to connectionist models by Hopfield (1984). In the following paragraph, the energy function for the selection network will be derived.

The use of the "sigma-pi" units requires that y_{ikjl}-values close to 1 or 0 have a clear reproduction of the retinal input. This constraint is satisfied by the energy function in a leaky integrator (for a discussion, see Hopfield, 1984):

$$E_{leak} = \sum_{i,k,j,l} \int_0^{y_{ikjl}} f^{-1}(x)dx \tag{2}$$

with the sigmoid function:

$$f(x) = \frac{1}{1+e^{-m(x-s)}}$$

and with $y_{iklj} = f(x_{ikjl})$.

According to the first constraint illustrated in Figure 6, only one unit in each control layer should be maximally active and all other units should have zero output activity. This suggests a winner takes all

(WTA) mechanism between units of a contol layer. The energy function for this type of behaviour can be defined as:

$$E_{WTA}(y_i) = a \cdot \left(\sum_i y_i - 1 \right)^2 - \sum_i y_i \cdot I_i \tag{3}$$

where I_i is the input. This energy function is minimal, when all y_i's are zero except one y_i and corresponding I_i has the maximal value of all I_is (see Mjolsness & Garrett, 1990). This equation would force one unit of the control layer to be 1; however, there should be the possibility for attention not to be allocated to any location. Thus, a two-state winner take all (WTA2) was introduced:

$$E_{\text{WTA2}}^{(1)}\left(y_{ikjl}\right) = \sum_{ij} \left(\sum_{k,l} y_{ikjl-1} \right)^2 \cdot \left(\sum_{k,l} y_{ikjl} \right)^2 \tag{4}$$

The multiplicational part of this equation introduces a second minimum into the energy function, where all units can stay zero and so attention is not directed to any location. This equation adds a threshold function to the WTA behaviour, whereby the output activity of the units stay zero as long as the input activity is below a certain level. The input to the WTA2 is built by the visual field and will be introduced below.

The second constraint illustrated in Figure 5 leads to a WTA2 behaviour between control layers as well, producing a second WTA2 energy function.

$$\left(E_{\text{WTA2}}^{(2)}\left(y_{ikjl}\right) \right)$$

The last constraint aims at preserving the neighbourhood relation between units. For this, the energy function should be minimal when adjacent units on the diagonal are active (Figure 5). This is achieved by the following equation:

$$E_{neighbour}\left(y_{ikjl}\right) = -\sum_{i,j,k,l} \sum_{s=-L}^{L} \sum_{r=-1}^{L} g_{sr} \cdot y_{ikjl} \cdot y_{i+r,k+s,j+r,l+s} \tag{5}$$

The coefficient g_{sr} introduces Gaussian weighting into the equation and operates so that units in the immediate neighbourhood are likely to be more active than ones further out. This implements a simple form of perceptual grouping determined by the proximity of the elements.

Finally, the visual field builds an input to each control layer. As in equation 3, this is given by the following energy function:

$$E_{input}\left(y_{ikjl}\right) = -\sum_{k,l} y_{ikjl} \cdot y_{kl}^{VF} \tag{6}$$

This leads to a preference for high input values over low (zero) input values.

Knowledge Network

The model presented so far does not include knowledge about objects. To introduce knowledge into SAIM, a simple template-matching approach was used. Here, the match between templates and contents of the FOA was determined using a scalar product as a similarity measure:

$$I_m^{temp} = \sum_{l=1}^{M} \sum_{j=1}^{M} y_{ij}^{FOA*} \cdot w_{ij}^{m} \tag{7}$$

where w_{ij}^{m}'s are the templates and M is the size of the FOA.

The templates are implemented in the knowledge network, where the templates are formed from the connecting weights into template units $\left(y_m^{temp}\right)$. The template unit with the best matching template should have the activity 1 and all other template units should have zero activity. To realize this function, again a simple WTA was used (equation 3):

$$E_{knowledge}\left(y_m^{temp}, y_{ikjl}\right) = a^{temp} \cdot \left(\sum_m y_m^{temp} = 1\right)^2 - \sum_m^K y_m^{temp} \cdot I_m^{temp} \tag{8}$$

where K is the number of template units.

To get the complete energy function which satisfies all constraints, one simply sums the different energy functions:

$$\begin{aligned} E_{total}\left(y_m^{temp}, y_{ikjl}\right) &= a_1 \cdot E_{WTA2}^{(1)}\left(y_{ikjl}\right) + a_2 \cdot E_{WTA2}^{(2)}\left(y_{ikjl}\right) \\ &+ b_1 \cdot E_{neighbour}\left(y_{ikjl}\right) + b_2 \cdot E_{input}\left(y_{ikjl}\right) + \\ &b_3 \cdot E_{knowledge}\left(y_m^{temp}, y_{ikjl}\right) + E_{leak1}\left(y_{ikjl}\right) + E_{leak2}\left(y_m^{temp}\right) \end{aligned} \tag{9}$$

The coefficients of the different energy functions weight the different constraints against each other.

Topology

The energy function introduced in the previous section defines mimima at certain values of y_{ikjl} and y_m^{temp}, where they satisfy the constraints for a correct functioning of SAIM. To find these values, a gradient descent was used as in Hopfield (1984):

$$\dot{x}_{ikjl} = -\frac{\partial E_{total}\left(y_{ikjl}, y_m^{temp}\right)}{\partial y_{ikjl}} \tag{10}$$

This leads to a set of differential equations. The solution of the differential equations determines the temporal behaviour of the selection network as it tries to minimize the energy of the whole system. In other words, each differential equation stands for a unit of the selection network and each unit tries to minimize the energy of SAIM (see Heinke & Humphreys, in prep., for details).

For the selection network, this leads to the topology depicted in Figure 5, where each unit in the selection network links to four different inputs. The first input $\left(I_{ikjl}^-\right)$ provides global inhibition, which comes from WTA2 behaviour. The second input is derived from the neighbourhood-preserving behaviour I_{ikjl}^+. The third input comes from the visual field $\left(y_{kl}^{VF}\right)$. The last input comes from the knowledge network and involves top-down modulation I_{ikjl}^{td}. In terms of this view, the mathematical description of each unit becomes:

$$\dot{x}_{ikjl} = -x_{ikjl} - I_{ikjl}^- + b_1 \cdot I_{ikjl}^+ + b_2 \cdot y_{kl}^{VF} + b_3 \cdot I_{ikjl}^{td} \tag{11}$$

Lesioning

SAIM can be lesioned in a variety of different ways. Because the selection network can be related to the parietal cortex (see main text), we concentrated on lesions at this location. Two ways of lesioning units were considered: intrinsic and total lesioning. The *intrinsic lesioning* only involved intrinsic inputs from within the selection network. This did not affect the input from the visual field or top-down modulation. In mathematical terms, the intrinsic lesioning is described by extending equation 11 to:

$$\dot{x}_{ikjl} = -x_{ikjl} + d_{ikjl}^{intr} \cdot \left(-I_{ikjl}^- + b_1 \cdot I_{ikjl}^+\right) + b_2 \cdot y_{kl}^{VF} + b_3 \cdot I_{ikjl}^{td} \tag{12}$$

where d_{ikjl}^{intr} is a "damage" factor. If d_{ikjl}^{intr} is set smaller than 1, it reduces the influence of the intrinsic inputs $\left(I_{ikjl}^-, I_{ikjl}^+\right)$ and leaves the input from the visual field and the knowledge network $\left(y_{kl}^{VF}, I_{ikjl}^{td}\right)$ unaffected.

There were two different spatial patterns of lesion, as depicted in Figure 9: The "vertical" lesion only affected the left part of the selection network and restricted the effect of the lesion to the left part of the visual field. The "horizontal" lesion affected inputs into the left side of the FOA for inputs across the visual field.

For vertical lesioning, the damage factor d_{ikjl} was:

$$d_{ikjl} = \begin{cases} d & 0 < k < N/2; 0 < l < N; 0 < i, j < M \\ 1 & \text{otherwise} \end{cases}$$

with $d < 1$. N is the size of the visual field and M is the size of the FOA. The condition $0 < k < N/2$ restricts the damage to the left side of the selection network.

For horizontal lesioning, the damage factor d_{ikjl} was:

$$d_{ikjl} = \begin{cases} d & 0 < i < M/2; 0 < j < M; 0 < k, l < N \\ 1 & \text{otherwise} \end{cases}$$

with $d < 1$. The condition $0 < i < M/2$ restricts the lesion to the lower part of the selection network and hence to the left part of the FOA.

Scanning

To produce scanning behaviour in SAIM, a top-down inhibition was introduced. This strategy consisted of two parts: First, SAIM had to decide when an object was to be inhibited and, second, how this object was to be inhibited.

Deciding when an object is to be inhibited was implemented by the activity of the template units in the knowledge network. If one of these units was above a certain threshold, then inhibition occurred. This can be related to the situation of "recognizing and object". After the threshold was passed, the inhibition y_{kl}^{inh} was active and reduced the activity in the visual field by:

$$I_{kl}^{VF}(\text{new}) = I_{kl}^{VF}(\text{old}) \cdot \left(1 - \tau \cdot y_{kl}^{inh}\right) \tag{13}$$

When y_{kl}^{inh} is zero, the activity in the visual field $\left(I_{kl}^{VF}\right)$ is unchanged, whereas when y_{kl}^{inh} is larger than zero, the activity of $\left(I_{kl}^{VF}\right)$ is reduced. τ controls the influence of the inhibition. The inhibition $\left(y_{kl}^{inh}\right)$ is stronger at locations where the content of the visual input matches the activated template. The reason for this lies in a possible spatial overlap of templates in the visual field. For instance, in the stimulus in Figure 13, the head of the arrow overlaps with the dash of the arrow. Inhibition from the left-hand template does not allow activation at the left pixel of the dash.

In addition to this inhibition of the visual field, the starting conditions of the whole network are set to zero.

VISUAL COGNITION, 1998, *5* (1/2), 49–79

Two Roles for Attention in Shape Perception: A Structural Description Model of Visual Scrutiny

John E. Hummel and Brian J. Stankiewicz

Department of Psychology, University of California, Los Angeles, CA, USA

This paper presents MetriCat, a model of the human capacity to recognize objects both as members of a general class (e.g. "chair") and as specific instances ("my office chair"), and of the role of visual attention in this capacity. MetriCat represents the attributes of an object's parts and their relations in a non-linear fashion that provides a natural basis for recognition at both the class and instance levels (Stankiewicz & Hummel, 1996). Like previous structural description models (e.g. Hummel & Biederman, 1992), MetriCat represents part attributes and relations independently, dynamically binding them into structural descriptions. The resulting representation suggests two roles for visual attention in shape recognition: attention for binding and attention for signal-to-noise control. MetriCat implements both functions as special cases of a single mechanism for controlling the synchrony relations among units representing separate object parts. The model accounts for the time course of class- and instance-level classification, and makes several predictions about the relationships between attention, time and levels of classification.

INTRODUCTION

Human object recognition is remarkably flexible. Upon viewing a novel instance of a known object class, it is usually possible to recognize the object immediately as a member of that class. For example, in a furniture store, we effortlessly recognize the chairs as chairs, the tables as tables, and so forth, even if we have never seen those specific chairs or tables before. At the same time, it remains possible to tell the difference between one chair and another. Although these observations conform closely to common sense, it is challenging to understand how the visual representation of shape makes this kind of multi-level classification possible (Marr, 1982). Computational models of

Requests for reprints should be addressed to John E. Hummel, Department of Psychology, University of California Los Angeles, 405 Hilgard Avenue, Los Angeles, CA 90095-1563, USA.
This research was supported by NSF grant SBR-9511504.

object recognition are divided with respect to their capacity to account for classification at different levels of abstraction. Models based on categorical structural descriptions (Biederman, 1987; Dickenson, Pentland, & Rosenfeld, 1992; Hummel & Biederman, 1992; Hummel & Stankiewicz, 1996a) provide a natural account of our ability to recognize objects as members of general classes (e.g. "chairs"), but do not provide a clear basis for distinguishing similar members of the same class. View-based models (Bülthoff & Edelman, 1992; Bülthoff, Edelman, & Tarr, 1995; Edelman, Cutzu, & Duvdevani-Bar, 1996; Poggio & Edelman, 1990; Tarr, 1995) are adept at classifying objects as individual instances, but are not well-suited to account for our ability to recognize novel instances of known object classes. A clear computational account of how both instance- and class-level recognition obtain simultaneously has yet to be developed.

A related question concerns the role of visual attention in shape perception and object recognition. A growing body of evidence suggests that we can recognize objects without attending to them (Tipper, 1985; Tipper & Driver, 1988; Treisman & DeSchepper, 1996). However, this does not imply that attention plays no role in object recognition. Attention is known to play an important role in many basic visual tasks, including feature selection (see Bundesen, this issue) and visual binding (e.g. Treisman, 1982; Treisman & Gelade, 1980; but see Kanwisher & Wojculik, this issue). Using a priming paradigm, Stankiewicz, Hummel and Cooper (in press) recently showed that attention also plays a role in the visual representation of object shape. Specifically, we found that attended images visually prime both themselves and their left–right reflections, whereas ignored images prime only themselves (see also Stankiewicz & Hummel, in prep.). Thus, although it does not determine *whether* an object will be recognized, attention seems to affect the qualitative *form* of the visual representations mediating recognition. This fact suggests the beginnings of an answer to the question of how we recognize objects at multiple levels of abstraction: Perhaps attention serves to "tune" the representation of object shape, alternating between coarse, categorical representation (e.g. for class-level recognition) and more precise representations (e.g. for instance-level classification). This idea is intuitive, and similar ideas have been proposed before (e.g. Biederman, 1987; Hummel & Stankiewicz, 1996a; Marr, 1982; Olshausen, Anderson, & Van Essen, 1993). But to turn this intuitive idea into a falsifiable theory, it is necessary to specify both the form of the visual representations that are subjected to this attention-based "tuning", and the nature of the attentional mechanisms that perform the tuning.

This paper presents *MetriCat* (for *metric* and *cat*egorical properties), a model of shape recognition that addresses the question of how we recognize objects at multiple levels of abstraction (Stankiewicz & Hummel, 1996) and the role of visual attention in this capacity. MetriCat is an extension of our previous work on structural descriptions of object shape (Hummel & Biederman's, 1992,

JIM; and Hummel & Stankiewicz's 1996a, *JIM.2*). Like JIM and JIM.2, MetriCat represents object shape in terms of the qualitative properties of volumetric parts (i.e. geons; Biederman, 1987) and the qualitative relations among them. Also like its predecessors, it represents geon attributes and relations *independently* of one another. These properties give MetriCat the capacity for class-level recognition enjoyed by models based on categorical structural descriptions. However, MetriCat differs from these models in that its representation of shape attributes and relation is not strictly categorical. Rather, part attributes and relations are represented in a non-linear form that emphasizes differences across categorical boundaries without discarding all metric information within those boundaries. This property permits the model to represent and match object shape at multiple levels of numerical specificity, and provides a natural basis for classifying objects at multiple levels of abstraction (Stankiewicz & Hummel, 1996).

This approach to the representation of object shape suggests two separate but related roles for attention in shape perception. Coding part attributes independently of their relations makes it necessary to bind them dynamically (i.e. actively) into part-based groups (Hummel & Biederman, 1992). Attention is known to play a central role in binding independent visual attributes (see Schneider, 1995, for a thorough review), and therefore figures prominently in the generation of structural descriptions from object images (Hummel & Biederman, 1991, 1992; Hummel & Stankiewicz, 1996a; Stankiewicz et al., in press; see also Logan, 1994). Like its predecessors, MetriCat requires attention to bind attributes into part-based structural descriptions (although it implements attention more explicitly than either JIM or JIM.2). It also uses attention to generate the metrically detailed representations that permit classification at progressively finer levels of specificity (e.g. from *chair*, to *office chair*, to *my office chair*). Both these operations—attribute binding and the generation of detailed representations of shape—are performed by a single mechanism; namely, by enhancing the ability of object parts to inhibit one another in the competition for binding and processing resources. The model's attention mechanism thus unifies the binding and selective processing functions performed by visual attention (see Schneider, 1995). (However, we should note that the model is not intended as a general theory of visual attention. Among other things, it does not explicitly address such phenomena as location-based visual search, visual neglect following brain damage, etc. Rather, our current focus is strictly on the role of attention in the representation and classification of object shape.) The resulting model makes testable predictions about the roles of time and attention in recognition at different levels of visual specificity, suggests a specific basis for intelligent search for diagnostic features for subordinate- and instance-level classification, and generates testable predictions about the relationship between levels of classification and the effects of viewpoint on recognition performance.

THEORIES OF OBJECT RECOGNITION

Recent theories of object recognition fall into two general classes with respect to their ability to account for shape classification at different levels of abstraction. One class of theories assumes that objects are represented as "structural descriptions" specifying an object's parts in terms of their categorical attributes and relations to one another (Biederman, 1987; Dickenson et al., 1992; Hummel & Biederman, 1992; Hummel & Stankiewicz, 1996a). For example, a table might be represented as a horizontal slab on top of four vertical posts; a coffee mug might be represented as a squat vertical cylinder with a curved cylinder attached to its side (see Biederman, 1987). Categorical representations of this type have several desirable properties, including robustness to noise and variations in viewpoint, and a natural capacity to generalize over variations in object shape (see Biederman, 1987; Pinker, 1984). As a consequence, they provide a natural account of our ability to recognize objects in novel viewpoints (Biederman & Cooper, 1991a, 1992; Biederman & Gerhardstein, 1993; Cooper, Biederman, & Hummel, 1992), our ability to recognize objects in the presence of noise or occlusion, and our ability to recognize novel instances of known object classes (Biederman, 1987; Clowes, 1967). Some structural description models also account for a variety of more subtle properties of human shape perception, including the role of convex parts in shape perception (Biederman, 1987; Biederman & Cooper, 1991b; Hoffman & Richards, 1985; Tversky & Hemenway, 1984), the role of categorical relations in shape perception and object recognition (Hummel & Stankiewicz, 1996b; Saiki & Hummel, in press), and the role of time and attention in shape perception and objection recognition (Hummel & Stankiewicz, 1996a; Stankiewicz et al., in press).

For the same reason that they support recognition at the level of object classes, categorical structural descriptions are insufficient to make some within-class distinctions. For example, a categorical structural description of a robin would be indistinguishable from a categorical structural description of a blue jay: On the basis of such a description alone, both objects would simply be recognized as birds. In such cases, people search for distinguishing features (such as the red breast on the robin, or the blue crest on the jay) as a basis for classifying these objects at the subordinate-levels of "robin" and "blue jay" (Biederman, 1987; Biederman and & Schiffrar, 1987). But while such features play a critical role in subordinate-level recognition, it is unlikely that they constitute our only basis for distinguishing structurally similar objects. Although it is difficult, we can discriminate objects that differ only in their metric properties (Bülthoff & Edelman, 1992; Edelman et al., 1996; Hummel & Stankiewicz, 1996b).

In contrast to structural description models, "view-based" models represent objects as holistic "views" specifying the two-dimensional coordinates of their features as they appear in specific views (Bülthoff & Edelman, 1992; Bülthoff et al., 1995; Edelman et al., 1996; Poggio & Edelman, 1990; Tarr, 1995; Vetter, Poggio, & Bülthoff, 1994). This approach differs from the structural description approach in that (a) there is no explicit decomposition of an object into its parts, and (b) an object's features are represented in terms of their numerical coordinates in the view, rather than their categorical (e.g. "above/below") relations to one another. This kind of representation is metrically precise and information-rich, making it suitable for distinguishing structurally similar objects (Bülthoff et al., 1995; Tarr, 1995). There is substantial support for the idea that some instance-level classification tasks—most notably face recognition—are mediated by this type of holistic representation of object shape (e.g. Farah, 1992; Tanaka & Farah, 1993). In addition, there is evidence for the role of view-like representations in our capacity to recognize objects without attending to them (Stankiewicz et al., in press), although the views implicated in automatic recognition may differ substantially from the metrically precise, information-rich representations postulated in current view-based models (see Hummel & Stankiewicz, 1996a).

If the view-based approach provides a general account of instance-level classification (i.e. beyond the case of faces and similar objects), then our capacity for multi-level classification may simply reflect the simultaneous operation of both views (for instance recognition) and structural descriptions (for class recognition). However, not all subordinate- or instance-level recognition is performed on the basis of holistic views. For example, Biederman and Schiffrar (1987) showed that categorical features play the central role in chick-sexing,[1] a decidedly subordinate-level classification task, and Hummel and Stankiewicz (1996b) report evidence against the role of holistic views in the recognition of structurally similar objects. Thus, although holistic views probably play an important role in face recognition, and although diagnostic categorical features probably play an important role in subordinate- and instance-level recognition, neither proposal provides a complete account of our ability to recognize objects at multiple levels of abstraction. As such, we believe it is worth considering alternative explanations for this capacity.

A UNIFIED MODEL OF INSTANCE- AND CLASS-LEVEL RECOGNITION

As noted previously, categorical representations (as postulated in structural description theories) naturally support recognition at the entry- or class-level, while metrically rich representations (as postulated in view-based theories) naturally support instance- and subordinate-level recognition. MetriCat is

[1] Chick-sexing is the task of deciding, on the basis of the appearance of the genitalia, whether a given chick is male or female.

based on a single representation that captures both these properties. The basis of MetriCat is a simple extension of the representations postulated in categorical structural description models. A categorical representation entails a non-linear mapping from a stimulus domain to the perceptual representation of that domain. For example, consider an image containing two figures, A and B. The relation "Above(A,B)" is strictly categorical if it evaluates to *true* (or 1) for all locations of A and B such that Y_A (the location of A on the vertical axis, Y) is greater than Y_B, and to false (or 0) for all locations such that $Y_A \leq Y_B$. In this case, the mapping from the stimulus domain (coordinates in the image) to the relation is a step function (i.e. Above(A,B) is 1 for all ($Y_A - Y_B > 0$, and 0 for all ($Y_A — Y_B \leq 0$). A step function is strictly categorical in the sense that its value (0 or 1) changes only at the categorical boundary (i.e. the derivative is infinite at the categorical boundary and zero everywhere else), discarding all information on either side of the boundary. However, a step is a special case of a more general class of non-linear functions whose derivative is a maximum over some point (such as a categorical boundary), and reduced elsewhere. A common example is the logistic function:

$$y = \frac{1}{1+e^{-x}} \tag{1}$$

Like a step function y changes fastest over a single points in x (specifically, $x = 0$) but, unlike a step, it continues to change (although progressively less so) as x deviates further from zero. This "softer" non-linearity is meaningfully categorical in that, like a step function, it emphasizes differences across categorical boundaries (e.g. from Above to Below). [Indeed, in the literature on categorical perception, this kind of function is the behavioural manifestation of categorical perception (see e.g. Foster & Ferraro, 1989).] But the logistic function has the advantage that it does not discard all information on either side of the boundary.

We argue that extant structural description models are insufficient for instance-level recognition largely because they are based on categorical properties defined by step functions. MetriCat uses logistic (rather than step) non-linearities to represent categorical properties (such as whether one part is above or below another, and whether a geon's major axis is straight or curved). In other respects, MetriCat is like its predecessors, JIM and JIM.2: It represents part attributes and relations explicitly and independently, and binds those properties into relational structures dynamically; that is, the representations in MetriCat are structured rather than holistic (see Hummel & Biederman, 1992). The resulting representations have all the advantages of a categorical structural description, but also permit fine metric discriminations when necessary. In combination with an appropriate set of routines for matching these representations to object memory, the result is a unified account of both class- and instance-level recognition. Moreover, this approach to representing object shape suggests a unifying account of two seemingly different functions of visual attention. In MetriCat, a single mechanism controls attention for binding (e.g. as discussed by Treisman and others) and attention for signal-to-noise control (e.g. as discussed by LaBerge and others).

Assumptions and Relation to Prior Work

The focus of the MetriCat model is the representation of object shape and the operations that match those representations to memory. (Specifically, it is an extension of the upper layers of JIM and JIM.2, which are responsible for shape representation and object classification; the lower layers of these models are responsible for image segmentation, etc.) MetriCat takes a description of an object's parts and their spatial relations as input. Rules for segmenting images into part-based groups, and for recovering the parts' attributes and spatial relations, are described elsewhere (Dickenson et al., 1992; Hummel & Biederman, 1992; Hummel & Stankiewicz, 1996a), so for the purposes of the current model, we shall simply assume that these operations have taken place.

Overview

As input, MetriCat takes a numerical representation of a geon's shape attributes and relations to other geons (Figure 1, "Input"). One such pattern is given for each geon in an object. In the model's first layer (Figure 1, "Layer 1"), separate collections of units respond to: (1) the parallelism of a geon's sides, (2) the curvature of its major axis, (3) the curvature of its cross-section, (4) its aspect ratio, (5) the pointedness of its major axis (i.e. is the major axis pointed, as in a cone, or truncated, as in a cylinder or funnel), (6) whether the geon is above or below any other geons, and (7) whether it is beside or centred on any other geons. (This is an admittedly simplified set of attributes. Among other potentially important properties, we are omitting the geons' connectedness relations. For a richer set of geon and relation descriptors, see Biederman, 1987.) Shape attributes and relations are represented independently, in the sense that separate collections of units represent separate attributes. Unit are bound into geon-based set by synchrony of firing (Hummel & Biederman, 1992): If two units "fire" (i.e. become active) in synchrony with one another, then they are treated as belonging to separate geons. Synchrony and, more importantly, *asynchrony*, are established by means of oscillatory gates associated with the geons: The gates interact so as to "open", sending the properties of the corresponding geon to the model's first layer, one at a time. There is evidence for synchrony-based binding in biological visual systems (see König & Engel, 1995, for a thorough review).

In broad strokes, the model works as follows. When an object is presented for recognition, its geons begin to fire out of synchrony, generating separate patterns of activation on the attribute and relation units in Layer 1. In the best

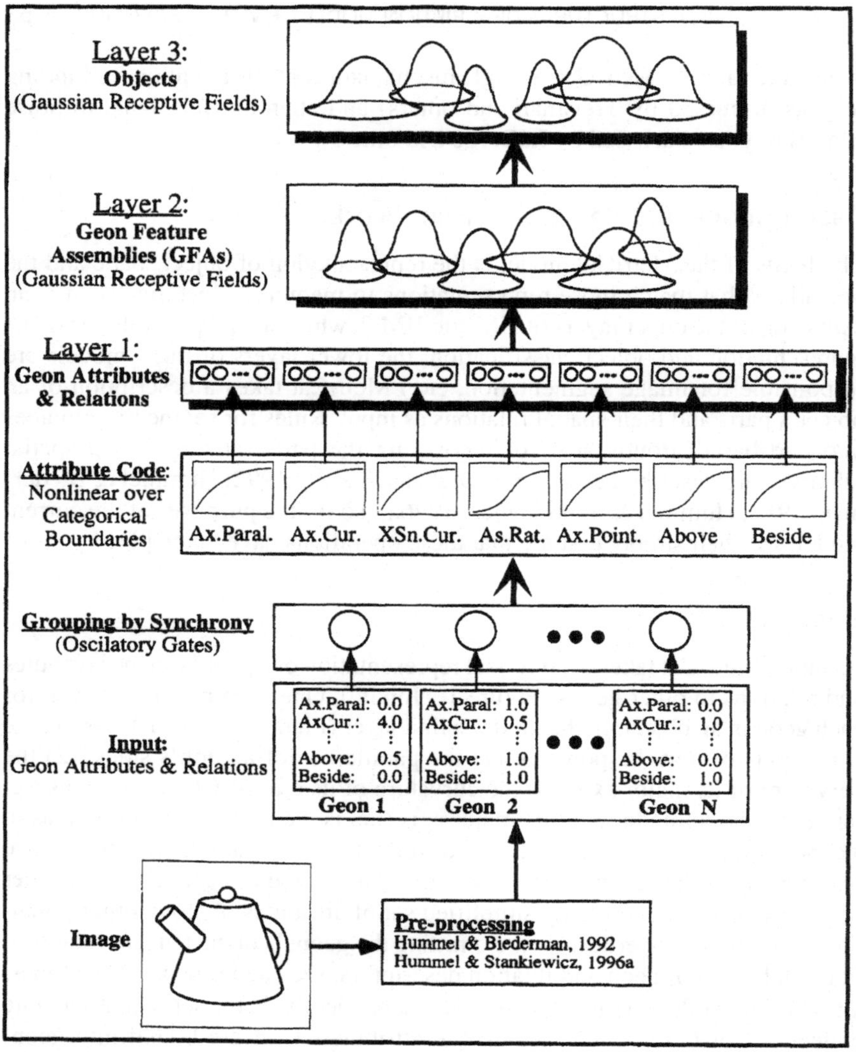

FIG. 1. The MetriCat architecture. As input, the model takes a numerical description of an object's constituent geons and their interrelations (Input). Geon attributes are grouped by synchrony induced by the action of oscillatory gates (Grouping by Synchrony). Each geon is characterized by five shape attributes, parallelism of main axis (Ax.Paral.), curvature of main axis (Ax.Cur.), curvature of cross section (XSn.Cur,), aspect ratio (As.Rat.) and pointedness of main axis (Ax.Point), and two spatial relations, above/below (Above) and centred/beside (Beside). The numerical value of each attribute is passed through a logistic non-linearity (Attribute Code), the result of which is represented on a bank of 50 units in the model's first layer (Layer 1). Patterns of activation in Layer 1 activate Geon Feature Assembly (GFA) units with Gaussian receptive fields in Layer 2. The outputs of GFA units activate object units with Gaussian receptive fields (Layer 3).

case, one geon will fire at a time, but as described shortly, the geons' ability to fire cleanly out of synchrony is a function of how much "attention" is directed to the object. The model's second layer (Layer 2) consists of Geon Feature Assembly units (GFA units; Hummel & Biederman, 1992) that take their inputs from the attribute and relation units, thereby responding to particular geons in particular relations to other geons. The model's third layer (Layer 3) consists of object units that take their inputs from the GFA units. Object units sum their inputs over time, "reassembling" a collection of GFAs (geons in particular relations) into a representation of a whole object.

GFA and object units (*classifier* units) have Gaussian receptive fields (RFs) in their input spaces, where the mean of the Gaussian determines a unit's preferred input pattern, **p**, and the standard deviation, σ, determines the unit's tolerance for deviations from that pattern (see Poggio & Girosi, 1990). GFA units have RFs in the space of geon attributes and relations, and object units have RFs in the space of GFAs. Classifier units with wide RFs (i.e. large σ) respond to a wider range of input than units with narrow RFs; that is, wide units are better able to tolerate to deviations from their preferred patterns than are narrow units. This variable-tolerance encoding has several importance implications. First, classifier units with wide RFs respond to whole classes of objects, whereas units with narrow RFs tend to respond selectively to individual instances (Stankiewicz & Hummel, 1996). Second, wide (class-level) units are able to respond earlier in processing than narrow (instance-level) units, as elaborated shortly. As a result, MetriCat predicts that objects will be recognized at the class-level before they are recognized as individual instances. And third, wide units are more robust to noise in their input vectors, and are therefore better able to respond when an object is not fully attended: MetriCat predicts that greater attention (e.g. visual scrutiny) is required to recognize objects at the instance-level. Each of these properties is illustrated and elaborated in the "Simulations" section.

Representation of Attributes and Relations

Each attribute (or relation) is represented by a bank of units that coarsely code the numerical value of that attribute (Figure 2). The coded value for any attribute is obtained by passing the attribute's raw numerical value through a logistic function (Hummel & Stankiewicz, 1996b; Stankiewicz & Hummel, 1996). For example, consider the relation Above(i, j), which codes the location of geon i relative to geon j on the vertical image axis, Y. $P_Y(i, j)$ is the scaled location of i relative to j on Y:

$$P_Y(i,j) = (Y_i - Y_j) / (l_{Yi} + l_{Yj}) \tag{2}$$

where Y_i and Y_j are the Y-coordinates of the centroids of i and j, respectively, and l_{Yi} and l_{Yj} are the lengths of i and j along Y. $P_Y(i, j)$ is unbounded. It will be

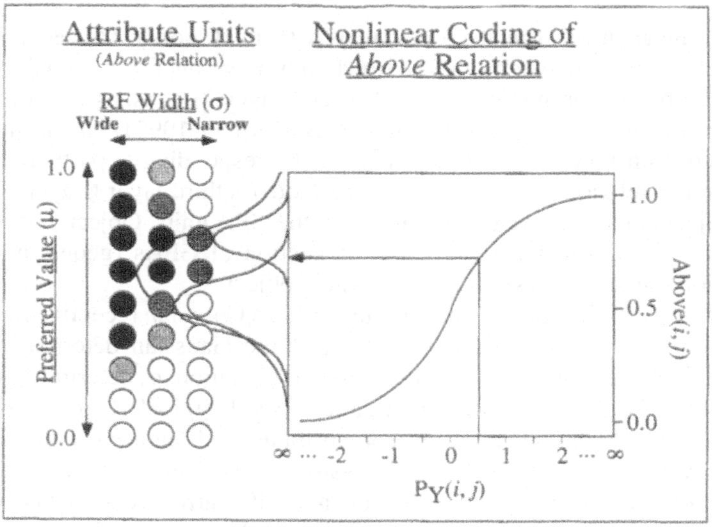

FIG. 2. Detail of the representation of object attributes (in Layer 1), illustrated with the Above relation. The raw value of an attribute or relation is passed through a logistic non-linearity, and the resulting value is coarsely coded on 50 units with Gaussian receptive fields in the space of logistic values (0. . .1). Units are depicted as circles, receptive fields are depicted as Gaussian curves, and activation as shades of grey, with more active units in darker shades. The relation represented corresponds to $P_Y(i, j) = 0.5$, or "geon *i* is above geon *j* at a distance that is half the sum of their heights".

negative whenever *i* is below *j*, and positive whenever *i* is above *j*. Scaling *P* by the parts' lengths makes it scale-invariant: *P* will not change with the absolute size of the object's image. Human object recognition is also scale-invariant in this way (Biederman & Cooper, 1992). For an image of a fixed size, $P_Y(i, j)$ changes linearly with the location of geon *i* relative to geon *j* along Y. Above(*i*, *j*), the above/below location of *i* relative to *j* that is used for shape classification, is computed by passing $P_Y(i, j)$ through the logistic function:

$$\text{Above}(i, j) = \frac{1}{1 + e^{-\kappa P_y(i,j)}} \tag{3}$$

where κ is a scaling constant. Although $P_Y(i, j)$ is unbounded, Above(*i*, *j*) is bounded between 0 and 1; it will be less than 0.5 whenever *i* is below *j* (i.e. when $P < 0$) and greater than 0.5 whenever *i* is above *j* (when $P > 0$). Like a categorical relation, Above( ) changes fastest about the categorical boundary, $P = 0$ (where $Y_i = Y_j$). However, as noted previously, Above( ) does not discard all metric differences within categorical boundaries. κ determines the steepness of Above( ) about the categorical boundary $P = 0$; when $\kappa = \infty$ Above( ) is a step function that evaluates to 0 for all $P < 0$ and to 1 for all $P > 0$.

The left–right relation, *Beside*, is computed in the same way as the Above relation, except that left/right distinctions are discarded, so the function effectively computes centredness versus off-centredness with respect to the horizontal axis:

$$\text{Beside}(i, j) = 2\left(\frac{1}{1+e^{-\kappa|P_x(i,j)|}} - 0.5\right) \tag{4}$$

As a result, Beside(i, j) is invariant with left–right reflection (Hummel & Biederman, 1992). It evaluates to zero when geon i is exactly centred on geon j (on the X-axis), and to values closer to 1.0 as i moves farther to the left or right j.

Equations (3) and (4) express the functions for computing all attributes in MetriCat. Equation (3) expresses the form for any attribute with two continuous regions separated by a categorical boundary. These include the Above relation (one geon can be more or less extreme in its location either above or below another geon) and aspect ratio [a geon can be more or less squat (e.g. a coin is a squat cylinder) or more or less elongated (e.g. a pipe is an elongated cylinder)]. Equation (4) expresses the form for an attribute with one continuous region and one singularity. For example, in the case of the Beside relation, *off-centre* (or "beside") is a continuous region and *centred* is a singularity (a geon can be more or less distant from the midline of another, but there is only one point where it is exactly centred). Most of the properties in MetriCat are of this latter variety. These include parallel sides (singularity) versus non-parallel sides (continuous), straight cross-section (singularity) versus *curved* cross-section (continuous), *pointed* major axis (singularity) versus *truncated* major axis (continuous), and *straight* major axis (singularity) versus *curved* major axis (continuous).

The model's input layer consists of seven banks of units (one bank for each attribute), each with 50 units. Units within a bank respond to logistic values given by equations (3) and (4) (depending on the attribute). Units have Gaussian receptive fields over the range of logistic values (0 . . . 1) with varying centres (means) and receptive field sizes (standard deviations). As illustrated in Figure 2, the result is a population coding for the logistic value of each attribute (Stankiewicz & Hummel, 1996).

Model Operation

The model's operation is described here in general terms only. The details of its operation (including equations and operating parameters) are given in the Appendix.

Oscillators and Visual Attention. An object's geons are induced to fire out of synchrony by means of a collection of oscillatory gates. There is one gate associated with each geon. By virtue of the interaction between an excitatory unit (E_i) and an inhibitory unit (I_i), each gate, *i*, oscillates between a state of activity ($E_i > 0$), in which the gate is "open", and inactivity ($E_i = 0$), in which the gate is "closed" (see Hummel & Stankiewicz, 1996a; von der Malsburg & Buhman, 1992). When a gate is open (i.e. $E_i > 0$), the attributes of the corresponding geons are passed to (i.e. represented on) the attribute units. If more than one gate opens at a time, then the attributes of multiple geons will be superimposed on the attribute vectors. The result is a binding error (or "superposition catastrophe"; von der Malsburg, 1981), because it is impossible to determine which attributes belong together as properties of the same geon. The gates act to prevent such errors by inhibiting one another, thereby opening (or "firing") at different times (i.e. out of synchrony with one another; Figure 3c).

The model's ability to keep separate geons firing out of synchrony with one another is dependent on the gates' ability to inhibit one another. In turn, the lateral inhibition between the different gates is modulated by a global parameter, α. Figure 3 illustrates the effect of α on the gates. When α is large (e.g. 1.5), the gates inhibit one another strongly and therefore fire cleanly out of synchrony (figure 3c); when α is zero, the gates cannot inhibit one another at all, and therefore never fire out of synchrony (although they continue to oscillate; Figure 3a); at intermediate values of α, the gates fire somewhat out of synchrony (Figure 3b). We assume that α is proportional to the amount of attention directed to an object. Our claim is that the function of attention (at least in the context of object recognition) is to enable separate groups of units to fire *out* of synchrony with one another. In so doing, attention serves both to control the dynamic binding of geon attributes and relations (Hummel & Biederman, 1991, 1992; Hummel & Stankiewicz, 1996a), and to control the signal-to-noise ratio of attended objects (e.g. LaBerge & Brown, 1989): Note that the pattern of asynchrony is cleaner for "strongly attended" objects (Figure 3c) than for "weakly attended" objects (Figure 3b). The effect of α on model performance is discussed in greater detail in the "Simulations" section.

Coarse Coding of Attribute Values. Each geon attribute is represented as a pattern of activation distributed over a bank of 50 *attribute* units (Figure 2). Attribute units have overlapping receptive fields over the range of logistic values of the corresponding attribute (equation 3 or 4, depending on the attribute). A complete geon is represented by a 350-dimensional (50 units × 7 attributes) vector, **a**.

Part Classification. GFA units have Gaussian RFs in the 350-dimensional space of attribute units. Each GFA unit receptive field has a mean, **p**, a vector that corresponds to the unit's preferred stimulus pattern, and a standard deviation, σ, which defines the width of the unit's receptive field (i.e. its tolerance for deviations from **p**). The simulations reported here were run with three sizes of GFA unit RFs, $\sigma = 0.10$, 0.25, and 0.35. Units with small σ respond to very

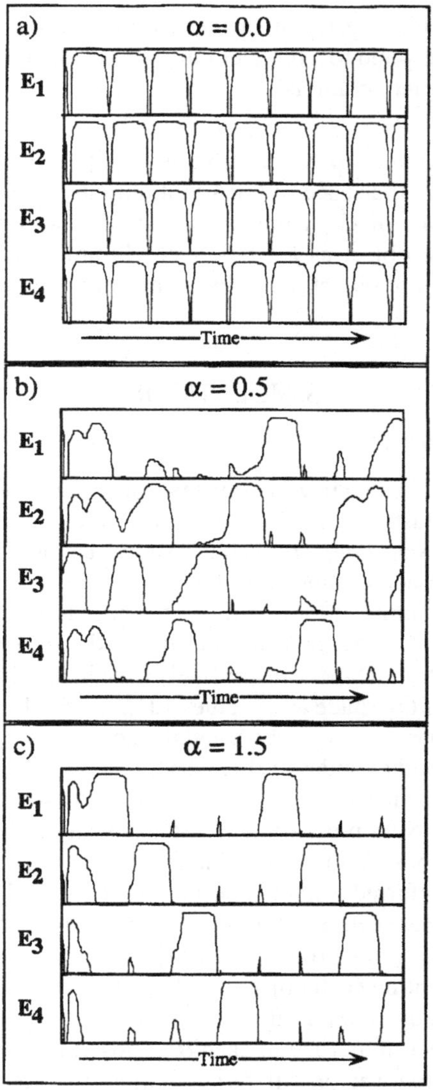

FIG. 3. Simulation results illustrating the effect of attention (α) on MetriCat's ability to make separate geons fire out of synchrony. Each frame shows the activation of four gates ($E_1 \ldots E_4$) as a function of time and α. Activation ($E_i = 0 \ldots 1$) is depicted on the ordinate of each curve. (a) With $\alpha = 0$ (no attention), all four gates (geons) fire in synchrony with one another. (b) With $\alpha = 0.5$ (limited attention), the gates fire out of synchrony, but there is substantial overlap in their activity. (c) With $\alpha = 1.5$ (strong attention), the gates fire cleanly out of synchrony.

specific attribute vectors (i.e. to parts with specific shapes in specific relations); those with larger σ respond to a broader range of vectors (and thus to a broader range of part shapes and relations).

Object Classification. GFA units sum their outputs over time. Object units have Gaussian RFs in the space of GFA unit outputs. As a result, object units respond to collections of GFA units, reassembling an object's parts into a representation of the object as a whole (see Hummel & Biederman, 1992). There were two sizes of object unit RFs in the simulations reported here, σ = 0.10 and 0.5.

SIMULATIONS

Simulation Procedure

We trained the model to recognize 16 objects, comprising four instances of each of four classes. As illustrated in Figure 4, we will refer to the classes as *teapots*, *lamps*, *cars* and *nonsense objects*. Table 1 shows the attribute values of each part of each object. Each instance difference from the next nearest member of its class by 0.5 raw[2] units on one critical attribute dimension (Table 1). The teapots differed in the aspect ratio of the truncated cone (raw values 1.0, 1.5, 2.0 and 2.5 for $teapot_1 \ldots teapot_4$, respectively), the lamps differed in the degree of non-parallelism of the shade (raw values 1.0 . . . 2.5), the cars differed in the aspect ratio of the chassis (2.5 . . . 1.0), and the nonsense objects differed in the curvature of the curved cylinder (1.0 . . . 2.5).

Training took place in two steps. The model was first trained to classify the individual object parts by presenting each part one at a time, and running the model for 100 iterations. At the end of this time, we compared the attribute unit vector, **a**, to the preferred vectors, $\mathbf{p}_i$, of all existing GFA units, *i*. If the Euclidean distance between **a** and $\mathbf{p}_i$ was greater than 0.05 for all *i*, then we created three new GFA units (one at each σ) with $\mathbf{p} = \mathbf{a}$. Next, we trained the object units by presenting each object part for 100 iterations and allowing it to activate all the GFA units. After all the parts of an object had been presented, we created two object units (one at each σ) whose means (**p**) were set to the value of the GFA output vector. All the simulations reported in the next section were run by presenting a single object as input and allowing the model to run for 500 iterations. Except where noted otherwise, α was 1.5 in all simulations. The data reported are means over 10 simulation runs. Simulations were run with multiple objects, but because the results were always qualitatively very

---

[2] "Raw" units are units that serve as the input to (rather than the output of) the logistic functions (equations 3 and 4).

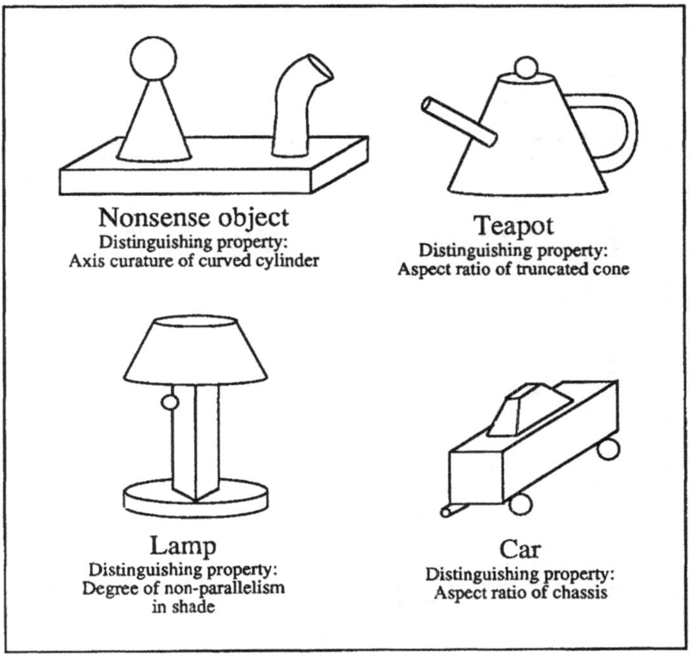

FIG. 4. Illustration of the four object classes MetriCat was trained to recognize.

similar for all objects, each set of results is reported in terms of a set of runs with one object.

Multi-level Classification

The most basic test of the model's capacity for multi-level classification is its response to a stimulus on which it was trained. If MetriCat can recognize objects at both the instance- and class-levels, then the following results should be obtained. Given a stimulus such as car_1(the first member of the category car), the model should activate both the instance-level (i.e. small σ) and class-level (i.e. large σ) object units recruited during training with that stimulus. It should also activate the class-level units recruited for different instances in the same class (here, car_2, car_3 and car_4), but it should not activate the instance-level units recruited for those objects. It should not activate the class- or instance-level units for any other objects (i.e. $teapot_1$ . . . $nonsense\text{-}object_4$). Figure 5 shows the model's response to the stimulus car_1. Figure 5a shows the mean responses (over 10 runs) of the instance-level unit (triangles) and class-level unit (circles) recruited for car_1. Figure 5b shows the mean responses of the instance- and class-level units for car_2, the nearest other instance of the same object class.

TABLE 1
Attribute Values of the 16 Objects MetriCat was Trained to Recognize[a]

	Object Part	*Axis Parallelism*	*Cross-Section*	*Aspect Ratio*	*Axis Curvature*	*Axis Point*	*Above*	*Beside*
Nonsense-object	Curved cylinder	4	−4	4	**1, 1.5, 2, 2.5**	0	4	4
	Brick	0	4	−4	0	4	−4	4
	Cone	4	−4	4	0	0	4, −4	4
	Sphere	4	−4	0	0	0	4	0
Teapot	Truncated cone	4	−4	**1, 1.5, 2, 2.5**	0	4	4, 4	4
	Curved cylinder	0	−4	−4	4	4	0	4
	Sphere	4	−4	0	0	0	4	0
	Cylinder	0	−4	4	0	4	0	4
Lamp	Truncated cone	**1, 1.5, 2, 2.5**	−4	4	0	0	4	0
	Vertical brick	0	4	4	0	4	4, −4	0
	Sphere	4	−4	0	0	0	0	4
	Horizontal brick	0	4	−4	0	4	−4	0
Car	Truncated pyramid	4	4	**−1.0, −1.5, −2.0, −2.5**	0	4	4	0
	Brick	0	4	4	0	4	4, −4	4
	Horizontal cylinder	0	−4	−4	0	4	−4	4
	Sphere	4	−4	0	0	0	−4	0
	Sphere	4	−4	0	0	0	−4	4

[a]The four instances of each class are distinguished by their values on one critical attribute (depicted in **bold** in table cells).

(Recall that car_1 and car_2 differ by only 0.5 raw units in the aspect ratio of one part.) Figure 5c shows the mean responses of the instance-level and class-level units for the central-most instance in the class *lamp* ($lamp_1$). These results indicate that the model correctly recognized car_1 at both the instance- and class-levels of abstraction: Both the instance- and class-level units recruited for car_1 became active; the class-level unit, but not the instance-level unit for car_2 became active; and none of the units corresponding to $lamp_1$ became active.

Figure 5 also shows the time course of recognition at the class- and instance-levels. Note that class-level units (circles) become active faster than instance-level units (triangles): Consistent with human recognition performance (Jolicoeur, Gluck, & Kosslyn, 1984; Rosch et al., 1976), MetriCat recognizes objects at the class-level faster than it recognizes them at the instance level. This property is a natural consequence of MetriCat's multi-level approach to object recognition. Recall that class-level units have wider receptive fields (larger σ) than instance-level units (this is true of both object units and GFA units). As a result, a given deviation (distance) between a stimulus pattern (**a** in the case of GFA units and **o** in the case of object units) and a unit's preferred stimulus pattern (**p**) has a greater impact on the response of a narrow (instance-level) unit than on the response of a wide (class-level) unit.[3] Stimuli tend to deviate more from the trained patterns (i.e. the units' preferred patterns) earlier in processing than later in processing. At the level of the GFA unit inputs (**a**), this early deviation results from the time it takes for an object's geons to become out of synchrony with one another (see Figure 3b,c), causing the properties of different geons to be "mixed" early in processing (as elaborated below). At the level of object unit inputs, this early deviation results both from the initially weak activation of the GFA units and from the time it takes for all an object's geons to have the opportunity to fire. Early in processing, the GFA outputs, O_i, will be zero for all GFA units, i, whose preferred geons have not yet fired, causing **o** to differ from the object unit's **p**. Here, too, class-level units, which have wide receptive fields, will respond more strongly to these imperfect inputs than instance-level units, with their narrow receptive fields.

Recognition of Novel Instances of Known Classes

People easily recognize novel instances of known object classes, appreciating both that the novel instance both belongs to the familiar class and that it nonetheless differs from all previous instances of that class. We tested Metri-

[3]Consider two Gaussian distributions, G_1 with σ_1, with G_2, with σ_2, where $\sigma_1 > \sigma_2$ (i.e. G_1 is wider than G_2), and let G_1 and G_2 be normalized to have equal heights at their means. For any distance, $d > 0$, from their means, the height of the wide Gaussian, G_1, will be greater than the height of the narrow Gaussian, G_2. That is, $G_1(d) > G_2(d)$ when $d > 0$ [$G_1(d) = G_2(d)$ when $d = 0$].

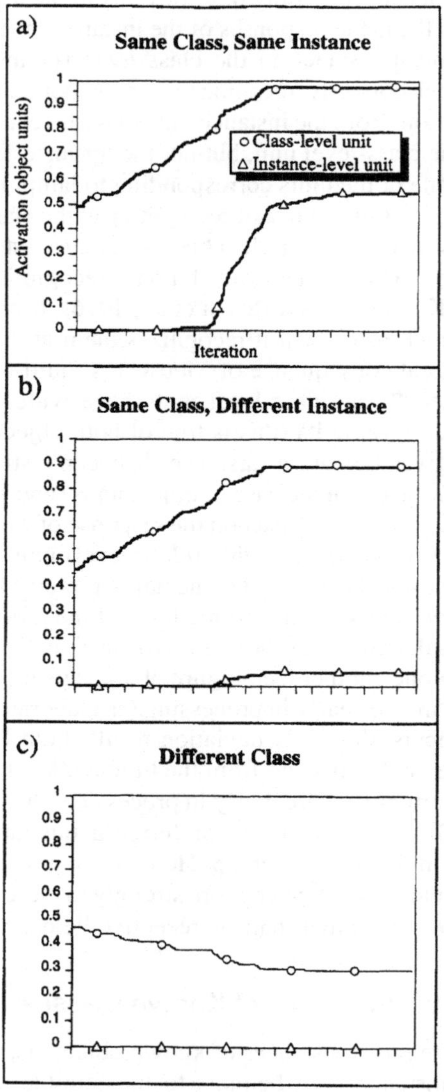

FIG. 5. Response of various object units to the stimulus car_1. (a) Activation of the class (circules) and instance (triangles) object units recruited in response to car_1 as a function of time (iterations). (b) Activation of the class and instance object units for car_2. (c) Activation of the class and instance object units for $lamp_1$.

Cat's ability to do this by presenting it with a new member of the class *nonsense-object*. We created this instance by distorting nonsense-object$_1$. Distortions were introduced by changing the raw values of each attribute by a random amount between – 0.01 and 0.01 (20% of the distance between adjacent members of the class on the critical attribute). Figure 6 shows the model's response to the resulting novel instance. Circles indicate the mean activation of the class-level unit for nonsense-object$_1$, and triangles indicate the response of the instance-level unit for that object (which is the closest instance to the novel one). Note that the model correctly recognized the novel instance as a member of the same class, but it did not mistake it for a familiar instance (as indicated by the low activation of the instance-level unit).

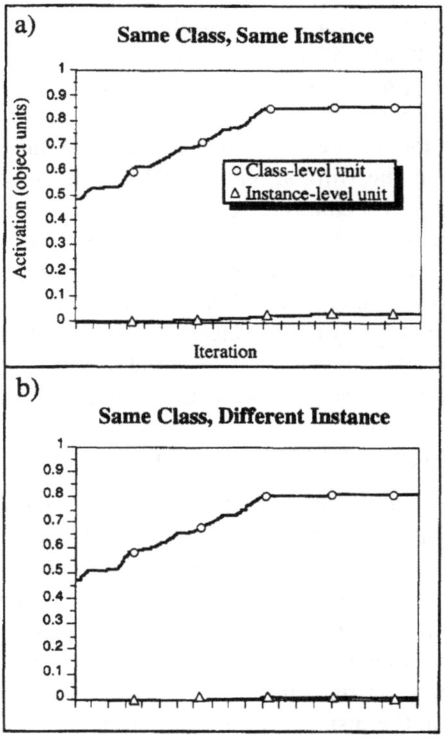

FIG. 6. Response to a novel instance of a known class. (a) Activation of the class (circles) and instance (triangles) object units recruited in response to the stimulus object as a function of time (iterations). (b) Activation of the class and instance object units for a different member of the same class.

Sensitivity to Noise

MetriCat is subject to intrinsic system-level noise introduced by the operations that establish asynchronous firing of an object's geons (Figure 3). This noise manifests itself as random variations in the patterns of activation generated on the attribute units. MetriCat's ability to recognize trained objects in spite of this noise shows that the model is at least somewhat noise-tolerant. To further observe the model's sensitivity to noise, we tested its ability to recognize stimuli corrupted by variable, random input noise. We generated these stimuli by starting with a trained object and varying each attribute value by a random amount between -0.01 and 0.01. The noise was re-randomized on each iteration. The resulting variable noise can either be thought of as stimulus noise, such as static in the image, or as additional system-level noise. Because the noise was re-randomized on each iteration, the mean value of each attribute (over several iterations) tends to approach the value of that attribute in the original stimulus. If MetriCat can tolerate this kind of noise, then it should recognize the stimulus at both the class- and instance-levels (although recognition should take longer than in the no-additional-noise case). Figure 7 shows the model's response to a noisy version of nonsense-object$_1$. As expected, the model recognized the stimulus at both the class- and instance-levels, although classification took longer and did not reach as high a level as in the basic simulations reported above. These results are especially interesting in comparison with the results of the simulations for "Novel-instance" simulations reported above. The only procedural difference between the current simulations and the novel-instances simulations is that the current simulations varied the noise on every iteration, whereas the deviations in the novel-instances simulations did not vary. MetriCat responded appropriately in both cases: It treated the constant noise as a property of the object, classifying the stimulus as a novel exemplar of a known class; and it treated the variable noise as noise, recognizing the stimulus as a familiar (albeit noisy) instance of a familiar class.

Attention in Instance-level Classification

In MetriCat, attention modulates the lateral inhibition that causes an object's geons to fire out of synchrony. If two (or more) geons drift into synchrony with one another, then the properties of one will interfere with the interpretation of the other. As noted previously, GFA and object units are not all equal in their capacity to tolerate this type of processing noise: Units with wide RFs (large σ) are better-suited to tolerate deviations from their trained patterns than are narrow (small σ) units. At the same time, narrow units are better suited to discriminate objects at the instance-level than are wide units. Together, these properties predict that, with reduced attention, class-level recognition will be possible but instance-level recognition will not (especially if the object is depicted in a novel view; see Hummel & Stankiewicz, 1996a). This property

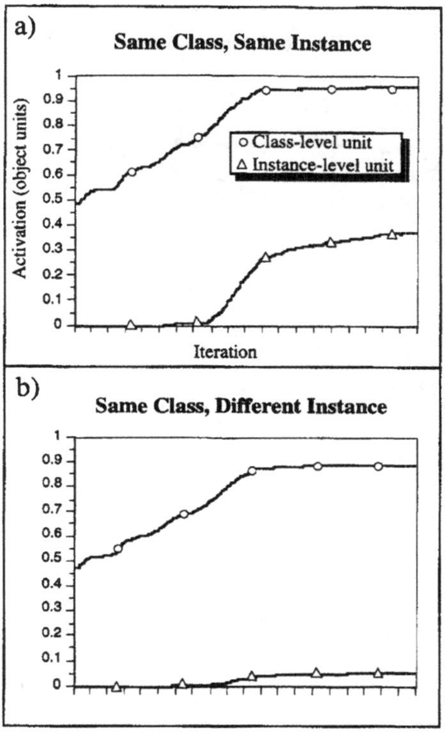

FIG. 7. Response to a stimulus created by adding variable noise to a trained instance. (a) Activation of the class (circles) and instance (triangles) object units recruited in response to the stimulus object as a function of time (iterations). (b) Activation of the class and instance object units for a different member of the same class.

is illustrated in Figure 8a, which shows the response of the model to nonsense-object$_1$ when the attention parameter, α, was set to 0.5 (rather than 1.5, the value used in the previous simulations). Note that MetriCat recognized the stimulus as a member of the class nonsense-object, but did not recognize it as the instance nonsense-object$_1$.

Figure 8b shows the model's performance with α set to zero—that is, when the stimulus is not attended at all. Here, the object is recognized neither at the instance- nor class-levels. This result seems to predict that object recognition requires attention. However, recall that MetriCat is intended, not as a stand-alone model, but as a component of the upper layers of Hummel and Stankiewicz's (1996a) JIM.2. Specifically, Layer 1 of MetriCat corresponds to the Independent Geon Array (IGA) of JIM.2, and the classification layers of MetriCat correspond to the classification layers of JIM.2. Like Layer 1 of MetriCat, the IGA represents shape attributes independently, is dependent on

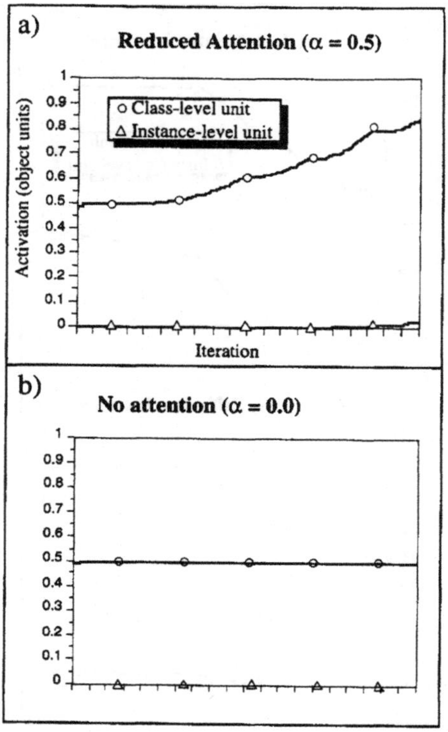

FIG. 8. Response to a trained stimulus under reduced attention. Circles depict the activation of the class-level unit recruited in response to the stimulus. Triangles depict the response of the instance-level unit recruited in response to the stimulus. (a) Model response with reduced attention ($\alpha = 0.5$); (b) model response without attention ($\alpha = 0$).

dynamic binding, and is responsible for recognition by structural description. However, JIM2 has an additional component, the Substructure Matrix (SSM), which does not require dynamic binding. For familiar object views, the SSM is sufficient for rapid recognition without attention. The IGA and SSM represent object shape in qualitatively different ways. JIM.2 predicts, not that unattended objects will not be recognized, but that recognition of unattended objects will differ *qualitatively* from the recognition of attended objects (see Hummel & Stankiewicz, 1996a). Stankiewicz et al. (in press; see also Stankiewicz & Hummel, in prep.) report experimental findings that are strikingly consistent with the specific predictions of JIM.2. For simplicity, we have left the SSM out of MetriCat, but, in principle, the SSM could be part of MetriCat just as it is part of JIM.2. Thus, we take the simulation results in Figure 8b to predict that structural description (and recognition on the basis of a structural description) will require attention, not that recognition *at all* will require visual attention.

DISCUSSION

MetriCat is a structural description model of multi-level shape classification. Like its predecessors, JIM and JIM.2, MetriCat represents object shape as a collection of parts in particular spatial relations. Part attributes and relations are represented independently, and are dynamically bound into structural descriptions by synchrony of firing. However, MetriCat departs from its predecessors in that its representation of part attributes and relations is not strictly categorical. MetriCat's representations are categorical in the sense that they are non-linear over categorical boundaries in attribute dimensions, but they are metric in that they preserve metric differences within categorical boundaries. With the appropriate routines for matching shape representations to object memory (here, Gaussian RFs with varying standard deviations), the resulting metric/categorical representation supports classification at multiple levels of abstraction as a natural consequence. Simulation results show that, counter to popular wisdom, structural descriptions need not be limited to recognition at the level of object classes.

The MetriCat approach to shape classification also suggests a unified account of the role (and mechanisms) of visual attention in shape perception. Due to the logistic representation of metric properties, metric differences within categorical boundaries are reduced in magnitude relative to metric differences across boundaries. As a result, the former are more sensitive to noise than are the latter. MetriCat uses attention to recover such purely metric differences and classify objects as individual instances. In this role, attention serves to increase the signal-to-noise ratio in the representation of a geon, allowing small metric differences to express themselves. The same mechanism serves to maintain the dynamic binding of shape attributes and relations into sets. In both cases, the mechanism is a simple parameter, α, that determines the strength with which geons inhibit one another in the competition for the opportunity to fire: The greater the inhibition, the cleaner the asynchrony, and the higher the signal-to-noise ratio.

Given the benefits of attention to MetriCat, it is reasonable to ask why α should even be a variable: Why not leave it set to a maximum value all the time? The reason is that the privilege of firing cleanly out of synchrony is a finite resource (Hummel & Biederman, 1991). To the extent that one geon is firing all by itself (and thereby maximizing its binding and its signal-to-noise ratio), then, by definition, no other geons can be firing at all. All the simulations reported here were run with stimuli consisting of single objects. In such situations, it is sensible to leave α at a maximum value, devoting as much processing as possible to the one object in the visual field. But in more realistic situations there are many objects in the visual field, so it may be sensible as a default to devote only a moderate amount of attention to any one object. Such a default would permit rapid classification at the class-level without necessarily excluding the processing of all other objects in the visual field (cf. Stankiewicz et al., in press). When it becomes necessary to recognize an object as an instance, it may be worth "turning attention up", temporarily processing that object to the exclusion of others. Clearly, at this point in time, these considerations are merely speculation. But MetriCat suggests a specific mechanism for thinking about the implementation and consequences of visual attention in shape perception.

Relation to Other Models of Object Recognition

MetriCat bears important similarities to current view-based models of object recognition. First, like the models of Poggio and his colleagues (e.g. Edelman et al., 1996; Poggio & Edelman, 1990; Vetter et al., 1994), MetriCat uses units with Gaussian receptive fields as the basis for object classification. However, it is important to recognize that MetriCat differs markedly from any view-based model in the *representational space* over which the Gaussians are defined. In all extant view-based models, shape classification is performed by basis functions defined in the space of the two-dimensional coordinates of object features: The representational assumption underlying these models is that objects are represented and matched to memory in terms of the coordinates of their features (hence the name "view-based"). The psychological plausibility of this assumption is questionable (Hummel & Stankiewicz, 1996b). By contrast, in MetriCat, the Gaussian RFs are defined in the space of categorical attributes and relations. As a consequence, the models have very different properties. In particular, it is not clear how view-based models could be adapted to account for the role of categorical properties in shape perception (as summarized in the Introduction; see also Biederman & Gerhardstein, 1995). More importantly, the representations in MetriCat are *structured* (i.e. attributes are represented independently of their relations), whereas current view-based models are strictly holistic. This difference has important implications for the models' ability to generalize from known to novel instances (cf. Fodor & Pylyshyn, 1988; Hummel & Biederman, 1992; Hummel & Stankiewicz, 1996b).

A second similarity between MetriCat and view-based models is the shared emphasis on metric properties in the representation of object shape. But here, too, the differences are more important than the similarities. The most important difference is that, in view-based models, the representational space (feature coordinates) is perfectly linear in (indeed, identical to) the perceptual domain from which it derives (feature coordinates as they appear in the image). By contrast, in MetriCat, the representational space (the logistic representation attribute values) is non-linear in the perceptual domain from which it derives (the numerical values of the attributes). This difference is important because the non-linearity plays a critical role in the behaviour of MetriCat, and the linearity plays an equally critical role in the view-based models. It is doubtful that the principles underlying MetriCat could be adapted to operate with a linear representation of attributes, and it is equally doubtful that the principles underlying the view-based approach could be adapted to work with a non-linear representation of coordinates (Hummel & Stankiewicz, 1996b).

Extensions

The simulations reported here suggest that MetriCat has promise as an account of our ability to recognize objects at multiple levels of abstraction. However, numerous additional tests are required to evaluate MetriCat as a general model of object recognition. Doing so will require integrating MetriCat with a front-end (such as the early layers of JIM) that can automatically recover geon attributes and relations from line drawings or grey-level images. At this point, it is nonetheless possible to speculate about some other implications of the MetriCat approach to object recognition. One particularly interesting implication concerns the relationship between levels of classification and sensitivity to variations in viewpoint. In general, categorical attributes and relations are more robust to variations in viewpoint than otherwise equivalent metric attributes (Biederman, 1987). For example, a representation that describes the axis of a curved cone simply as "curved" will remain the same in many views of the cone, whereas a representation that specifies its numerical degree of curvature (e.g. as given by the curvature of the cone's bounding edges) will change as the cone is rotated in depth. MetriCat relies more heavily on precise metric properties for instance-level recognition than for class-level recognition. (This is true because of the way it codes numerical attributes and the way it matches those attributes to memory for recognition.) It therefore predicts that instance-level recognition will tend to be more view-sensitive than class-level recognition. There is some indirect support for this prediction (see Biederman & Gerhardstein, 1995; Bülthoff et al., 1995; Tarr & Bülthoff, in press).

MetriCat as a Model of Visual Attention

As a model of attention, MetriCat is still in an early stage of development. The mechanism it uses to implement attentional selection—enhanced inhibition for asynchrony—is motivated strictly by the problem of generating structural descriptions in a neural network for shape recognition. Conspicuously absent from the discussion so far is any basis for deciding *when* attention should be directed to an object and *where* to direct it. One particularly interesting property of MetriCat is that an answer to the first question (How do we know when to direct attention?) may serve as a partial answer to the second (How do we know where to direct it?). Note that α is a global parameter. It does not operate on any particular location in the visual field, or even on any particular object. Rather, it serves only to enhance the ability of whatever is currently firing to inhibit anything else that might attempt to fire in the near future: α is directed in time rather than space. Any given object (or part) exists at a particular location in the visual field, and fires at a particular time. Thus, knowing *when* to direct attention is tantamount to knowing *where* to direct it: Directing attention to whatever is firing at a given time implicitly directs attention to a particular object occupying a particular location in the visual field.

How can MetriCat figure out when to direct its attention? Part of the answer to this question must depend on the system's processing goals, and this part of the question is clearly beyond the scope of our current research. However, given that the system knows that it cares about a particular object, there is a straightforward basis for dynamically directing attention to various parts of that object. This basis relates to the relationship between the activation of object units and the utility of object parts for discriminating one object from another. Ambiguity about an object's identity consists of simultaneous activation in multiple, inconsistent object units. For example, if the units for both "teapot" and "lamp" are equally active at some instant, then at that instant, MetriCat is undecided about whether the object is a teapot or a lamp. Imagine that the system is processing some (as yet unrecognized) stimulus, and that, on the basis of the geon that is currently firing, there is no way to decide whether the object is a teapot or a lamp. As long as the current (uninformative) geon continues to fire, the activations of the "lamp" and "teapot" units will remain unchanged. Then the current geon stops firing, and some new geon starts to fire. If this new geon is informative, then the activations of the object units will begin to change—say, "teapot" beings to decline and "lamp" begins to grow. This change in activation can serve as a signal that the geon under consideration is informative, and that attention should be directed to it (so it can inhibit its competitors and remain active longer without interference). Once the informative geon has done all it can in the way of indicating whether the object is a teapot or a lamp, the object units' activations will once again stop changing. Attention should now be moved away from this geon and onto a different one. Thus, one way to direct attention dynamically may be to set α to a value proportional to the change in the activation of object units. We have implemented an early version of this mechanism and the results so far have been promising. Augmented with a learning algorithm for keeping track of which parts are diagnostic for the recognition of which objects, this temporal search mechanism might serve as one way to search for diagnostic features for object recognition (e.g. as discussed by Biederman, 1987).

It is still unlikely, however, that this simple mechanism could constitute a complete solution to the problem of allocating visual attention. Among other things, it provides no clear way to explain phenomena such as visual search or visual neglect, which seem to have a decidedly spatial component. However, it is tempting to speculate that this type of mechanism might constitute at least one basis for attentional selection in human shape perception.

Selective Processing of Visual "Features"

One other extension of MetriCat is worth mentioning here. MetriCat uses Gaussian receptive fields with variable standard deviations (σ) to classify objects at multiple levels of abstraction. In the model's current form, σ for any given unit is a scalar. Implicitly, this convention sets σ to the same value for all attribute dimensions. An extension (and generalization) of this approach would be to make σ a vector that can take different value on different dimensions (as **p** is currently). For example, a given GFA might select for cones with a very particular aspect ratio (i.e. by setting σ to a small value on the dimension *aspect ratio*), without being as selective for particular values on other dimensions (σ would be larger on these dimensions). This kind of selective narrowing of the units' receptive fields would allow MetriCat to choose diagnostic stimulus dimensions for instance-level classification, and constitutes another way the architecture might account for the use of diagnostic features for visual scrutiny.

SUMMARY AND CONCLUSIONS

MetriCat is in an early stage of development, but the approach is promising. The fundamental principles underlying the model are that: (1) Objects are visually represented as collections of part attributes and relations, which are dynamically bound into structural descriptions (Hummel & Biederman, 1992); (2) part attributes and relations are represented in a non-linear fashion that emphasizes categorical boundaries without discarding all metric information (Stankiewicz & Hummel, 1996); and (3) attention enables parts to inhibit one another so that they can fire cleanly out of synchrony. Together, these principles provide a preliminary account of the human capacity to classify objects at multiple levels of abstraction, and suggest a theory of the mechanism of attention in shape perception.

REFERENCES

Biederman, I. (1987). Recognition-by-components: A theory of human image understanding. *Psychological Review, 94*, 115–147.

Biederman, I., & Cooper, E.E. (1991a). Evidence for complete translational and reflectional invariance in visual object priming. *Perception, 20*, 585–593.

Biederman, I., & Cooper, E.E. (1991b). Priming contour deleted images: Evidence for intermediate representations in visual recognition. *Cognitive Psychology, 23*, 393–419.

Biederman, I., & Cooper, E.E. (1992). Size invariance in visual object priming. *Journal of Experimental Psychology: Human Perception and Performance, 18*, 121–133.

Biederman, I., & Gerhardstein, P.C. (1993). Recognizing depth-rotated objects: Evidence and conditions for 3-dimensional viewpoint invariance. *Journal of Experimental Psychology: Human Perception and Performance, 19*, 1162–1182.

Beiderman, I., & Gerhardstein, P.C. (1995). Viewpoint-dependent mechanisms in visual object recognition: A critical analysis. *Journal of Experimental Psychology: Human Perception and Performance, 21*, 1506–1514.

Biederman, I., & Schiffrar, M.M. (1987). Sexing day-old chicks: A case study and expert systems analysis of a difficult perceptual-learning task. *Journal of Experimental Psychology: Learning, Memory and Cognition, 13*, 640–645.

Bülthoff, H.H., & Edelman, S. (1992). Psychophysical support for a two-dimensional view interpolation theory of object recognition. *Proceedings of the National Academy of Science, 89*, 60–64.

Bülthoff, H.H., Edelman, S.Y., & Tarr, M.J. (1995). How are three-dimensional objects represented in the brain? *Cerebral Cortex, 3*, 247–260.

Clowes, M.B. (1967). Perception, picture processing and computers. In N.L. Collins & D. Michie (Eds), *Machine intelligence* (Vol. 1, pp. 181–197). Edinburgh: Oliver & Boyd.

Cooper, E.E., Biederman, I., & Hummel, J.E. (1992). Metric invariance in object recognition: A review and further evidence. *Canadian Journal of Psychology, 46*, 191–214.

Dickenson, S.J., Pentland, A.P., & Rosenfeld, A. (1992). 3-D shape recovery using distributed aspect matching. *IEEE Transactions on Pattern Analysis and Machine Intelligence, 14*, 174–198.

Edelman, S., Cutzu, F., & Duvdevani-Bar, S. (1996). Similarity to reference shapes as a basis for shape representation. *Proceedings of the 18th Annual Conference of the Cognitive Science Society*, pp. 260–265. Mahwah, NJ: Lawrence Erlbaum Associates, inc.

Farah, M. (1992). Is an object an object an object: Cognitive and neuropsychological investigations of domain-specificity in visual object recognition. *Current Directions in Psychological Science, 1*, 164–169.

Fodor, J.A., & Pylyshyn, Z.W. (1988). Connectionism and cognitive architecture: A critical analysis. In S. Pinker & J. Mehler (Eds), *Connections and symbols* (pp. 3–71). Cambridge, MA: MIT Press.

Foster, D.H., & Ferraro, M. (1989). Visual gap and offset discrimination and its relation to categorical identification in brief line-element displays. *Journal of Experimental Psychology: Human Perception and Performance, 15*, 771–784.

Hoffman, D.D. & Richards, W.A. (1985). Parts of recognition. *Cognition, 18*, 65–96.

Hummel, J.E., & Biederman, I. (1991). Binding by phase locked neural activity: Implications for a theory of visual attention. Paper presented at the *Annual Meeting of the Association for Research in Vision and Ophthalmology*, Sarasota, FL, May.

Hummel, J.E., & Biederman, I. (1992). Dynamic binding in a neural network for shape recognition. *Psychological Review, 99*, 480–517.

Hummel, J.E., & Holyoak, K.J. (1997). Distributed representations of structure: A theory of analogical access and mapping. *Psychological Review, 104*, 427–466.

Hummel, J.E, & Stankiewicz, B.J. (1996a). An architecture for rapid, hierarchical structural description. In T. Inui & J. McClelland (Eds). *Attention and performance XVI: Information integration in perception and communication* (pp. 93–121). Cambridge, MA: MIT Press.

Hummel, J.E., & Stankiewicz, B.J. (1996b). Categorical relations in shape perception. *Spatial Vision, 10*, 201–236.

Jolicoeur, P., Gluck, M.A., & Kosslyn, S.M. (1984). Picture and names: Making the connection. *Cognitive Psychology*, 16, 243–275.

König, P., & Engel, A.K. (1995). Correlated firing in sensory-motor systems. *Current Opinion in Neurobiology, 5*, 511-519.

LaBerge, D., & Brown, V. (1989). Theory of attentional operations in shape identification. *Psychological Review, 96*, 101–124.

Logan, G.D. (1994). Spatial attention and the apprehension of spatial relations. *Journal of Experimental Psychology: Human Perception and Performance, 20,* 1015–1036.

Marr, D. (1982). *Vision.* San Francisco, CA: Freeman.

Olhausen, B.A., Anderson, C.H., & Van Essen, D.C. (1993). A neurobiological model of visual attention and invariant pattern recognition based on dynamic routing of information. *The Journal of Neuroscience, 13,* 4700–4719.

Pinker, S. (1984). Visual cognition: An introduction. In S. Pinker (Ed.), *Visual cognition* (pp. 1–62). Amsterdam, Elsevier.

Poggio, T., & Edelman, S. (1990). A neural network that learns to recognize three-dimensional objects. *Nature, 343,* 263–266.

Poggio, T., & Girosi, F. (1990). Regularization algorithms that are equivalent to multilayer networks. *Science, 277,* 978–982.

Rosch, E., Mervis, C.B., Gray, W.D., Johnson, D.M., & Boyes-Braem, P. (1976). Basic objects in natural categories. *Cognitive Psychology,* 8, 382–439.

Saiki, J., & Hummel, J.E. (in press). Connectedness and the integration of parts with relations in shape perception. *Journal of Experimental Psychology: Human Perception and Performance.*

Schneider, W.X. (1995). VAM: A neuro-cognitive model for visual attention control of segmentation, object recognition, and space-based motor action. *Visual Cognition, 2,* 331-375.

Stankiewicz, B.J., & Hummel, J.E. (1996). MetriCat: A representation for basic and subordinate-level classification. *Proceedings of the 18th Annual Conference of the Cognitive Science Society,* pp. 254–259. Mahwah, NJ: Lawrence Erlbaum Associates, inc.

Stankiewicz, B.J., & Hummel, J.E. (in prep.). Automatic priming for translation- and scale-invariant representations of object shape.

Stankiewicz, B.J., Hummel, J.E., & Cooper, E.E. (in press). The role of attention in priming for left–right reflections of object images: Evidence for a dual representation of object shape. *Journal of Experimental Psychology: Human Perception and Performance.*

Tanaka, J.W., & Farah, M.J. (1993). Parts and wholes in face recognition. *Quarterly Journal of Experimental Psychology: Human Experimental Psychology, 146A,* 225–245.

Tarr, M.J. (1995). Rotating objects to recognize them: A case study on the role of viewpoint dependency in the recognition of three-dimensional objects. *Psychonomic Bulletin and Review, 2,* 55–82.

Tarr, M.J., & Bülthoff, H. (in press). Conditions for viewpoint-dependence and viewpoint-invariance: What mechanisms are used to recognize an object? *Journal of Experimental Psychology: Human Perception and Performance.*

Tipper, S.P. (1985). The negative priming effect: Inhibitory effects of ignored primes. *Quarterly Journal of Experimental Psychology, 37A,* 571–590.

Tipper, S.P., & Driver, J. (1988). Negative priming between pictures and words in a selective attention task: Evidence for semantic processing of ignored stimuli. *Memory and Cognition, 16,* 64–70.

Treisman, A. (1982). Perceptual grouping and attention in visual search for objects. *Journal of Experimental Psychology: Human Perception and Performance, 8,* 194–214.

Treisman, A., & Gelade, G. (1980). A feature integration theory of attention. *Cognitive Psychology, 12,* 97–136.

Tresiman, A., & DeSchepper, B. (1996). Object tokens, attention, and visual memory. in T. Inui & J.L. McClelland (Eds), *Attention and performance XVI.* Cambridge, MA: MIT Press.

Tversky, B., & Hemenway, K. (1984). Objects, parts, and categories. *Journal of Experimental Psychology: General, 113,* 169–193.

Vetter, T., Poggio, T., & Bülthoff, H.H. (1994). The importance of symmetry and virtual views in three-dimensional object recognition. *Current Biology, 4,* 18–23.

von der Malsburg, C. (1981). *The correlation theory of brain function.* Internal Report 81-2. Department of Neurobiology, Max-Planck-Institute for Biophysical Chemistry, Göttingen, Germany.

von der Malsburg, C., & Buhmann, J. (1992). Sensory segmentation with coupled neural oscillators. *Biological Cybernetics, 67*, 233–242.

APPENDIX

Oscillatory Gates

Each gate, i, has two components, an excitor, E_i, and an inhibitor, I_i, which interact to cause E_i to oscillate. E_i changes according to:

$$\Delta E_i = \left[0.9(1 - E_i)(1 - 2I_i)\right] - 0.5(1 - E_i) - \sum_{j \neq i} L_j \tag{5}$$

where I_i is the activation of the corresponding inhibitor and L_j is the inhibitory strength of gate j (see equation 7). I_i changes according to:

$$\Delta I_i = \begin{cases} \left.\begin{cases} 0.005(E_i) \text{ iff } I_i < 0.2 \\ 0.5(E_i) \text{ iff } I_i \geq 0.2 \end{cases}\right\} \text{if } r_i \\ \left.\begin{cases} -0.1 \text{ iff } I_i < 0.9 \\ -0.5 \text{ iff } I_i \leq 0.9 \end{cases}\right\} \text{otherwise} \end{cases} \tag{6}$$

where r_i is a Boolean variable that is set to *true* whenever $I_i < 0.1$ and to false whenever $I_i > 0.995$; r_i remains at its last set value whenever $0.1 < I_i < 0.995$. Together, (5) and (6) cause E_i to oscillate, as illustrated in Figure 3 (Hummel & Stankiewicz, 1996a; Hummel & Holyoak, 1997). In combination with the inhibition between competing gates (L), the result is that separate E_i tend to oscillate out of synchrony with one another. L_i, the inhibitory strength of gate i is:

$$L_i = E_i P_i \alpha \tag{7}$$

where P_i, the priority of gate i, modulates the ability of i to inhibit other gates, j, and α modulates the global ability of all gates to inhibit one another. A gate's priority is:

$$P_i = \begin{cases} 0 \text{ if } I_i > 0.2 \text{ and } \Delta I_i = (-0.5) \\ P_i = P_i + \left(0.001 + \left[0.01(1 - P_i)\right]\right) \text{otherwise} \end{cases} \tag{8}$$

By (6) and (8), P_i will go to zero immediately after i fires and then gradually grow toward 1.0. P_i helps the gates to "time-share" by ensuring that a gate will have little ability to inhibit other gates (and therefore little opportunity to fire) if it has fired in the recent past. α corresponds to the amount of attention directed to an object. When α is large (e.g. 1.5), the various gates inhibit one another strongly (equation 7) and therefore fire cleanly out of synchrony; when α is zero, the gates cannot inhibit one another at all, and therefore never fire out of synchrony; at intermediate values of α, the gates fire somewhat out of synchrony.

Attribute Units

Each attribute unit, i, has a Gaussian receptive field (RF) with a centre, μ_i, in the range of logistic values (0.0 . . . 1.0) and a standard deviation, σ_i, in the range 0.0 . . . 0.25. The input to attribute unit i, from all geons, j, is:

$$I_i = \sum_j E_j G(\|\mu_i - l_j\|, \sigma_i) \tag{9}$$

where E_j is the value of the excitatory gate on geon j, l_j is the logistic value of geon j on the corresponding attribute, and G( ) is the Gaussian. The activation of an attribute unit grows as:

$$\Delta a_i = 0.5I_i - 0.05a_i \tag{10}$$

GFA Units

GFA units have Gaussian RFs in the 350-dimensional (50 units × 7 attributes) space of attribute units. The activation of GFA unit i in response to attribute vector **a** is:

$$A_i = G\left(\left[\frac{\|\mathbf{p}_i - \mathbf{a}\|}{\sqrt{d}}\right], \sigma_i\right) \tag{11}$$

where $\mathbf{p}_i$ is the mean (centre) of i's RF, σ_i is its standard deviation, and d is the dimensionality of the attribute vector (here 350). The output of GFA unit i at time t is:

$$O_i^t = \begin{cases} A_i^t \text{ if } A_i^t > O_i^{t-1} \\ O_i^{t-1} \text{ otherwise} \end{cases} \tag{12}$$

Object Units

Object units have Guassian RFs in the space of GFA unit outputs. The activation of object unit i is:

$$B_i = G\left(\left[\frac{\|\mathbf{p}_i - \mathbf{o}\|}{\mathbf{p}_i}\right], \sigma_i\right) \tag{13}$$

where $\mathbf{p}_i$ is the mean (centre) of i's RF. **o** is the vector of GFA unit outputs, and σ_i is the standard deviation of i's receptive field. The normalization by $\|\mathbf{p}_i\|$ (the length of the object unit's receptive field vector) serves to correct for the dimensionality of the GFA vector. (Note that, as more objects are learned, the number of object parts stored in memory grows, changing the dimensionality of both the GFA output vector and an object unit's receptive field.)

VISUAL COGNITION, 1998, *5* (1/2), 81–107

Selective Dorsal and Ventral Processing: Evidence for a Common Attentional Mechanism in Reaching and Perception

Heiner Deubel, Werner X. Schneider and Ingo Paprotta

Institut für Psychologie, Allgemeine und Experimentelle Psychologie, Ludwig-Maximilians-Universität, München, Germany

The primate visual system can be divided into a ventral stream for perception and recognition and a dorsal stream for computing spatial information for motor action. How are selection mechanisms in both processing streams coordinated? We recently demonstrated that selection-for-perception in the ventral stream (usually termed "visual attention") and saccade target selection in the dorsal stream are tightly coupled (Deubel & Schneider, 1996). Here we investigate whether such coupling also holds for the preparation of manual reaching movements. A dual-task paradigm required the preparation of a reaching movement to a cued item in a letter string. Simultaneously, the ability to discriminate between the symbols "E" and "Ǝ" presented tachistoscopically within the surrounding distractors was taken as a measure of perceptual performance. The data demonstrate that discrimination performance is superior when the discrimination stimulus is also the target for manual aiming; when the discrimination stimulus and pointing target refer to different objects, performance deteriorates. Therefore, it is not possible to maintain attention on a stimulus for the purpose of discrimination while directing a movement to a spatially separate object. The results argue for an obligatory coupling of (ventral) selection-for-perception and (dorsal) selection-for-action.

INTRODUCTION

Our knowledge about the architecture of the visual system of primates has increased enormously during the last two decades. There is growing consensus that visual processing occurs in parallel and interaction streams at different,

Requests for reprints should be addressed to Heiner Duebel, Institut für Psychologie, Ludwig-Maximilians-Universität, Leopoldstr. 13, D-80802 München, Germany. E-mail: deubel@psy.uni-muenchen.de

This research was supported by the Deutsche Forschungsgemeinschaft, SFB 462 ("Sensomotorik").

quasi-hierarchical levels (e.g. DeYoe & van Essen, 1988; Livingstone & Hubel, 1988; Milner & Goodale, 1995; Zeki, 1993. A number of suggestions have been made how this parallel and distributed processing of visual information might be functionally organized. Based on lesion work in monkeys, Mishkin, Ungerleider and Macko (1983) claimed that the visual system consists of two main pathways, namely the dorsal "where"-pathway and the ventral "what"-pathway. The suggested function of the "what"-pathway is to recognize objects based on their visual appearance. The "where"-pathway, on the other hand, computes spatial information about objects. At the cortical level, the segregation of both pathways can be tracked back to the primary visual cortex, area V1. From there, the "where"-pathway runs dorsally into the posterior parietal lobe, whereas the "what"-pathway leads ventrally to the inferior temporal lobe. Since this proposal, a large body of research has supported this distinction of two main pathways (but see Zeki, 1993). For instance, patients with brain lesions restricted to the inferior temporal cortex have problems recognizing objects by sight, a symptom called "visual agnosia" (e.g. Farah, 1990; Kolb & Whishaw, 1990). At the same time, spatial abilities, such as pointing to an object, are left intact. When agnosia is purely visual, recognition by other senses, such as touch, is still intact. Lesions restricted to the superior parietal areas of the dorsal "where"-pathway, on the other hand, can cause a symptom called "optic ataxia" (e.g. Milner & Goodale, 1995). These patients are able to identify objects due to their visual appearance, but they exhibit misreaching (mislocation) towards the same objects.

The labelling of the ventral and dorsal pathways as a "what"- and a "where"-pathway, respectively, was recently criticized by Goodale and Milner (1992; Milner & Goodale, 1995). Though they ascribe the computation of "what"-aspects—that is, the identification of objects—to the ventral pathway, they disagree about the function of the dorsal pathway. They do not see perception of the spatial layout of the external world as its main task, but instead computation of spatial information for motor actions such as a saccade or a reach towards an object. In other words, Goodale and Milner (1992) suggest a shift in emphasis from spatial perception to spatial information for action. Their view of dorsal processing is supported by human neuropsychological studies and neurophysiological work in macaques, especially by single-cell recordings (see Milner & Goodale, 1995). The literature reviewed indicates that the idea of a single representation of external space is probably wrong, and that instead several spatial-motor representations—sometimes called "processing streams"—exist in parallel for different kinds of motor actions (see e.g. Graziano & Gross, 1994; Milner & Goodale, 1995; Rizzolatti, Riggio, & Sheliga, 1994; Stein, 1992). For instance, information about saccade landing points is probably computed and coded in the lateral intraparietal area (LIP), while endpoints for grasping movements are computed in area 7b (both are part of the parietal lobe). Therefore, the brain seems to code spatial information for different effectors—that is, for different action classes—in different parts of the brain. In summary, Goodale and Milner (1992) suggest that the ventral stream is involved in visual perception and identification, whereas the dorsal stream computes information for spatial-motor actions. A related distinction was recently suggested by Jeannerod (1994), who differentiated between a "semantic mode" of processing, located in the temporal lobe (ventral stream), and a "pragmatic mode", located in the parietal cortex (dorsal stream).

Visual processing in both streams does not occur in a purely automatic, "bottom-up" driven manner. Rather, control of processing is task-dependent; this type of selectivity of visual processing has been called "endogenous visual attention" (e.g. Posner, 1980). Much research in experimental psychology and the neurosciences has investigated the properties of these selection processes in vision (for overviews, see Bundesen, 1990; Desimone & Duncan, 1995; Posner & Petersen, 1990; Schneider, 1993; Treisman, 1988; van der Heijden, 1992). Traditional experimental psychology has focused on the function of visual attention in the ventral stream; that is, on "selection-for-visual-perception". For instance, experiments on visual search (for overviews, see Treisman & Gormican, 1988; Wolfe, 1994) have attempted to determine how fast and how accurate certain visual attributes and their conjunctions can be "perceived" to be signalled. In most of these investigations, "ventral" attributes such as colour, orientation, and so on, served as the properties that defined the search target. Therefore, selection-for-visual-perception (in contrast to selection-for-spatial-motor-control—the dorsal processing domain) has been the main topic of search tasks. Another research tool for the effects of visual attention in ventral processing is the spatial pre-cueing paradigm (e.g. Eriksen & Hoffman, 1973, Posner, 1980; van der Heijden, 1992). Experiments have shown that pre-knowledge about the possible location of a target leads to faster and more accurate responses to visual aspects such as alphanumeric identity or simple shape features, such as curved versus straight (for overviews, see Posner & Raichle, 1994; van der Heijden, 1992).

This bias in measuring the effect of visual attention mainly for ventral visual processing can be traced back to the suggested functions of attention. Attention is assumed to facilitate detection (Posner, 1980), to allow "feature integration" (Treisman & Gelade, 1980), "object recognition" (LaBerge & Brown, 1989; Schneider, 1995) and "entry to visual short-term memory" (Bundesen, 1990; Duncan & Humphreys, 1989). However, these assumptions do not imply that the selection mechanism itself is located in the ventral stream only. Instead, several theories have suggested a central role of the dorsal stream in controlling the attentional mechanism, sometimes called the "spatial attention mechanism" (e.g. La Berge & Brown, 1989; Posner & Petersen, 1990; Schneider, 1995; van der Heijden, 1992).

Compared to the large body of theoretical work on the relationship between attention and (ventral) perceptual processing, there are scant data on the role of visual attention in dorsal processing; more precisely, the role of attention in spatial-motor control. Allport (1987) and Neumann (1987) suggested that spatial motor actions, such as grasping one object from among other objects, may also be a selection process, what Allport (1987) called "selection-for-action". Natural environments usually contain several objects, and only one of them should be used as the target for an individual action. For instance, grasping a pen among other pens requires the motor system to receive spatial information, probably in arm-centred coordinates (Graziano & Gross, 1994), of the intended pen only. Information from other pens has to be excluded from controlling the grasping action. In other words, an attentional mechanism is needed that selects the spatial information of the movement target. Because spatial information is provided by the visual system (the dorsal pathway), Allport (1987, 1989) and Neumann (1987, 1990) have suggested that visual attention is involved in this selection process. Another example of selection-for-spatial-motor-action refers to the control of saccadic eye movements. Before each saccade, the next fixation point has to be selected among many potential candidates in the environment.

Unfortunately, there has not been much experimental work on selection-for-spatial-motor-action. Tipper, Lortie and Baylis (1992) investigated the role of visual attention for manual reaching in an interference paradigm. They wished to determine if the interference effects found for ventral visual processing (e.g. Eriksen & Eriksen, 1974) can also be obtained for spatial-motor actions. The degree of interference is usually considered as a measure of the efficiency of attentional processes. In these experiments, subjects had to reach, as fast and as precisely as possible, from a starting position to one of nine locations indicated by a red light (the target). In some trials, a yellow light (the distractor) appeared, simultaneously with the red target light, at a different location. Substantial interference effects were obtained; response latencies were prolonged compared to trials where no distractor appeared. This interference effect was only observed when the distractor was located between the starting position and the target. Tipper et al. (1992) argued that their results reflect "action-centred attention", emphasizing that the location of the movement target is most relevant to the amount of interference. In summary, these results show that interference effects by nearby objects can also be obtained for spatial-motor action such as reaching, suggesting that visual attention processes are also involved in selection-for-spatial-motor-action. A similar conclusion was reached by Castiello (1996). In one of his experiments, subjects had to grasp a target as their primary task. A secondary, non-spatial task was required for a different object located close to the target. Castiello observed interference effects of the secondary task on the kinematics of the primary grasping movement, given the subject performed a subsidiary task which involved the distractor.

Another line of research dealing with dorsal selection concerns the relationship between eye movement control and visual attention. The question is whether visual attention for perceptual processing on the one hand, and selection of a target for a saccade on the other, are independent or not. The results of early experiments on this issue were controversial (e.g. Klein, 1980; Posner, 1980), partly due to methodological problems (see Shepherd, Findlay, & Hockey, 1986). More recent studies (Deubel & Schneider, 1996; Hoffman & Subramaniam, 1995; Kowler, Anderson, Dosher, & Blaser, 1995; Schneider & Deubel, 1995) have clearly demonstrated a strict link between ventral selection-for-perception and dorsal selection-for-a-saccade.

In the experiments of Deubel and Schneider (1996), subjects had to saccade to locations within horizontal letter strings left or right of a central fixation cross. The performance in discriminating between the "E" and "Ǝ" presented tachistoscopically before the saccade within the surrounding distractors was taken as a measure of visual attention in perception. The results showed that discrimination performance is best when discrimination target and saccade target refer to the same object. The findings argue for an obligatory and selective coupling of dorsal processing for saccade programming and ventral processing for perception and discrimination; this coupling is restricted to one common target object at a time.

Based on these results and other computational considerations, Schneider (1995) postulated a Visual Attention Model (VAM) that suggests a common selection mechanism for both processing streams. In line with two-stage models of perception and attention (Neisser, 1967), a first stage of low-level visual processing computes, in parallel in early visual areas of the brain (e.g. V1, V2), elementary visual information in the form of "primitive" object structures (visual units). Higher-level visual processing in the dorsal and ventral stream is assumed to be capacity-limited; that is, it occurs only for one visual unit (one "object") at a time. In the model, visual attention is the mechanism that determines the unit, carries out the selection, and gates the information flow from low- to high-level vision in a way that only information from one object is further processed. The VAM claims that visual attention selects one low-level visual object at a time, leading to prioritized perceptual processing in the ventral stream (i.e. the object is recognized). Simultaneously, possible spatial-motor actions (saccade, pointing, reaching, grasping, etc.) towards this object are programmed in the dorsal stream. Only the (effector-specific) "go" signal is necessary to convert the programs into overt action.

Such attention-mediated and object-specific coupling of dorsal and ventral processing has already been demonstrated for eye movement control and perceptual selection (Deubel & Schneider, 1996). More than just for saccades, however, VAM predicts that the same coupling should also hold for aiming, reaching and grasping (Schneider, 1995, p. 363). In the present study, we analysed the coupling of reaching movements and visual discrimination. For this purpose, a dual-task paradigm similar to that used in our previous studies was developed. The primary task was to make a goal-directed reaching movement to a cued object, measuring selection-for-spatial-motor-action in the dorsal stream. Prior to the movement, a secondary task required subjects to discriminate between the characters "E" and "Ǝ", measuring selection-for-perception ("traditional" visual attention) in the ventral stream. It is hypothesized that the programming of the reaching movement yokes the visual attention mechanism, so that during this selection process no other object can be processed in high-level ventral vision. Consequently, discrimination performance should be best when discrimination target and reaching target refer to the same object. For non-corresponding reaching and discrimination targets, better than chance performance should be possible only when visual attention shifts first to the discrimination target and then to the reaching target. In this case, longer initiation latencies for the movement should be expected.

METHODS

Subjects

Five subjects participated in the experiments; their age ranged from 22 to 28 years. They had normal vision and normal motor behaviour. All subjects were experienced in a variety of experiments in oculomotor research. One subject was one of the authors of the study, the others were naive with respect to the aim of the experiments.

Experimental Set-up

Figure 1 shows a sketch of the experimental set-up. The subject was seated in a dimly lit room. The visual stimuli were presented on a fast 21 inch colour monitor (CONRAC 7550 C21), visible through a one-way mirror. The monitor provided a frame frequency of 100 Hz at a spatial resolution of 64 pixels per inch. The active screen size was 40 × 30 cm; the viewing distance was 57.7 cm. The video signals were generated by a freely programmable graphics board (Kontron KONTRAST 8000), controlled by a PC via the TIGA (Texas Instruments Graphics Adapter) interface. The stimuli appeared on a grey background adjusted to a mean luminance of 2.2 cd/m^2. The luminance of the stimuli was 23 cd/m^2. The relatively high background brightness is essential to avoid the effects of phosphor persistence (Wolf and Deubel, 1997).

The use of a one-way mirror allowed free hand movements to the stimuli without visual feedback about hand position. Reaching movements were recorded with a Fastrak electromagnetic position and orientation measuring

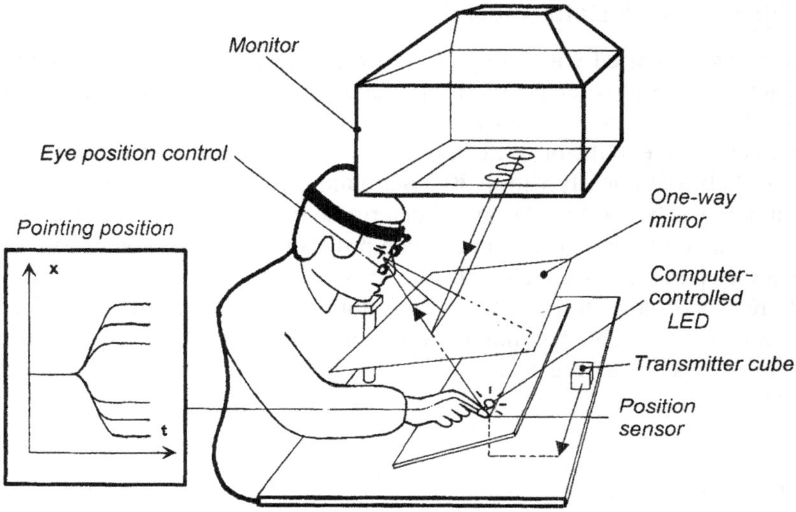

FIG. 1. Experimental apparatus.

system (Polhemus Inc., 1993) and sampled at 400 Hz. The sender device was fixed 60 cm in front of the subject. The sender emits time-multiplexed, orthogonal electromagnetic fields of 10 kHz frequency. From induction in the receiver, which was mounted on the fingertip of the subject's right hand, the orientation relative to the sender device is calculated by a central processing unit. From the intensity of the electromagnetic field, the distance between sender and receiver is determined. The position in space is calculated from distance and orientation by use of a specific digital signal processor (TI320C30). The device allows for a maximum translation range of 10 feet, with an accuracy of 0.03 inches RMS. The frequency response is 120 Hz; without further filtering, the phase lag response is 4 msec. Connected on the receiver was a red LED (5 mm diameter), controlled by the PC. The LED allowed us to provide controlled visual feedback about the spatial position of the fingertip.

Eye fixation was monitored by an infrared eyetracker (IRIS, Skalar Medical) with a temporal bandwidth of 240 Hz. This device measures the reflection difference between the sclera and iris by infrared LEDs and phototransistors that are situated next to the subject's eyes. Head movements were restricted by an adjustable chin rest. The experiments were controlled by a 486 PC. The PC also served for the automatic off-line analysis of the pointing movement data, for which movement latencies and start and end positions of the manual responses were determined.

Calibration and Data Analysis

Each session started with calibration of the eyetracker, the subject having to sequentially fixate three positions arranged on a horizontal line at distances of 8.5°. Also, the origin and coordinate alignment frame of the position sensor were set relative to the projected position of the monitor's centre. The position sensor behaved linearly within 30 cm around the central position. The overall accuracy was better than 2 mm. To determine latency, amplitude and duration of the reaching movements, an off-line program for evaluation of movement trajectory parameters searched the movement record for the transgression and subgression of a vectorial velocity threshold of 10 mm/s (which is equivalent to about 1°/sec). The beginning and the end of the reaching movement were calculated as linear regressions in a 200 msec time window around these points.

Experimental Paradigm

After an initial training block that was not included in the data analysis, each subject underwent six blocks (three blocks per day) of each of the experiments; each block consisted of 120 single trials. The subject performed a dual task involving both manual reaching and visual discrimination. In each experimental trial, the reaching movement was guided by a central, symbolic cue that indicated the movement target (MT) within a string of letters. Moreover, the subject had to report the identity of a discrimination target (DT) presented tachistoscopically in the string. Two experiments were performed. In Experiment 1, the DT appeared *before* the hand movement. For each experimental block, the position of the DT was held constant, either on the right or on the left, and on the central position of the string. Experiment 2 was similar to Experiment 1, except that the DT was presented *at the onset* of the reaching movement.

Figure 2 shows an example for the sequence of stimuli in a single trial of Experiment 1. Each trial started with the presentation of a small fixation cross in the centre of the screen, with a size of 0.25°. Simultaneously, two strings of pre-mask characters appeared to the left and right of the central fixation, each consisting of five pre-mask items resembling the number "8". The width of each item was 0.9° of visual angle; its height was 1.4°. The distance between the items was 2.4°, with the central item of the five letters being presented at an eccentricity of 7.65°. The three central items of each letter string appeared on ellipses coloured red (r), green (g) and blue (b), as indicated in Fig. 2. Colour intensities of the ellipses were adjusted by flicker-photometry to make them equally salient.

The subject was asked to maintain strict fixation at the centre of the screen, initially indicated by a central fixation cross, throughout the trial. Maintenance

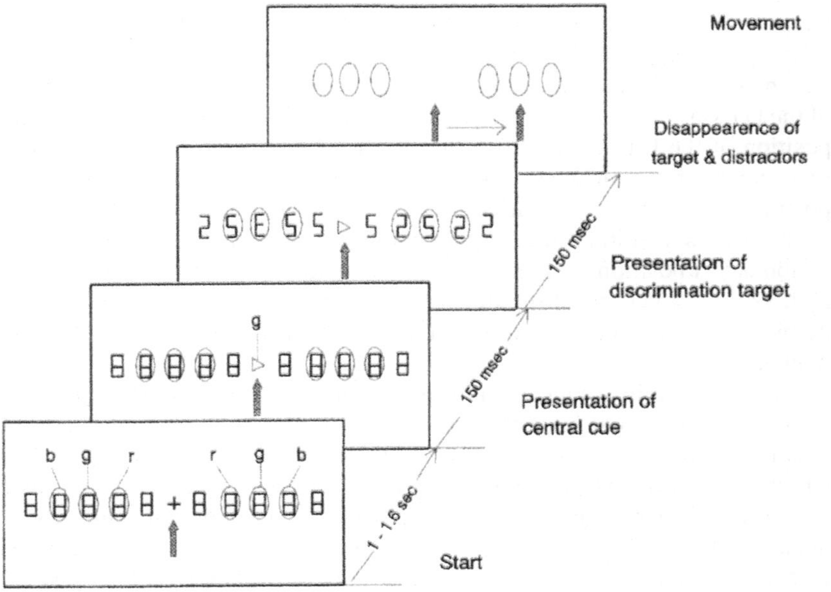

FIG. 2. Stimulus sequence in Experiment 1. The trial starts with the presentation of a small fixation cross and two strings of characters to the left and right of the central fixation. The three central items of each letter string appear on ellipses coloured red (r), green (g), and blue (b). Initially, the subject positions his or her fingertip on the location of the central cross (fingertip position is indicated by the arrowhead). After a delay of 1–1.6 sec, a symbolic cue in the form of a red, green or blue triangle appears in the centre of the screen, pointing either to the right or to the left side; this cue specifies the movement target within the string. Then, 150 msec later, the pre-mask characters change into nine distractors and one discrimination target ("E" or "Ǝ"). The target and distractors remain visible for 150 msec. Then, the characters and the central cue are removed and only the coloured ellipses remain.

of fixation was monitored by the IRIS oculometer. At the beginning of the trial, the subject had to position his or her fingertip on the location of the central cross. The position of the fingertip is indicated by the arrowhead in Fig. 2. In this phase, the LED was switched on, aiding precise positioning. After a delay of 1000–1600 msec, a symbolic cue in the form of a red, green or blue triangle appeared in the centre of the screen, pointing either to the right or to the left side. Colour and pointing direction of the triangle thus unequivocally indicated a specific item, the movement target (MT), within the string. The primary task was to "point to this target as fast and precisely as possible". Simultaneously with cue onset, the LED was switched off to disable any further visual feedback of hand or pointing position. Then, 150 msec after the appearance of the cue, well before the onset of the pointing movement, the pre-mask characters changed into nine distractors and one discrimination target. The distractors were randomly selected among the characters "S" and "Ƨ". The central character on one of both sides was replaced by the discrimination target (DT), which consisted either of the letter "E" or its mirror image ("Ǝ"). The position of the DT was constant during each block and known to the subject (e.g. central position of the DT was constant during each block and known to the subject (e.g. central position in the string on the right side). The movement target positions, however, were varied independently within the central three items of the strings, resulting in 12 combinations of movement target and discrimination target positions. All experimental conditions occurred with equal probability. The target and distractors remained visible for 150 msec. Then, the items and the central cue were removed and only the coloured ellipses remained.

Due to the timing of the stimulus presentation, the discrimination target was no longer present 300 msec after the appearance of the coloured triangle. As a result, most reaching movements were initiated well *after* the disappearance of target and distractors (see Figure 5). To eliminate occasional responses that occurred too early, the off-line data analysis discarded movements with latencies shorter than 200 msec. Also, trials with movement velocities smaller than 11 mm/s^2 and durations shorter than 50 msec and longer than 600 msec, were not considered in the analysis. This accounted for less than 2% of all trials.

One second after the onset of the reaching movement, the LED was switched on again to enable control of visual feedback of the finger position reached. Finally, the subject indicated, without time pressure, the identity of the discrimination target ("E" or "Ǝ") by pressing one of two buttons (2AFC task). The central fixation cross reappeared after the subject's decision and the next trial was initiated by the computer.

In separate sessions, two types of "single-task" controls were run. A first control task ("no discrimination–reaching only" single-task condition) served to assess pointing reaction times in a single-task situation. For this purpose, the subject was asked to point to the indicated position, but was not required to discriminate. A second control task ("no reaching–discrimination only" single-task condition) served to test discrimination performance without pointing. Here, the subject was only asked to indicate the identity of the discrimination target; no reach was required. Each subject performed two blocks of each control task.

Experiment 2 was very similar to Experiment 1 except that the presentation of the discrimination stimulus occurred at the *onset* of the reaching movement. For this purpose, the computer performed an on-line calculation of movement velocity. Stimulus presentation was triggered when the velocity exceeded a threshold of 1°/sec.

RESULTS

Experiment 1

Movement Performance. After the initial training block, all five subjects were able to produce reaching movements with surprisingly consistent accuracy and latency. Figure 3 gives examples of several manual responses from one of the subjects. The graph displays the registered finger position as a function of time, for the different movement target eccentricities. It can be seen from the raw data that the end positions of the movements correlate well with the MT positions. Some of the responses showed a small overshoot with respect to the movement end position. The amplitude data reported in the following refer only to the final movement position. Moreover, the movements were in general very consistent with respect to their velocity profiles; only a few movements with multiple velocity peaks were observed.

The impression of the homogeneity of movement responses is confirmed by analysis of the movement data. Figure 4a shows mean movement amplitudes and Figure 4b mean movement durations as a function of the movement target location. The vertical bars denote the standard error; they are only visible for the cases where the error exceeds symbol size. The data are plotted separately for the cases where the discrimination stimulus was present at the central position on the right (open circles) and on the left (solid circles). It is easy to see that the amplitudes are independent of the position of the discrimination target. One rationale of the experimental approach was that the discrimination task should not interfere with the reaching task; this analysis of amplitudes suggests that this was indeed the case. Moreover, the mean movement amplitudes demonstrate that the reaching movements were very precise; mean amplitudes were highly correlated with the given MT positions ($r = 0.99$). A further data analysis in the form of a two-way ANOVA (repeated measures) confirmed a highly significant main effect of MT position, $F(5,20) = 1078$, a non-significant effect of DT position, $F(1,4) = 0.9, p > .1$, and a non-significant interaction, $F(5,20) = 0.89$.

A similar conclusion holds for the movement durations (Figure 4b). Average movement durations were 202, 260 and 315 msec for the small, medium and large target eccentricities respectively. Again, the data are independent of DT location, suggesting that the execution of the movement itself is not affected by the presentation of the test item. Accordingly, ANOVA showed a highly significant main effect of MT position, $F(5,20) = 263.7$, a non-significant effect of DT position, $F(1,4) = 0.44$, and a non-significant interaction, $F(5,20) = 0.80$.

Figure 5a displays mean movement onset latencies and standard errors as a function of MT location. Again, the data are given separately for the blocks where the discrimination target was on the right (open circles) and where DT

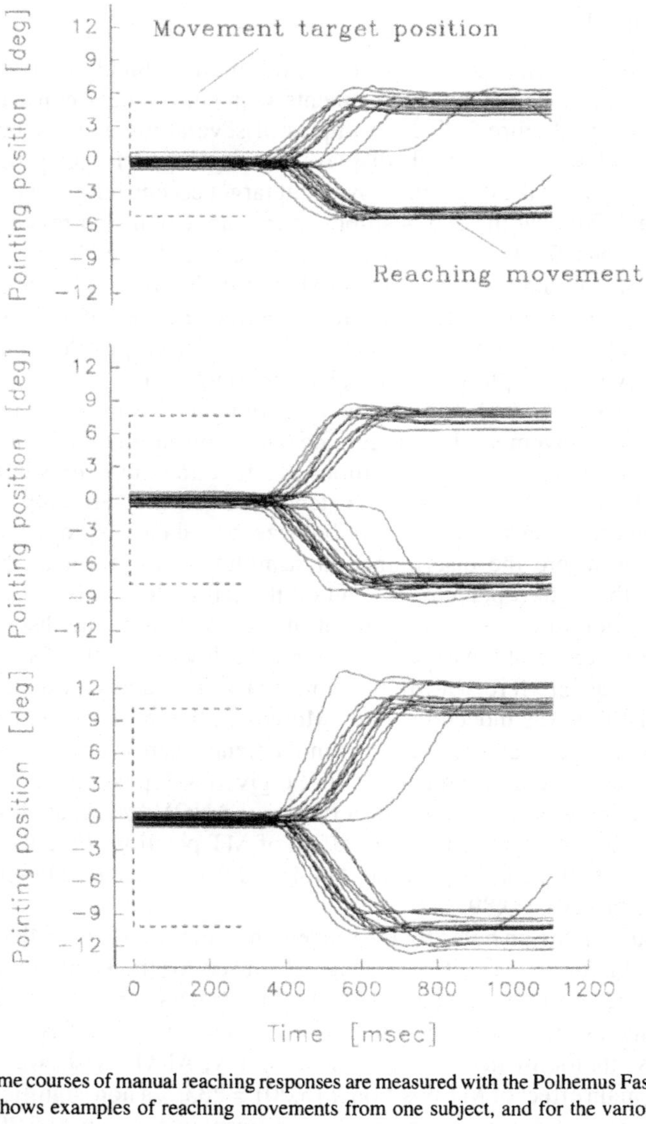

FIG. 3. Time courses of manual reaching responses are measured with the Polhemus Fastrack system. The graph shows examples of reaching movements from one subject, and for the various movement target eccentricities.

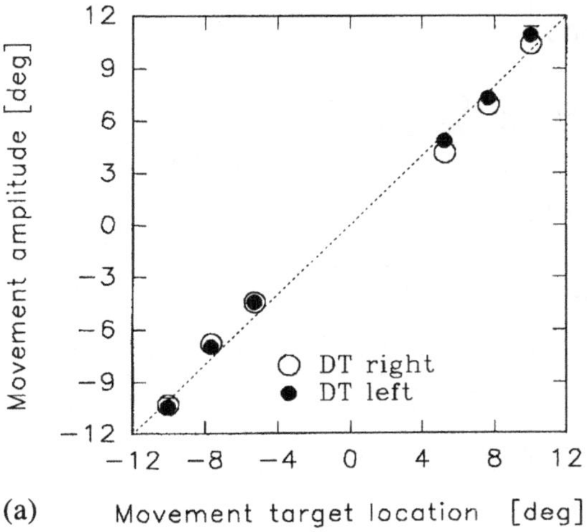

(a)

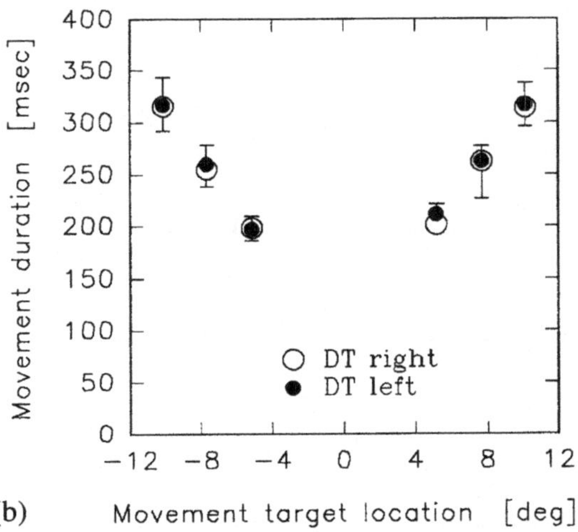

(b)

FIG. 4. (a) Mean movement amplitudes as a function of the movement target location in Experiment 1. Vertical bars denote standard errors. Data are plotted separately for the cases where the discrimination stimulus was present at the central position on the right (open circles) and on the left (solid circles). (b) Movement durations.

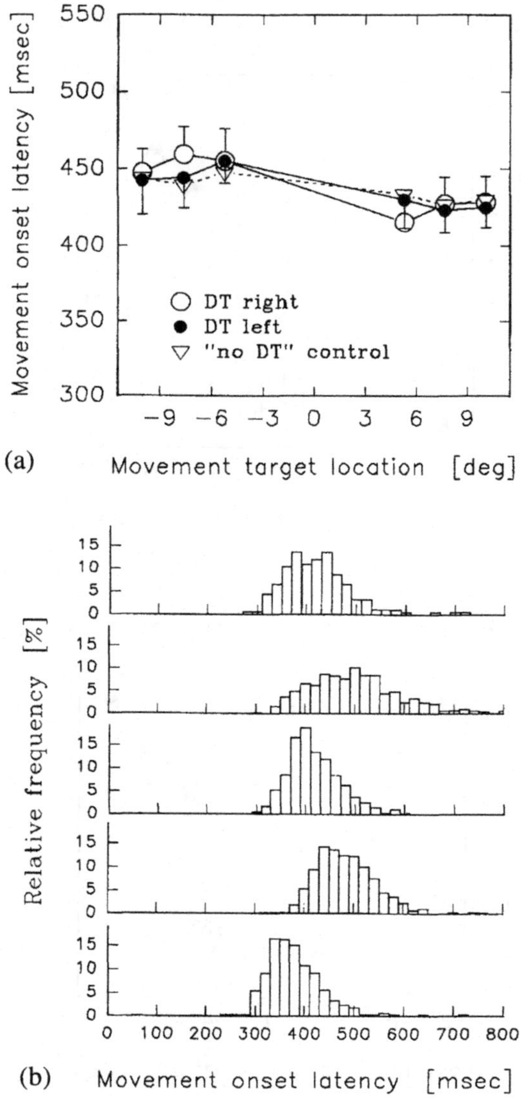

FIG. 5. (a) Mean movement onset latencies and standard errors as a function of MT location. Data are given separately for the blocks where the discrimination target was on the right (open circles) and on the left (solid circles). Open triangles display the latency data from the "no discrimination – reaching only" single-task control condition. (b) Histograms of the latency distribution, presented individually for the five subjects.

was on the left (solid circles). Mean movement onset latency averaged over all conditions was 437.8 msec. A two-way ANOVA revealed that the latencies depended neither on MT location, $F(5,20) = 0.74$, nor on DT location, $F(1,4) = 0$. Also, the interaction was not significant, $F(5,20) = 2.1$, $p > .05$. The open triangles in the graph display the latency data from the "no discrimination–reaching only" single-task control condition. For this type of experiment, mean latency was 436.9 msec. Again, the response latency was independent of MT location, $F(5,20) = 1.34$; $p > .1$.

Figure 5b shows histograms of the distribution of the movement onset latencies, individually for the five subjects who participated in the experiment. It can be seen that, while mean latency varies, the distributions for all subjects are unimodal and are skewed with the long tail towards longer latencies.

Perceptual Performance. The subjects reported that they had no difficulties pointing quickly to the indicated target item in the string. However, initially, they were very uncertain about their ability to discriminate between the DT items. Performance improved considerably after some practice. Therefore, the first session served for training and was not included in the data analysis. After the experiment, the subjects were asked for their subjective impression and how they solved the task. They reported that the peripheral items that were indicated as movement targets seemed to "light up" in a row in an almost unstructured visual field. They also had the impression that they could identify the distractor ("2" or "5") exactly when it appeared at the movement target position.

Our indicator for the momentary allocation of attention in the ventral stream is the accuracy with which the discrimination target can be identified. Discrimination performance can be expressed as the percentage of correct decisions of target identity; chance level is 50% correct. Figure 6 presents discrimination performance as a function of movement target location. Since performance was not significantly different for DT on the left or on the right, data from the two conditions were pooled in Figure 6 such that the position of the discrimination target always refers to the position indicated in the graph (at + 7.65°). In other words, negative MT locations refer to the cases where MT and DT were in opposite hemifields.

Figure 6a shows discrimination performance as a function of relative MT position for all response latencies (solid squares). The horizontal line represents the discrimination performance from the "no reaching–only discrimination" control task. The data suggest that performance depends on the relationship between the position of the discrimination stimulus and the location of the indicated movement target position; performance is best when the MT and DT positions coincide (DT = MT). When the movement is not directed to the critical item, performance decreases sharply. Performance is worst when the subject points to a direction opposite to the DT position. The performance advantage for the coincidence of MT and DT positions was confirmed by

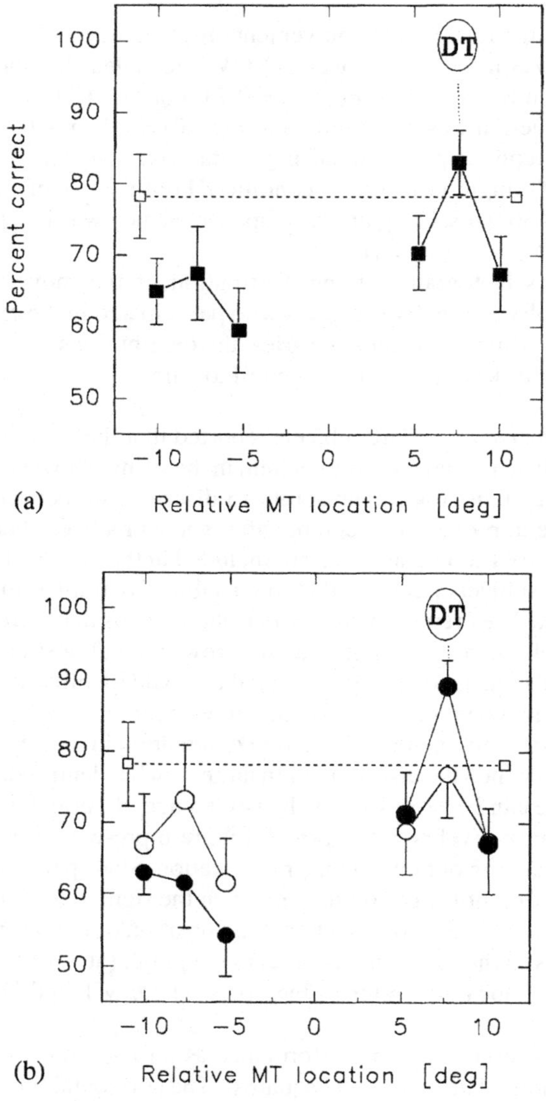

FIG. 6. (a) Discrimination performance as a function of movement target location. Data for DT on the left and on the right are pooled such that the position of the discrimination target always refers to the position indicated in the graph at + 7.65°. Vertical bars indicate standard errors. Horizontal line represents discrimination performance from the "No reaching – only discrimination" control trials. (b) Discrimination performance data after median split. Solid circles are for the fast half of responses; open circles are for the slow half of responses.

further statistical analysis: ANOVA showed a highly significant effect of relative MT position, $F(5,20) = 15.12$, $p < .0001$. In a *post-hoc* Student-Newman–Keuls test, the performance at DT = MT proved to be superior to all other cases, which did not differ significantly ($p < .01$).

Upon questioning after the experiments, subjects occasionally reported that they had the feeling that they performed better in the discrimination task when they delayed the manual response. An interpretation of this observation is that, in these cases, DT is discriminated first, and only later is movement programming initiated. This should result in longer movement latencies. In other words, one should expect an interaction between movement latency and perceptual performance. Therefore, we analysed performance for each subject separately for the fast half of responses (i.e. faster than the median latency of the subject) and for the slow half of responses. The averaged data are shown in Figure 6b. For the fast responses (solid circles), performance superiority at DT = MT was still more pronounced. For these fast responses directed to the discrimination stimulus, performance was even superior to discrimination performance in the "no movement" control condition (89.1 *vs* 78.3% correct). For the slow portion of responses (open circles), the spatial selectivity all but disappeared. Compared to the fast reactions, there was also a general tendency for discrimination to improve in those cases where MT and DT were presented in opposite directions. A two-factor ANOVA showed a significant main effect of relative MT position, $F(5,20) = 14.73$, $p < .0001$, and a non-significant main effect of latency, $F(1,4) = 0.05$. As expected, the interaction between response latency and MT position was significant, $F(5,20) = 4.14$, $p < .01$. *Post-hoc* Newman-Keuls tests showed that, for the fast half of responses, performance at MT = DT was significantly better than for the other relative MT positions ($p < .01$). For the slow responses, the superiority of MT = DT with respect to the other relative movement positions disappeared ($p > .05$). In summary, the data show that the ability to discriminate between objects in a multi-object scene during the preparation of a reaching movement is spatially selective, and superior at the movement goal. This is most pronounced for fast manual reactions.

Experiment 2

Movement Performance. In Experiment 2, the presentation of the discrimination target occurred at the *onset* of the manual response. The mean (± SE) movement onset latency was 441.2 ± 45 msec. Since the characteristics of the latency data in this experiment were identical to those of Experiment 1, the data are not presented in more detail here.

In this experiment, the discrimination stimulus appeared at movement onset and was present during most of the movement. Therefore, the question arises whether presence of the DT affected the precision of the reaching movement and/or its dynamic properties. For this reason, we again analysed the dependence of movement amplitude and duration on DT location. The results are shown in Figure 7. Figure 7a displays movement amplitude as a function of MT position. It can be seen that, as in Experiment 1, the overall movement was rather precise and there was no effect of DT position. Accordingly, a two-way ANOVA yielded a highly significant main effect of MT position, $F(5,20) = 410.8$, a non-significant effect of DT position, $F(1,4) = 3.41$, $p > .1$, and no interaction, $F(5,20) = 1.41$, $p > .1$.

Figure 7b displays mean movement durations. Although there seemed to be a general tendency for movements to be shorter for DT appearing in the right hemifield, this effect did not reach statistical significance. ANOVA yielded a significant main effect of MT position, $F(5,20) = 20.48$, $p < .0001$, but a non-significant effect of DT position, $F(1,4) = 0.09$, and a non-significant interaction, $F(5,20) = 0.73$. In summary, as in the previous experiment, there was no indication that the movement itself was affected by the presentation of the DT.

Perceptual Performance. Figure 8 gives discrimination performance in Experiment 2 as a function of the relative position of the movement target, pooled over five subjects. In this case also, discrimination was superior when DT and MT referred to the same object. Accordingly, ANOVA yielded a significant effect of relative MT position, $F(4,5) = 4.42$, $p < .01$. A *post-hoc* Newman-Keuls test confirmed a significant difference in the DT = MT condition with respect to the other conditions ($p < .05$). All other data points did not differ significantly.

DISCUSSION

The main aim of this study was to determine if and how selection in the ventral stream ("selection-for-perception") and selection of visual targets for reaching movements in the dorsal stream ("selection-for-spatial-motor-action") are coupled. This study developed from the theoretical perspective provided by VAM (Schneider, 1995), a recently developed model of the control of visual attention, and from empirical evidence confirming such coupling in the preparation of saccadic eye movements (Deubel & Schneider, 1996; Hoffman & Subramaniam, 1995; Kowler et al., 1995).

VAM states that a common selection mechanism exists for dorsal and ventral processing. This mechanism is suggested to select one object at a time in the "early" stages of the visual system, resulting in an increased activation of the visual representations of this object in higher-level ventral and dorsal visual areas. This increased activation allows the selective perceptual analysis of the selected object to the level of recognition, and the selective computation of its spatial parameters such that saccading, reaching and grasping movements are prepared. Therefore, VAM suggests a strict one-object-at-a-time rule: When-

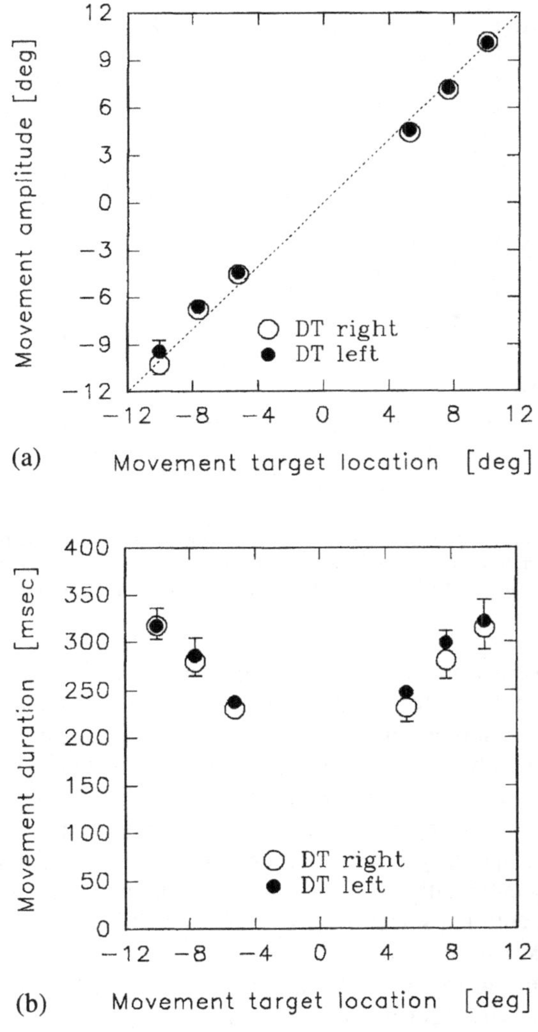

FIG. 7. (a) Mean movement amplitudes as a function of the movement target location in Experiment 2. Vertical bars denote standard errors. Data are plotted separately for the cases where the discrimination stimulus was present at the central position on the right (open circles) and on the left (solid circles). (b) Movement durations.

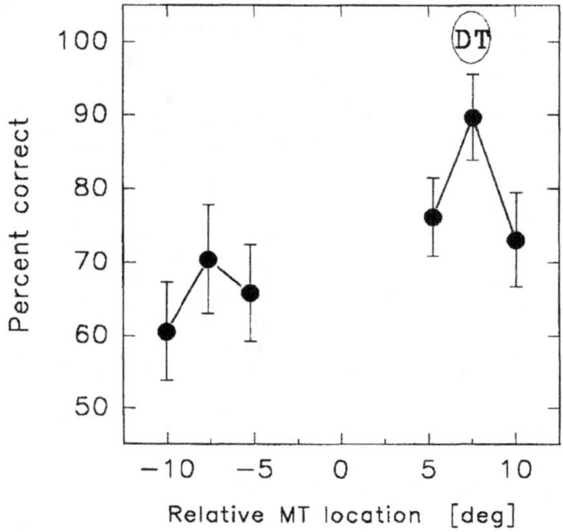

FIG. 8. Discrimination performance as a function of movement target location in Experiment 2. Data for DT on the left and on the right are pooled such that the position of the discrimination target always refer to the position indicated in the graph at + 7.65°. Vertical bars indicate standard errors.

ever a goal-directed action towards an object is prepared, only this movement target can be perceptually processed in higher-level ventral areas. On the other hand, whenever visual attention focuses on an item for the purpose of object recognition, no other objects can be selected for goal-directed actions. According to VAM, dissociations can only occur by a serial process, implying that the visual recognition of an object should considerably delay a motor response towards a different, spatially separate target. It should also be emphasized that the selection is object-specific; this is in contrast to others, who assume a spatial organization of attentional selection (e.g. Hughes & Zimba, 1987; Rizzolatti, Riggio, Dascola, & Umiltà, 1987).

The results from our experiments are perfectly consistent with these theoretical conjectures. The discrimination data from Experiment 1 demonstrate that well before movement onset, perceptual performance depends strongly on where in space the reaching movement is directed. Discrimination is best when the reaching movement and perceptual task refer to the same object, and is strongly reduced prior to a reach when an object other than the movement target has to be perceptually analysed. Our interpretation is that the (dorsally based) preparation of a goal-directed motor response, here a reaching movement, binds the (perceptual) processing capacities of the ventral stream to the same object. During the preparation phase, objects other than the movement target are temporarily excluded from ventral high-level visual analysis. Similar results have been obtained by Irwin and Gordon (this issue) for the coupling of saccade programming and encoding of visual-perceptual information into trans-saccadic memory.

The amount of spatial selectivity reflected in our data is surprising. It reflects the current spatial location of a common selection mechanism for dorsal and ventral processing. The fact that spatial selectivity was so clear in our experiments is probably due to the brief presentation time of the stimuli, thus preventing additional attentional shifts. In contrast, investigations using reaction time paradigms, where attentional shifts cannot be excluded, often reveal a rather broad gradient of attentional effects as a result of cueing (e.g. Downing & Pinker, 1985).

The object specificity of the coupling is in line with the findings of Castiello (1996), who determined if the kinematics of the target movement are influenced by non-target objects. Castiello's results indeed demonstrated interactions when the distractor object had to be used also for carrying out a simultaneous, secondary task. However, interference disappeared when the secondary, purely perceptual task (counting the number of times an object was illuminated) referred to the same object, which also served as the reaching target. This suggests that preparing and executing a reaching movement cannot be done simultaneously with attentional selection in the ventral stream when the two selection processes refer to different objects. When both tasks referred to the same object, parallel selection was possible.

The fact that the coupling between perception and action in our experiments occurred in spite of the subject's complete knowledge of the location where the discrimination target was presented, argues for the assumption that the coupling is obligatory. Even with the incentive for separating visual perception and motor programming, subjects do not succeed in decoupling both processes. On the other hand, it is well known that visual attention can be shifted without concomitant eye or hand movements (e.g. Posner, 1980). Like Rizzolatti et al. (1987), we think that the strict coupling holds for the preparation and programming of the movement but does not necessarily require, or entail, its overt initiation. Therefore, in cases where visual attention but not the hand moves, we assume that the spatial parameters for the potential movement are available and provided by the attentional mechanism, but that the movement is prevented from being converted into overt action due to the non-release of the "go" signal.

An interesting aspect of our data results from the median split analysis of discrimination performance based on movement latencies (Figure 6). The results suggest that the coupling is restricted mainly to the fast responses; slower responses seem to allow better perception of the discrimination target in the non-corresponding cases. Again, this is consistent with our theoretical considerations. In cases where the initiation of the reach is not done as fast as possible (long latencies), it should be possible to undertake the discrimination task first, then the reaching task. Viewed from VAM's perspective, this means that the unitary visual attention mechanism first shifts to the known discrimination target location, allowing for discrimination and storage in short-term memory. Only then does attention shift to the movement target occur and the programming is continued.

The instructions required the subjects to give priority to the reaching task, which had to be performed as fast and as precisely as possible; visual discrimination was the secondary task. This is of some importance for the interpretation of the results, since we wanted to avoid any crossover when measuring perceptual performance on the motor action. Our results suggest that this aim was indeed fulfilled. Neither response latency and amplitude nor movement duration depended on the presentation of the discrimination target. This contrasts with the findings of Tipper et al. (1992) and Pratt and Abrams (1994), who showed that distractors that appear on the way to the movement target lead to delayed latencies of the reaching movement. Two reasons may account for this discrepancy. First, in the study of Tipper et al., the distractors appeared simultaneously with the movement target, whereas in our study, the discrimination target was presented 150 msec *after* movement cue onset. Therefore, one can assume that the programming of the movement might already have been completed before distractor onset. Second, the distractors used by Tipper et al. were coloured objects appearing abruptly in the visual field; such sudden onsets are generally assumed to attract attention automatically (Jonides, 1981; Yantis & Jonides, 1984). Similar reasoning holds for the results of Pratt and Abrams (1994). In our paradigm, on the other hand, the transients at the moment of DT presentation were equally distributed over all 10 items in the visual field (for each of the items, two lines elements disappeared). In consequence, it is unlikely that the presentation of the DT *per se* attracted attention. Finally, it is important to note that the targets did not "pop out" from the distractors because of figural reasons, which would again entail an automatic attraction of attention to the discrimination target. Similar approaches were used by Cheal and Lyon (1988) and Nakayama and Mackeben (1989).

The second experiment showed that coupling between dorsal and ventral processing is effective even during movement execution. It appears that visual attention remained on the movement target even during execution of the movement. We assume that this continuous coupling is necessary because subjects may evaluate movement success by means of the visual feedback provided by the LED after the reach. Correspondingly, the average movements were amazingly precise and consistent as reflected in the high accuracy and low variability of the movement data. However, we do not claim that movement execution is necessarily accompanied with a binding of the attentional mechanism at the movement target position. Attention should only be allocated to the future movement target, when it is necessary to evaluate the success of the movement by comparing (proprioceptive or visual) information about the actual movement end position with the intended target position. This comparison can probably not be done pre-attentively. On the other hand, when a movement is highly practised—this touches the issue of "automaticity" (for overviews, see Neumann, 1984; Shiffrin, 1988)—and does not require feedback control, then attention to the results of the action may not be necessary. An example of such an action might be shifting gears while driving a car.

The results obtained here for reaching movements are, to a significant degree, similar to our previous findings on the relation of saccades and object recognition (Deubel & Schneider, 1996; Schneider & Deubel, 1995). These experiments revealed a similar amount of spatial restriction of perceptual capabilities to the intended saccade target. Also, despite their knowledge of the location of the discrimination stimulus, it was not possible for the subjects to recognize the object while preparing a saccade to a different target. Finally, as in the present experiments, performance for non-target stimuli improved with longer saccadic latencies (unpublished observations). These coincidences provide strong support for VAM's assumption of a control mechanism that is common for saccades and reaching, and possibly for other types of goal-directed motor actions.

Two further attentional theories explicitly include selection in the dorsal stream, namely the "premotor hypothesis" of Rizzolatti et al. (1987, 1994) and the "integrated competition hypothesis" of Duncan (1996). The central claim of the premotor theory is that the control of "spatial attention" originates in the dorsal spatial-motor areas. In the original proposal, only areas related to eye movements were suggested to control spatial attention (Rizzolatti et al., 1987). In contrast to VAM, the premotor theory does not state whether separate mechanisms exist for dorsal and ventral visual processing, nor how they are related. Moreover, in contrast to Posner and Petersen (1990) and VAM, Rizzolatti, Gentilucci and Matelli (1985) claim that multiple attentional centres exist and that there is no need for a unitary mechanism for attentional control (see also Allport, 1993). Our results argue for just the opposite, namely for the existence of a unitary visual attention mechanism that controls both ventral and dorsal processing.

Duncan (1996) also proposed a framework for attentional processes in the primate brain that incorporates dorsal spatial-motor processes. According to his "integrated competition hypothesis", "attention" is considered to be an emerging state in which visual representations of one object win the competition against representations of other objects. Biasing the competition towards one object is assumed to be controlled by the current task instruction and to originate in brain areas where the task-relevant attributes are computed. Therefore, analogous to VAM, the integrated competition hypothesis predicts an object-specific coupling between the ventral and dorsal stream (see also Duncan, 1984). When reaching or saccading form the primary task, the target should win the competition in both streams. Other objects should be temporarily decoupled from action control and their perceptual representations properly accessed.

We have previously noted the lack of behavioural investigations analysing the relationship between selection-for-perception and selection-for-action. The situation is similar with respect to neurophysiological studies on this issue. To our knowledge, only one prominent single-cell study has directly addressed the effects of (eye) movement programming on ventral processing. Chelazzi, Miller, Duncan and Desimone (1993) studied the activity of neurons in the inferior temporal cortex (IT) in tasks involving the preparation and execution of saccades in target/distractor configurations. These IT neurons are assumed to compute the identity of objects based on visual shape (see Oram & Perrett, 1994). The results of Chelazzi et al. (1993) demonstrated that the preparation of a goal-directed saccade to a target surrounded by distractors leads to a decrease in firing rate of the neurons that represent a distractor; this decrease occurred shortly (90–120 msec) before saccade initiation. Therefore, selection of an object as a movement target is coupled with ventral suppression of distractor information, suggesting a neural mechanism for target selection. Based on our results, we predict similar patterns of neural activity for other types of goal-directed movements such as reaching and grasping.

In summary, our study is the first to demonstrate directly an obligatory, spatially highly selective coupling of selection-for-object-recognition and selection-for-action in a task involving manual reaching. In line with previous theoretical considerations, our findings argue for a unitary control mechanism of visual attention. This mechanism selects objects for perceptual processing (object recognition) and, at the same time, provides the spatial parameters for goal-directed actions such as reaching and grasping.

REFERENCES

Allport, D.A. (1987). Selection for action: Some behavioural and neurophysiological considerations of attention and action. In H. Heuer & A.F. Sanders (Eds), *Perspectives on perception and action* (pp. 395–419). Hillsdale, NJ: Lawrence Erlbaum Associates Inc.

Allport, D.A. (1989). Visual attention. In M.I. Posner (Ed.), *Foundations of cognitive science* (pp. 631–682). Cambridge, MA: MIT Press.

Allport, D.A. (1993). Attention and control. Have we been asking the wrong questions? A critical review of twenty-five years. In D.E. Meyer & S. Kornblum (Eds), *Attention and performance XIV: Synergies in experimental psychology, artificial intelligence, an cognitive neuroscience* (pp. 183–218). Cambridge, MA: MIT Press.

Bundesen, C. (1990). A theory of visual attention. *Psychological Review, 97*, 523–547.

Castiello, U. (1996). Grasping a fruit: selection for action. *Journal of Experimental Psychology: Human Perception and Performance, 22*, 582–603.

Cheal, M. & Lyon, D.R. (1988). Central and peripheral precuing of forced-choice discrimination. *Quarterly Journal of Experimental Psychology, 43A*, 859–880.

Chelazzi, L., Miller, E.K., Duncan, J., & Desimone, R. (1993). A neural basis for visual search in inferior temporal cortex. *Nature, 363*, 345–347.

Desimone, R., & Duncan, J. (1995). Neural mechanisms of selective visual attention. *Annual Review of Neuroscience, 18*, 193–222.

Deubel, H. & Schneider, W.X. (1996). Saccade target selection and object recognition: Evidence for a common attentional mechanism. *Vision Research, 36*, 1827–1837.

DeYoe, E.A., & van Essen, D.C. (1988). Concurrent processing streams in monkey visual cortex. *Trends in Neurosciences, 11*, 219–226.

Downing, C.J., & Pinker, S. (1985). The spatial structure of visual attention. In M.I. Posner & O.S.M. Martin (Eds), *Attention and performance XI* (pp. 171–187). Hillsdale, NJ: Lawrence Erlbaum Associates Inc.

Duncan, J. (1984). Selective attention and the organization of visual information. *Journal of Experimental Psychology: General, 113*, 501–517.

Duncan, J. (1996). Coordinated brain systems in selective perception and action. In T. Inui & J.L. McClelland (Eds), *Attention and performance XVI* (pp. 549–578). Cambridge, MA: MIT Press.

Duncan, J., & Humphreys, G.W. (1989). Visual search and stimulus similarity. *Psychological Review, 96*, 433–458.

Eriksen, B.A., & Eriksen, C.W. (1974). Effects of noise letters upon the identification of a target letter in a nonsearch task. *Perception and Psychophysics, 16*, 143–149.

Eriksen, C.W., & Hoffman, J.E. (1973). The extent of processing of noise elements during selective encoding from visual displays. *Perception and Psychophysics, 1*, 155–160.

Farah, M.J. (1990). *Visual agnosia: Disorders of object recognition and what they tell us about normal vision*. Cambridge, MA: MIT Press.

Goodale, M.A., & Milner, A.D. (1992). Separate visual pathways for perception and action. *Trends in Neurosciences, 15*, 20–25.

Graziano, M.S.A., & Gross, C.G. (1994). Mapping space with neurons. *Current Directions in Psychological Science, 3*, 164–167.

Hoffman, J.E., & Subramaniam, B. (1995). The role of visual attention in saccadic eye movements. *Perception and Psychophysics, 57*, 787–795.

Hughes, H.C., & Zimba, L.D. (1987). Natural boundaries for the spatial spread of directed visual attention. *Neuropsychologia, 25*, 5–18.

Jeannerod, M. (1994). The representing brain: Neural correlates of motor intention and imagery. *Behavioral and Brain Sciences, 17*, 187–245.

Jonides, J. (1981). Voluntary vs. automatic control over the mind's eye's movement. In J. Long & A. Baddeley (Eds), *Attention and performance IX* (pp. 187–203). Hillsdale, NJ: Lawrence Erlbaum Associates Inc.

Klein, R. (1980). Does oculomotor readiness mediate cognitive control of visual attention? In R. Nickerson (Ed.), *Attention and performance VIII* (pp. 259–276). Hillsdale, NJ: Lawrence Erlbaum Associates Inc.

Kolb, B., & Whishaw, I.Q. (1990). *Fundamentals of human neuropsychology*. New York: W.H. Freeman.

Kowler, E., Anderson, E., Dosher, B., & Blaser, E. (1995). The role of attention in the programming of saccades. *Vision Research, 35*, 1897–1916.

LaBerge, D., & Brown, V. (1989). Theory of attentional operations in shape identification. *Psychological Review, 96*, 101–124.

Livingstone, M.S., & Hubel, D. (1988). Segregation of form, color, movement, and depth: Anatomy, physiology, and perception. *Science, 240*, 740–749.

Milner, A.D., & Goodale, M.A. (1995). *The visual brain in action*. New York: Oxford University Press.

Mishkin, M., Ungerleider, L.G., & Macko, K.A. (1983). Object vision and spatial vision: Two cortical pathways. *Trends in Neurosciences, 6*, 414–417.

Neisser, U. (1967). *Cognitive psychology*. New York: Appleton-Century-Crofts.

Nakayama, K., & Mackeben, M. (1989). Sustained and transient components of focal visual attention. *Vision Research, 29*, 1631–1647.

Neumann, O. (1984). Automatic processing: A review of recent findings and a plea for an old theory. In W. Prinz & A.F. Sanders (Eds), *Cognition and motor processes* (pp. 227–267) (pp. 255–293). Heidelberg: Springer-Verlag.

Neumann, O. (1987). Beyond capacity: A functional view of attention. In H. Heuer & A.F. Sanders (Eds), *Perspectives on perception and action* (pp. 361–394). Hillsdale, NJ: Lawrence Erlbaum Associates Inc.

Neumann, O. (1990). Visual attention and action. In O. Neumann & W. Prinz (Eds), *Relationships between perception and action: Current approaches* (pp. 227–267). Berlin: Springer-Verlag.

Oram, M.W., & Perrett, D.I. (1994). Modeling visual recognition from neurobiological constraints. *Neural Networks, 7*, 945–972.

Posner, M.I. (1980). Orienting of attention. *Quarterly Journal of Experimental Psychology, 32*, 3–25.

Posner, M.I., & Petersen, S.E. (1990). The attention system of the human brain. *Annual Review of Neuroscience, 13*, 25–42.

Posner, M.I., & Raichle, M.E. (1994) *Images of Mind*. New York: Scientific American Library.

Pratt, J., & Abram, R.A. (1994). Action-centered inhibition: Effects of distractors on movement planning and execution. *Human Movement Science, 13*, 245–254.

Rizzolatti, G., Gentilucci, M., & Matelli, M. (1985). Selective spatial attention: One center, one circuit, or many circuits? In M.I. Posner & O.S.M. Marin (Eds), *Attention and performance XI* (pp. 251–265). Hillsdale, NJ: Lawrence Erlbaum Associates Inc.

Rizzolatti, G., Riggio, L., Dascola, I., & Umiltà, C. (1987). Reorienting attention across the horizontal and vertical meridians: Evidence in favor of a premotor theory of attention. *Neuoropsychologia, 25*, 31–40.

Rizzolatti, G., Riggio, L. & Sheliga, B.M. (1994). Space and selective attention. In C. Umiltà & M. Moscovitch (Eds), *Attention and performance XV: Conscious and nonconscious information processing* (pp. 231–265). Cambridge, MA: MIT Press.

Schneider W.X. (1993). Space-based visual attention models and object selection: Constraints, problems, and possible solutions. *Psychological Research, 56*, 35–43.

Schneider, W.X. (1995). VAM: A neuro-cognitive model for visual attention control of segmentation, object recognition, and space-based motor action. *Visual Cognition, 2*, 331–375.

Schneider, W.X., & Deubel, H. (1995). Visual attention and saccadic eye movements: Evidence for obligatory and selective spatial coupling. In J.M. Findlay, R. Walker, & R.W. Kentridge (Eds), *Eye movement research* (pp. 317–324). Amsterdam: Elsevier.

Shepherd, M., Findlay, J.M., & Hockey, R.J. (1986). The relationship between eye movements and spatial attention. *Quarterly Journal of Experimental Psychology, 38A*, 475–491.

Shiffrin, R.M. (1988). Attention. In R.C. Atkinson, R.J. Herrnstein, G. Lindsay, & R.D. Luce (Eds), *Stevens's handbook of experimental psychology* (2nd edn, Vol.2, pp. 739–811). New York: Wiley.

Stein, J.F. (1992). The representation of egocentric space in the posterior parietal cortex. *Behavioral and Brain Sciences, 15*, 691–700.

Tipper, S.P., Lortie, C., Baylis, G.C. (1992). Selective reaching: Evidence for action-centred attention. *Journal of Experimental Psychology: Human Perception and Performance, 18*, 891–905.

Treisman, A. (1988). Features and objects: The fourteenth Bartlett memorial lecture. *Quarterly Journal of Experimental Psychology, 40*, 201–237.

Treisman, A., & Gelade, G. (1980). A feature-integration theory of attention. *Cognitive Psychology, 12*, 97–136.

Treisman, A., & Gormican, S. (1988). Feature analysis in early vision: Evidence from search asymmetries. *Psychological Review, 95*, 15–48.

Van der Heijden, A.H. (1992). *Selective attention in vision.* London: Routledge.

Wolf, W., & Deubel, H. (1997). P31 phosphor persistence at photopic luminance level. *Spatial Vision, 10*, 323–333.

Wolfe, J.M. (1994). Guided search 2.0: A revised model of visual search. *Psychonomic Bulletin and Review, 1*, 202–238.

Yantis, S., & Jonides, J. (1984). Abrupt visual onsets and selective attention: Evidence from visual search. *Journal of Experimental Psychology: Human Perception and Psychophysics, 10*, 601–620.

Zeki, S.M. (1993). *A vision of the brain*. Oxford: Blackwell Scientific.

VISUAL COGNITION, 1998, *5* (1/2), 109–125

Visuomotor Priming

Laila Craighero, Luciano Fadiga, Giacomo Rizzolatti and Carlo Umiltà

Istituto di Fisiologia Umana, Università di Parma, Parma and Dipartimento di Psicologia Generale, Università di Padova, Padova, Italy

Two experiments were performed to explore a possible visuomotor priming effect. The participants were instructed to fixate a cross on a computer screen and to respond, when the cross changed colour ("go" signal), by grasping one of two objects with their right hand. The participants knew in advance the nature of the to-be-grasped object and the appropriate motor response. Before (100 msec), simultaneously with or after (100 msec) the "go" signal, a two-dimensional picture of an object (the prime), centred around the fixation cross, was presented. The prime was not predictive of the nature of the to-be-grasped object. There was a congruent condition, in which the prime depicted the to-be-grasped object, an incongruent condition, in which the prime depicted the other object, and a neutral condition, in which either no prime was shown or the prime depicted an object that did not belong to the set of to-be-grasped objects. It was found that, in the congruent condition, reaction time for initiating a grasping movement was reduced. These results provide evidence of visuomotor priming.

INTRODUCTION

Object grasping is a highly complex motor behaviour that requires the capacity to configure the hand according to the shape of a potentially limitless number of known and unknown objects (see, e.g. Jeannerod, Arbib, Rizzolatti, & Sakata, 1995). The physical characteristics of the objects, such as size, shape and orientation, must be visually perceived and used to select the most appropriate hand shaping. One possible way that the brain can compute this

---

Requests for reprints should be addressed to Carlo Umiltà, Dipartimento di Psicologia Generale, Università di Padova, Via Venezia 8, 35131 Padova, Italy.

We thank S. Maasen, W.X. Schneider, E. Wojciulik and two anonymous reviewers for their critical comments of an earlier draft of the manuscript. The work was supported by EEC Contract Biomed/H4 CT95-0789 and a grant from the Italian CNR to L.F. and G.R., and by grants from the Italian CNR and MURST to C.U. Some of the results of Experiment 2 were briefly reported in Criaghero, Fadiga, Umiltà and Rizzolatti (1996).

visuomotor transformation is to link automatically the object representation (i.e its visual properties) to a specific, predetermined grasping movement. Such a linkage would allow for rapid selection of specific object-related motor programs. In other words, and as also suggested by Goldberg and Seagraves (1987) for eye movements, to speed up response selection, it would be beneficial to select the appropriate motor program from an already existing repertoire of motor programs, rather than generate it anew (see Tucker & Ellis, in press).

Milner and Goodale (1995; Goodale & Milner, 1992) have recently proposed that the primate cortical visual areas are formed by two functional pathways. One, the "dorsal stream", has direct links to motor control systems. The other, the "ventral stream", is connected to systems that subserve perception and memory. The computations carried out in the ventral stream produce perceptual and cognitive representations of the visual characteristics of objects and their significance.

In the posterior parietal cortex, which belongs to the dorsal stream, these are neurons that are sensitive to the visual characteristics of the objects that are to be grasped. Each region within the posterior parietal cortex projects to separate regions within the premotor areas of the frontal lobes, where movements are programmed. Thus, the dorsal stream performs the sensorimotor transformations required for visually guided actions, such as grasping a specific object (for reviews, see Jeannerod et al., 1995; Milner & Goodale, 1995; Rizzolatti, Riggio, & Sheliga, 1994).

If size and orientation of a to-be-grasped object are processed by the dorsal stream, it is conceivable that such visual primes invoke stored information about the nature of the object, which in turn might determine the action programs initiated with respect to the object.

The notion that the representations of objects include, in addition to those visual characteristics which are computed in the dorsal stream, information about the actions that can be performed on those same objects, is not new (see, e.g. Eimer, Hommel, & Prinz, 1995). In this context, the term "affordances" has been used to refer to the fact that the actions appropriate for an object may be intrinsic to its representation (see Jeannerod, 1994; Tucker & Ellis, in press). This possibility is supported by neurophysiological and neuropsychological evidence.

In the monkey, neurons in the anterior intraparietal area (AIP) and in the ventral part of frontal premotor area 6 (F5) respond to visual objects in the absence of hand movements and are selectively sensitive to different types of grasping (for reviews, see Jeannerod et al., 1995; Milner & Goodale, 1995; Rizzolatti et al., 1994). It appears that the representation they compute is not concerned with object recognition, but rather with the appropriate object-related hand movement. Thus, areas AIP and F5 form a circuit that transforms visual information about the intrinsic properties of objects into hand movements aimed at interacting with those same objects.

In area F5, there are neurons that respond both when the monkey performs an action on an object and when it observes a similar action made by another monkey or by the experimenter. Rizzolatti and his colleagues (Di Pellegrino et al., 1992; Gallese, Fadiga, Fogassi, & Rizzolatti, 1996; Rizzolatti, Fadiga, Gallese, & Fogassi, 1996a) called these neurons "mirror neurons" and proposed that they compute an abstract representation of a specific action.

Fadiga, Fogassi, Pavesi and Rizzolatti (1995) stimulated the motor cortex of normal human participants (transcranial magnetic stimulation) and simultaneously recorded motor-evoked potentials. They reasoned that, if the observation of a movement activates the premotor cortex, this activation should induce an enhancement of motor-evoked potentials elicited by the magnetic stimulation of the motor cortex. Fadiga et al. found that motor-evoked potentials were selectively enhanced when the participants observed the experimenter grasping objects. Based on this result, they suggested that there is a brain system which is sensitive to both action observation and execution in humans. This issue was also addressed by the use of positron emission tomography (Rizzolatti et al. 1996b). The main finding was the presence of a selective activation in the posterior part of the left inferior frontal gyrus when participants observed the experimenter in the act of grasping objects.

A well-known single case study (Goodale, Milner, Jacobson, & Carey, 1991) reported results that are congruent with the neurophysiological findings we have summarized above. It showed that a brain-damaged patient retained the ability to execute appropriate automatic reaching and grasping responses to objects whose orientation, size and shape she could not explicitly report. The patient failed in a task requiring her to match the orientation of a hand-held card with the orientation of a slot. In contrast, when she was asked to reach out and "post" the card through the slot, her performance was excellent. When presented with pairs of plastic plaques, the patient could not tell whether they were same or different. Similarly, she could not estimate, with her index finger and thumb, the size of the plaques when they were shown one at a time. In contrast, when the patient was asked to grasp the plaques, her performance was indistinguishable from that of normal controls. This patient's behaviour clearly suggests the existence of a direct link between object qualities, such as orientation, size and shape, and reaching and grasping responses that are guided by the same qualities.

In spite of the increasing neurophysiological and neuropsychological evidence, the behavioural evidence to date that the sight of an object also activates the representation of the actions that can be performed on it is somewhat sparse and indirect.

The most relevant study is that by Tucker and Ellis (in press). They addressed the issue of whether visual objects potentiate actions that may be performed on them, even in the absence of explicit intentions to act. They used a stimulus–response compatibility paradigm with photographs of common graspable objects as stimuli. The participants had to decide as fast as possible, by performing a keypress response with either the left or the right hand, whether each object was upright or inverted. Tucker and Ellis reasoned that if a visual object activates the hand most suited to perform a reach-and-grasp movement, facilitation should occur when the simple keypress response is executed with the congruent hand. Conversely, interference should occur when the response is executed with the incongruent hand. The results showed that the pictures automatically activated the hand that was more compatible with grasping the depicted object in a given orientation.

Of some relevance is a study by Tipper, Lortie and Baylis (1992). In a task that required selective reaching for a target with nearby distractors, they found interference on response latency if the distractor was on or near the hand's trajectory to the target. They suggested that the distractors were automatically processed and motor programs were specified for them, thus producing the interference effect.

In conclusion, neurophysiological and neuropsychological evidence points to the existence of a direct visual route from objects to action. What is still lacking is clear evidence of the behavioural effects caused by this route. On the basis of the studies we have reviewed so far, it can be predicted that the motor program that is most appropriate for grasping an object is automatically activated by the visual presentation of that same object. To test this idea, we used an experimental paradigm similar to that used in classical studies of repetition and semantic priming, which showed that recognition of a stimulus is facilitated by having previously processed the same or a related stimulus (i.e. the prime; Bruce, 1983; Kutas & Hillyard, 1984; Meyer & Schvaneveldt, 1971; Warren & Morton, 1982). However, instead of exploring the effects of the prime on stimulus recognition, we tested its effects on object-determined motor responses.

It is worth noting that patients with frontal lobe lesions show a compulsive response that is known as "utilization behaviour" (e.g. Lhermitte, 1983). Utilization behaviour is characterized by the fact that visual stimuli may automatically—that is, in the absence of an intention to act—elicit motor responses, such as reaching and grasping. This compulsive response is perhaps an exaggeration of the type of normal visuomotor priming that is demonstrated in the present study. Pathologically enhanced visuomotor priming would manifest itself when control is lost due to frontal damage, and thus existing visuomotor connections cannot be suppressed.

EXPERIMENT 1

In this experiment, the two to-be-grasped objects required precision grips of comparable difficulty. The two objects differed in their orientation in relation to the participants' body midline. Note that orientation is among the object features to which neurons in areas AIP and F5 are known to respond selectively (e.g. Jeannerod et al., 1995; Milner & Goodale, 1995).

Method

Participants. Ten students attending the University of Parma volunteered to take part in the experiment in exchange for a small fee. All of the students were right-handed, had normal or corrected-to-normal visual acuity, and were unaware of the purpose of the experiment.

Apparatus and Materials. The experiment took place in a sound-attenuated cubicle and ambient light was provided from the ceiling by a halogen lamp. Each participant was seated in a chair with the head positioned on a chin rest.

A computer screen was located 57 cm from the participant's orbital plane. The stimuli on the screen were a white or red fixation cross, each arm of which subtended 1° of visual angle, and the white outline drawing of a rectangle (width 2°, height 5°), which could be rotated 45° either clockwise or counterclockwise. On the right side of the participant's body midline there was a switch, on which the participant placed the hand to start the trial. The to-be-grasped object was a rectangular bar (width 2.5 cm, height 6.0 cm), which could be rotated 45° either clockwise or counterclockwise in relation to the sagittal plane of the participant's body. The bar was positioned in a rectangular hole hollowed out of a plastic disk. The hole was larger than the bar, so that the participant could insert his or her thumb and index finger into it to grasp the bar.

Procedure. Each participant was instructed to fixate the white fixation cross and to respond, when it turned red ('go' signal), by grasping and lifting the object with the right hand. Reaction time (RT) was measured between onset of the "go" signal and release of the switch at the start position. The instructions stressed both speed and accuracy. An electronic device monitored whether the object was lifted from its support. If the participant failed to do so, then that trial was discarded and replaced.

On each trial, the sequence of events was as follows (see Figure 1, in which the experimental events are represented as schematic computer displays). Before the beginning of a trial, the experimenter positioned one of the two objects (50% each, according to a random sequence) on the support in front of the participant. Then the participant pressed the switch with the hand shaped in a pinch position. This caused the appearance of the word "destra" ("right", signalling a clockwise rotation) or "sinistra" ("left", signalling a counterclockwise rotation) on the screen. Because the word always indicated the object that was to be grasped, the participant was fully informed about the nature of the to-be-grasped object before the beginning of each trial. It must be stressed that

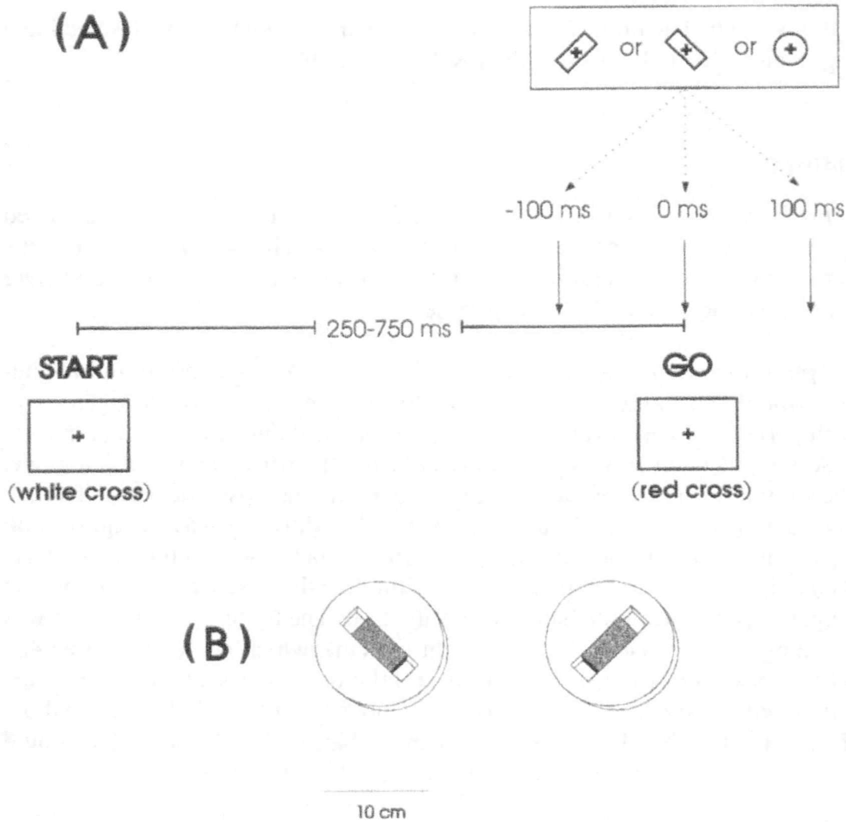

FIG. 1. (A) Schematic representation of the procedure for Experiments 1 and 2. Note that in Experiment 1 the circle was not used. (B) The to-be-grasped objects that were used in Experiments 1 and 2.

the participant was not able to see either the object or the hand, and thus the grasping response did not occur under visual feedback.

The beginning of the trial was marked by the appearance of the white cross on the screen. After a variable interval (250–750 msec), the cross turned red, that is the signal to execute the response. On the experimental trials, before (stimulus onset asynchrony = – 100 msec), simultaneously with (SOA = 0 msec), or after (SOA = 100 msec) the "go" signal, one of the two pictures (i.e. the prime) was presented. The three SOAs were randomly intermixed and occurred with equal probability (about 33% each).

The relations between the prime and the to-be-grasped object yielded a congruent condition (the two objects were the same, 35% of the trials) and an incongruent condition (the two objects were different, 35% of the trials). On 18% of the trials, no prime was presented, which yielded a neutral, control condition. Finally, on about 12% of the trials, the prime was presented but the "go" signal was not delivered. These were catch trials, in which the participant had to refrain from responding.

Every participant produced 204 trials: 144 experimental trials (that is, 12 trials for each combination of to-be-grasped object, congruence condition and SOA), 36 neutral trials and 24 catch trials.

Results and Discussion

Reaction times for neutral trials were analysed separately (see below), because on neutral trials the SOA factor was absent (no prime was presented).

Reaction times for experimental trials were submitted to an analysis of variance (ANOVA), in which the three within-subjects factors were orientation of the to-be-grasped object (clockwise *vs* counterclockwise), type of trial (congruent *vs* incongruent) and SOA (–100, 0 or 100 msec).

The three main effects were significant [orientation: $F(1,9) = 9.37, p < .05$; SOA: $F(2,18) = 6.59, p < .01$; type of trial: $F(1,9) = 6.23, p < .05$]. Reaction time was faster for the clockwise than for the counterclockwise orientation (342 *vs* 348 msec), and was faster for the –100 msec SOA and 0 msec SOA (339 and 340 msec) than for the 100 msec SOA (356 msec). Pairwise comparisons (Newman-Keuls test) showed that the RTs in the – 100 msec SOA and the 0 msec SOA did not differ, whereas they both differed significantly from RT with the 100 msec SOA condition ($p < .05$ and $p < .01$, respectively). More interestingly, RT was faster on congruent than incongruent trials (342 *vs* 348 msec).

Also, the interaction between the type of trial and SOA was significant, $F(2,18) = 7.95, p < .005$. As shown in Figure 2, this indicated that the advantage of congruent over incongruent trials was present and significant ($p < .01$) with the – 100 msec SOA (330 *vs* 348 msec). A similar, but non-significant trend was noted with the 0 msec SOA (336 *vs* 345 msec). In contrast, with the 100 msec SOA, incongruent trials were non-significantly faster than congruent trials (352 *vs* 361 msec).

In the ANOVA for neutral trials, the only within-subjects factor was orientation. It was not significant, although RTs were somewhat faster for the clockwise than the counterclockwise orientation (358 *vs* 362 msec).

The results clearly showed a priming effect. The task-irrelevant bi-dimensional drawing acted as a prime and decreased the latency for performing a grasping response towards a congruent real object.[1]

Two response components can be distinguished in a RT task—selection of which response is needed and programming of the selected response (e.g.

---

[1]No doubt, under the present experimental conditions, the participants were prepared to grasp objects. This was probably instrumental in producing the priming effect. It remains to be seen whether a comparable priming effect can be found in the absence of a readiness to grasp objects.

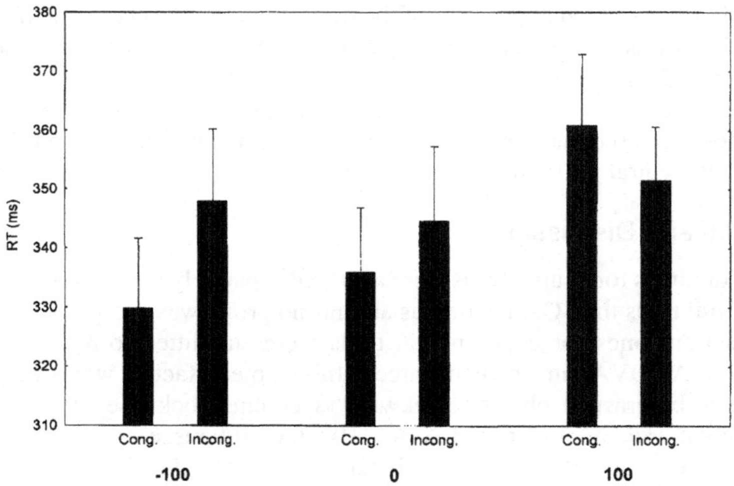

FIG. 2. The two-way interaction (type of trial × SOA) obtained in Experiment 1.

Klapp, 1995). Both components must be completed before the response is initiated, so that both can contribute to RT. In the present experiment response uncertainty and stimulus–response compatibility— that is, the factors that are known to influence response selection—were held constant. Therefore, the experimental manipulations affected programming rather than selection. It appears that the prime facilitated the programming of the appropriate response for grasping the target object.

It is important to point out that the priming effect was very clear only if the prime preceded the "go" signal. This must not be interpreted as an indication that the priming effect is weak and difficult to obtain. Rather, it indicates that, as is to be expected, the priming effect manifests itself only if the prime is shown while the response has yet to be programmed. When the prime appears simultaneously with or after the "go" signal—that is, when the programming of the response is already completed or nearly completed—the priming effect is much diminished or altogether absent.

The neutral condition, in which no visual prime was presented, was meant to provide a baseline to measure priming benefits and priming costs. The idea was that congruent trials might have produced faster RTs than neutral trials (i.e. benefits), whereas incongruent trials might have produced slower RTs than neutral trials (i.e. costs). Contrary to expectations, RT on neutral trials was somewhat slower than on incongruent trials.

There are two possible explanations for this. One is that the prime, which was present on congruent and incongruent trials and absent on neutral trials, had a non-specific arousing effect, thus speeding up response execution. The other possibility is that the prime produced benefits in the absence of costs. That is, the prime facilitated the corresponding response, if congruent. However, it did not cause inhibition of the alternative response. This issue was addressed in Experiment 2.

The orientation and SOA main effects are only moderately interesting. Apparently, programming a clockwise grasping response was slightly easier than programming a counterclockwise grasping response. When presented after the "go" signal, the prime could not act as a warning. Because of that, RT was slower than with the other two SOAs.

EXPERIMENT 2

The aims of this experiment were to replicate the results of Experiment 1 and explore whether costs could be obtained on incongruent trials. The main experimental manipulation concerned neutral trials, in which a visual object was presented that was not included in the set of to-be-grasped objects.

Method

Participants. Seventeen students attending the University of Parma participated in the experiment. They were selected on the basis of the same general characteristics as the participants in Experiment 1. None of them had taken part in the previous experiment.

Apparatus, Materials and Procedure. These were the same as for Experiment 1, except for neutral trials. On neutral trials, the prime was the white outline of a circle (3° in diameter). Remember that, in the previous experiment, no prime was presented on neutral trials. Apart from that, congruent, incongruent, neutral and catch trials, SOAs and the event sequence were as in Experiment 1 (see Figure 1). Because of the additional 12 catch trials with the circle, overall there were 216 trials.

Results and Discussion

Reaction times were submitted to an ANOVA in which the three within-subject factors were orientation of the to-be-grasped object (clockwise *vs* counterclockwise), type of trial (congruent, incongruent or neutral) and SOA (–100, 0 or 100 msec).

The trial and SOA main effects were significant, $F(2,32) = 8.25, p < .01$ and $F(2,32) = 17.78, p < .001$, respectively. Reaction time was significantly faster for congruent trials (349 msec) than for incongruent (358 msec) or neutral (355 msec) trials ($p < .01$ and $p < .05$, respectively; Newman-Keuls test), whereas neutral and incongruent trials did not differ. Reaction time was significantly faster with the –100 msec SOA (348 msec) and the 0 msec SOA (346 msec) than with the 100 msec SOA (367 msec; both *ps* $< .001$), whereas the –100 and 0 msec SOAs did not differ.

The interaction between type of trial and SOA was also significant, $F(4,64) = 3.05$, $p < .05$ (see Figure 3). It showed an advantage of congruent trials that was significant with the –100 msec SOA (congruent trials, 337 msec; incongruent trials, 355 msec; neutral trials, 353 msec; $p < .001$ and $p < .01$, respectively). In contrast, it disappeared at the 0 msec SOA (congruent trials, 346 msec; incongruent trials, 348 msec; neutral trials, 345 msec) and the 100 msec SOA (congruent trials, 364 msec; incongruent trials, 371 msec; neutral trials, 367 msec).

The results of the significant interaction between orientation, trial and SOA, $F(4,64) = 2.52$, $p < .05$, are reported in Figure 4. In summary, this interaction showed that, with the –100 msec SOA, congruent trials were faster than incongruent ($p < .001$) and neutral ($p < .01$) trials for the counterclockwise orientation. With the 0 and 100 msec SOAs, RTs for the three types of trial were not significantly different regardless of orientation and SOA.

As in Experiment 1, congruent trials were faster than incongruent trials only when the prime preceded the "go" signal. This confirmed that the priming effect manifests itself only if the prime is shown while the response has yet to be programmed.

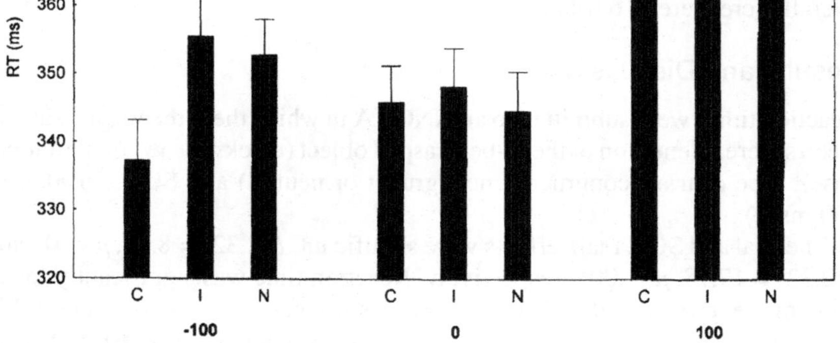

FIG. 3. The two-way interaction (type of trial × SOA) obtained in Experiment 2.

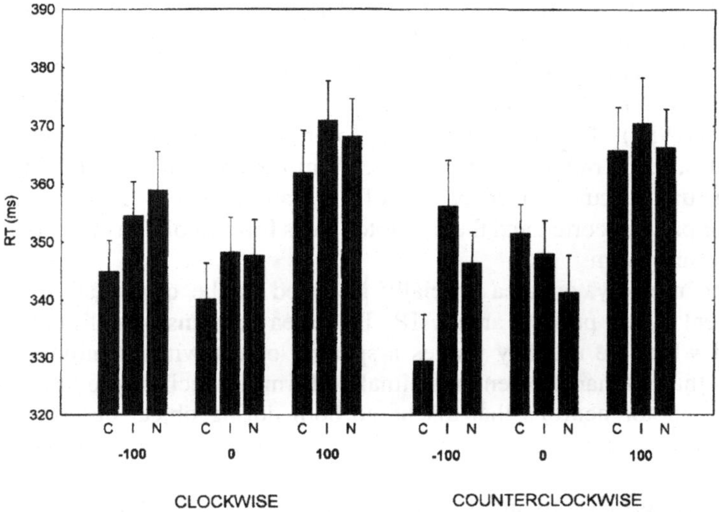

FIG. 4. The three-way interaction (type of trial × to-be-grasped object × SOA) obtained in Experiment 2.

In Experiment 2, however, the three-way interaction was also significant. This indicated that the priming effect, though present for both orientations, reached statistical significance with the *post-hoc* test for the counterclockwise orientation only. Although the lack of a significant priming effect for the clockwise orientation may be attributable to a Type II error, we cannot explain why the priming effect was greater for the counterclockwise orientation.

As in the previous experiment, RT for neutral trials was not faster than RT for incongruent trials. Because in the present experiment a visual prime was shown on neutral trials, an explanation in terms of a non-specific effect of the prime can be ruled out. However, it would be premature to conclude that priming benefits occur in the absence of priming costs. The neutral prime in fact represented an object different from the to-be-grasped one. From this point of view, neutral and incongruent trials were equivalent. The issue of costs is in need of further exploration.

GENERAL DISCUSSION

The visual cortical system of primates is formed by a large number of interconnected areas in which two broad "streams" can be recognized: A ventral stream largely projecting to the inferior temporal lobe and a dorsal stream that terminates in the inferior parietal lobe (Ungerleider & Mishkin, 1982). The ventral stream is responsible for the analysis of the qualities of objects. The dorsal stream is responsible for space computation (Ungerleider & Mishkin, 1982) and for object analysis for action (Goodale & Milner, 1992; Milner & Goodale, 1985). The posterior parietal cortex, in which the dorsal stream terminates, sends rich projections to the premotor areas of the frontal lobes, in which neural circuits are in charge of programming movements. Thus, the posterior parietal cortex and the premotor areas form a complex parieto-frontal visuomotor system.

In the monkey, an area crucially involved in the organization of hand movement is the parietal area, AIP. This area contains visual neurons that respond when the monkey fixates a specific object without moving, motor neurons that discharge when the animal performs a specific type of hand grip, and visuomotor neurons that discharge both during object observation and object-directed movements (Taira et al., 1991; see Jeannerod et al., 1995, for a review).

Area AIP projects to area F5, which belongs to the frontal premotor areas. Most neurons of area F5 discharge during goal-related hand movements, such as grasping, holding and manipulating (Rizzolatti et al., 1988; see Jeannerod et al., 1995, for a review). Many of these neurons are specific for particular types of hand prehension, such as precision grip, finger prehension and whole-hand prehension. The neurons of area F5 also discharge upon visual presentation of three-dimensional objects. Even more interestingly, the discharge often occurs only if the object's size or orientation matches the type of grip to which the neuron is selectively sensitive. Finally, some neurons of area F5 respond both when the monkey manipulates a given object or when it observes the experimenter manipulating that same object (the so-called "mirror" neurons; Di Pellegrino et al., 1992; Gallese et al., 1996; Rizzolatti et al., 1996).

There is compelling evidence that AIP and F5 form a cortical network that transforms visual information into hand movements, which allow the monkey to interact appropriately with objects (Jeannerod et al., 1995). Motor information is then transferred to area F1 (precentral motor cortex), to which F5 is directly connected, as well as to several subcortical centres, for movement execution (Jeannerod et al., 1995). If a similar network exists in man, as some recent evidence suggests (Grafton, Arbib, Fadiga, & Rizzolatti, 1996), then it should be possible to prime a grasping response by presenting a prime depicting the object that "affords" that particular type of grasping.

In the present study, normal participants were primed, while ready to execute a grasping movement, by the visual presentation of task-irrelevant bi-dimensional drawings of objects. The results showed that drawings that were visually congruent with the to-be-grasped object reduced RT for the grasping response. This is evidence of visuomotor priming: seeing an object facilitates an action congruent with the visual properties of that same object.[2] This is clearly in accord with the available neurophysiological evidence (e.g. Di Pellegrino et al., 1992; Gallese et al., 1996; Rizzolatti et al., 1996a).

It would also appear that the type of compulsive behaviour known as "utilization behaviour" (e.g. Lhermitte, 1983) is a pathological release of the normal, automatic object-to-action transformation process. Our findings indicate that the mere presentation of visual objects automatically evokes object-related motor responses. In patients in whom frontal control is severely impaired because of a lesion (e.g. Shallice, 1988), this mechanism may capture the motor system and determine the utilization behaviour. In normals, it represents a useful way for fast programming object-related actions.

It should be noted at this point that some studies with patients and normal subjects have addressed a related, but different, issue. They investigated whether there is a direct visual route that subserves the selection of learned actions to be performed on seen objects.

Riddoch and Humphreys (1987) described a patient who demonstrated impaired semantic information about seen objects and was poor at naming them. However, he could make specific learned gestures to the same objects. For example, when presented with a knife or a fork, the patient made correct cutting and prodding gestures, but failed when his semantic knowledge about the knife and the fork was tested. Riddoch and Humphreys argued that the patient's relatively preserved ability to make gestures to visually presented objects was attributable to the operation of a direct route to action, which bypasses the semantic system (see also Riddoch, Humphreys, Coltheart, & Funnell, 1988).

Patients who, despite moderate to severe loss of semantic (functional and associative) object knowledge, were nevertheless able to perform almost normally on single-object use, have been described by Buxbaum, Schwartz and Carew (1997), Hillis and Caramazza (1995) and Sirigu, Duhamel and Poncet (1991). The opposite dissociation was found in other patients, who showed good visual object recognition and naming, but were impaired at making gestures to seen objects (Buxbaum et al., 1997; Motomura & Yamadori, 1994; Pilgrim & Humphreys, 1991; Riddoch, Humphreys, & Price, 1989).

[2]It should be noted that there is an alternative explanation of the results of the present study. Because the participants did not see the to-be-grasped object, they may have formed a visual image of it before the "go" signal was presented. If the image was congruent with the task-irrelevant prime, facilitation may have resulted. It is clear, however, that an incongruent prime should have disrupted the image of the to-be-grasped object, thus causing interference. Therefore, this alternative explanation also has difficulties explaining why interference was not found on incongruent trials.

These neuropsychological findings have led to the notion that there are two independent routes from seen objects to action (e.g. Riddoch et al., 1988; Rumiati & Humphreys, in press): One route that is mediated by the visual activation of semantic/functional knowledge about objects; a second route that is mediated solely by visual information derived from the objects. The direct visual route is thought to operate through associations between stored visual representations of objects and learned actions. The stored visual representations would belong to a structural description system, separate from semantic memory.

Klatzky, Pellegrino, McCloskey and Lederman (1993; see also Klatzky, Pellegrino, McCloskey, & Doherty, 1989) showed that normal people possess strong associations between objects and the actions commonly carried out with them. In their study, they explored people's knowledge about the movements underlying functional interactions with objects. On the basis of clustering and multidimensional scaling analyses, they demonstrated that movement features were incorporated into the cognitive representation of objects. Subsequently, Klatzky, Fikes and Pellgrino (1995) showed that knowledge about objects and their functions could trigger an appropriate hand shape and the required configuration could be primed, before the onset of reaching, by the object's colour.

In a study by Rumiati and Humphreys (in press), participants were asked to name or to make gestures to drawings of objects (e.g. writing to a pen, pounding to a hammer). Because the instructions were to respond as rapidly as possible without being too concerned about accuracy, errors were elicited. The errors could be visual (e.g. "hammer" for "razor"), semantic (e.g. "saw" for "hammer") or mixed (e.g. "match" for "cigarette"). It was found that, in gesturing, participants made more visual errors and fewer semantic or mixed errors in comparison to naming. According to Rumiati and Humphreys, the fact that gesturing responses produced more visual errors is evidence of a direct visual route from objects to action.

At first sight, it would appear that these studies with patients and normal observers addressed a problem that is similar, if not identical, to the one explored in the present study—that is, whether there is a direct link between seen objects and actions that can be performed on them. There is, however, a profound difference that should not be overlooked. Here we dealt with a very simple action, grasping, that is guided by elementary object qualities, such as orientation, shape and size. In contrast, the other studies were concerned with the way objects are used. That these issues are different is attested by the fact that it makes sense to ask whether there is a direct route from an object to its use (and the studies reported above suggest there is), or rather the correct use of an object requires recognizing the object and accessing semantic information about it. In contrast, it makes little sense to ask whether the act of grasping an object is mediated by semantic information. In fact, no doubt we can grasp objects we do not recognize.

The results of the present study could also be relevant to the premotor theory of spatial attention (Rizzolatti et al., 1994; Rizzolatti, Riggio, Dascola, & Umiltà, 1987; Umiltà, Riggio, Dascola, & Rizzolatti, 1991). According to this hypothesis, space is represented in several pragmatic maps.[3] Some of them control oculomotion, whereas others control movements of the arm and other body parts. Spatial attention is thought to depend on the fact that, when the observer prepares to perform a goal-directed movement, neurons in the corresponding pragmatic map become active and facilitate sensory maps located upstream.

To date, evidence in favour of the premotor hypothesis has originated mainly from the role of the oculomotor system in spatial attention (see, e.g. Kustov & Robinson, 1996; for a review, see Rizzolatti et al., 1994). When the observer attends to a given location in space, a program for a shift of gaze to that location is prepared. For example, when attention is primed to the right side, the eyes, though still directed at fixation, are "implicitly" shifted to the right. This facilitates the sensory centres located on that side, which, in turn, facilitates detection of stimuli located in that region of space.

Considering that the basic neurophysiological organization of the non-oculomotor spatial maps is similar to the organization of the map that controls eye movements, the premotor hypothesis should also apply to other effector systems. Thus, directing attention to an object of a certain size, shape and orientation should result from the preparation of a specific motor program for grasping that object, in the same way as directing attention to a location in space results from the preparation of an eye movement to that location.

In the experiments described here, the participants were asked to maintain fixation when the "go" signal appeared in non-catch trials. Because the irrelevant visual object encircled the fixation cross, this object primed a motor response program for grasping a similar three-dimensional object. According to the premotor theory of attention, the reverse should also be true. When a subject is ready to grasp an object, RT to a picture of that object should decrease, because the motor program for grasping automatically activates the neural system that codes the representation of the object's intrinsic properties. Thus,

[3]Cortical pragmatic maps are maps that transform spatial information into movements (e.g. Rizzolatti et al., 1994). The premotor hypothesis maintains that spatial attention can be subserved by any pragmatic map. In humans and primates, however, as a consequence of the strong development of foveal vision and the neural mechanisms related to foveation, a central role in spatial and selective attention would be played by those maps that code space for oculomotion.

the experimental paradigm presented in the present paper (or a variation of it) might also be used for studying object-related attentional phenomena.

REFERENCES

Bruce, V. (1983). Recognizing faces. *Philosophical Transactions of the Royal Society, London, B302*, 423–436.

Buxbaum, L.J., Schwartz, M.F., & Carew, T.G. (1997). The role of semantic memory in object use. *Cognitive Neuropsychology, 14*, 219–254.

Craighero, L., Fadiga, L., Umiltà, C., Rizzolatti, G. (1996). Evidence of visuomotor priming effect. *Neuroreport, 7*, 347–349.

Di Pellegrino, G., Fadiga, L., Fogassi, L., Gallese, V., & Rizzolatti, G. (1992). Understanding motor events: A neurophysiological study. *Experimental Brain Research, 91*, 176–180.

Eimer, M., Hommel, B., & Prinz, W. (1995). S-R compatibility and response selection. *Acta Psychologica, 90*, 301–313.

Fadiga, L., Fogassi, L., Pavesi, G., & Rizzolatti, G. (1995). Motor facilitation during action observation: A magnetic stimulation study. *Journal of Neurophysiology, 73*, 2608–2611.

Gallese, V., Fadiga, L., Fogassi, L., & Rizzolatti, G. (1996). Action recognition in the premotor cortex. *Brain, 119*, 593–609.

Goldberg, M.E., & Seagraves, M.A. (1987). Visuospatial and motor attention in the monkey. *Neuropsychologia, 25*, 107–118.

Goodale, M.A., & Milner, D.A. (1992). Separate visual pathways for perception and actions. *Trends in Neuroscience, 15*, 20–25.

Goodale, M.A., Milner, D.A., Jacobson, L.S., & Carey, D.P. (1991). A neurological dissociation between perceiving objects and grasping them. *Nature, 349*, 154–156.

Grafton, S.T., Arbib, M.A., Fadiga, L., & Rizzolatti, G. (1996). Localization of grasp representations in humans by PET: 2. Observation versus imagination. *Experimental Brain Research*, 111, 103–111.

Hillis, A., & Caramazza, A. (1995). Cognitive and neural mechanisms underlying visual and semantic processing: Implications from "optic aphasia". *Journal of Cognitive Neuroscience, 7*, 457–478.

Jeannerod, M. (1994). The representing brain: Neuronal correlates of motor intention and imagery. *Behavioral and Brain Sciences, 17*, 187–202.

Jeannerod, M., Arbib, M.A., Rizzolatti, G., & Sakata, H. (1995). Grasping objects: The cortical mechanisms of visuomotor transformation. *Trends in Neuroscience, 18*, 314–320.

Klapp, S.T. (1995). Motor response programming during simple and choice reaction time: The role of practice. *Journal of Experimental Psychology: Human Perception and Performance, 21*, 1015–1027.

Klatzky, R.L., Pellegrino, J.W., McCloskey, B.P., & Doherty, S. (1989). Can you squeeze a tomato? The role of motor representations in semantic sensibility judgments. *Journal of Memory and Language, 28*, 56–77.

Klatzky, R.L., Pellegrino, J.W., McCloskey, B.P., & Lederman, S.J. (1993). Cognitive representations of functional interactions with objects. *Memory and Cognition, 21*, 294–303.

Klatzky, R.L., Fikes, T.G., & Pellegrino, J.W. (1995). Planning for hand shape and arm transport when reaching for objects. *Acta Psychologica, 88*, 209–232.

Kustov, A.A., & Robinson, D.L. (1996). Shared neural control of attention shifts and eye movements. *Nature, 384*, 74–77.

Kutas, M., & Hillyard, S.A. (1984). Brain potentials during reading reflect word expectancy and semantic association. *Nature, 307*, 161–163.

Lhermitte, F. (1983). Utilisation behaviour and its relation to lesions of the frontal lobes. *Brain, 106*, 237–255.

Meyer, D.E., & Schvaneveldt, R.W. (1971). Facilitation in recognizing pairs of words: Evidence of a dependence between operations. *Journal of Experimental Psychology, 90*, 227–234.

Milner, A.D., & Goodale, M.A. (1995). *The visual brain in action.* Oxford: Oxford University Press.

Motomura, N., & Yamadori, A. (1994). A case of ideational apraxia with impairment of object use and preservation of object pantomime. *Cortex, 30*, 167–170.

Pilgrim, E., & Humphreys, G.W. (1991). Impairment of action to visual objects in a case of ideomotor apraxia. *Cognitive Neuropsychology, 8*, 459–473.

Riddoch, M.J., & Humphreys, G.W. (1987). Visual object processing in the case of optic aphasia: A case of semantic access agnosia. *Cognitive Neuropsychology, 4*, 131–185.

Riddoch, M.J., Humphreys, G.W., Coltheart, M., & Funnell, E. (1988). Semantic systems or system? Neuropsychological evidence reexamined. *Cognitive Neuropsychology, 5*, 3–25.

Riddoch, M.J., Humphreys, G.W., & Price, C.J. (1989). Routes to action: Evidence from apraxia. *Cognitive Neuropsychology, 6*, 437–454.

Rizzolatti, G., Riggio, L., Dascola, I., & Umiltà, C. (1987). Reorienting attention across the horizontal and vertical meridians: Evidence in favor of a premotor theory of attention. *Neuropsychologia, 25*, 31–40.

Rizzolatti, G., Camarda, R., Fogassi, M., Gentilucci, M., Luppino, G., & Matelli, M. (1988). Functional organization of inferior area 6 in the macaque monkey. II. Area F5 and the control of distal movements. *Experimental Brain Research, 71*, 491–507.

Rizzolatti, G., Riggio, L., & Sheliga, B.M. (1994). Space and selective attention. In C. Umiltà & M. Moscovitch (Eds), *Attention and performance XV* (pp. 231–265). Cambridge, MA: MIT Press.

Rizzolatti, G., Fadiga, L., Gallese, V., & Fogassi, L. (1996a). Premotor cortex and the recognition of motor actions. *Cognitive Brain Research, 3*, 131–141.

Rizzolatti, G., Fadiga, L., Matelli, M., Bettinardi, V., Paulesu, E., Perani, D., & Fazio, F. (1996b). Localization of grasp representations in humans by PET: 1. Observation versus execution. *Brain Research, 111*, 246–252.

Rumiati, R.I., & Humphreys, G.W. (in press). Recognition by action: Dissociating visual and semantic routes to action in normal observers. *Journal of Experimental Psychology: Human Perception and Performance.*

Shallice, T. (1988). *From neuropsychology to mental structure.* Cambridge University Press.

Sirigu, A., Duhamel, J.R., & Poncet, M. (1991). The role of sensorimotor experience in object recognition. *Brain, 114*, 2555–2573.

Taira, M., Mine, S., Georgopoulos, A.P., Murata, A., & Sakata, H. (1991). Parietal cortex neurons of the monkey related to the visual guidance of hand movements. *Experimental Brain Research, 83*, 29–36.

Tipper, S.P., Lortie, C., & Baylis, G.C. (1992). Selective reaching: Evidence for action-centred attention. *Journal of Experimental Psychology: Human Perception and Performance, 18*, 891–905.

Tucker, M., & Ellis, R. (in press). On the relations between seen objects and components of actions. *Journal of Experimental Psychology: Human Perception and Performance.*

Umiltà, C., Riggio, L., Dascola, I., & Rizzolatti, G. (1991). Differential effects of central and peripheral primes on the reorienting of spatial attention. *European Journal of Cognitive Psychology, 3*, 247–267.

Ungerleider, L.G., & Mishkin, M. (1982) Two cortical visual systems. In D.J. Ingle, M.A. Goodale, & R.J.W. Mansfield (Eds), *Analysis of visual behavior* (pp. 549–586). Cambridge, MA: MIT Press.

Warren, C., & Morton, J. (1982). The effect of priming on picture recognition. *British Journal of Psychology, 73*, 117–129.

VISUAL COGNITION, 1998, *5* (1/2), 127–155

Eye Movements, Attention and Trans-saccadic Memory

David E. Irwin and Robert D. Gordon

Department of Psychology, University of Illinois at Urbana-Champaign, Champaign, IL, USA

The eyes make rapid, saccadic movements from point to point in space several times each second. It is generally assumed that some mental representation of the visual environment is maintained across eye movements in a *trans-saccadic memory*. We examined the role of attention in the encoding of information into trans-saccadic memory using a partial report procedure. A letter array was presented in one fixation, then a bar marker probed report of one array position after a saccade was made to a new location. Accuracy was high for positions that subjects had been told to attend to, but it was also high for positions near the saccade target, even if subjects had been instructed to attend elsewhere. These results indicate that attention determines what information is encoded into trans-saccadic memory and hence remembered across eye movements. Because attention automatically precedes the eyes to the saccade target location, information near the saccade target is likely to be encoded. The results are discussed in terms of VAM, the neurocognitive model of visual attention proposed by Schneider (1995).

INTRODUCTION

We inspect the visual world by means of saccades, rapid shifts of gaze that occur 3–4 times each second. Although we perceive the world to be a continuous panorama, considerable evidence (reviewed below) suggests that memory across eye movements (i.e. *trans-saccadic memory*) is severely limited. This implies that our impression of a unified and coherent visual environment is due

---

Requests for reprints should be addressed to David E. Irwin, Department of Psychology, University of Illinois at Urbana-Champaign, 603 E. Daniel St., Champaign, IL 61820, USA. E-mail: dirwin@s.psych.uiuc.edu

This research was supported by National Science Foundation Grant SBR 93-09564 to D.E.I. We thank Alan Allport, Art Kramer, Gordon Logan and Kevin O'Regan for helpful comments on the research, and Caprice Anderson, Sang Du, Rita Polonus and Ana Zorzopolous for their assistance with data collection.

---

to the contents of individual eye fixations, rather than to any richly detailed mental representation that is built up across saccades (Irwin, 1991; O'Regan, 1992). Nonetheless, some information appears to be maintained from one eye fixation to the next; in the research reported below, we investigated what information is remembered and the role attention plays in this process.

Several findings support the argument that relatively little information is remembered across eye movements. For example, McConkie (1991) reported that people viewing pictures frequently fail to detect object displacements, object deletions and changes in the physical characteristics of objects that occur across successive fixations. Such changes should be quite noticeable if trans-saccadic memory maintains a detailed representation of a scene. Other research has shown that people are unable to integrate visual patterns viewed in successive fixations to perceive some composite pattern (e.g. Bridgeman & Mayer, 1983; Irwin, Brown, & Sun, 1988; Irwin, Yantis, & Jonides, 1983; O'Regan & Levy-Schoen, 1983; Rayner & Pollatsek, 1983). Rather, the first pattern appears to vanish when the eyes move. Integration performance does not fall to chance, however, because the positions of a few pattern elements are maintained in trans-saccadic memory. Irwin (1991) showed that people were able to judge whether visual patterns viewed in successive fixations were identical or different, but accuracy was affected strongly by pattern complexity. Based in part on these results, Irwin (1993) estimated that between three and six elements of a visual pattern are maintained in memory across a saccade. This estimate is consistent with research by Hayhoe and colleagues using a shape-integration task. Hayhoe, Lachter and Feldman (1991) found that people could judge very precisely whether or not three points viewed in successive fixations (one point per fixation) formed a right triangle, but Lachter, Hayhoe and Feldman (1991) found that performance fell dramatically when the locations of six points had to be remembered. Using a priming paradigm, rather than an explicit memory test, Henderson (1994; Henderson & Anes, 1994) found that position-specific priming effects across saccades were limited to only a single item. Thus, the results from several different experimental paradigms converge in showing that trans-saccadic memory has a limited capacity.

But what determines what information is remembered from one fixation to the next? This question has received little investigation; in almost all of the studies reviewed above, the information to be remembered was presented in a unique and well-specified spatial location, usually at the saccade target, and the question of interest was whether the information could be combined or compared with information presented in a subsequent fixation. Research by Bryden (1961) and by Crovitz and Daves (1962) suggests that information appearing near the saccade target is more likely to be remembered than other information in a display. For example, Crovitz and Daves (1962) presented an array of digits for 100 msec while subjects fixated a central point; after display offset, the subjects were allowed to move their eyes wherever they pleased while they attempted to report all of the digits in the array. Digits on the side of the array to which the first eye movement was made were recalled better than digits on the opposite side of the array. This result suggests that making an eye movement to some location improves recall of information that was presented at that location before the eyes moved. Because subjects were allowed to move their eyes wherever they pleased, however, an alternative explanation is that one side of the array was more memorable than the other, hence more likely to draw the eyes. In sum, because the eyes moved freely, the direction of the effect cannot be determined.

This problem was eliminated by Irwin (1992). In this study, subjects were presented with an array of letters while they fixated a central point; a peripheral saccade target indicated the direction that the eyes should move on each trial. Following the eye movement, a partial-report cue (e.g. an arrow) appeared near one of the previously occupied array positions. Subjects were required to report the letter that had occupied the spatial location indicated by the report cue. To respond correctly, subjects had to remember the position and the identity of the cued letter across the eye movement. Irwin found that subjects could remember only 3–4 letters (i.e. position + identity units) across an eye movement, regardless of the number of letters presented in the letter array. Report of the letters spatially near the saccade target was much more accurate than report of other letters in the array, however. This suggests that information near the saccade target is more likely to be encoded into trans-saccadic memory than is other information in the display. Irwin also found that intra-array errors (erroneous report of a non-cued letter from the array) were much more frequent than extra-array errors (erroneous report of a letter not contained in the array), suggesting that subjects remembered the identities of the letters in the array but not their locations.

These results were replicated by Irwin and Andrews (1996), who found in addition that colour information about the probed letters could be retained along with position and identity information with no reduction in accuracy. They argued that trans-saccadic memory retains a limited number of integrated object files (colour + position + identity units in this case) for the contents of a display. Furthermore, Irwin and Andrews found that memory for position and identity information was improved only slightly when subjects made two as opposed to one fixation on the letter array, suggesting that limited information accumulation occurs across multiple eye movements. Thus, the results of Irwin (1992) and Irwin and Andrews (1996) suggest that some kinds of information (identity) are remembered better than others (location), and that the information at some spatial locations (near the saccade target) is remembered better than information at other spatial locations.

Why is information near the saccade target remembered better? Irwin (1992) suggested that this was caused by attention preceding the eyes to the saccade target, thereby increasing the likelihood that letters near that location would be encoded into trans-saccadic memory at the expense of other letters in the array. Several investigators have argued that attention movements precede eye movements to some location, based on the fact that the detection and the identification of stimulus items presented at the saccade target location are facilitated relative to items presented at other locations (e.g. Deubel & Schneider, 1996; Henderson, Pollatsek, & Rayner, 1989; Hoffman & Subramaniam, 1995; Klein, 1980; Klein & Pontefract, 1994; Kowler, Anderson, Dosher, & Blaser, 1995; Rayner, McConkie, & Ehrlich, 1978; Shepherd, Findlay, & Hockey, 1986). This is so even if the stimulus is presented before the saccade actually occurs and subjects are instructed to attend to a location other than the saccade target (e.g. Deubel & Schneider, 1996; Hoffman & Subramaniam, 1995; Kowler et al. 1995). Because attention was not manipulated directly in the experiments of Irwin (1992) and Irwin and Andrews (1996), however, their conclusion that attention causes information near the saccade target to be remembered better than information in other display locations is somewhat tenuous.

In the research reported below, we further investigated the relationship between attention movements and eye movements in the encoding of information into trans-saccadic memory. Subjects were instructed to attend to one region of a display while they moved their eyes either to the region they were attending or to a different spatial region. Because previous work has shown that attention movements obligatorily precede eye movements (e.g. Deubel & Schneider, 1996; Hoffman & Subramainiam, 1995; Kowler et al., 1995; Shepherd et al., 1986), we expected recall of the letters near the saccade target location would be high even when subjects were instructed to attend elsewhere. We also investigated the spatial distribution of attention, by examining if only information directly near the saccade target was encoded into memory, or if the recall of display locations in-between a starting fixation location and the saccade target was also facilitated.

EXPERIMENT 1

On each trial in Experiment 1, an array of 10 letters was presented while subjects viewed a central fixation point. The array disappeared when a saccade was initiated to one of two saccade targets. After the saccade, a partial-report probe appeared near one of the previously occupied letter positions and subjects attempted to report the identity of the letter that had appeared there, as well as the spatial position of the probe (i.e. Array Location 1–10). Saccade direction varied from trial to trial and was cued by a tone that was presented at the beginning of the trial. Subjects were instructed to pay more attention to one side of the letter array than the other. The side of the array that subjects were instructed to attend was probed much more often than the other side of the array to encourage subjects to follow the attentional instruction. On half of the trials the subjects moved their eyes towards the side of the array they were told to attend to, and on half of the trials they moved their eyes away from the side they were told to attend to. Of interest was how voluntary attentional allocation (manipulated by instruction) and saccade-induced attention shifts would influence memory across the saccade.

Method

Subjects. Nine subjects, including the first author, participated in Experiment 1. Except for the author, the subjects were undergraduate and graduate students at the University of Illinois at Urbana-Champaign who were naive about the experimental hypotheses. All subjects had normal or corrected-to-normal vision. The naive subjects were paid $5 per hour for participating, plus an additional bonus for responding accurately.

Stimuli. Each stimulus array consisted of 10 letters, displayed in a two-row × five-column format. The 10 letters were selected randomly prior to each trial from the set of all consonants, excluding the letter Y. A short vertical bar presented either above (top row) or below (bottom row) one of the array locations was used as the partial-report cue. The bar probe did not occur equally often at each array location. Rather, the four array locations (two in the top row and two in the bottom row) which were on the side of the array that a subject was instructed to attend were each probed on 30 of 156 trials, whereas the six remaining array locations were each proved on 6 of 156 trials.

Apparatus. Stimuli were presented on a Tektronix 608 oscilloscopic display equipped with P15 phosphor, which has no detectable persistence (Groner et al., 1993). Stimulus presentation was controlled with a Gateway 2000 486 50 MHz computer. The x- and y-coordinates and the intensity value of each point to be plotted were stored in a plotting buffer, which is able to transfer values to the oscilloscope at a rate of 2000 points per millisecond (Finley, 1985). A refresh rate of 1000 Hz was used during the experiment (i.e. each point we displayed on the oscilloscope was refreshed once every millisecond). The computer also recorded the output from an Applied Science Laboratories Model 210 scleral reflectance eyetracker by means of an analog-to-digital converter. The eyetracker was mounted on eyeglass frames that were held in place on the subject's head with a headband. The eyetracker was configured to record horizontal movements of the left eye only. Eye position was sampled once every millisecond. A bite bar with dental impression compound was used to keep the subject's head steady during the experiment. Subjects completed a calibration sequence (described later) before every experimental trial. The accuracy of the eyetracker under these conditions is ± 0.3°.

During the experiment, subjects were positioned 57 cm from the display. At this viewing distance, the total display area subtended a visual angle of 12°

horizontally and 10° vertically. The letter arrays subtended 5.1° horizontally and 2.9° vertically. Each letter subtended a visual angle of approximately 0.3° horizontally and 0.5° vertically. The letters were separated by 0.9° horizontally and 1.9° vertically. The vertical bar probe was 0.45° high and 0.05° wide; it was separated from the probed letter by 0.2°. The central fixation cross and the two saccade targets, which were used during the calibration and the experimental trials, each subtended 0.2° vertically and horizontally. During the experimental trials, each saccade target was separated from the central fixation cross by 2.4°.

The experimental chamber was illuminated by overhead fluorescent lights. The luminance of the display screen was 68 cd/m^2. The effective luminance of the stimulus display was 552 cd/m^2. This luminance was obtained by measuring the luminance of a 31 × 31 dot-matrix plotted within an 8 × 8 mm area that was refreshed every millisecond.

Procedure. The typical sequence of events for a trial in the saccade condition is depicted in Fig. 1. Each trial began with a calibration routine during which a calibration point (a plus sign) stepped across the display at three locations separated by 2.4°. Each point was presented for 1500 msec, and the subject was instructed to fixate each carefully. Eye position at each location was sampled (at a rate of 1000 Hz) for 100 msec near the middle of this interval. These recordings served to calibrate the output of the eyetracker against spatial position.

Following calibration, a single fixation cross was presented at the centre of the display, where the central calibration point had appeared. The subject was instructed to fixate this cross carefully. After 500 msec, a tone was played for 250 msec. This tone indicated the direction in which the subject was to make a saccade when the letter array appeared. A low tone (300 Hz) indicated a saccade to the left; a high tone (1000 Hz) indicated a saccade to the right. Following the offset of the tone, the central fixation cross was presented alone for an interval of 1000, 1250 or 1500 msec. A variable interval was used to discourage anticipatory eye movements that might not have allowed adequate processing of the letter array. At the end of this interval, the letter array and two additional plus signs, the potential saccade targets, were presented simultaneously. One plus sign appeared at each end of the letter array, 2.4° away from the central fixation cross in each direction, centred between the terminal letters in the array. The letter array remained visible until the subject initiated a saccade towards the appropriate saccade target. Saccade onset was defined as a change in eye position with a velocity greater than 50°/s in the same direction for three consecutive milliseconds. After the saccade was initiated, the letter array was removed, leaving only the central fixation cross and the two potential saccade targets visible. Then, an interval of 50 msec elapsed before the bar probe was presented for 33 msec. After probe presentation, the subject attempted to report

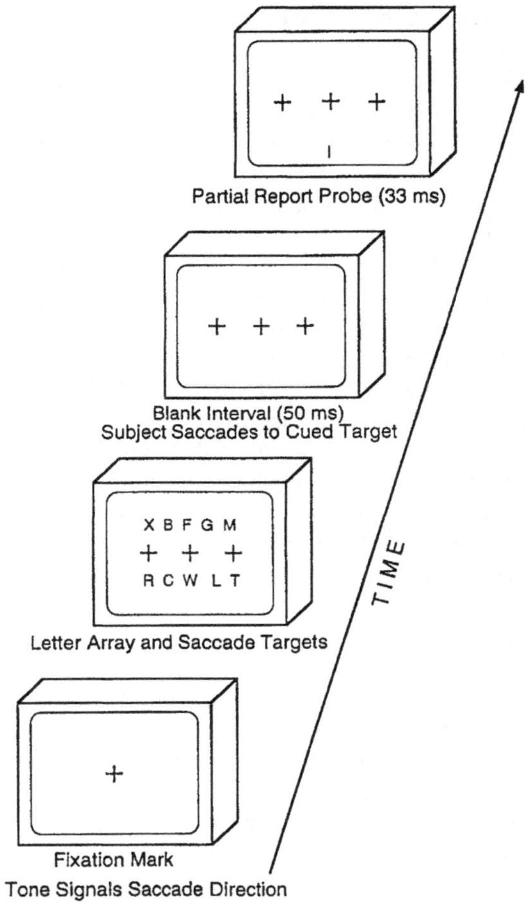

FIG. 1. Schematic illustration of the procedure for trials in the saccade condition of Experiment 1.

the letter that had occupied the probed location, as well as the spatial position of the probe (i.e. Array Location 1–10). These responses were typed into the computer terminal keyboard. After each trial, the subject received feedback which indicated whether or not each response was correct. At the end of the experiment, subjects received a half-cent bonus for each correct response.

The subject's eye movement had to have a latency of 100–1000 msec for the trial to be acceptable. This criterion eliminated anticipatory saccades that might not have allowed for adequate processing of the letter array, and delayed saccades potentially indicative of attention lapses. In addition, only trials in which the initial saccade was in the correct (cued) direction were accepted. Furthermore, the subject had to fixate within 1° of the central fixation cross before the saccade, and had to execute a saccade that landed outside this region, in order for the trial to be accepted. Averaged across subjects, 20.6% (SE = 6.0%) of the trials failed one or more of these criteria and were excluded from the analysis.

Throughout the experimental trials, subjects were instructed to attend to one side of the letter array, and they were told that positions on that side of the array would be probed five times as often as positions on the other side of the array. We will call the side of the array that the subject was supposed to attend and that was probed more often the "high-probability" side of the array, and we will call the other side of the array the "low-probability" side of the array. Five of the subjects were instructed to attend to the left side of the display; the remaining four subjects were instructed to attend to the right side of the display.

Each subject completed four blocks of 39 trials each. Saccade direction and probe position were sequenced randomly across trials. Data were collected over the course of two sessions. Before beginning the experimental trials, each subject completed a control experiment in which no attention instructions were given and each array location was probed an equal number of times. Thus, subjects were quite familiar with the basic partial-report procedure before participating in Experiment 1.

Results and Discussion

To simplify the data exposition and to increase the number of observations in each cell of the experimental design, in the analyses reported below we averaged over the spatial direction of the saccade (left *vs* right) and collated the data based on whether the saccade was made to the high-probability side of the array (the left side for five subjects, the right side for four subjects) or to the low-probability side of the array.

Preliminary analyses performed on the eye-movement data showed that the attentional instructions influenced eye-movement behaviour. The mean saccade latency (hence, the exposure duration of the letter array) was longer when the eyes moved to the low-probability side of the array (287 msec, SE = 27 msec) than when the eyes moved to the low-probability side of the array (257 msec, SE = 19 msec), $F(1,8) = 7.0$, $p < .03$, MSe = 5770. The mean saccade latency in the control experiment that subjects completed before participating in Experiment 1 was 252 msec, so it would appear that the difference in saccade latency in Experiment 1 was due to a cost in moving away from the high-probability side, rather than a benefit in moving towards it. Saccades made towards the high-probability side of the array also had a significantly shorter duration (23.2 msec, SE = 1.3 msec) than saccades made towards the low-probability side of the array (26.0 msec, SE = 1.2 msec), $F(1,8) = 9.7, p < .02$, MSe = 36.5. This was most probably due to a difference in the landing position of the eye with respect to the saccade target, which produced a difference in saccade length. Saccades made towards the low-probability side of the array were longer, more accurate, but more variable (mean = 0.10° long of the target, SE = 0.10°) than saccades made towards the high-probability side of the array (mean = 0.34° short of the target, SE = 0.08°, $F(1,8) = 9.4$, $p < .02$, MSe = 0.96. The initial fixation location (i.e. the position of the eyes before the saccade) did not vary as a function of saccade direction (mean = 0.02° towards the high-probability side of the central fixation point, SE = 0.035°). Although the attentional instructions influenced eye-movement behaviour, the effects were rather small in absolute terms; furthermore, even 400 msec differences in exposure duration have been found to have no significant effect on letter-report accuracy in previous research using the trans-saccadic partial-report task (Irwin & Andrews, 1996). Thus, it seems unlikely that the results described below can be attributed to differences in eye-movement behaviour across experimental conditions.

Accuracy. On each trial, subjects attempted to report the letter that had occupied the spatial position indicated by the partial-report probe, and the spatial position of the probe (Array Location 1–10). The subject's letter responses were classified as correct only if the letter they reported had appeared at the probed position. Averaged across subjects, saccade directions and array locations, mean letter-report accuracy in the saccade condition was 40.6% (SE = 10.1%). Multiplying percentage correct by the number of letters in the array yields an estimate of the number of elements (i.e. position + identity units) remembered from the display (Sperling, 1960), in this case 4.1. This is very similar to the results reported by Irwin (1992) and Irwin and Andrews (1996) when 10-letter arrays were used as stimuli (3.6 and 4.3 elements remembered, respectively). Thus, it appears that the attention instructions did not increase the amount of information that was stored in trans-saccadic memory. Subjects were highly accurate at reporting the probe's spatial position (mean = 93.6%, SE = 1.8%), so the low letter-report accuracy cannot be attributed to a failure to recognize which array location had been probed.

The major purpose of this experiment was to examine whether letters near the saccade target were reported more accurately than letters at other array locations even when subjects were instructed to attend away from the saccade target area. The relevant data are presented in Table 1, which shows letter-report accuracy as a function of probe position and saccade direction. The data have been collated such that columns 1 and 2 always refer to the high-probability side of the letter array, the side that subjects were instructed to attend to (the results for these positions are italicized to reflect the attentional instruction). Saccade direction in this case refers to whether the saccade was made towards the high-probability side of the array or to the low-probability side of the array.

An ANOVA was conducted on the data with factors of saccade direction, row probed (top *vs* bottom) and column probed (1–5). Letter-report accuracy

TABLE 1
Percentage Correct as a Function of Probe Position in Experiment 1

	Column				
	High-probability Side			*Low-probability Side*	
Condition	*1*	*2*	*3*	*4*	*5*
Top row					
Saccade to high-probability side	*92.0*	*43.7*	50.0	16.7	57.4
Saccade to low-probability side	*84.0*	*38.0*	33.3	24.1	100.0
Bottom row					
Saccade to high-probability side	*58.8*	*15.2*	16.7	0.0	20.2
Saccade to low-probability side	*54.9*	*14.6*	22.1	20.3	50.0

Note: Subjects were instructed to attend to the high-probability side of the letter array (columns 1 and 2), which was probed for report five times as often as the low-probability side. Saccades were made equally often towards the high-probability side and the low-probability side.

was higher when a position on the top row was probed than when a position on the bottom row was probed, $F(1,8) = 25.8$, $p < .001$, MSe = 0.124. Accuracy also varied as a function of which column was probed, $F(4,32) = 14.4$, $p < .001$, MSe = 0.136: Letter-report accuracy was higher when an end position was probed than when an interior position was probed. End-position advantages are frequently found in partial-report experiments using linear arrays (e.g. Mewhort, Campbell, Marchetti, & Campbell, 1981), presumably because there is less lateral masking for the items that appear in the end positions (van der Heijden, 1992). The column probed factor interacted with saccade direction, $F(4,32) = 6.5$, $p < .001$, MSe = 0.046. No other main effects or interactions were significant. The error term of the column probed by saccade direction interaction was used to construct a 95% confidence interval for several comparisons of interest; these are described in the next few paragraphs. Differences of 8.3% and above are significant.

First, did the attention instructions influence which items were remembered from the array? This can be assessed most clearly by examining the locations on the side of the array opposite the saccade target, because they are uncontaminated by any potential attentional benefits produced by the saccade itself. If the attention instructions influenced memory, letter-report accuracy for columns 1 and 2 when saccades were made to the low-probability side should be higher than letter-report accuracy for columns 4 and 5 when saccades were made to the high-probability side. Averaged across rows and the two column positions, these values were 47.9 and 23.6%, respectively. Thus, accuracy was much higher when high-probability positions were probed than when low-probability positions were probed, given that the eyes moved away from these positions. These results indicate that the attention instructions did influence which array positions were remembered. It is apparent from Table 1 that subjects were unable to attend equally to all four positions (two in the top row, two in the bottom row), however; letter-report accuracy varied from 84.0% (column 1, top row) to 14.6% (column 2, bottom row) among the positions subjects were instructed to attend. Nonetheless, accuracy was higher for each of these positions compared to the analogous position in the low-probability locations (e.g. 57.4% for column 5, top row and 0.0% for column 4, bottom row).

The second question of interest is whether making an eye movement towards the low-probability side of the array improved memory for the letters that appeared there, even though subjects were attempting to attend to the high-probability side of the array. This can be assessed by comparing letter-report accuracy for columns 4 and 5 when the saccade was made to the low-probability side of the array as opposed to the high-probability side of the array. Averaged across rows and the two column positions, these values were 48.6% and 23.6%, respectively. Thus, accuracy for the low-probability positions was much higher when the eyes moved towards them than when the eyes moved away, consistent with the conclusion that the act of making a saccade to some location causes attention to shift to that location before the saccade. Indeed, mean accuracy for the low-probability non-saccade positions (48.6%) was statistically identical to that of the high-probability non-saccade positions (47.9%) discussed in the preceding paragraph. It is apparent from Table 1 that the saccade-induced attention movement did not affect equally all four array positions near the saccade target, however; letter-report accuracy varied from 100% for the position above the saccade target to 20.3% for the position below and one column removed from the saccade target. Nonetheless, accuracy was higher for each of the low-probability positions when a saccade was made in their direction as opposed to the other side of the letter array. Thus, consistent with the results of previous investigators (e.g. Deubel & Schneider, 1996; Hoffman & Subramaniam, 1995; Kowler et al., 1995; Shepherd et al., 1986), it appears that attention moves to the saccade target location before the eyes move, even when subjects are trying to attend somewhere else; because of the attention shift, information near the saccade target location is encoded into trans-saccadic memory.

Two additional comparisons of interest concern possible additive effects of saccade-induced attention shifts with instruction-induced attention shifts. Is any additional benefit gained in moving the eyes to some location that is already being attended? This can be determined by comparing letter-report accuracy for columns 1 and 2 when saccades are made towards those positions as opposed to away from those positions. Averaged over rows and the two column positions, these values are 52.4 and 47.9%, respectively. This difference is not significant. Examination of Table 1 reveals a small but non-significant effect of the saccade on each of the four array locations in question. Another way of addressing this question is by examining whether any additional benefit is gained in instructing subjects to attend to the side of the array towards which they move their eyes; this can be assessed by comparing letter-report accuracy for columns 1 and 2 when saccades are made towards those positions with letter-report accuracy for columns 4 and 5 when saccades are made towards those positions. Averaged over rows and the two column positions, these values are 52.4 and 48.6%, respectively. This difference is not significant. Examination of Table 1 reveals a small effect of the attention instruction on only two of the four array locations in question. In sum, only a small and non-significant additional benefit is gained when the eyes move to a location that is already being attended or when attention is allocated via instruction to a location towards which the eyes will move.

Error Analyses. To obtain additional information about the way in which information is stored in memory, an analysis of the kinds of errors that subjects made was conducted. Because subjects were forced to respond on every trial (i.e. response omissions were not allowed), there were only two possible kinds of errors they could make—intra-array errors (report of a letter that had not appeared at the probed position but had appeared elsewhere in the letter array) and extra-array errors (report of a letter that had not appeared anywhere in the letter array). In partial-report research, intra-array errors are generally assumed to reflect loss of location information from memory, whereas extra-array errors are generally assumed to reflect loss of identity information (e.g. Irwin, 1992; Irwin & Yeomans, 1986; Mewhort et al., 1981; Townsend, 1973). In Experiment 1, intra-array errors were made on 48.4% (SE = 11.3%) of the trials, whereas extra-array errors were made on only 10.0% (SE = 5.8%) of the trials. These error patterns are very similar to those found by Irwin (1992) when 10-letter arrays were used as stimuli; in that study, 49.7% of the responses were intra-array errors and 14.9% were extra-array errors. As noted earlier, subjects were highly accurate at reporting the probe's spatial position, so the high percentage of intra-array errors cannot be attributed to a failure to recognize which array location had been probed. It is also important to note that the difference between the percentages of intra-array and extra-array errors cannot be explained through random guessing. Given the population of 20 letters that was used and the presentation of a 10-letter array on each trial, by chance there are nine ways to make an intra-array error and 10 ways to make an extra-array error. Thus, the finding that intra-array errors occurred much more often than extra-array errors in the saccade condition suggests that subjects lost location information about the letters in the display, but retained identity information. The spatial distribution of the intra-array errors was not random, however; 52.9% of them involved report of the letter vertically or horizontally adjacent to the probed letter. Thus, at least some coarse location information appears to be retained across eye movements.

Additional analyses of variance conducted on the error data with factors of saccade direction, row probed and column probed revealed that both intra-array and extra-array errors increased as accuracy decreased, and both kinds of errors were affected in the same way by the attentional instructions and by the saccade-induced attention shifts. Because these analyses provide no additional information about the questions of interest, they will not be discussed further.

Summary. Although subjects followed the instruction to attend to the high-probability side of the letter array, report of the letters above and below the saccade target was facilitated when a saccade was made to the low-probability side of the array. This result provides strong support for the conclusion that information near the saccade target location is encoded into trans-saccadic memory because attention shifts to the location of the saccade target before the eyes move. The attentional effect produced by the saccade was localized in space; the greatest benefit was found for the letter position above the saccade target, although some benefit was also found for the position below the saccade target. There was also a slight improvement in recall for the letters that appeared in-between the central fixation point and the saccade target, but accuracy was very low for these positions. The effect of making a saccade to some location yielded approximately as much benefit as biasing a subject to attend to that location through instruction and probe probability; little additional benefit was gained by having voluntary attention and saccade-induced attention directed to the same side of the letter array.

There was a cost in saccade latency in moving the eyes away from the side that one was instructed to attend to, however. It is one subject's introspection (D.E. Irwin) that when a saccade had to be executed to the low-probability side of the array, an attempt was made to encode the letters in the high-probability positions into memory before executing the saccade; in contrast, when a saccade had to be executed to the high-probability side of the array, less time was spent in encoding the letters before the saccade was executed. It is interesting that the amount of information that could be remembered across the saccade was not affected by the use of these different strategies. About four items were retained in memory across a saccade; what attention did was influence which items were remembered.

Most of the errors were intra-array rather than extra-array errors, suggesting that it is primarily location information (or the binding of location with identity information) that is lost from memory when the eyes move (cf. Irwin, 1992; Irwin & Andrews, 1996). The attentional instruction and the saccade-induced attention shift reduced both kinds of errors, indicating that attention improves the coding of both location and identity information in trans-saccadic memory.

EXPERIMENT 2

It is generally believed that one function of attention is to combine separate features (e.g. colour, shape) that appear at the same spatial location into an integrated whole or object (e.g. Treisman & Gelade, 1980); in the absence of attention, illusory conjunctions, or incorrect combinations of features, may occur. To obtain additional information about the effects of attention on trans-saccadic memory, in Experiment 2 we used a trans-saccadic partial-report task using letters that appeared in different colours. Subjects viewed an array of coloured letters in one fixation, then executed a saccade to a target. The letters disappeared when the saccade was initiated; after the saccade ended, a partial-report probe appeared near one of the previously occupied letter positions. Subjects attempted to report the identity and the colour of the letter that had been presented there. As in Experiment 1, subjects were instructed to pay attention to one side of the letter array, which was probed much more often than the other side; saccades (whose direction was cued by a tone) were made equally often to each side of the letter array. Letter report and colour report for the high-probability locations should be very accurate and few illusory conjunctions should occur if subjects follow the attentional instruction, because the features present at those locations should be accurately conjoined via attention into integral objects. Similarly, letter report and colour report for the items near the saccade target should be very accurate and few illusory conjunctions should occur if attention automatically precedes the eyes to the saccade target location. An array of 6 letters (2 rows × 3 columns) rather than 10 was used in this experiment for a number of reasons: It was difficult to generate a large population of unique colours to use as stimuli; overall accuracy was quite low (35–40%) when 10-letter arrays were used in Experiment 1; and the results of Experiment 1 indicated that subjects were unable to attend equally to four separate array locations. By instructing subjects to attend to only two locations (one in the top row and one in the bottom row, both on the high-probability side of the letter array), Experiment 2 may provide a stronger test of the relationship between voluntary attention and saccade-induced attention shifts.

Method

Subjects. Eight subjects, including the first author, participated in this experiment. Three of the subjects had participated in the first two experiments; the others were inexperienced. The subjects were paid $5 per hour for their participation, plus they received a one-cent bonus for each correct response.

Stimuli. The stimuli consisted of letter arrays containing six coloured letters in a two-row × three-column arrangement. The letters were drawn randomly without replacement on each trial from the set: D, F, J, L, N, S, T, Z. The colours were drawn randomly without replacement on each trial from the set (CIE coordinates in parentheses): light cyan (x = .218, y = .3, luminance = 103 cd/m^2; red (x = .538, y = .367, luminance = 22 cd/m^2); blue (x = .165, y = .102, luminance = 10 cd/m^2); magenta (x = .29, y = .178, luminance = 28 cd/m^2); brown (x = .506, y = .413, luminance = 26 cd/m^2; green (x = .294, y = .532, luminance = 122 cd/m^2); yellow (x = .398, y = .474, luminance = 153 cd/m^2); and white (x = .299, y = .314, luminance = 149 cd/m^2). An asterisk (*) appearing above (top row) or below (bottom row) one of the array locations was used as the partial-report cue. The two array locations (one in the top row and one in the bottom row) which were on the side of the array that a subject was instructed to attend were each probed on 72 of 192 trials, whereas the four remaining array locations were each probed on 12 of 192 trials.

Apparatus. Stimuli were presented at a refresh rate of 72 Hz on a NEC MultiSync 3FGx colour monitor equipped with a monitor lens that reduced screen reflectance. A Gateway 2000 486 50 MHz microcomputer controlled stimulus presentation with a VGA graphics adaptor. The computer also recorded the output from the eyetracker and collected keyboard responses, as in the first experiment.

During the experiment, subjects were seated 57 cm from the display monitor. At this viewing distance, the total display area subtended 26° of visual angle horizontally and 19.7° vertically. The letter arrays were presented in the centre of the display area. The letter arrays subtended 4.3° horizontally and 2.2° vertically. Each letter was 0.3° wide and 0.7° high. The spaces between letters were 1.7° horizontally and 0.8° vertically. The asterisk used as the bar probe was 0.3° wide and 0.4° high. It was presented 0.2° above or below the target letter position. Calibration, saccade target and fixation points used during the experiment subtended 0.2° horizontally and 0.4° vertically.

Characters were presented in graphics mode (640 x 200), using the default font which presents characters in an 8 x 8 grid. Colours were chosen from the standard PC colour palette to be maximally discriminable from each other. The display background was light grey (CIE coordinates: x = .302, y = .318, luminance = 68 cd/m^2) and it eliminated any phosphor persistence from the letter array. The calibration, saccade target, report probe and fixation points were dark grey (CIE coordinates: x = .306, y = .322, luminance = 17 cd/m^2).

Procedure. Each subject completed several preliminary procedures before participating in the eye-movement experiment. The purpose of these was to familiarize the subject with the stimuli and with the partial-report task. First, the subjects were shown the letter and colour sets to be used in the experiment. They were instructed to use the following colour names to refer to the colours: *sky* for light cyan, *red* for red, *blue* for blue, *purple* for magenta, *orange* for brown, *green* for green, *yellow* for yellow, and *white* for white. These names were chosen so that each colour could be referred to by a unique beginning initial — S, R, B, P, O, G, Y and W, respectively — when subjects typed their colour responses into the computer keyboard. Subjects were given several minutes to study these materials, and then they completed 50 trials in which a single colour letter was flashed for 100 msec on the display monitor. After each presentation, the subject entered the letter they had seen and the beginning initial of the letter's colour name into the computer keyboard. Half of the subjects responded letter first and colour second, whereas the other half responded colour first and letter second. Order of response was constant for an individual subject throughout all practice and experimental sessions. A chart listing the letter set and colour set (including names and initials) was available throughout all sessions for subjects to refer to. Accuracy on letter and colour naming was greater than 90% for all subjects in this familiarization task, indicating that they were able to use the response coding scheme accurately and that they had no serious colour vision deficiencies.

Next, each subject completed 50 partial-report trials while maintaining fixation on a central point. During these trials, a 2 × 3 array of coloured letters was presented for 250 msec, then the bar probe was presented for 42 msec immediately after stimulus offset. Probe position varied randomly from trial to trial. Each subject then completed 180 more partial-report trials while maintaining fixation, but on these trials the probe delay was either 56, 153 or 750 msec. Probe position and probe delay varied randomly from trial to trial. By the end of these practice blocks, subjects had become very familiar with the basic partial-report task, the experimental stimuli and the response scheme. Following this exposure they were introduced to the eye-movement (transsaccadic) version of the partial-report task. The procedure for these trials is described next.

The sequence of events for the saccade trials was very similar to that used in Experiment 1. After calibration, a fixation cross was presented at the centre of the display. After 500 msec, a high (1000 Hz) or low (300 Hz) tone was played for 250 msec to indicate the saccade direction for the current trial. The fixation cross remained on the display, and the array was presented after an interval of 1000, 1250 or 1500 msec. As described earlier, the six letters were chosen without replacement from a set of eight consonants, and they were displayed in six different colours, also chosen from a pool of eight alternatives. Two rows of three upper-case letters each were presented, with one letter situated 0.2° above and another letter situated 0.2° below each of the three calibration locations. The left and right saccade targets were presented simultaneously with the onset of the letter array. The letter array remained visible until a saccade was initiated in the direction indicated by the tone. After a delay of 56 msec, a bar probe was presented for 42 msec. Following probe presentation, the subject attempted to indicate the letter which had occupied the probed array location, as well as its colour. These responses were typed into the computer terminal keyboard. Order of report (letter/colour or colour/letter) was counterbalanced across subjects. After each trial, the subject received feedback which indicated whether or not each response was correct.

The subject's eye-movement and fixation behaviour had to satisfy the criteria described in Experiment 1 for the trial to be acceptable. Averaged across subjects, 25.9% (SE = 16.2%) of the trials failed one or more of these criteria, and were excluded from the analysis.

Throughout the experimental trials, subjects were instructed to attend to one side of the letter array (the high-probability side) because positions on that side of the array would be probed six times as often as positions on the other side of the array (the low-probability side). Four of the subjects were instructed to attend to the left side of the display; the remaining four subjects were instructed to attend to the right side of the display.

Each subject completed six blocks of 32 trials each in the saccade condition. Saccade direction and probe position were sequenced randomly across trials. Before beginning the experimental trials, each subject completed several practice blocks of saccade trials. Data for the experimental trials were collected over the course of two sessions.

Results and Discussion

To simplify the data exposition and to increase the number of observations in each cell of the experimental design, in the analyses reported below we averaged over the spatial direction of the saccade (left *vs* right) and collated the data based on whether the saccade was made to the high-probability side of the array (the left side for four subjects, the right side for four subjects) or to the low-probability side of the array.

Preliminary analyses performed on the eye-movement data showed that the attentional instructions influenced eye-movement behaviour. Unlike Experiment 1, saccades made towards the high-probability side of the array had a significantly longer duration (26.6 msec, SE = 0.7 msec) than saccades made towards the low-probability side of the array (24.8 msec, SE = 0.8 msec), $F(1,7) = 21.9$, $p < .002$, MSe = 3.8. As in Experiment 1, this difference in saccade duration is most probably due to a difference in the landing position of the eye with respect to the saccade target, which produced a difference in saccade length; subjects overshot the saccade target when they moved towards the high-probability side of the letter array (mean = 0.08° long of the target, SE = 0.11°), but when the saccade was made towards the low-probability side of the array, they undershot the saccade target (mean = 0.44° short of the target, SE = 0.06°). This difference was not significant, however. The initial fixation location (i.e. the position of the eyes before the saccade) did not vary as a function of saccade direction (mean = 0.05° towards the high-probability side of the central fixation point, SE = 0.032°). Unlike Experiment 1, the mean saccade latency (hence, the exposure duration of the letter array) did not vary significantly as a function of whether the eyes moved to the low-probability side of the array (mean = 257 msec, SE = 31 msec) as opposed to the high-probability side of the array (mean = 250 msec, SE = 34 msec). In sum, the attentional instructions influenced eye-movement behaviour less and in different ways than in Experiment 1; the significant effects were small in size, however, so it seems unlikely that the results described below can be attributed to differences in eye-movement behaviour across experimental conditions.

Accuracy. On each trial, subjects attempted to report the identity and the colour of the letter that had occupied the spatial position indicated by the partial-report probe. The most common response outcome was for both the identity and the colour of the probed item to be recalled correctly (mean = 64.5%, SE = 3.9%). Multiplying this value by the number of items in the array reveals that subjects remembered 3.9 position + identity + colour units from the letter display. This is very similar to the level of performance in Experiment 1, in which colour was not reported. These results thus replicate the finding of Irwin and Andrews (1996) that item colour can be remembered with item identity and item position at no additional cost, and they indicate that trans-saccadic memory stores integrated objects (coloured letters) rather than separate features (colours and letters). Correct identity report with incorrect colour report occurred on 10% (SE = 1.4%) of the trials; incorrect identity report with correct colour report occurred on 13.6% (SE = 2.2%) of the trials; and incorrect report of both identity and colour occurred on 11.9% (SE = 1.2%) of the trials. There was a high degree of contingency between identity report and colour report; the probability of correctly recalling the colour of the probed item conditionalized on correct recall of the identity of the probed item was 0.87. In the analyses reported below, we focus on the trials in which both identity and colour were reported correctly, because they represent trials in which features were conjoined and remembered successfully.

The data of primary interest are presented in Table 2, which shows the percentage of trials in which both the identity and the colour of the probed item were reported correctly as a function of probe position and saccade direction. The data have been collated such that column 1 always refers to the high-probability side of the letter array, the side that subjects were instructed to attend (the results for these positions are italicized to reflect the attentional instruction). Saccade direction in this case refers to whether the saccade was made towards the high-probability side of the array or to the low-probability side of the array.

An ANOVA was conducted on these data with factors of saccade direction, row probed (top *vs* bottom) and column probed (1–3). Accuracy was higher when a position on the top row was probed than when a position on the bottom row was probed $F(1,7) = 6.9, p < .05$, MSe = 0.071. As in Experiment 1, there was an end-position advantage such that accuracy was higher when an end

TABLE 2
Percentage of Identity Correct/Colour Correct Trials as a Function of Probe Position in Experiment 2

	Column		
	High-probability Side	*Low-probability Side*	
Condition	*1*	*2*	*3*
Top row			
Saccade to high-probability side	*93.8*	57.4	53.8
Saccade to low-probability side	*95.0*	53.0	77.0
Bottom row			
Saccade to high-probability side	*93.4*	18.8	52.9
Saccade to low-probability side	*71.0*	20.5	87.9

Note: Subjects were instructed to attend to the high-probability side of the letter array (column 1), which was probed for report six times as often as the low-probability side. Saccades were made equally often towards the high-probability side and the low-probability side.

position was probed than when the middle was probed, $F(2,14) = 30.0$, $p < .001$, MSe = 0.070. The interaction between row probed and column probed was significant, $F(2,14) = 8.3$, $p < .005$, MSe = 0.40, as was the interaction between saccade direction and column probed, $F(2,14) = 4.3$, $p < .05$, MSe = .079. These interactions were significant because the attentional instructions and the saccade-induced attention shifts influenced which positions were remembered. We discuss this further below, using the error term from the saccade direction × row probed × column probed interaction, $F(2,14) = 3.4$, $p < .06$, MSe = 0.021, to test several planned comparisons. Differences of 14% and above are significant at the .05 level.

First, did the attention instructions influence which array elements were remembered? If so, then accuracy for column 1 when saccades were made to the low-probability side of the array should be higher than accuracy for column 3 when saccades were made to the high-probability side of the array. Averaged across rows, these values were 83.0 and 53.4%, respectively. Thus, accuracy was much higher when high-probability positions were probed than when low-probability positions were probed when the eyes moved away from these positions. This was true for positions in both the top and bottom rows, but the difference was significantly larger for the top row (95.0 *vs* 53.8%) than for the bottom row (71.0 *vs* 52.9%). This suggests that subjects were unable to attend equally to both positions on the high-probability side of the array, but instead favoured the top row.

Did making an eye movement towards the low-probability side of the array improve memory for the items that appeared there, even though subjects were attempting to attend to the high-probability side of the array? This was examined by comparing accuracy for column 3 when the saccade was made to the low-probability side of the array as opposed to the high-probability side of the array. Averaged across rows, these values were 82.5 *vs* 53.8%, respectively. Thus, accuracy for the low-probability positions was much higher when the eyes moved towards them than when the eyes moved away, consistent with the conclusion that the act of making a saccade to some location causes attention to shift to that location before the saccade. As in Experiment 1, mean accuracy for the low-probability saccade positions (82.5%) was statistically identical to that of the high-probability non-saccade positions (83.0%) discussed in the preceding paragraph. The saccade-induced attention movement appeared to have a slightly larger effect on the bottom row (87.9 *vs* 52.9%) than on the top row (77.0 *vs* 53.8%), but this difference was not significant. These results support the conclusion that attention moves to the saccade target location before the eyes move, even when subjects are trying to attend somewhere else. Because of the attention shift, the letter identity and letter colour information near the saccade target location are conjoined and stored in trans-saccadic memory.

As in Experiment 1, we also examined whether saccade-induced attention shifts combined with instruction-induced attention shifts to provide an additional memory benefit. To determine whether an additional benefit is gained when the eyes move to a location that is already being attended, we compared accuracy for column 1 when the eyes moved towards that column as opposed to away from that column. Averaged over rows, these values are 93.6 and 83.0%, respectively. This difference is not significant. However, a significant benefit is found if the bottom row alone is considered (93.4 *vs* 71.0%); a ceiling effect may have occurred for the top row (93.8 *vs* 95.0%). There is also some evidence that an additional benefit is gained when subjects are instructed to attend to the side of the array towards which they move their eyes: Averaged over rows, accuracy for column 1 when saccades were made toward column 1 was 93.6%, whereas accuracy for column 3 when saccades were made towards column 3 was 82.5%. Although this overall difference is not significant, the difference for the top row alone is significant (93.8 *vs* 77.0%); the difference for the bottom row is small, however (93.4 *vs* 87.9%). In sum, in this experiment, there is some evidence that additional benefit is gained when the eyes move to a location that is already being attended or when attention is allocated via instruction to a location towards which the eyes will move. Our failure to find such an effect in Experiment 1 may have been due to a lack of power, or to the fact that subjects were unable to allocate their attention effectively to four separate locations.

Error Analyses. The percentage of intra-array and extra-array errors for both identity and colour responses were calculated as in the previous experiment. As reported above, letter identity was reported correctly on 74.5% of the trials; 22.4% (SE = 7.7%) of the identity responses were intra-array errors and 3.1% (SE = 2.2%) of the identity responses were extra-array errors. Letter colour was reported correctly on 78.1% of the trials; 17.3% (SE = 6.3%) of the colour responses were intra-array errors and 4.6% (SE = 3.2%) were extra-array errors. Thus, as in the previous experiment, most errors involved report of an identity or a colour that had been presented in the letter array, rather than a non-presented identity or colour. Of course, chance guessing favours intra-array over extra-array errors in this experiment, because the six items presented on each trial were chosen from a pool of only eight alternatives. Thus, given that an error occurred, the likelihood of an intra-array error is 5/7, while the likelihood of an extra-array error is only 2/7. In other words, chance guessing predicts that there should be about 2.5 times as many intra-array as extra-array errors. The observed ratio of intra-array to extra-array errors was considerably higher than the 2.5 times expected by chance guessing, however. Thus, it appears that location information is more likely to be lost than identity information when the eyes move. An analysis of the distribution of location errors showed that approximately 70% of them involved report of the identity or of the colour of the item horizontally or vertically adjacent to the probed position, however, indicating that some coarse coding of location apparently survives the saccade. This was true for both the identity and the colour response. There was very little contingency between identity and colour reports when an intra-array error occurred: The probability of reporting the colour of the erroneously reported identity when an identity intra-array error occurred was 0.16, and the probability of reporting the identity of the erroneously reported colour when a colour intra-array error occurred was 0.20. These values are not much different from chance (0.13). Thus, integrated identity + colour units did not "migrate" together to cause an error; rather, identity and colour were independent. In contrast, recall that there was a high contingency (0.87) between identity and colour reports when a correct response was made.

Additional analyses of variance conducted on the error data with factors of saccade direction, row probed and column probed revealed that both intra-array and extra-array errors increased as accuracy decreased, and both kinds of errors were affected in the same way by the attentional instructions and by the saccade-induced attention shifts. Because these analyses provide no additional information about the questions of interest, they will not be discussed further.

Instead, we will focus on another way of examining the error data, namely in terms of what Treisman (e.g. Treisman & Schmidt, 1982) called "feature errors" and "illusory conjunctions". A feature error occurs when the subject reports one dimension of the probed item correctly (e.g. identity) but makes an extra-array error on the other dimension (e.g. colour). In contrast, an illusory conjunction occurs when the subject reports one dimension of the probed item correctly, but makes an intra-array error on the other dimension. According to Treisman's Feature Integration Theory, illusory conjunctions should be more frequent than feature errors when attention is limited, because the features that are present in the display will not be conjoined correctly. Thus, we should find that illusory conjunctions, rather than feature errors, are affected by the attentional instruction that we used and by the saccade-induced attention shifts that we hypothesize affect task performance.

Tables 3 and 4 show the percentage of feature errors and illusory conjunctions as a function of probe position and eye-movement direction. Separate analyses of variance were conducted on these data with factors of saccade direction, row probed (top *vs* bottom) and column probed (1–3). No main effects or interactions were significant in the analysis of the feature errors, indicating that neither the attentional instructions nor saccade-induced attention shifts affected the likelihood that a feature error would occur. In the analysis of the illusory conjunctions, the column probed main effect was significant, $F(2,14) = 11.7$, $p < .001$, MSe = 0.066, as were the interactions between row probed and column probed, $F(2,14) = 5.3$, $p < .02$, MSe = 0.049, and saccade direction and column probed, $F(2,14) = 5.9$, $p < .02$, MSe = 0.034. These interactions were significant because the attentional instructions and the saccade-induced attention shifts influenced the likelihood that an illusory conjunction would occur. Put briefly, very few illusory conjunctions occurred when subjects moved their eyes towards a high-probability position and that position was probed (4.5%). Very many illusory conjunctions occurred when subjects moved their eyes away from a low-probability position and that position was probed (34.5%). High-probability positions that the eyes moved away from (12.9%) and low-probability positions that the eyes moved towards (11.2%) produced a fairly low level of illusory conjunctions when probed. Using the error term from the saccade direction x column probed interaction (the three-way interaction did not approach significance, $F < 1$), differences of 12.6% and above are significant at the .05 level. These results support the conclusion that attention precedes the eyes to the saccade target location, making it more likely

TABLE 3
Percentage of Feature Errors as a Function of Probe Position in Experiment 2

	Column		
	High-probability Side	*Low-probability Side*	
Condition	*1*	*2*	*3*
Top row			
Saccade to high-probability side	*2.9*	6.3	4.1
Saccade to low-probability side	*0.5*	10.8	5.3
Bottom row			
Saccade to high-probability side	*0.8*	6.8	8.4
Saccade to low-probability side	*6.1*	8.4	5.0

Note: Subjects were instructed to attend to the high-probability side of the letter array (column 1), which was probed for report six times as often as the low-probability side. Saccades were made equally often towards the high-probability side and the low-probability side.

TABLE 4
Percentage of Illusory Conjunctions as a Function of Probe Position in Experiment 2

	Column		
	High-probability Side	*Low-probability Side*	
Condition	*1*	*2*	*3*
Top row			
Saccade to high-probability side	*3.4*	28.1	39.6
Saccade to low-probability side	*4.6*	27.0	17.8
Bottom row			
Saccade to high-probability side	*5.5*	55.9	29.4
Saccade to low-probability side	*21.1*	47.5	4.6

Note: Subjects were instructed to attend to the high-probability side of the letter array (column 1), which was probed for report six times as often as the low-probability side. Saccades were made equally often towards the high-probability side and the low-probability side.

that the features that appear near that location will be correctly conjoined into objects that are stored in trans-saccadic memory. When attention is unlikely to be allocated to some position (i.e. a low-probability position that the eyes move away from), many illusory conjunctions occur when that position is probed. It is interesting that when the central array positions were probed, accuracy was quite low and many illusory conjunctions occurred; it appears that even though subjects fixated these letter positions before executing their saccades, they did not attend to the information that was present there. We note in passing that chance guessing favours illusory conjunctions over feature errors by a ratio of 2.5 to 1, but the observed ratios for the positions discussed above are considerably higher than that.

Summary. On most trials, subjects recalled both the identity and the colour of the probed item correctly. Even though colour, as well as position and identity, had to be remembered across the saccade, subjects still remembered close to four elements from the letter display, just as they did in Experiment 1 in which colour was not varied. These results provide additional support for the conclusion that the capacity of trans-saccadic memory is approximately four objects.

Report of letter and colour for the high-probability locations was very accurate and few illusory conjunctions occurred when these positions were probed, especially if a saccade was made in their direction. These results indicate that subjects followed the instruction to attend to the high-probability side of the letter array. Nonetheless, correct report of letter and colour for the array items that appeared near the saccade target was facilitated when a saccade was made to the low-probability side of the array, and few illusory conjunctions occurred. These results support the conclusion that attention shifts obligatorily to the location of the saccade target before the eyes move, thereby increasing the likelihood that features near that location will be conjoined and encoded as integrated objects into trans-saccadic memory. As in the previous experiment, the attentional effect produced by the saccade was localized in space; the greatest benefit was found for the position below the saccade target, although the position above the saccade target was facilitated as well. The effect of making a saccade to some location yielded approximately as much benefit as biasing a subject to attend to that location through instruction and probe probability; in this experiment, having voluntary attention and saccade-induced attention directed to the same side of the letter array led to additional improvements in memory.

Most of the errors were illusory conjunctions rather than feature errors. The attentional instruction and the saccade-induced attention shift influenced the number of illusory conjunctions that occurred, but had no effect on the feature error rate. These results support the conclusion that trans-saccadic memory consists largely of integrated objects formed when attention conjoins features that are present in the display.

Unlike Experiment 1, there was no significant difference in saccade latency when the eyes moved towards versus away from the high-probability side of the letter array. This may have occurred because there were fewer items in the letter array and subjects were instructed to attend to only two as opposed to four letter positions in the high probability side of the array. This may have decreased the amount of time required to encode the items in the high-probability positions into memory before the eyes moved to the low-probability side of the array. Using an Attention Operating Characteristic analysis, Kowler et al. (1995) reported that some attention can be diverted from the saccade goal without affecting latency, so perhaps this happened in Experiment 2.

GENERAL DISCUSSION

The main goal of the present research was to investigate what information is remembered across a saccade when subjects are instructed (and encouraged via a probability manipulation) to attend to one side of a display while they move their eyes either to that side or to the other, low-probability, side of the display. The results of two experiments showed that trans-saccadic memory for the high-probability side of the display was quite accurate, but that executing a saccade to the low-probability side of the display significantly improved recall of the items that appeared near the saccade target. Experiment 2 showed that attentional instruction and the saccade-induced attention shift exerted their effects by increasing the likelihood that the separate features present at each array location were accurately combined to form unified objects. In general, the effect of making a saccade to some location produced as much benefit as biasing a subject to attend to that location through instruction and probe probability. These results support the conclusion that attention movements precede eye movements in an obligatory fashion, as others have argued (e.g. Deubel & Schneider, 1996; Hoffman & Subramanian, 1995; Kowler et al., 1995; Shepherd et al., 1986). The results also show that both voluntary and saccade-induced attention shifts are very localized in space; subjects were unable to attend equally to multiple array locations, and the attentional effect produced by the saccade was always greater for one position than for others. These results are in agreement with those of Deubel and Schneider (1996), Henderson (1993) and Kowler (1995).

Several other findings are also of interest. In both experiments, subjects remembered approximately four items from the letter display, even when colour had to be remembered in addition to identity and position information. These results support the argument that the capacity of trans-saccadic memory is approximately four objects (e.g. Irwin, 1992, 1993; Irwin & Andrews, 1996). What attention does is influence which array elements are remembered, given these capacity limits. For example, one subject (D.E. Irwin) attempted to encode the contents of all of the array positions into memory before executing the saccade, giving highest priority to the high-probability positions; when the saccade was made to the low-probability side of the letter array, the saccade-induced attention shift facilitated the encoding of the items that appeared near the saccade target, bumping out of memory any low-priority information. If any of the attended positions was probed for report, accuracy was high; if an unattended position was probed, however, accuracy was low. Another general finding of interest is that, in both experiments, most errors seemed to be due to loss of location information about the array elements, rather than loss of identity information. This suggests that identity information may be retained better than location information when the eyes move. Alternatively, the binding of location with identity may be lost. However, most of the location errors involved the report of an item spatially near the correct item, suggesting that some coarse coding of location information survives a saccade. The results of the present research are consistent with the Object-File Theory of Trans-saccadic Memory recently proposed by Irwin and Andrews (1996; see also Irwin, 1996), which claims that trans-saccadic memory consists largely of a limited number of object files that are created when attention conjoins the stimulus features that co-occur in specific spatial locations into unitary wholes (cf. Kahneman & Treisman, 1984; Treisman, 1988).

In the spirit of this special issue of *Visual Cognition*, we conclude by offering some speculations about the neural basis of trans-saccadic memory. We do this within the context of VAM, the neurocognitive model of visual attention recently proposed by Schneider (1995). According to Schneider, the main function of visual attention is to implement *object tokens* that contain globally segmented information about individual objects in a display; in this respect,

VAM is nicely compatible with the object-file theory. VAM assumes a cortical processing architecture like that shown in Figure 2. The first cortical processing stage, area V1, computes local, low-level features (e.g. local colour and local orientation) in retinotopic modules. Following the registration of sensory information in these modules, further cortical processing is accomplished via two separate pathways, typically called the "where"- and "what"-pathways (e.g. Mishkin, Ungerleider, & Macko, 1983). The "where"-pathway, located dorsally and extending through area MT to the parietal cortex, is specialized for motion perception, spatial representation and spatial information processing, whereas the "what"-pathway, located ventrally and extending through V4, area IT and the STS, is specialized for the processing of higher-level form and colour information. According to VAM, various kinds of higher-level "type" information (e.g. shape primitives) are computed in the "what"-pathway for the purposes of object recognition. The receptive fields of neurons in the "what"-pathway are quite large, however, so that location coding is imprecise. In contrast, spatial coding is precise in the "where"-pathway, but this pathway contains no information about the features of objects in the environment. This creates a binding problem—somehow the perceptual system must figure out which features in the environment correspond to which locations in space for us to perceive the coherent world of localized objects that we ordinarily experience. According to VAM, this binding problem is solved via back-refer-

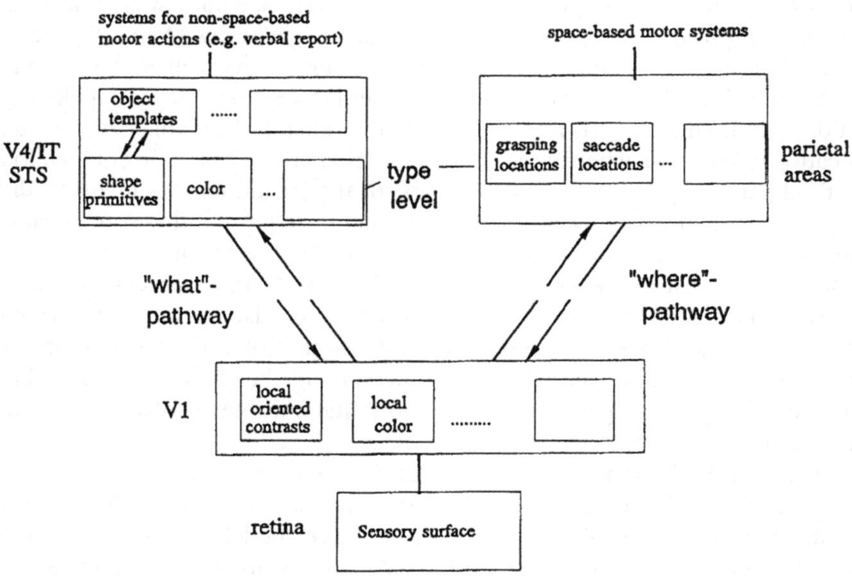

FIG. 2. A simplified and selective sketch of the primate visual system (reprinted with permission from Schneider, 1995).

encing to area V1. For example, the perceptual system can use a where-based attentional mechanism in posterior parietal cortex to scan a region of space, which causes an attention signal to be sent to V1. The retinotopic modules in V1 are connected via common locations, so the attention signal activates all the features that occupy the scanned region. The result of this activation is an object token which contains both "what and "where" information; VAM assumes that object tokens are stored in short-term memory for subsequent action, such as verbal report. "What"-based attentional selection can also occur, via back-projections from V4/IT to area V1 (to select all red objects, for example). In essence, VAM assumes that V1 acts as a location-based distributor of attentional signals.

VAM could account for the results of our trans-saccadic partial-report experiments in the following way. Based on the attentional instructions provided to subjects, the "where"-based attentional mechanism could be used to access and form tokens for the high-probability locations in the display. These tokens would be generated serially and stored in short-term memory. VAM assumes that a motor action can be directed only at the currently attended item, however, so programming a saccade to the saccade-target location would require attention to be redirected to that region of space; thus, tokens would be formed for objects near the saccade target location as well. Because short-term memory has a limited capacity, however, not all of the tokens that would be created could be remembered. Following saccade execution, when the partial-report probe is presented, report of the probed item would be successful only if the appropriate token could be retrieved from short-term memory. Because V1 is blank after the saccade (i.e. it contains only the partial-report cue and not the letter display), it is not possible to create a new object token for the probed location. Our results, and those of Irwin (1992) and Irwin and Andrews (1996), indicate that at most four tokens (object files) are held in short-term memory across the saccade, so overall accuracy would be limited to that amount. The fact that most errors are illusory conjunctions rather than feature errors suggests that unbound features of the display are also retained across the saccade, however. One possibility is that residual information about object features persists for some period of time after the saccade in areas V4/IT or the STS, where location coding is imprecise; the effect might also result from "broken" object tokens in short-term memory as its capacity is exceeded.

In conclusion, our results indicate that attention determines what information is encoded into trans-saccadic memory and hence remembered across eye movements. Because attention precedes the eyes to the saccade target location, information near the saccade target is likely to be encoded and remembered. We offer a possible neuropsychological account of our results in terms of VAM (Schneider, 1995). Although this account is clearly speculative, it may nonetheless serve as a useful starting point for further investigations into the cognitive neuroscience of trans-saccadic memory.

REFERENCES

Bridgeman, B., & Mayer, M. (1983). Failure to integrate visual information from successive fixations. *Bulletin of the Psychonomic Society, 21*, 285–286.

Bryden, M. (1961). The role of post-exposural eye movements in tachistoscopic perception. *Canadian Journal of Psychology, 15*, 220–225.

Crovitz, H., & Daves, W. (1962). Tendencies to eye movement and perceptual accuracy. *Journal of Experimental Psychology, 63*, 495–498.

Deubel, H., & Schneider, W.X. (1996). Saccade target selection and object recognition: Evidence for a common attentional mechanism. *Vision Research, 36*, 1827–1837.

Finley, G. (1985). A high-speed plotter for vision research. *Vision Research, 25*, 1993–1997.

Groner, R., Groner, M.T., Muller, P., Bischof, W.F., & Di Lollo, V. (1993). On the confounding effects of phosphor persistence in oscilloscopic displays. *Vision Research, 33*, 913–917.

Hayhoe, M., Lachter, J., & Feldman, J. (1991). Integration of form across saccadic eye movements. *Perception, 20*, 393–402.

Henderson, J. (1993). Visual attention and saccadic eye movements. In G. d'Ydewalle & J. Van Rensbergen (Eds), *Perception and cognition: Advances in eye-movement research* (pp. 37–50). Amsterdam: North-Holland.

Henderson, J. (1994). Two representational systems in dynamic visual identification. *Journal of Experimental Psychology: General, 123*, 410–426.

Henderson, J., & Anes, M. (1994). Roles of object-file review and type priming in visual identification within and across eye fixations. *Journal of Experimental Psychology: Human Perception and Performance, 20*, 826–839.

Henderson, J., Pollatsek, A., & Rayner, K. (1989). Covert visual attention and extrofoveal information use during object identification. *Perception and Psychophysics, 45*, 196–208.

Hoffman, J.E., & Subramaniam, B. (1995). The role of visual attention in saccadic eye movements. *Perception and Psychophysics, 57*, 787–795.

Irwin, D.E. (1991). Information integration across saccadic eye movements. *Cognitive Psychology, 23*, 420–456.

Irwin, D.E. (1992). Memory for position and identity across eye movements. *Journal of Experimental Psychology: Learning, Memory and Cognition, 18*, 307–317.

Irwin, D.E. (1993). Memory for spatial position across saccadic eye movements. In G. d'Ydewalle & J. Van Rensbergen (Eds), *Perception and cognition: Advances in eye-movement research* (pp. 323–332). Amsteram: North-Holland.

Irwin, D.E. (1996). Integrating information across saccadic eye movements. *Current Directions in Psychological Science, 5*, 94–100.

Irwin, D.E., & Andrews, R. (1996). Integration and accumulation of information across saccadic eye movements. In T. Inui & J.L. McClelland (Eds), *Attention and performance XVI: Information integration in perception and communication* (pp. 125–155). Cambridge, MA: MIT Press.

Irwin, D.E., & Yeomans, J.M. (1986). Sensory registration and informational persistence. *Journal of Experimental Psychology: Human Perception and Performance, 12*, 343–360.

Irwin, D.E., Yantis, S., & Jonides, J. (1983). Evidence against visual integration across saccadic eye movements. *Perception and Psychophysics, 34*, 49–57.

Irwin, D.E., Brown, J.S., & Sun, J.-S. (1988). Visual masking and visual integration across saccadic eye movements. *Journal of Experimental Psychology: General*, 117, 274–285.

Kahneman, D., & Treisman, A. (1984). Changing views of attention and automaticity. In R. Parasuraman & D. Davies (Eds), *Varities of attention* (pp. 29–61). New York: Academic Press.

Klein, R. (1980). Does oculomotor readiness mediate cognitive control of visual attention? In R.S. Nickerson (Ed.), *Attention and performance VIII* (pp. 259–276). Hillsdale, NJ: Lawrence Erlbaum Associates Inc.

Klein, R., & Pontefract, A. (1994). Does oculomotor readiness mediate cognitive control of visual attention? Revisited! In C. Umiltà & M. Moskovitch (Eds), *Attention and performance XV* (pp. 333–350). Cambridge, MA: MIT Press.

Kowler, E., Anderson, E., Dosher, B., & Blaser, E. (1995). The role of attention in the programming of saccades. *Vision Research, 35*, 1897–1916.

Lachter, J., Hayhoe, M., & Feldman, J. (1991). Capacity limitations in the integration of information across saccades. *Investigative Ophthalmology and Visual Science, 32*, 1025.

McConkie, G.W. (1991). Perceiving a stable visual world. Paper presented at the *Sixth European Conference on Eye Movements*, Leuven, Belgium.

Mewhort, D.J.K., Campbell, A., Marchetti, F., & Campbell, J. (1981). Identification, localization, and "iconic" memory: An evaluation of the bar-probe task. *Memory and Cognition, 9*, 50–67.

Mishkin, M., Ungerleider, L., & Macko, K. (1983). Object vision and spatial vision: Two cortical pathways. *Trends in Neurosciences, 6*, 414–417.

O'Regan, J.K. (1992). Solving the "real" mysteries of visual perception: The world as an outside memory. *Canadian Journal of Psychology, 46*, 461–488.

O'Regan, J.K., & Levy-Schoen, A. (1983). Integrating visual information from successive fixations: Does trans-saccadic fusion exist? *Vision Research, 23*, 765–768.

Rayner, K., & Pollatsek, A. (1983). Is visual information integrated across saccades? *Perception and Psychophysics, 34*, 39–48.

Rayner, K., McConkie, G., & Ehrlich, S. (1978). Eye movements and integrating information across fixations. *Journal of Experimental Psychology: Human Perception and Performance, 4*, 529–544.

Schneider, W.X. (1995). VAM: A neuro-cognitive model for visual attention control of segmentation, object recognition, and space-based motor action. *Visual Cognition, 2*, 331–375.

Shepherd, M., Findlay, J., & Hockey, R. (1986). The relationship between eye movements and spatial attention. *Quarterly Journal of Experimental Psychology, 38A*, 475–491.

Sperling, G. (1960). The information available in brief visual presentations. *Psychological Monographs, 74*(11, Whole No. 498).

Townsend, V.M. (1973). Loss of spatial and identity information following a tachistoscopic exposure. *Journal of Experimental Psychology*, 98, 113–118.

Treisman, A., (1988). Features and objects: The Fourteenth Bartlett Memorial Lecture. *Quarterly Journal of Experimental Psychology, 40A*, 201–237.

Treisman, A., & Gelade, G. (1980). A feature integration theory of attention. *Cognitive Psychology, 12*, 97–136.

Treisman, A., & Schmidt, H. (1982). Illusory conjunctions in the perception of objects. *Cognitive Psychology, 14*, 107–141.

Van der Heijden, A.H.C. (1992). *Selective attention in vision.* London: Routledge and Kegan.

VISUAL COGNITION, 1998, *5* (1/2), 157–181

Implicit but not Explicit Feature Binding in a Balint's Patient

Ewa Wojciulik

Department of Psychology, University of California at Los Angeles, CA and Department of Psychology, Harvard University, Cambridge, MA, USA

Nancy Kanwisher

Department of Psychology, Harvard University, Cambridge, MA, USA

Visual perception is often conceptualized as a process of extracting visual attributes from the stimulus, from simple features like colour and orientation to high-level identities of words and objects. However, an important further task for vision is to solve the "binding problem"—to determine which visual attributes go together to form one object (e.g. Treisman & Gelade, 1980). Recent evidence suggests that the parietal lobes are critical for feature binding (e.g. Friedman-Hill, Robertson, & Treisman, 1995). We examined a patient with bilateral parieto-occipital damage and found that, while he was at chance on an explicit binding task (reporting which of two words was coloured), an implicit reaction time measure showed that correct colour-word bindings were nonetheless represented in his visual system. These results (1) show a dissociation between implicit and explicit binding and (2) suggest that the parietal lobes may be critical for explicit but not implicit binding. The implications of these results for feature integration theory are discussed.

INTRODUCTION

There now exists a large body of evidence, spanning human neuropsychology (e.g. Rafal & Robertson, 1995; Rizzolatti & Berti, 1993), functional imaging

---

Requests for reprints should be addressed to Ewa Wojciulik, Institute of Cognitive Neuroscience, Alexandra House, University College London, Gower Street, London WC1E 6BT, UK. E-mail: e.wojciulik@ucl.ac.uk

We would like to thank RM for his participation, and Lynn Robertson, Robert Rafal, Anne Treisman, Molly Potter, Stacia Friedman-Hill, Jon Driver, Glyn Humphreys and an anonymous reviewer for comments and discussions of an earlier draft of the manuscript. This research was supported by a doctoral fellowship from the Natural Sciences and Engineering Research Council of Canada to EW, and NIH grant MH 45245 to NK. Preliminary results were reported at the 24th Annual Meeting of the Society for Neuroscience, November 1994 (Wojciulik, Robertson, & Kanwisher).

(e.g. Corbetta, Miezin, Shulman, & Petersen, 1993; Corbetta, Shulman, Miezin, & Petersen, 1995; Köhler et al., 1995) and monkey neurophysiology (e.g. Colby, 1991; Maunsell, 1995; Mishkin, Ungerleider, & Macko, 1983), pointing to the importance of the parietal lobes in visual attention and spatial processing. Unilateral parietal damage in humans often leads to a variety of attentional (e.g. Posner, Walker, Friedrich, & Rafal, 1984) and spatial (e.g. Bisiach, Luzzatti, & Perani, 1979) deficits. The present study investigated the role of the parietal lobes in binding, a process which is responsible for integrating visual features into coherent objects and which is hypothesized to depend on attention (e.g. Treisman & Gelade, 1980). In particular, we tested whether patient RM, who suffered bilateral parietal damage, might be able to bind visual features at an implicit level, even though his overt reports indicate a marked impairment in feature binding (Friedman-Hill, Robertson, & Treisman, 1995).

Evidence for the attentional basis of parietal deficits comes from studies using several different experimental paradigms. For example, Posner et al. (1984) showed that patients with parietal damage are especially slow to detect a stimulus in the contralesional field if it is preceded by a cue in the ipsilesional field, suggesting a difficulty in disengaging attention from the good field. Eglin, Robertson and Knight (1989) showed that parietal patients are very impaired on visual search tasks. When a target was defined by a conjunction of features and the distractors were present on both sides of the display, patients' response times were much slower for detection of a target on the contralesional than on the ipsilesional side. Cohen and Rafal (1991) also found that unilateral damage can lead to a large number of illusory conjunction errors in the contralesional field: Their patient, who suffered a left temporo-parietal lesion, often perceived two features (colour and shape) as belonging to the same object, when in fact they belonged to two different objects.

Corbetta et al. (1995) used positron emission tomography to investigate the neural mechanisms underlying feature binding in normal human subjects. Their subjects searched for a target defined by a single feature (colour or speed of motion) or by a conjunction of features (colour and speed). They found that the right superior parietal lobule, which is active during spatial attentional shifts (Corbetta et al., 1993), was also more active during conjunction search than during feature search. Wojciulik, Kanwisher and Driver (1997) further found that the intraparietal sulci of both hemispheres were also more active during conjunction than feature search when the stimuli were presented in rapid serial visual presentation.

These results are interesting for two reasons. First, numerous findings suggest that the primate visual system is composed of many distinct areas, each processing a different set of visual attributes, such as motion, colour or orientation (e.g. Corbetta et al., 1990; Livingstone & Hubel, 1988). Our perception, however, is not of a random collection of features, but of stable unified objects. The results of Cohen and Rafal (1991), Corbetta et al. (1995),

Eglin et al. (1989) and Wojciulik et al. (1997) suggest that the parietal lobes may play an important role in integrating individual features into stable object representations.

Second, these results are important because the task of feature integration has been ascribed to visual attention (Treisman & Gelade, 1980). According to Treisman's feature integration theory, features are detected pre-attentively and in parallel across the visual field, but their integration into single objects requires focused attention to each object's location in turn. Taxing attentional resources, whether by short exposures, dual tasks, or some kinds of brain damage, results in miscombinations of features or illusory conjunctions (e.g. Arguin, Cavanagh, & Joannette, 1994; Cohen & Rafal, 1991; Treisman & Schmidt, 1982). Thus, these data suggest that the parietal lobes may play a critical role in the proper working of the attentional mechanism involved in the integration of features.

A recent study by Friedman-Hill et al. (1995) supports the notion that the parietal lobes are critical for feature integration (or "binding"). This study is especially important because it suggests that the binding deficit is due to a spatial impairment, in accord with Treisman's theory. Friedman-Hill et al. studied the performance of patient RM with bilateral parietal damage on feature conjunction and spatial tasks. They found that: (1) RM made many illusory conjunction errors (e.g. he often reported seeing a red X or a blue O when the display consisted of a red O and a blue X), even with exposure durations as long as 10 sec; (2) the illusory conjunction errors were due to spatial, not temporal binding problems (i.e. RM made more illusory conjunction errors with simultaneous than with sequential presentations of two objects); and (3) RM also had gross impairments in his spatial abilities (e.g. he was at chance when deciding whether one letter was to the left or right of a second letter). According to feature integration theory, correct identification of a conjunction of features requires that the object be correctly localized. The theory accounts very well for RM's performance: He is unable to bind features correctly because of his poor localization abilities (see also Coslett & Saffran, 1991, for a similar explanation of simultanagnosia). Thus, the results presented by Friedman-Hill et al. (1995) suggest that the parietal lobes are critical for the correct binding of features, which is dependent on correct localization of these features.

In recent years, however, many dissociations have been observed between conscious (explicit) and non-conscious (implicit) processing of visual information in neurological disorders, such as unilateral neglect, simultanagnosia, blindsight, or prosopagnosia (e.g. Berti & Rizzolatti, 1992; Coslett & Saffran, 1991; Weiskrantz, Barbur, & Sahraie, 1995; Young, Hellawell, & DeHaan, 1988). Brain-damaged patients often possess high-level visual knowledge of which they are unaware. Patients with neglect, for example, may deny that an object is present in the contralesional visual field, and yet show semantic priming from that object (Berti & Rizzolatti, 1992).

We tested whether a similar dissociation might be observed for integration of features: Is it possible that RM had the correct binding information at some level in his visual system but was simply not aware of it? In the feature conjunction experiments conducted by Friedman-Hill et al. (1995), RM was asked to make explicit conjunctions. They were explicit in the sense that he had to have conscious access to both features of the target object and their conjunction. Thus, in the colour-and-shape conjunction task, RM had to report verbally both the identity and colour of the letter; in the size-and-shape conjunction task, he had to first decide which of two shapes was taller and then report the identity of that shape. It is possible that, even when RM reported illusory conjunctions, the correct conjunctions were nonetheless correctly registered at some level in his visual system. So, for example, when shown a red X and a blue O, could he have implicitly known that the X was really red, even when he reported seeing a blue X?

The answer to this question is important if we are to accept that the parietal lobes are critical for binding. If RM could be shown to have implicit binding in the absence of explicit knowledge of that information, the idea that the brain regions which are damaged in RM (parieto-occipital junctions, the angular gyri and the superior parietal lobules bilaterally; see Case description) are necessary for binding will have to be revised. Instead, we would have to conclude that the role of the parietal lobes is to make the binding information explicit (or consciously accessible), rather than to compute the binding in the first place. Here, we present exactly such evidence: Even when RM reports an illusory conjunction, some part of his visual system nonetheless "knows" the correct combination of features present in the display.

To address the question of whether features can be correctly bound implicitly without being consciously accessible, we tested RM on a modified Stroop task. In the original Stroop paradigm (Stroop, 1935), words that name colours (e.g. the word "BROWN") are written in ink colours that are inconsistent with the words (e.g. the colour green). The subject's task is to name the colour of the ink as quickly as possible. In the control condition, no words are present and the subject names the ink colour of coloured squares. Subjects' response times (RTs) are slower when naming the ink colours of the inconsistent words than when naming the ink colours of the coloured patches (see MacLeod, 1991, for explanations of this interference effect).

Kahneman and Henik (1981) used a variant of the Stroop task to show that interference from the inconsistent colour-name word is greater when it is conjoined with the colour in the same object than when the word and colour belong to two separate objects. When attention is directed to a particular object (and/or its location), all its attributes are selected so that both relevant (the colour) and irrelevant (the word) dimensions are processed (see also Duncan, 1984). Thus, although the inconsistent word may interfere with the response even when the word is not conjoined with the colour in one object, this interference is greater when the two attributes constitute parts of the same object.

This task is well suited to answering the question about implicit conjunctions, because the required response is a feature response: The only thing that is relevant to the task is the colour present in the display and the subject need not even be aware of the identity of the words. The presence of conjunction information would be evident in the relative amounts of interference found for the same versus different object cases: When the colour and word are features of the same object, the interference should be greater than when they constitute features of two separate objects.

EXPERIMENT 1

In this experiment, we used a modified version of Kahneman and Henik's (1981) Stroop task. The display consisted of two colour-name words presented on a black background. One word was coloured in one of four possible colours, while the other word was always displayed in white. RM's task was to name the colour of the coloured word as quickly as possible (see Fig. 1). This adapted Stroop task allowed us to test whether RM could bind features correctly at an implicit level when he was at chance for reporting explicit conjunctions (as assessed by an independent test; see below).

The crucial comparison involves the "same-object" and "different-object" conditions (Fig. 1). In these two cases, the component "features" are exactly the same: There are two colours (e.g. green and white) and two words, one inconsistent and the other consistent with the response (e.g. BROWN and GREEN, respectively). The response ("green" in this example) is also the same. The only thing that differs between these two conditions is the conjunction of the words with colours: In the different-object case, the incompatibility comes from a different object than the colour response; in the same-object case, the incompatibility comes from the same object as the colour response. If RM has no conjunction information, then there should be no difference in RTs to name the colour in these two conditions, because all the features are exactly the same. If, on the other hand, he does correctly conjoin the words with colours, then he should be slower in the same-object than in the different-object condition.

Such a result on its own would not show evidence for *implicit* conjunction information until an additional requirement is met: We also have to show that it is not due to RM's limited residual capacity to bind features explicitly. After all, Friedman et al. (1995) showed that at exposure durations from 0.5 to 10 sec RM's performance on the feature conjunction tasks was well above chance. To assess whether RM can bind features implicitly while he has no conscious access to that information, the displays must be presented at sufficiently short durations to keep performance at chance on an explicit task requiring feature conjunction.

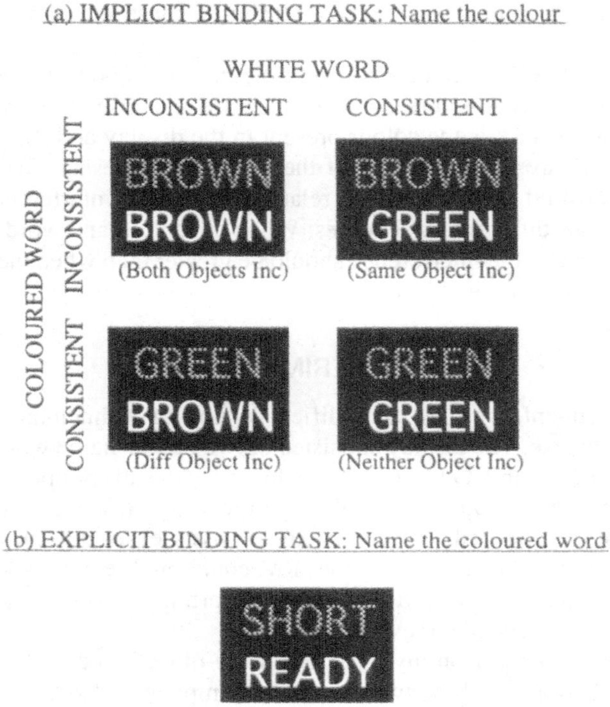

FIG. 1. Design and sample displays used in Experiment 1: (a) Stroop (implicit binding) task and (b) explicit binding task. The coloured word is shown stippled (top word); in this example, the colour of the coloured word is green.

To eliminate the possibility that RM might occasionally make correct explicit conjunctions, and to be able to claim the presence of implicit conjunctions in the Stroop task, we interleaved an additional explicit conjunction task between each block of the Stroop task. The ideal task for this explicit conjunction control would have been to display the very same stimuli as in the Stroop task and ask RM to report the identity of the coloured *word* rather than its *colour*. So, to perform correctly on this task, the subject would have to first figure out *which* word is coloured *and* identify that word—that is, he would have to make an explicit conjunction. In Fig. 1, for example, the correct responses would be GREEN and BROWN in the same-object and different-object conditions, respectively. This task, however, proved impossible for RM; he was so practised at naming the colours[1] that he could not switch to naming

[1]RM had already been tested on a version of this Stroop task 7 months earlier.

the words. He found this new task very difficult and confusing, took a very long time to respond, and kept naming the colour rather than the word.

Consequently, for the explicit conjunction control task, the display looked exactly like the two-word Stroop display except that the words were changed to neutral (i.e. non-colour-word) adjectives (e.g. SHORT), matched to the colour words for frequency, length and probability of word recognition on the basis of the first letter only. RM's task here was to identify the coloured word rather than the colour; that is, he had to report an explicit conjunction.

In the experiment, each block of trials in the explicit conjunction task followed a block of trials in the Stroop (implicit conjunction) task, forming an implicit–explicit pair. If RM's performance on the explicit control block was at chance, the data from the paired (i.e. preceding) Stroop block were entered into the analysis. If, on the other hand, RM's explicit conjunctions were above chance (due to continued practice on the task), the block was rejected, the exposure duration of the displays reduced and the next paired block of the implicit Stroop task followed by the explicit control was run. This procedure guaranteed that the data collected in the Stroop task could not be due to RM's occasional explicit conjunctions and, indeed, reflected the workings of an implicit binding mechanism whose output was not consciously accessible.

Method

Case Description. RM was in his fifties when he suffered two successive embolic strokes, the first in June 1991 and the second in March 1992. He showed severe spatial disorientation and had to be escorted into the hospital. He reported being blind and could not accomplish the most rudimentary tasks without help. Clinical evaluation (by Dr R. Rafal) in the autumn of 1992 indicated that RM had Balint's syndrome (see Rafal, 1996): He had difficulty perceiving more than one object at a time (simultanagnosia); he could not easily redirect his eyes away from a fixated object but, when he did, his eye movements were inaccurate (ocular apraxia); and he showed a deficit in using visual information to guide hand movements, resulting in misreaching (optic ataxia). He also had some dysarthria (slurring of speech), but no aphasia. Automated static perimetry revealed an inferior arc of hemianopia about 10° from the fovea. Goldmann perimetry performed in June 1994 showed full visual fields with some inferior nasal depression in the left eye. RM could not tell which of two objects was in front of the other (or which was closer to him) even when they were 20 cm apart, but his stereopsis, tested with random dot stereograms, was normal. Colour vision, uncorrected visual acuity and contrast sensitivity were normal. RM showed no deficits in object, face or word recognition (for other details of this case, see Baylis, Driver, Baylis, & Rafal, 1994; Friedman-Hill et al., 1995). There was no evidence of colour-specific anomia: On multiple tests in which two words (either neutral adjectives or colour-name words) were presented simultaneously, one coloured and one white, RM named the colour with better than 95% accuracy, even with very brief (105 msec) exposures.

By the time he was tested, RM still suffered some spatial disorientation (e.g. he had to be escorted from the waiting room to the experimental room in the hospital), but family members reported that he could navigate in and around his house. His gaze moved over the visual field. Optic ataxia improved but was still evident. He needed only intermittent help in his daily activities.

RM's visual abilities continued to improve over time. In August 1993, during pilot tests for Experiment 1 (conducted in March 1994), he could already sometimes identify more than one object at a time, but his performance was heavily dependent on display durations. In one test, two colour-name words (randomly chosen from a set of four: BROWN, GREEN, PURPLE and YELLOW) were presented simultaneously one above the other; both words were presented in white on a black background, with no forward or backward masks. RM always reported at least one word correctly; he reported both words correctly on 13 of 24 trials (54%) with 5.1 sec exposures, and 6 of 24 trials (25%) with 3 sec exposures. One week later, after much practice with these and similar displays, his performance on the same tests improved: He reported both words correctly on 17 of 24 trials (71%) with 3 sec display durations, but only 6 of 24 trials (25%) with 1.5 sec exposures. These tests show that, with sufficiently long exposures, RM could partly overcome his simultanagnosia and report both words, but his performance was still quite poor, even though the task was made relatively easy by limiting the word pool. [In addition, Baylis et al. (1994) found that RM's reading of four-letter words (3 sec exposures) was very accurate, but when the letters were rearranged to form unpronounceable nonwords, he reported only two letters on average. Due to time constraints, it was impossible to assess RM's simultanagnosia during the period when Experiment 2 was conducted (March 1996).]

Computed tomography (CT) scans revealed nearly symmetrical parieto-occipital lesions in both hemispheres and a small infarct in the right cerebellum. As described in Friedman-Hill et al. (1995), three-dimensional magnetic resonance imaging (MRI) confirmed the CT results, showing that the lesions were concentrated in Brodmann's area 39 (angular gyri) and the lateral aspects of area 7 (superior parietal lobules) and extended into the white matter. The lesions possibly also included lateral aspects of areas 19 and 5. There was also a small lesion in Brodmann's area 6 (supplementary motor area) of the right hemisphere and small asymmetrical lesions in the cerebellum (for CT and MRI reconstructions of RM's brain lesions, see Baylis et al., 1994; Friedman-Hill et al., 1995).

Design. This experiment used a 2×2 repeated-measures design. The compatibility of the two words (i.e. coloured and white) was manipulated independently, resulting in four conditions: (1) both words inconsistent with the colour response (both-objects-inconsistent); (2) coloured word inconsistent and white word consistent (same-object-inconsistent); (3) coloured word consistent and white word inconsistent (different-object-inconsistent); and (4) both words consistent (neither-object-inconsistent).

Materials and Apparatus

1. *Stroop: Implicit Conjunction Task.* Each trial started with a white fixation cross (about 0.7° high and wide) displayed in the centre of the monitor for 495 msec. A warning beep occurred at the onset of the fixation cross. The fixation cross was then replaced by a two-word display. The presentation duration of the words was changed from block to block, as described in the Procedure section below.

The display consisted of two colour-words, in upper-case Geneva font, size 48, presented one above the other on a black background in the centre of the monitor. RM was seated approximately 60 cm from the monitor. The display was 3.5° high and from 5.5° to 7° wide (depending on the particular words). Each word was 1.35° high; a vertical gap of 0.8° separated the two words.

The coloured word was displayed in one of four colours, while the other word was displayed in white. The colour-words and colours used were GREEN, PURPLE, BROWN and YELLOW. These colours were chosen so that the colour-words had approximately the same length (e.g. RED was not used because the subject could have been able to make the appropriate conjunction without knowing the identity of the word, but solely on the basis of its length).

Each block was composed of 48 trials, so that there were 12 trials in each of the four conditions. In the both-objects-inconsistent condition, two types of trials were included: Either the two words were different or they were the same, but in both cases each word was inconsistent with the response. The trials were presented in a pseudorandomized order: At most three trials from the same condition, and at most three trials with the same response, could occur consecutively.

Each colour and each word appeared equally often in each of the conditions, but the particular combinations of words and colours were determined by the four conditions. The coloured word appeared in the top position on one half of the trials, and in the bottom position on the other half. The position of the coloured word varied pseudorandomly from trial to trial, with the constraint that not more than three successive trials presented the coloured word in the same position.

There were four buffer trials at the beginning of each block, which were not included in the analysis. The purpose of these trials was to reduce the possibility of errors and increased variance due to a difficulty of changing tasks between the implicit and explicit blocks. The buffer trials included one trial from each of the four conditions and used a different colour on each trial.

2. *Control: Explicit Conjunction Task.* The display in the control task looked exactly like the Stroop display except that the colour-words were changed to the following neutral adjectives: SHORT, READY, CASUAL and USEFUL. Thus, the display consisted of two words, presented one above the other. One of the words was coloured in one of the four colours, while the other was always presented in white. The two words were always different. As in the Stroop task, the presentation duration was changed from block to block (see Procedure). The size and font of these words was the same as for the Stroop words.

To make the Stroop and control words as similar as possible in terms of their ease of recognition, the control words were chosen with the following constraints: They matched the colour words in (1) number of letters, (2) frequency of occurrence in written English (Kučera and Francis, 1967), and (3) probability of word recognition on the basis of the first letter only (i.e. all the neutral words started with different first letters, as was true for the colour words).

Each word appeared equally often in each of the four colours and in white. The coloured word was presented in the top position on one half of the trials, and in the bottom position on the other half. The position of the coloured word varied pseudorandomly from trial to trial, as described for the Stroop task. Each block was composed of 24 experimental trials, preceded by four buffer trials. The buffer trials were not included in the analysis.

The experiment was run on a Macintosh LC II computer. The stimuli were displayed on a Macintosh Apple-Color RGB monitor. The programs were written in MacProbe software (Hunt, 1994) and were used to display the stimuli and to collect the responses.

Procedure. In the Stroop task, RM was asked to name the colour present in the display as quickly as possible. The dependent variable was the time RM took to name the colour. Because of a technical problem with the microphone, voice RTs could not be recorded. Instead, the experimenter pressed one of four keyboard buttons which corresponded to RM's response. The experimenter sat next to the subject and could not see the display from her position. Although this procedure was not optimal due to the increased variance (i.e. the variance in the experimenter's button press RTs was added to the patient's variance in his verbal RTs) and produced an increase in RM's own RTs, to the extent that the different comparisons were significant, this does not present a problem for the interpretation of the data. We estimated that the experimenter added approximately 600 msec to RM's verbal RTs, based on 16 blocks of a similar task run on normal subjects, where we had collected both the subjects' verbal RTs and the experimenter's key press RTs. The data in Table 2 are corrected accordingly (i.e. we subtracted 600 msec from the RTs).

In the control (explicit conjunction) task, RM was asked to say which word was coloured. The dependent variable was accuracy in naming the correct word.

RM was informed about the colours used in the Stroop task and the words used in the control task.

Each block of the implicit Stroop task was paired with a block of the explicit control task in the following way. The experiment started with a block of the control task, with display duration set to 300 msec, to determine the presentation duration at which RM had no explicit conjunction information. In other words, if RM reported the coloured word on about one half of the trials, and the white word on the other half, this result was interpreted as showing no explicit information about the conjunctions of words with colours. Then, a block of the Stroop task, paired with the next block of the control task, were run in succession. If this control block still showed chance performance (between 42 and 54% correct[2]) on naming the coloured word, then the paired Stroop data were entered into the analysis. If, on the other hand, RM showed better than chance performance due to continued practice with short exposures, the previous paired block was rejected, the presentation duration was further reduced by 15 or 30 msec (depending on how good RM's performance was on the control task), and another paired block of the Stroop task, followed by the control task, was run. These paired implicit–explicit blocks were run until 10 blocks of analysable data (i.e. blocks where RM's performance was at chance on the explicit conjunction task) were collected. The mean exposure duration of the displays (in both tasks) over these 10 blocks averaged 159 msec (median = 180 msec) and ranged from 210 to 105 msec.

Note that this procedure of rejecting the paired blocks where RM's explicit performance was above chance does not underestimate RM's explicit binding ability at the short exposure durations we used in this experiment. At any given display duration, RM often started at chance and would remain at chance for a block, sometimes two blocks, or even three blocks (see Table 1). Then, with this practice, he would improve and perform above chance, at which point we rejected that paired block and again reduced the display durations until he was at chance. (On two occasions, after RM's performance increased above chance at a given exposure duration, two or three successive reductions were necessary to bring him down to chance.) The same sequence then followed: He would remain at chance for a block or two, at the shorter display durations, and then improve. In other words, the rejected blocks reflected his improvement after practice at these brief exposure durations, rather than variation in sampling from

[2]There were no explicit conjunction blocks in which RM had 55–58% accuracy, but there were three blocks in which RM was 42–45% accurate at naming the correct word. We decided to include these blocks in the analysis, since in these blocks RM's explicit conjunctions were more often incorrect than correct, and that could only reduce the difference between the same-object and different-object conditions in the Stroop task. Even when the three corresponding Stroop blocks are excluded from the analysis, the comparison between same-object and different-object conditions remains significant, $t(6) = 4.6$, $p < .005$.

TABLE 1
Block by Block Rejection Procedure

Exposure Duration (msec)	*Block Number*	*Accuracy on Coloured Word*	*Accept the Paired Implicit Block?*
Session 1			
210	1	12/24	Accept
210	2	17/24	Reject
180	3	10/24	Accept
180	4	10/23	Accept
195	5	13/24	Accept
195	6	15/24	Reject
180	7	11/23	Accept
Session 2			
195	8	11/22	Accept
195	9	19/24	Reject
180	10	15/24	Reject
165	11	16/24	Reject
135	12	13/24	Accept
135	13	16/24	Reject
120	14	15/24	Reject
105	15	12/24	Accept
105	16	11/24	Accept
105	17	10/24	Accept

Note that there were two exceptions to the general procedure of reducing exposure durations: We increased them by 1 screen refresh (15 msec) when RM indicated that the task was becoming too hard (after block 4) and at the beginning of session 2, which was run one day later.

the same population. Because RM's task changed between blocks, he was instructed at the beginning of each block which task he would be doing next.

This experiment was run in two separate sessions, on two successive days in March 1994. Five analysable blocks were collected during each of the sessions. The first Stroop block, run during the first session, for which explicit conjunctions were at chance, was treated as a practice block and was not entered into the analysis.

Results

The analyses of both tasks were performed on only those paired blocks where RM's accuracy on the explicit conjunction task was close to chance (i.e. 42–54% accuracy[2]). A total of 10 blocks satisfied this requirement (7 blocks were rejected). For these blocks of the explicit conjunction task, RM named the coloured word an average of 48% of the time, and the white word 50% of the time, $t(9) = 0.9$, $p = .38$. This result shows unambiguously that RM correctly perceived at least one of the two words present in the display: 98% of his responses were of words actually presented and only 2% were intrusion errors (where he named one of the other two words not present in the display). Yet only half of his responses were of the coloured word: he was at chance for reporting the coloured word. In other words, he had no explicit information of the colour and word conjunctions.

RM's median RTs to name the colour in each of the 10 paired Stroop blocks were entered into the analysis. Table 2 shows the means of the median RTs in the four conditions. RM was 96% accurate in naming the colour of the coloured word and only the correct responses were included in the analysis. The critical comparison of same-object versus different-object was significant, $t(9) = 6.2$, $p = .0002$: RM took longer to name the colour when it was inconsistent with the same object (836 msec) than when it was inconsistent with a different object (671 msec). The ANOVA also showed that the main effects of coloured-word and white-word compatibility were both significant, $F(1,9) = 119.3, p < .0001$, and $F(1,9) = 26.1, p = .0006$, respectively: His RTs were longer for inconsistent than consistent coloured words (906 *vs* 646 msec) and for inconsistent than consistent white words (823 *vs* 729 msec). The interaction was also significant, $F(1,9) = 7.4, p = .02$, suggesting that RM processed both words in the display: When the coloured word was consistent, an inconsistent white word (different-object) added a cost of 50 msec over a consistent white word (neither-object), $t(9) = 3.2$, $p = .01$; but when the coloured word was inconsistent, this cost (both-objects *vs* same-object) was 139 msec, $t(9) = 4.4, p = .002$.

Discussion

This experiment shows that RM had implicit binding information at some level in his visual system which he could not access explicitly. This conclusion is based on two results. First, in the Stroop task, RM's response times to name the colour were slower in the same-object condition, where the colour and the inconsistent word were conjoined in the same object, than in the different-object condition, where the colour and the inconsistent word belonged to two separate

TABLE 2
Means of RM's Median RTs (in msec) to Name the Colour of the Coloured Word in the Stroop Task (Standard Error of the Mean in Parentheses)

	White Word	
Coloured Word	*Inconsistent*	*Consistent*
Inconsistent	975 (33)	836 (19)
Consistent	671 (15)	621 (19)

Note that these RTs are corrected for experimenter's keypress RTs (see Method).

objects, despite the fact that these two displays were composed of precisely the same features. This result shows that he did have the correct conjunction information at least some of the time. Second, this difference was obtained in the absence of explicit conjunction information: RM was at chance when he was asked to report which word was coloured in the explicit conjunction control, suggesting that the correct feature binding observed in the Stroop task could not be due to explicit binding.

One potential shortcoming of the explicit control task is that RM was simply asked to name the coloured word. His chance performance on this task was assumed to reflect his inability to explicitly conjoin the colour with the coloured word. It is possible, however, given RM's deficits at seeing more than one object at a time, that he sometimes perceived only one word. Thus, on occasions when he saw only the white word, he could have known that the word was actually white, but reported it nonetheless, given it was the only word he saw. In other words, he could have had some explicit conjunction information, despite his chance performance: Of the 50% white words reported, some could have been correctly conjoined with the white colour; added to the 48% of coloured words reported, this number would have been higher than chance. If so, our Stroop results could be explained by explicit, not implicit, binding.

However, a different version of the explicit task showed that, at these short exposure durations, RM did not know which colour belonged to the word he reported.[3] In this task, RM was presented with the displays used in the explicit conjunction task (see Method), with exposure durations of 119 msec. He was asked to name one word and its colour, with "white" being a legitimate colour response. RM reported the coloured word and its colour on 21/26 trials (81%), but also reported the white word *and* the coloured word's colour on 16/21 trials (71%) (2-tailed Fisher exact test $p = .73$; see Table 3). These results show that, although RM had a large bias to name the colour rather than white, he simply did not know whether the word he reported was actually coloured or white: He called the reported word coloured just as often when he named the white word

TABLE 3
RM's Responses in an Alternative Explicit Conjunction Task, where RM was Asked to Report One Word and Its Colour, with "White" a Possible Answer

	Coloured Word	*White Word*
Overall	26/47 (55%)	21/47 (45%)
And colour	21/26 (81%)	16/21 (76%)
And white	5/26 (19%)	5/21 (24%)

[3]We would like to thank Lynn Robertson for proposing and testing this alternative explanation.

as when he named the coloured word. Thus, these data support our claim that when RM is asked to name just the coloured word and he is at chance on this task, he does not know whether it is white or coloured. In other words, his chance performance in our explicit task reflects his actual inability to explicitly bind a word with its colour. The results we obtained in the Stroop task cannot therefore be explained by explicit binding and reflect instead the presence of implicit binding.

Another alternative account to implicit binding posits that the crucial difference between the same-object and different-object conditions is due to differential priming in the two conditions.[4] This alternative priming hypothesis assumes that RM sees only one word, either the coloured word, on half the trials, or the white word, on the other half. In the different-object condition, when RM sees the (consistent) coloured word, there is facilitation; when he sees the (inconsistent) white word, there is interference. In the same-object condition, however, when RM sees the (inconsistent) coloured word, there is interference, but in addition this word's colour primes the name of the white word (same as colour name), which activates the conflicting colour white, thereby further slowing the RTs. When he sees the (consistent) white word, it facilitates the response but also primes the colour, which activates the (inconsistent) coloured word, thus slowing the RTs. Overall, the same-object condition produces slower RTs than the different-object condition. To summarize, this account posits that only one word (either coloured or white) is perceived in the different-object condition; in the same-object condition, however, although only one word is perceived at first, the other word is also activated through priming, which strengthens the interference.

EXPERIMENT 2

To test the "priming account", we changed the *consistent* colour-words to neutral words in the Stroop task. That is, in the same-object condition, the coloured word was inconsistent with the colour response (e.g. word BROWN displayed in green), while the other word was a neutral adjective (e.g. the word SHORT displayed in grey; see below). In the different-object condition, the coloured word was a neutral adjective (e.g. the word SHORT displayed in green), while the other word was inconsistent with the response (e.g. the word BROWN displayed in grey). Because there were no consistent words in this version of the Stroop task, no priming could occur.

By the time we conducted this test in March 1996, RM's vision had improved substantially, despite his having suffered a subdural frontal haematoma in June 1995. In particular, RM's explicit conjunction performance was above chance

[4]We thank Anne Treisman for pointing out this possibility

even with exposure durations of only 15 msec. To bring his explicit conjunction performance to chance, we changed the display as follows: (1) The words were presented on a white background, with the non-coloured (previously white) word displayed in grey; (2) the colours were less saturated; (3) the brightness of the coloured words was roughly matched to the brightness of the grey words.

These changes also allowed us to test another alternative account.[5] With displays similar to our original displays (saturated coloured words and white words on a black background), when RM reported the white word to be coloured, on a few occasions he also reported the colour to be paler (Lynn Robertson, personal communication). These reports suggested that, perhaps when RM perceived the white word as coloured, the white made the colour appear less saturated, diluting the Stroop effects: A coloured word conjoined with a saturated colour may facilitate or interfere more with the response than might a white word perceived to be conjoined with a less saturated colour. According to this account (the "dilution account"), the difference between the same-object and different-object conditions could have been caused by the dilution of Stroop effects through explicit binding (though not necessarily correct binding; that is, of the coloured word with a saturated colour on one half of trials, and of the white word with a less saturated colour on the other half of trials), rather than by implicit binding of the coloured word with its colour.

Method

Design. In this experiment, we were mainly concerned with testing the difference between the same-object and different-object conditions. However, to keep this experiment as similar as possible to Experiment 1, trials from the other two conditions—both-objects-inconsistent and neither-object-inconsistent (i.e. both words neutral adjectives)—were also included.

Materials and Apparatus. The materials and apparatus were the same as used in Experiment 1, except that the background was white, the colours were less saturated, and the non-coloured word (previously displayed in white) was shown in grey, roughly matching the brightness of the coloured word. As explained above, trials in the same-object condition were composed of one inconsistent word, displayed in colour, and one neutral word, displayed in grey; in the different-object condition, the inconsistent word was displayed in grey, whereas the neutral word was coloured. Other than the conjunction of words with colours, these two conditions were identical in all other respects (i.e. component features and the response).

[5]We thank Lynn Robertson for pointing out this possibility

Procedure. The procedure was the same as in Experiment 1. That is, the Stroop blocks were interleaved with the explicit conjunction control task, where RM had to report the coloured word. Only those Stroop blocks which were paired with explicit conjunction performance at chance were included in the analysis; if the explicit conjunctions were above chance, the paired preceding Stroop block was rejected, and the exposure durations for the next paired block were reduced.

RM's verbal RTs to name the colour were recorded with a microphone.

Results and Discussion

Fifteen paired Stroop–control blocks were run, of which 11 satisfied the requirement of chance performance on the explicit control task. As before, explicit conjunctions were considered to be at chance if the accuracy of the coloured word report was between 42 and 54%.[6] These 11 blocks were entered into the analysis, while the other 4 blocks were rejected.

The mean exposure duration in these blocks was 83 msec (median 75 msec; range 75–105 msec), or about twice as fast as the exposure durations in Experiment 1. In the explicit control task, RM named the coloured word 47% of the time, and 48% of the time he named the grey word, $t(10) = 0.4$, $p = .7$. Thus, RM was at chance on explicit conjunctions: 95% of his responses were of words which were present in the display (5% were intrusion errors), but only half of these responses were of the correct coloured word.

For each of the 11 paired Stroop blocks, RM's median RTs in the same-object and different-object conditions were calculated for correct colour responses only. With the changed displays and much shorter exposure durations, RM's colour report was 86% correct, a 10% decrease in accuracy compared to Experiment 1. Only the correct responses were entered into the analysis. RM's RTs in the same-object condition (1207 msec) were slower than in the different-object condition (1173 msec), but this difference did not reach significance, $t(10) = 1.39$, $p = .10$ (one-tailed). The fact that this comparison was not significant was surprising, considering that his RTs in the same-object condition were slower than in the different-object condition in 9 of the 11 blocks. An inspection of the distribution of the differences showed two outliers, one at each end of the distribution. We therefore conducted a non-parametric statistical test, the sign test, which showed the median difference of 38 msec between the same-object and different-object conditions (9 of 11) to be signifi-

[6]There were no blocks where explicit conjunctions were 55–58% correct, but there were two blocks where RM named the coloured word on 42% of trials.

cant, $p = .03$ (one-tailed).[7] We conclude that RM did show the predicted difference of slower RTs in the same-object than in the different-object case, supporting our hypothesis that RM has implicit conjunction information in the absence of explicit access to this knowledge.

Discussion

The results of this experiment support the implicit binding hypothesis: RM was slower in the same-object than in the different-object condition, while he was at chance for naming the coloured word. The alternative priming and dilution accounts predicted no difference between these two conditions, and are thus inconsistent with these findings. Nonetheless, the observed difference was smaller than in Experiment 1. It may be that priming, or dilution of Stroop effects, or both contributed to the large difference we found in the earlier version of this experiment. However, there are at least three other reasons for this reduction. First, in Experiment 2, the difference reflects *only interference*—there is more interference from the inconsistent word in the same-object than in the different-object condition. In contrast, in Experiment 1, this difference reflects *the sum of facilitation* from the consistent word *and interference* from the inconsistent word, both of which are larger for the coloured than the white word (i.e. facilitation is large for the consistent coloured word in the different-object condition than for the consistent white word in the same-object condition, and interference is larger for the inconsistent coloured word in the same-object condition than for the inconsistent white word in the different-object condition). Second, the much shorter exposure durations and less saturated colours made the task more difficult for RM overall, evidenced by much longer RTs (400 msec on average) and increased intrusion rates (for both colours and words), which reduced the number of observations per cell, thereby reducing the power of these tests. Third, the much longer RTs might also be responsible for the decrease in the size of the difference.

GENERAL DISCUSSION

Our results provide evidence for a dissociation between implicit and explicit knowledge of visual attribute binding. When asked to name the colour of the coloured word, RM showed more interference when the inconsistent word was conjoined with the colour in the same object than when the inconsistent word constituted a different object, despite the fact that the words and colours were exactly the same in the two cases. Yet, he could not say which of the two words

[7] If we exclude the two outliers (one at each end of the distribution), the mean difference between the same-object and the difference-object conditions is 42 msec, and is significant by a t-test as well, $t(8) = 3.3$, $p = .005$ (one-tailed).

was coloured. These findings indicate that RM did have the correct binding information implicitly, despite his lack of awareness of that information. Furthermore, they suggest that the parietal lobes (or at least the areas damaged in RM, which include primarily Brodmann's areas 39 and 7, but possibly also parts of areas 19 and 5) are not critical for all types of binding; in particular, while explicit binding may require parietal involvement, implicit binding seems to depend on earlier areas of the visual pathway.

Two questions remain: (1) What do we mean when we say RM has implicit binding information? (2) What is required to make this binding information explicit? There are two possible answers to the first question. Feature integration theory allows for features to be bound in early vision, after which they are analysed in separate modules, and finally reconjoined through focused attention to an object's location (Treisman, 1988), specified in the master map of locations in the parietal lobe (Friedman-Hill et al., 1995). Indeed, the existence of the McCollough effect (McCollough, 1965) when attention is tied up during adaptation shows that some features (orientation and colour) are bound very early on without attention (Houck and Hoffman, 1986). This kind of early binding could depend on cells in V1 which respond to particular combinations of colours and orientations (e.g. Leventhal et al., 1995). Thus, there are at least two levels at which features may be conjoined: One in early processing, which does not require attention, and one in later processing, which, according to the theory, does require attention. Implicit binding could exist at either of these levels.

Yet, for Stroop interference to occur, the conflicting word has to be recognized. It is very unlikely that stimuli as complex as words would be recognized in V1; certainly, word recognition requires processing beyond V1. Thus, the implicit conjunctions observed in our experiment cannot occur at this level. But how can such "high-level" conjunctions arise? One possibility is that features may be processed separately after the initial joint coding in V1 (see Treisman, 1988), but once the features are coded in their specialized functional modules, they become (implicitly) bound through links between those modules, with common location specifying which features are part of one object. The primate visual cortex is composed of many different areas, with many forward, backward and lateral connections between them (Felleman & Van Essen, 1991). On this account, these connections would facilitate binding at an implicit level without the involvement of the parietal lobes and the master map of locations, which is hypothesized to be represented there.

The other possibility is that the features which are originally bound in V1 never do come apart and are simply analysed together through most stages of processing. There is evidence to suggest that some areas which were once thought to be specialized for analysis of a particular feature dimension (e.g. V4 for colour; Zeki, 1980) are actually involved in much more complex processing (e.g. Ferrera, Rudolph, & Maunsell, 1994; Schein & Desimone, 1990; Schiller,

1995; Schiller & Lee, 1991). Schiller (in press) proposes that, "each extrastriate visual area, rather than performing a unique, one-function analysis, is engaged, as are most neurons in the visual system, in many different tasks", so that the process of perceptual analysis "is performed interactively by *areas and neurons with multipurpose properties*" (emphasis added; see also Desimone & Duncan, 1995; DeYoe & Van Essen, 1988). The idea of feature conjunctions being processed together, without them coming apart, is consistent with this view.[8]

But what is required to make the implicit binding information explicit? The results of Friedman-Hill et al. (1995) showing that RM has gross impairments in spatial localization suggest that accurate localization of objects, mediated by focused attention, may be necessary to accomplish this task. Many studies have shown that attention is necessary to bind features correctly, in accord with Treisman's feature integration theory (e.g. Arguin et al., 1994; Briand & Klein, 1987; Eglin et al., 1989; Prinzmetal, Presti, & Posner, 1986; Treisman & Gelade, 1980; Treisman & Schmidt, 1982; but see also Nakayama & Silverman, 1986). To the extent that RM has a deficit in reporting the correct conjunction information (i.e. explicit conjunctions), his deficit would appear to be due to an attentional impairment. On the other hand, we showed that an accurate representation of these conjunctions does exist at some level in his visual system. What, then, are the implications of this finding for feature integration theory?

To answer this question, we need to consider the extent of RM's attentional impairment. If his attentional processing is completely compromised by the lesions, or is partially operational but overtaxed by the brief exposure durations, then our results would suggest that attention is not necessary for feature integration *per se*. Rather, the role of attention would then be to make the already existing implicit conjunctions explicit. This possibility is consistent with feature integration theory only to the extent that both see attention as a binding mechanism, since it further specifies that binding is pre-attentive and attention only serves to make the binding explicit.

It is possible, however, that despite RM's brain damage and the short exposure durations, he may actually have some attentional resources left intact. These residual resources could be sufficient to create the implicit conjunctions we observed but not sufficient to make them explicit. In other words, the amount

[8]One potential problem for this proposal is the existence of illusory conjunctions, both in normal subjects (Treisman & Schmidt, 1982) and in RM's explicit conjunction tasks. A possible solution is that explicit binding requires an additional and separate process, beyond the processing required for implicit integration. This mechanism in RM is either damaged or disconnected from those parts of visual cortex which contain the implicit information about conjunctions. When illusory conjunctions occur in normal subjects, the process is not impaired but is stressed by heavy attentional load (divided attention). It remains to be seen whether normals will also show implicit binding under conditions where explicit binding does not occur or is incorrect.

or strength of available attentional resources would determine whether an implicitly perceived conjunction becomes a consciously accessible one. This possibility is also consistent with Treisman's theory. The only problem is that the theory specifies that accurate localization is necessary for feature integration, whereas we showed that RM can implicitly bind features correctly, despite gross impairments in spatial localization. Indeed, Friedman-Hill et al. (1995) propose that *explicit* localization is necessary for correct binding.

Although we did not undertake an extensive assessment of RM's spatial abilities with our displays, we did run two short localization tests, one at the end of each experiment. In the first test, we asked RM to indicate which of the two words, top or bottom, was coloured as well as to name the colour of the coloured word. For this task, the displays consisted of the neutral word displays (i.e. those used for the explicit control task in Experiment 1). The exposure duration was set to 210 msec, which was the longest exposure duration used in the implicit–explicit conjunction task. RM named the correct location on only 12 of 27 (44%) trials,[9] but named the correct colour on 26 of 27 (96%) trials. In the second test, we asked RM to report the coloured word and say whether it was the top or the bottom word. Here we used the neutral word displays of Experiment 2 and set the exposure duration to 75 msec, the median duration used in that experiment. RM was close to chance on both responses: He named the coloured word on 12 of 23 (52%) trials and the white word on 9 of 23 (39%) trials. Of the trials where he named the coloured word correctly, he localized it correctly on 5 of 12 (42%) trials; if we conditionalize his localization performance on the word he reported (whether coloured or white), his accuracy at localizing it remained unchanged (10/23 trials, or 43%). These data are consistent with the results reported by Friedman-Hill et al. (1995), who found that RM was at chance for deciding whether one letter was above or below (or to the right or left of) another at much longer exposure durations.

Thus, RM was able implicitly to bind features correctly without explicit location information. Nonetheless, to the extent that feature integration theory does not require *explicit* spatial localization for the correct binding of features, our data can be accommodated within this framework. Although our two short localization tests and the results of Friedman-Hill et al. (1995) show that RM's spatial localization is severely disrupted, all of these experiments used explicit measures. Indeed, Robertson, Treisman and Friedman-Hill (1995) tested RM on a spatial version of the Stroop task and found evidence for implicit spatial processing, despite near chance performance on explicit report of an object's location. It appears that implicit spatial information may be sufficient to support

[9]In this task, RM made many responses such as "bottom-right" or "bottom-left", although the words were displayed one above the other and centred. Such responses were counted as correct if, as in this example, the coloured word was the bottom one.

implicit binding, but it remains to be seen whether it can also support explicit binding. The results of Friedman-Hill et al. (1995) suggest that this may be the case: Whereas RM was more than 80% accurate on an explicit conjunction task at exposure durations of 500 msec, he was at chance on localizing (explicitly) one letter with respect to another at exposure durations which were twice as long. However, more direct tests are required to determine the precise role of implicit and explicit location information in both types of binding.

To summarize, our results are consistent with the notion that attention serves to bind features, but the precise role of attention in binding needs further clarification. We have suggested two possibilites: The first account suggests that attention works to make implicit binding explicit (with integration accomplished without attention) and the second proposes that all binding is dependent on attention, but a certain minimum of resources (and perhaps explicit localization) are necessary to make this information consciously accessible. A third possibility is that implicit and explicit binding are mediated by different attentional mechanisms. Clearly, the notion of pre-attentive binding of high-level visual attributes, such as word identity and colour (i.e. the first account), is not consistent with feature integration theory, but further research is necessary to determine which of these alternative accounts is correct.

One more question deserves consideration. It is possible that our implicit binding results may be accounted for by the standard Stroop effect. Perhaps RM processed all the features pre-attentively, and then, on the basis of colour, restricted his attentional window to the coloured word. That word would then have a higher activation than the white word, and would therefore produce more interference. According to this account, RM took longer to name the colour in the same-object condition than in the different-object condition, because in the first case the coloured word was inconsistent with the response, but consistent in the other. But if RM was able to narrow down his processing to the coloured word only, so that it was more strongly activated than the white word, he should have been able to use this information in the explicit conjunction task to report the coloured word more often than the white word. Yet his chance performance in the explicit task suggests that he was unable to do that. This presents a paradox if one assumes that implicit and explicit binding rely on the same underlying representation. In such a case, if the explicit task has a well-defined probability of guessing by chance (and equal to the guessing probability in the implicit task), any information evident in the implicit task should be available to support better than chance guessing on the explicit task. In our experiment, the guessing probabilities were matched in the two tasks. As such, these data argue against the notion that the same representation underlies both implicit and explicit information, with the only difference being the quality of the information represented (cf. Farah, 1994; Farah, Monheit, & Wallace, 1991). Instead, we suggest that implicit and explicit binding may rely on qualitatively distinct representations.

Finally, why should the visual system represent conjunctions in two ways? One possibility is that there is a limit on how many bindings (and separate objects) can be represented *explicitly* at any one time in the visual system, and implicit bindings may provide a way to bypass this capacity limit. Another possibility is that implicit binding is used for object recognition, carried out in the ventral pathway (e.g. Mishkin et al., 1983), whereas explicit binding may make this information available to other functional domains (e.g. action, language), such that the system as a whole can use it for goal-directed action (Baars, 1988).

The last point of this Discussion concerns the relationship between attention, in particular feature binding, and awareness. Many scholars often assume a causal relationship between attention and awareness (e.g. Crick and Koch, 1990a,b; Posner et al., 1984). According to Crick and Koch (1990a,b), visual awareness arises from the workings of an attentional mechanism responsible for feature binding. Our present results show that correct binding information may exist at some level in the visual system at which it is not yet consciously accessible. Therefore, it seems that feature binding alone is insufficient for conscious perception of correct conjunctions.

In summary, we showed that RM, who has bilateral parietal damage, has an accurate representation of feature conjunctions of which he is unaware. We conclude that the parietal lobes (at least those parts damaged in RM) are not critical for implicit binding, although they may be involved in constructing explicit representations of feature conjunctions.

REFERENCES

Arguin, M., Cavanagh, P., & Joannette, Y. (1994). Visual feature integration with an attention deficit. *Brain and Cognition, 24*, 44–56.

Baars, B.J. (1988). *A cognitive theory of consciousness*. New York: Cambridge University Press.

Baylis, G.C., Driver, J., Baylis, L.L., & Rafal, R.D. (1994). Reading of letters and words in a patient with Balint's Syndrome. *Neuropsychologia, 32*, 1273–1286.

Berti, A., & Rizzolatti, G. (1992). Visual processing without awareness: Evidence from unilateral neglect. *Journal of Cognitive Neuroscience, 4*, 345–351.

Bisiach, E., Luzzatti, C., & Perani, D. (1979). Unilateral neglect, representational schema and consciousness. *Brain, 102*, 609–618.

Briand, K.A., & Klein, R.M. (1987). Is Posner's "beam" the same as Treisman's "glue": On the relation between visual orienting and feature integration theory. *Journal of Experimental Psychology: Human Perception and Performance, 13*, 228–241.

Cohen, A., & Rafal, R.D. (1991). Attention and feature integration: Illusory conjunctions in a patient with a parietal lobe lesion. *Psychological Science, 2*, 106–110.

Colby, C.L. (1991). The neuroanatomy and neurophysiology of attention. *Journal of Child Neurology, 6* (suppl.), S90–S118.

Corbetta, M., Miezin, F.M., Dobmeyer, S., Shulman, G.L., & Petersen, S.E. (1990). Attentional modulation of neural processing of shape, color, and velocity in humans. *Science, 248*, 1556–1559.

Corbetta, M., Miezin, F.M., Shulman, G.L., & Petersen, S.E. (1993). A PET study of visuospatial attention. *Journal of Neuroscience, 13*, 1202–1226.

Corbetta, M., Shulman, G.L., Miezin, F.M., & Petersen, S.E. (1995). Superior parietal cortex activation during spatial attention shifts and visual feature conjunction. *Science, 270*, 802–805.

Coslett, H.B., & Saffran, E. (1991). Simultanagnosia: To see but not two see. *Brain, 114*, 1523–1545.

Crick, F., & Koch, C. (1990a). Towards a neurobiological theory of consciousness. *The Neurosciences, 2*, 263–275.

Crick, F., & Koch, C. (1990b). Some reflections on visual awareness. *Cold Spring Harbor Symposia on Quantitative Biology, LV*, 953–962.

Desimone, R., & Duncan, J. (1995). Neural mechanisms of selective visual attention. *Annual Review of Neuroscience, 18*, 193–222.

DeYoe, E.A., & Van Essen, D.C. (1988). Concurrent processing streams in monkey visual cortex. *Trends in Neurosciences, 11*, 219–226.

Duncan, J. (1984). Selective attention and the organization of visual information. *Journal of Experimental Psychology: General, 113*, 501–517.

Eglin, M., Robertson, L.C., & Knight, R.T. (1989). Visual search performance in the neglect syndrome. *Journal of Cognitive Neuroscience, 1*, 372–385.

Farah, M. (1994). Visual perception and visual awareness after brain damage: A tutorial overview. In C. Umiltà & M. Moscovitch (Eds), *Attention and performance XV: Conscious and nonconscious information processing* (pp. 37–76). Cambridge, MA: MIT Press.

Farah, M.J., Monheit, M.A., & Wallace, M.A. (1991). Unconscious perception of "extinguished" visual stimuli: Reassessing the evidence. *Neuropsychologia, 29*, 949–958.

Felleman, D.J., & Van Essen, D.C. (1991). Distributed hierarchical processing in the primate cerebral cortex. *Cerebral Cortex, 1*, 1–47.

Ferrera, V.P., Rudolph, K.K., & Maunsell, J.H.R. (1994). Responses of neurons in the parietal and temporal visual pathways during a motion task. *Journal of Neuroscience, 14*, 6171–6186.

Friedman-Hill, S.R., Robertson, L.C., & Treisman, A. (1995). Parietal contributions to visual feature binding: Evidence from a patient with bilateral lesions. *Science, 296*, 853–855.

Houck, M.R., & Hoffman, J.E. (1986). Conjunction of color and form without attention: Evidence for an orientation-contingent color aftereffect. *Journal of Experimental Psychology: Human Perception and Performance, 12*, 186–199.

Hunt, S. (1994). MacProbe: A Macintosh-based experimenter's workstation for the cognitive sciences. *Behavior Research Methods, Instruments and Computers, 26*, 345–351.

Kahneman, D., & Henik, A. (1981). Perceptual organization and attention. In M. Kubovy & J.R. Pomerantz (Eds), *Perceptual organization* (pp. 181–211). Hillsdale, NJ: Lawrence Erlbaum Associates Inc.

Köhler, S., Kapur, S., Moscovitch, M., Winocur, G., & Houle, S. (1995). Dissociation of pathways for object and spatial vision: A PET study in humans. *NeuroReport, 6*, 1865–1868.

Kučera, H., & Francis, W.N. (1967). *Computational analysis of present-day American-English.* Providence, RI: Brown University Press.

Leventhal, A.G., Thompson, K.G., Liu, D., Zhou, Y., & Ault, S.J. (1995). Concomitant sensitivity to orientation, direction, and color of cells in layers 2, 3, and 4 of monkey striate cortex. *Journal of Neuroscience, 15*, 1808–1818.

Livingstone, M., & Hubel, D. (1988). Segregation of form, color, movement, and depth: Anatomy, physiology, and perception. *Science, 240*, 740–749.

MacLeod, C.M. (1991). Half a century of research on the Stroop effect: An integrative review. *Psychological Bulletin, 109*, 163–203.

Maunsell, J.H.R. (1995). The brain's visual world: Representation of visual targets in cerebral cortex. *Science, 270*, 764–769.

McCollough, C. (1965). Color adaptation of edge-detectors in the human visual system. *Science, 149*, 1115–1116.

Mishkin, M., Ungerleider, L.G., & Macko, K.A. (1983). Object vision and spatial vision. Two cortical pathways. *Trends of Neurosciences, 6*, 414–417.

Nakayama, K., & Silverman, G.H. (1986). Serial and parallel processing of visual feature conjunctions. *Nature, 320*, 264–265.

Posner, M.I., Walker, J.A., Friedrich, F.J., & Rafal, R.D. (1984). Effects of parietal injury on covert orienting of attention. *Journal of Neuroscience, 4*, 1863–1874.

Prinzmetal, W., Presti, D.E., & Posner, M.I. (1986). Does attention affect visual feature integration? *Journal of Experimental Psychology: Human Perception and Performance, 12*, 361–370.

Rafal, R. (1996). Balint's syndrome. In T.E. Feinberg & M.J. Farah (Eds), *Behavioral neurology and neuropsychology* (pp. 337–356). New York: McGraw-Hill.

Rafal, R., & Robertson, L. (1995). The neurology of visual attention. In Gazzaniga (Ed.), *Cognitive neurosciences* (pp. 625–648). Cambridge, MA: MIT Press.

Rizzolatti, G., & Berti, A. (1993). Neural mechanisms of spatial neglect. In I.H. Robertson & J.C. Marshall (Eds), *Unilateral neglect: Clinical and experimental studies* (pp. 87–105). Hillsdale, NJ: Lawrence Erlbaum Associates Inc.

Robetson, L.C., Treisman, A., & Friedman-Hill, S. (1995). Spatial deficits: Effects on feature integration. Paper presented at the *36th Annual Meeting of the Psychonomic Society*, Los Angeles, CA, November.

Schein, S.J., & Desimone, R. (1990). Spectral properties of V4 neurons in the macaque. *Journal of Neuroscience, 10*, 3369–3389.

Schiller, P.H. (1995). Effect of lesions in visual cortical area V4 on the recognition of transformed objects. *Nature, 376*, 342–344.

Schiller, P.H. (in press). Past and present ideas about how the visual scene is analyzed by the brain. *Cerebral Cortex.*

Schiller, P.H., & Lee, K. (1991). The role of the primate extrastriate area V4 in vision. *Science, 251*, 1251–1253.

Stroop, J.R. (1935). Studies of interference in serial verbal reactions. *Journal of Experimental Psychology, 18*, 643–662.

Treisman, A. (1988). Features and objects: The Fourteenth Bartlett Memorial Lecture. *Quarterly Journal of Experimental Psychology, 40A*, 201–237.

Treisman, A., & Gelade, G. (1980). A feature-integration theory of attention. *Cognitive Psychology, 12*, 97–136.

Treisman, A., & Schmidt, H. (1982). Illusory conjunctions in the perception of objects. *Cognitive Psychology, 14*, 107–141.

Weiskrantz, L., Barbur, J.L., & Sahraie, A. (1995). Parameters affecting conscious versus unconscious visual discrimination with damage to the visual cortex (V1). *Proceedings of the National Academy of Sciences, 92*, 6122–6126.

Wojciulik, E., Kanwisher, N., & Driver, J. (1997). Activation of intraparietal sulci in nonspatial visual search. Poster presented at the *Annual Meeting of the Society for Cognitive Neuroscience*, Boston, MA, March.

Young, A.W., Hellawell, D., & DeHaan, E.H.F. (1988). Cross-domain semantic priming in normal subjects and a prosopagnosic patient. *Quarterly Journal of Experimental Psychology, 40A*, 561–580.

Zeki, S.M. (1980). The representation of colours in the cerebral cortex. *Nature, 284*, 412–418.

VISUAL COGNITION, 1998, *5* (1/2), 183–216

Event Files: Evidence for Automatic Integration of Stimulus–Response Episodes

Bernhard Hommel

Max-Planck-Institute for Psychological Research, Cognition and Action, München, Germany

One of the main functions that visual attention serves in perception and action is feature binding; that is, integrating all information that belongs to an object. The outcome of this integration has been called "object file", a hypothetical memory structure coding episodic combinations of stimulus features. Action-oriented approaches to attention, however, suggest that such a purely perceptual or perceptually derived structure may be incomplete: If attention subserves action control, object files may include action-related information as well. That is, feature binding may not be restricted to stimulus features but also include features of the responses made to the respective stimulus. In three experiments, subjects performed simple, already prepared left- or right-key responses (R1) to the mere presence of "Go" signals (S1) that varied randomly in form, colour and location. Shortly after the prepared response, a binary choice reaction (R2) to the form or colour of a second stimulus (S2) was made. The results show that benefits due to stimulus-feature repetitions (S1–S2) interact: Form repetition only facilitates performance if colour is also repeated, and repeating the relevant stimulus feature (form or colour) only facilitates performance if stimulus location is repeated. This can be taken as evidence for object-file formation. But there was also evidence for bindings between stimulus and response features: Repetition benefits associated with both the relevant stimulus feature and stimulus location depended on response repetition. This suggests that object files represent only one component of more complex "event files" that link information about stimulus and response aspects of an experienced episode.

Requests for reprints should be addressed to Bernhard Hommel, Max-Planck-Institute for Psychological Research, Cognition and Action, Leopoldstr. 24, D-80802 München, Germany. E-mail: hommel@mpipf.muenchen.mpg.de

I would like to thank Benjamin Beyer, Irmgard Hagen and Albrecht Schnabel for their assistance in collecting the data; Marie Accardo for checking the English; John Henderson, Werner X. Schneider and an anonymous reviewer for helpful comments; and Sabine Maasen and Werner X. Schneider for organising a stimulating conference.

INTRODUCTION

When we look around, we see objects and events, made up of particular combinations of particular features, located in particular positions in space. How does the cognitive system deal with the information delivered by vision and the other senses? As we now know, visual information is registered in various features maps distributed throughout the visual cortex (e.g. Cowey, 1985; DeYoe & Van Essen, 1988), not speaking of the information propagated directly to the colliculus superior, to the frontal eye fields, and so forth. How do the systems involved in perception "know" which feature belongs to which object? According to which rules and principles are codes of these features related to each other?

There are several answers to this question and most have a great deal to do with location. As a first approximation, Treisman (1988; Treisman & Gelade, 1980) suggested that visuospatial attention serves to integrate the information belonging to one object. Visual attention is assumed to work like a spotlight with an adjustable size that can be directed to certain locations on, and moved across, a so-called "master map of locations". This location map, which, according to Treisman (1993), might be fed by the dorsal "where" path suggested by Ungerleider and Mishkin (1982), is connected to all (or at least many of) the other, also spatially organised, representational maps, which code simple features, such as form, colour and orientation, and thus could represent a stage in Ungerleider and Mishkin's ventral "what" path. Focusing attention onto a master-map location results in the integration of all features registered in the corresponding locations of the connected representational maps. Based on the assumption that corresponding map locations represent features from the same location in the visual world, and given that features belonging to the same object usually occupy the same environmental location, such an integration mechanism could well serve to integrate object-specific information. If all we needed to know about our visual environment was whether or not registered features belong to a common object, this integration-by-attending-to-location mechanism would be all that we needed.

But what do we need to know about features and objects? Many of the possible answers to this question have to do with orientation and anticipation: If we know that two or more features belong to the same object, we can discriminate between several objects sharing certain features; or expect the presence of one feature of an object when seeing another; or anticipate what will happen to one by observing another; or experience object constancy despite changes over time in some of the features. Yet, none of these functions could be served by a merely temporary integration through attending: As soon as the attentional spotlight moves to the next location, all the work would be lost again. Thus, what we also need is some kind of memory that preserves the outcome of feature integration over time.

Object Files

Kahneman and Treisman (1984; Kahneman, Treisman, & Gibbs, 1992; Treisman, 1993) have suggested a mechanism that may serve the function of preserving the products of feature-integration processes. Building upon Treisman's feature-integration theory, they assume that the result of the integration process, possibly enriched by long-term knowledge, is temporarily stored in what they call an "object file". Object files thus contain (or represent), among other things, knowledge about feature conjunctions that specify the corresponding object, together with information about the current object location. Once formed, object files do not allow for cross-referencing of object-specific features, but keep track of objects in spite of changes in their location or in some of their features over time: If the changes are small enough or only refer to relative location, new visual events (i.e. changes in features or feature values in a particular location) do not require the formation of a new file, just an update of the old file. While forming a new file may correspond to the experience of a novel object, file updating could correspond to the experience of object reappearance, hence underlying perceived object constancy and continuity.

There are at least two types of experimental evidence to support the object-file approach—the effect of "negative priming" and the "reviewing effect". Negative priming was first reported by Allport, Tipper and Chmiel (1985; for reviews, see Fox, 1995; May, Kane, & Hasher, 1995). Allport et al. had their subjects work through lists or sequences of superimposed pairs of letters or pictures. One member of each pair was the to-be-named target, printed in a particular target colour (e.g. red), while the other member served as a distractor printed in a different colour (e.g. green). Importantly, the trials on which the current target matched the preceding distractor were associated with slower reaction times (RTs) than trials without such a match. One interpretation offered by Allport et al. (1985) and recently revived by Park and Kanwisher (1994) comes close to the object-file concept. It holds that, in a given trial, the features of target and distractor are integrated (i.e. linked cross-domains) automatically and separately. If, in the next trial, the available features combine in the same fashion, integration is easier or faster for these than for new combinations, which require the formation of new cross-domain links. Obviously, this is the same idea underlying the object-file concept, only that integration here is assumed to precede rather than to follow attentional orienting (Allport et al., 1985).

Further evidence for the existence of object files has been reported by Kahneman et al. (1992). They presented their subjects with a sequence of two displays, a multi-letter preview or prime display, which did not require any response, and a single-letter probe display, which required naming the letter. In some trials, the letter that eventually appeared in the probe display was already part of the prime display. If this was the case, the responses were sometimes, but not always, faster than when the probe letter did not match any one of the prime letters. However, this preview effect was also much larger when the matching prime letter appeared in the same (relative or absolute) location as the probe letter. The authors interpreted this finding as evidence that prime-letter identities and locations were integrated into letter-specific object files. If the particular identity-location conjunction of the probe letter matched one of the object files formed during the preview, integration was faster or even superfluous. This produced an "object-specific preview benefit", which Kahneman et al. contrast with the much weaker "non-specific preview benefit" that occurred if prime and probe matched as to identity, but not location. Object-specific preview benefits have also been reported by Henderson (1994; Henderson & Anes, 1994), although in this studies considerable non-specific benefits were also found.

Non-specific and specific preview effects have different theoretical implications. Non-specific effects are usually attributed to the priming of "type" representations; that is, stored descriptions of object features in (semantic?) long-term memory. Only one code or representation is assumed to exist for every feature in the world, so that, if a feature is shared by more than one object in the field, the activation of a code does not unambiguously identify its source. Object-specific effects, in contrast, as observed in negative-priming and preview tasks, imply that encountering a visual event does not only result in the priming of object types, but also in separate episodic bindings of the features belonging to the objects perceived (i.e. object files). If the same object appears again and, thus, the particular feature conjunction is repeated, the corresponding object file is retrieved, or revived, and updated. If, in contrast, a novel object appears, the object-specific features are integrated and information about their conjunction is stored in a newly created object file. Importantly for the present study, the latter case should be associated with slower processing times than the former.

Event Files

A number of studies have demonstrated binding effects (i.e. effects of feature-conjunction repetitions versus non-repetitions) in a variety of tasks with different kinds of stimuli and responses. For instance, evidence for the binding of visual stimulus features has been reported for form and colour (Allport et al., 1985), form and location (Kahneman et al., 1992) and colour and location (Tipper, Weaver, & Houghton, 1994), independent of whether or not the prime stimulus or stimuli must be "selected-against" alternative stimuli (Park & Kanwisher, 1994). However, until now, binding effects have only been sought between (visual) stimulus features, not between stimulus and response features.

Considering that the object-file concept was originally invoked to account for the integration of distributed sensory information, this is hardly surprising; yet, there are some indications that object files are not purely perceptual or object-related structures, but include action-related information as well.

First, Treisman (1992) reported experiments in which subjects learned to perform certain tasks with, or mental operations on, a number of nonsense patterns. Although performance improved with practice, there was little transfer to other tasks using the same patterns. As Treisman argued, this may indicate that repeated experience with new objects—and, thus, repeated formation of object files for these objects—leads to the integration of task- or response-related information, so that the files or traces of the overlearned patterns can no longer be used if the responses change.

Second, Danzinger and Robertson (1994) conducted a series of negative-priming experiments using a variant of Allport and co-workers' (1985) dual-letter design. Subjects were presented with pairs of letters—one of two possible target letters together with one of two possible distractors—and were asked to respond manually to the identity of the target. Performance was better if the colour or the location of the target (both irrelevant stimulus features) was repeated rather than alternated, but this repetition benefit was mainly restricted to cases where target identity was also repeated—hence, there was evidence for the integration of stimulus features, as expected from an object-file perspective. In a further experiment, two target letters were assigned to each response key, so that the effects of identity repetition and of response repetition could be separated. Although the relevant statistical tests are not reported, the results suggest that response alternation reduced the beneficial effect of stimulus-feature repetition. Again, this may indicate that stimulus and response features were integrated into a common episodic structure.

Based on these observations, it may be that, somewhat paradoxically, there is more in an object file than information about an object. In fact, if object files were really the basis of our episodic long-term memory, it would make sense not only to link codes of sensory features common to an object, but also to store what this feature conjunction is useful for, what action this object affords. If so, the original object-file concept may in fact be too narrow and may need to be merged with, or even replaced by, the concept of an "event file"; that is, an episodic memory trace linking codes of features belonging to an action-relevant object with codes of features characterising the corresponding action.

Such an event-file concept stresses the possibly action-related function of stimulus-feature integration and, thus, fits well with the action-oriented approach to visual attention proposed by Allport (1987), Neumann (1990) and Van der Heijden (1992). Allport (1987) pointed out that traces of episodic object-action couplings may serve to guide action on subsequent occasions. In the same vein, Logan (1988) proposed that instances of stimulus–response combinations may be stored over time, and Henderson (1996) considered this possibility, in particular for spatial information from stimulus- and response-related maps. Until now, however, all we have is casual observations, while systematic investigations of possible event-file-formation processes are lacking. The present study was aimed to tap into these hypothetical processes to demonstrate the existence of event files and to unravel their structure.

If event files really do exist, they may take one of at least three kinds of structure. An obvious possibility is that action-related information is just another ingredient of object files, so that event files could be viewed as extended, informationally enriched object files. If so, stimulus location should be crucial in addressing the corresponding episodic structure, just as proposed originally by Kahneman et al. (1992). They assumed that location information provides the "label" that is attached to an object file, whereas information about other stimulus features—and maybe about the response as well—forms the file's "contents". This suggests that integrated response information can be accessed only if some spatial continuity of the stimulus is given; hence, response-repetition effects unfold only, or more strongly, if stimulus location is also repeated. In other words, an "extended-object-file hypothesis" predicts that effects of response repetition and of stimulus-location repetition interact in an underadditive fashion (i.e. especially good performance if both response and stimulus location is repeated).

A second possibility is that everything is integrated into a single, uniform event file. On the one hand, it is true that the results of Henderson (1994), Henderson and Anes (1994) and Kahneman et al. (1992) provide substantial support for the assumption that codes of stimulus form and location are bound together. On the other hand, these features were the only two investigated (apart from a combination of form and colour in study 6 of Kahneman et al.), so that we do not know what will happen if more features are involved, especially response-related ones. Possibly, all available stimulus and response features become interconnected, so that the emerging event file can be accessed via every feature involved, not just in the case of spatial stimulus continuity. If so, repeating a particular stimulus or response feature should produce beneficial effects only, or at least to a greater extent, if other features are repeated as well. In other words, a "uniform-event-file hypothesis" would predict a higher-order interaction of all feature-repetition effects involved, regardless of whether the feature belongs to the stimulus or to the response.

Third, event files may have a more differentiated structure. It may be that object files—whether they have a spatial "label" or not—are only part of a more complex, perhaps highly structured event file comprising both object- and action-related information. Some stimulus-feature codes may be strongly associated with codes representing stimulus location, whereas others are associated with response-related codes. Or the same code may be part of several, different episodic linkages, perhaps depending on its role or importance in the task at hand. Consequently, there may be a set of different, co-existing interactions between the effects of stimulus- and response-feature repetitions in a particular task that do not need to be further modified by a higher-order interaction. *A priori*, such a "structured-event-file hypothesis" does not allow for positive predictions of the same precision as the extended-object-file hypothesis or the uniform-event-file hypothesis; it is clear, however, that both interactions between stimulus-feature repetitions and between stimulus and response-feature repetitions should be involved.

The Task

The task used to investigate the existence and structure of event files was based on Kahneman and co-workers' (1992) preview design. The basic experimental ideal was to extend the prime–probe design of Kahneman et al. (1992) in a way that allows for a temporal coupling between the prime and a systematically varied response. To achieve an orthogonal manipulation of prime stimulus and prime-related response, however, the response should only accompany, but not depend on, the features of the prime. That is, the identity of the response should be signalled by a stimulus other than the prime.

Figure 1 shows the task resulting from these considerations. Each trial started with the presentation of a response cue, indicating which response (R1) was to be made to the prime (S1). Between the response cue and presentation of S1, ample time was given to prepare the response. Although the form, colour and location of the prime varied, subjects were only to respond to the *presence* of the (temporally predictable) prime, independently of its features. In this way,

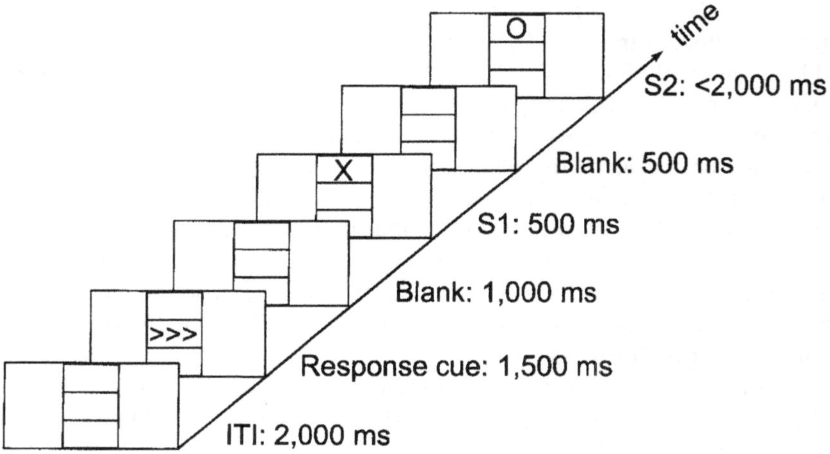

FIG. 1. Schematic illustration of the displays and the timing of events in Experiments 1–3.

any possible combination of S1 and R1 features could be realised. One second after prime presentation, the probe (S2) appeared. The probe always varied on the same dimensions as the prime, so that S1 and S2 could match or mismatch as to form, location or colour. The response to the probe (R2) was not known in advance, but was signalled by one of the S2 features (form in Experiments 1 and 3, colour in Experiment 2). That is, while R1 was a simple reaction to the presence of S1, R2 was a binary-choice reaction to the task-relevant feature of S2.

This task has several relevant characteristics. Importantly, S1 and R1 overlap in time, or at least occur in close temporal proximity, so that the preconditions for integrating stimulus and response information into a single event file are given: Temporally, S1 and R1 belong to the same event. However, the relationship between S1 and R1 features is completely arbitrary; that is, in no way task relevant or informative. Moreover, S1 is not only temporally predictable, it is also the only stimulus that appears, so that it must not be "selected-against" a distractor or alternative stimulus. That is, no single feature of S1 is to be coded or even identified to perform properly—only its presence matters. If, under such circumstances, S1 and R1 features were integrated, this would suggest a high degree of autonomy and automaticity of event integration.

EXPERIMENTS 1A AND 1B

Experiment 1 was conducted as a first test of whether response-related information is really integrated together with stimulus-related information into a common memory structure. Of the three stimulus dimensions—form, colour and location—only form was relevant to the task (i.e. to the second response); only one response dimension, location, was also task-relevant. Each stimulus dimension could take one of two values, so that form, colour and location could be repeated or alternated from S1 to S2. The same was true for the response dimension: Response location could be repeated or alternated from R1 to R2. In Experiment 1A, a third response condition was added, where no R1 was required. This single-response condition was considered to be a neutral condition for comparisons, which in the case of response repetition–alternation effects may help to decide whether repetition was beneficial or alternation was detrimental for performance.

Experiment 1 can be expected to produce three types of results that differ widely in their theoretical implications. The most obvious outcome would be main effects of repeating or alternating stimulus or response features. As already discussed, effects of this kind do not indicate the integration of feature information, but can be regarded as non-specific[1] (i.e. object- or event-unspecific) effects that may result from the priming of type representations in long-term memory.

A second outcome that was expected refers to the effects of repeating versus alternating the features for S1 and S2. The available evidence strongly suggests that different stimulus features of the same object are integrated into an object file, so that it should matter whether the particular stimulus-feature conjunction in S1 is or is not repeated. More precisely, repeating a stimulus feature should be beneficial only, or to a larger extent, if other stimulus features are also repeated. Consequently, the effects of stimulus-feature repetition were expected to interact: While repeating the particular conjunction of features from S1 to S2 should facilitate R2, repeating only some of the features should produce less benefit or none at all.

However, it is an open question whether interactions are to be found among all stimulus features, as the original object-file concept would suggest. On the one hand, previous studies have shown that form, colour and location can all participate in object-file formation, so that contributions from all of the present stimulus dimensions are possible. On the other hand, in most previous experiments, the respective dimension was relevant to the task, while only form is relevant there. Thus, the question is whether irrelevant stimulus dimensions are also integrated. As far as location is concerned, the answer seems to be yes. In the study of Kahneman et al. (1992), for instance, subjects were only asked to name a single letter in the probe display after having seen the prime—yet, naming was especially fast if both letter identity *and* relative location were repeated. Together with the very similar results of Henderson (1994: Henderson & Anes, 1994), this suggests that stimulus location information is combined with the relevant stimulus feature even if location is irrelevant to the task, just as Kahneman and co-workers' (1992) "location-label" assumption implies. Therefore, integration of form, the relevant stimulus feature and stimulus location was expected in the present experiment, and hence an interaction between form repetition and location repetition.

---

[1]Strictly speaking, the main effects of (stimulus-) feature repetition reported here, and summarized in part in Fig. 5, do not correspond exactly to—and thus cannot be compared directly with—the non-specific preview effects reported by Kahneman et al. (1992) or Henderson (1994). In the present study, each stimulus-feature repetition effect is computed across several response conditions (two to four, depending on the experiment) and several other stimulus-repetition or alternation conditions. In contrast, Kahneman et al. and Henderson only compared conditions where the target letter did not match the two or more (not responded-to) preview letters with conditions where it matched one of them in identity but not location. However, despite these differences in computational details, main effects of feature repetition do represent preview effects that are not object- or event-specific, and thus should measure the same thing (e.g. priming of feature- or dimension-specific nodes) as non-specific preview effects.

But what about non-spatial irrelevant features? According to the approach of Kahneman and Treisman (1984; Treisman, 1988), all features that belong to an object are integrated into an object file, independent of their task relevance. This would suggest that colour and form would be integrated as well as colour and location, corresponding to interactions between colour repetition and form repetition and between colour repetition and location repetition, or even a three-way interaction, as implied by the "location-label" assumption. However, the task relevance of non-spatial stimulus dimensions has been shown to affect the role of the respective feature in negative priming (Milliken, Tipper, & Weaver, 1994; Tipper et al., 1994). If at least some part of the negative priming phenomenon is due to the formation of object files (Allport et al., 1985; Park & Kanwisher, 1994), this would suggest that task relevance may also affect performance in the present experiment. Accordingly, it may be that location, but not colour, repetition effects interact with the effect of form repetition, much as the structured-event-file account implies.

A third type of expected outcome refers to the interaction between the effect of response (R1–R2) repetition versus alternation on the one hand and the effects of repeating versus alternating (S1–S2) stimulus features on the other. The basic idea pursued here is that response information may be integrated together with stimulus information into something like an event file. If so, the effect of response repetition should depend on whether or not the respective stimulus features are also repeated and vice versa. More precisely, while repeating the particular conjunction of stimulus (S1) and response (R1) features should facilitate the second response (R2), a partial repetition should produce no (at least not that much) better performance than a complete non-repetition. One may even expect partial repetitions to produce worse performance than non-repetitions: If, for instance, the combination of stimulus feature S_A and response R_X is followed by the combination of S_A and R_Y (i.e. another response), re-viewing S_A may activate the associated (by now incorrect) response R_X, thus yielding a response conflict that would not be present if S_A and R_Y had been preceded by S_B and R_X. *A priori* it is not clear whether all of the three stimulus features participate in the event-file formation. If, according to the uniform-event-file hypothesis, integration is fully non-selective, only a four-way interaction should be obtained, hence performance should be best if everything is repeated (or everything is alternated). Yet, it may also be that response information is associated with the relevant stimulus feature only (i.e. form) or with stimulus location, which is known to be a likely ingredient of object files. Accordingly, lower-order interactions involving the R1–R2 relationship were to be expected.

In the original design of the experiment, reported here as Experiment 1A, the letters X and O where used to manipulate stimulus form, as in many previous studies. However, as form was the task-relevant stimulus feature, this choice may lead to a possible confounding. Although X and O clearly differ in form, they represent familiar and nameable stimulus configurations for the subjects investigated and thus may be processed in a somewhat different way, or on a different level, than the colour or location of the stimulus. Thus, if different outcomes were obtained for form on the one hand and colour or location on the other—and this turns out to be the case—it would be difficult to tell whether this asymmetry is due to some peculiarity of form processing (or processing the task-relevant stimulus feature) or a result of using familiar symbols as stimuli. To rule out the latter possibility, a control experiment (Experiment 1B) was run with a limited number of conditions (excluding the single-response condition), where horizontal and vertical lines were used as stimuli. If possible asymmetric findings in Experiment 1A could be replicated in 1B, we would be sure that they are not due to the use of familiar symbols as relevant stimuli.

Method

Subjects. Eight paid volunteers (5 females and 3 males, aged 21–35 years) took part in Experiment 1A and another eight (7 females and 1 male, aged 23–35 years) in Experiment 1B. All reported having normal or corrected-to-normal vision, and were not familiar with the purpose of the experiment.

Apparatus and Stimuli. Both experiments were controlled by a Hewlett Packard Vectra QS20 computer, attached to an Eizo 9080i monitor via an Eizo MD-B11 graphics adaptor. From a viewing distance of about 60 cm, the subjects faced three 1.2° × 1.2° grey square outlines, vertically arranged (see Fig. 1). The stimuli were presented in red or green in the top or bottom frame. The form of the stimuli was different in the two experiments. The upper-case letters O and X (0.3° × 0.4°) were used in Experiment 1A, while a thin vertical line (0.07° × 0.6°) and a somewhat thicker horizontal line (0.3° × 0.11°) were used in Experiment 1B. The middle box, positioned at the centre of the screen, was used for response (R1) cue presentation only. The response cues were rows of three white left- or right-pointing arrows, or hyphens, indicating a left, a right or no response (R1), respectively. Responses were made by pressing the left or right of two microswitches mounted on a board with the index or middle finger of the right hand, respectively.

Procedure and Design. In a given trial, subjects made one or two responses. If required, the first response (R1) was always a simple reaction. The type of response (i.e. left or right keypress) was indicated by the response cue, which was to be carried out as soon as the first stimulus (S1) appeared. Subjects were told that there would be no systematic relationship between S1 and R1, so that they should perform the precued response at S1 onset, disregarding the form, colour and location of S1. The second response (R2)—or first, if R1 was not required—was always a binary-choice reaction to the second stimulus (S2).

The critical stimulus feature was S2 form: Half of the subjects responded to an O (Experiment 1A) or a vertical line (Experiment 1B) by pressing the left key, and to an X (Experiment 1A) or a horizontal line (Experiment 1B) by pressing the right key; the other half received the opposite mapping. Subjects were told that colour or location of S2 would be unimportant and uninformative, and hence should be ignored.

The sequence of events in each trial is illustrated in Fig. 1. After an inter-trial interval of 2000 msec, R1 was signalled by the response cue for 1500 msec, followed by a blank interval of 1000 msec. Then S1 appeared for 500 msec, followed by a further blank interval of 500 msec. If R1 was incorrect or missing, a new trial was started. Otherwise, S2 was presented and remained on until the end of the trial. The program waited until R2 was given but no longer than 2000 msec. If R1 or R2 was incorrect or missing, auditory error feedback was provided, and the trial was recorded and repeated at some random position in the remainder of the block.

In Experiment 1A, a session consisted of three blocks of 192 randomly ordered trials each, one for practice only and two experimental blocks. A short break was allowed after the first two blocks. Each block was composed of a factorial combination of S2 form (O *vs* X, corresponding to left *vs* right R2), colour (red *vs* green) and location (top *vs* bottom box), the possible relationships between S1 and S2 (i.e. repetition *vs* alternation) regarding form, colour and location, and the three possible relationships between R1 and R2 (repetition, alternation, or single response).

In Experiment 1B, a session consisted of two experimental blocks of 128 trials each, preceded by 40 randomly drawn practice trials. Each block was composed as in Experiment 1A, except that the single-response condition was dropped. That is, R2 was always preceded by a (same or different) R1.

Results

In Experiment 1A, R1 responses were missing, incorrect or anticipated (RT<100 msec) in 1.4, 1.5 and 2.0% of the trials, respectively. In Experiment 1B, the corresponding rates were 1.0, 1.0 and 0.4%. Correct R1 responses were given within 342 msec (Experiment 1A) and 376 msec (Experiment 1B) on average. R1 data were not analysed further.

Trials with missing R2 responses (Experiment 1A, 0.03%; Experiment 1B, 0.05%), or anticipations (Experiment 1A, 2.3%; Experiment 1B 0.5%), were also excluded from analysis. For the remaining data, mean RTs and proportions of errors (PEs) were calculated for each experiment as a function of the four possible relationships between the stimuli and the responses of the two subtasks; that is, according to whether the form, colour or location of S1 and S2 was repeated or alternated, and whether R2 was preceded by a same, a different or no response (See Table 1 and 2 for means). Analyses of variance (ANOVA) were performed by using a four-way design for repeated measures.

TABLE 1
Means of Mean Reaction Times (RT; in msec) and Percentages of Errors (PE) for R2 in Experiment 1A as a Function of the Relationship Between S1 and S2 and Between R1 and R2 (R2 Repeated, Alternated or Single)

	Response					
	Repeated		*Alternated*		*Single*	
Stimulus Feature Repeated	*RT*	*PE*	*RT*	*PE*	*RT*	*PE*
Neither	514	7.6	431	2.1	464	0.7
L(ocation)	510	7.3	479	0.7	495	2.2
F(orm)	488	2.9	477	1.4	516	2.2
C(olour)	543	5.5	449	0.0	474	2.1
LF	441	0.7	493	7.1	524	2.0
LC	524	1.5	488	3.2	517	1.4
FC	481	3.9	471	4.7	495	2.1
LFC	432	0.0	504	10.0	526	4.1

Reaction Times. There were only two significant main effects: One of response relation in Experiment 1A, $F(2,14) = 4.58$, $p < .05$, where responses were faster with response alternation (474 msec) than with repetition (491 msec), and slowest in the single-response condition (501 msec); and one of colour repetition in Experiment 1B, $F(1,7) = 6.09$, $p < .05$, where repeating stimulus colour yielded faster responses than alternating (447 *vs* 460 msec).

More important, however, was whether the benefit of the repetition of stimulus form, colour or location would depend on (and thus interact with) the

TABLE 2
Means of Mean Reaction Times (RT; in msec) and Percentages of Errors (PE) for R2 in Experiment 1B as a Function of the Relationship Between S1 and S2 and Between R1 and R2 (R2 Repeated or Alternated)

	Response			
	Repeated		*Alternated*	
Stimulus Feature Repeated	*RT*	*PE*	*RT*	*PE*
Neither	487	7.6	424	2.2
L(ocation)	468	4.9	442	1.5
F(orm)	466	1.5	485	9.7
C(olour)	485	3.4	408	0.0
LF	414	0.7	492	14.0
LC	477	7.2	447	6.2
FC	434	2.1	454	10.0
LFC	393	2.3	476	12.6

relationship between R1 and R2. If so, a RT benefit would be expected if the two responses were the same but not if they were different. Figure 2 shows, for the two experiments, the relative repetition benefit for each stimulus dimension (i.e. mean RT for alternation of form, colour or location, minus mean RT for repetition) as a function of the relationship between R1 and R2. Clearly, repeating stimulus form or location produced a benefit with response repetition but not with response alternation or single responses, where repetition costs

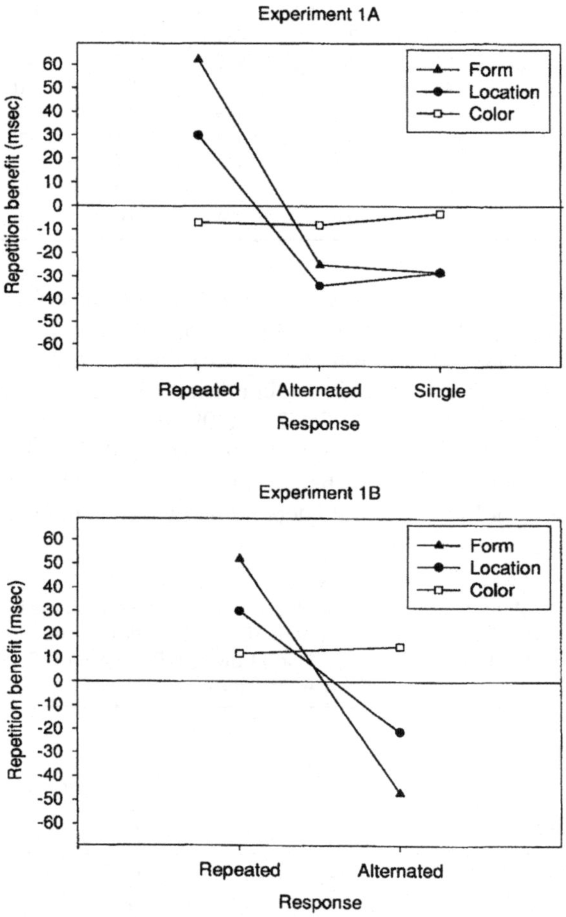

FIG. 2. Stimulus (S1–S2) repetition benefits ($RT_{alternation}$–$RT_{repetition}$) for stimulus form (F), colour (C) and location (L) in Experiments 1A (upper panel) and 1B (lower panel) as a function of response relation (R1–R2 repetition or alternation, or single). $RT_{alternation}$ corresponds to the mean of all conditions involving alternation of the respective stimulus feature (e.g. conditions Neither, L, C and LC, for stimulus form) in the given response condition, while $RT_{repetition}$ corresponds to the mean of all conditions involving repetition of that feature (e.g. conditions F, LF, FC and LFC).

were obtained. This pattern produced a highly significant interaction between response relationship and form repetition in Experiment 1A, $F(2,14) = 22.30$, $p < .001$, and Experiment 1B, $F(1,7) = 58.18$, $p < .001$, and an interaction between response relationship and stimulus-location relation in Experiment 1A, $F(2,14) = 34.98$, $p < .001$, and Experiment 1B, $F(1,7) = 23.04$, $p < .005$. However, there was no interaction of response relationship and colour in either experiment ($F < 1$). A separate ANOVA on alternate- and single-response trials only in Experiment 1A did not reveal any interaction involving response relation, showing that both conditions played a comparable role.

Single comparisons, (*t*-tests, two-tailed) confirmed that, in Experiment 1A, all response-specific repetition benefits and costs associated with form and location (Fig. 2) were significantly different from zero ($p < .05$), except the location-repetition benefit with response repetition and the form-repetition cost in the single-response condition. However, even these latter effects approached significance ($p < .08$ and $p < .07$, respectively). A similar picture was obtained in Experiment 1B, where all form- and location-related costs and benefits were significant or nearly so, as in the case of location-repetition costs with response alternation ($p < .06$). Colour-related effects were all far from significance, except the repetition benefit with response repetition in Experiment 1B ($p < .07$).

There were two further commonalities between the two experiments: First, form and colour repetition interacted in Experiment 1A, $F(1,7) = 5.71$, $p < .05$, as well as in Experiment 1B, $F(1,7) = 10.10$, $p < .05$. In both cases, this was due to faster responses if form and colour were either both repeated or both alternated (483 and 447 msec for Experiment 1A and 1B, respectively) than if only one, but not the other, was repeated (494 and 459 msec, respectively). Second, there was a very similar interaction between form and location, which was clearly significant in Experiment 1A, $F(1,7) = 11.74$, $p < .05$, but only marginally so in Experiment 1B, $F(1,7) = 3.97$, $p < .09$: Responses were faster if the two stimulus attributes were either both repeated or both alternated (483 and 447 msec for Experiments 1A and 1B, respectively) than if only one, but not the other, attribute was repeated (495 and 459 msec, respectively).

Errors. In Experiment 1A, there were just two significant effects, both mirroring the RT results. An interaction of response relation and stimulus location, $F(2,14) = 5.01$, $p < .05$, showed that repeating stimulus location decreased the error rates with response repetitions (2.4 and 5.0% for location repetition and alternation, respectively), but increased rates with response alternations (5.2 and 2.0%, respectively) and single responses (2.4 and 1.8%, respectively). In the same vein, an interaction of response relation and stimulus form, $F(2.14) = 7.47$, $p < .01$, indicated that repeating form decreased the error rates with response repetitions (1.9 and 5.5% for form repetition and alternation, respectively), but increased rates with response alternations (5.8 and 1.5%, respectively) and single responses (2.6 and 1.6%, respectively). Both interactions disappeared in a separate ANOVA on alternation and single-response trials only, suggesting that response repetition was the crucial condition.

In Experiment 1B, repeated responses produced smaller error rates (3.7%) than response alternations (7.0%), $F(1,7) = 6.67$, $p < .05$, and form repetitions yielded larger rates (6.6%) than form alternations (4.1%), $F(1,7) = 18.54$, $p < .005$. The two variables also interacted, $F(1,7) = 27.59$, $p < .001$, replicating the corresponding pattern in Experiment 1A: Again, repeating stimulus form decreased the error rates with response repetitions (1.6 and 5.8% for form repetition and alternation, respectively), but increased rates with response alternations (11.6 and 2.5%, respectively).

Discussion

The results reveal two theoretically important patterns. First, pure repetition effects of stimulus dimensions are virtually absent; the common pattern is an interaction between form—the task-relevant stimulus feature—and colour on the one hand, and between form and location on the other. These interactions do not seem to result from priming feature-specific type nodes, but rather from re-addressing structures of integrated feature conjunctions. As already mentioned, this finding is not new: Interactions between (relevant) form and (irrelevant) location have been reported by Henderson (1994; Henderson & Anes, 1994) and Kahneman et al. (1992), and colour-related effects have also been found previously (e.g. Allport et el., 1985). However, the present results also show that stimulus features do not seem to be integrated non-selectively, as both the original object-file concept and the uniform-event-file view would have led us to expect. If they were, a three-way interaction should have been observed, implying that only repeating the complete stimulus produced a benefit, while partial repetitions are ineffective. Yet, the results suggest that there is not one global binding of all features, but two different, local bindings, one between the two non-spatial stimulus features and one between the task-relevant stimulus feature and stimulus location. In contrast, there is no evidence for binding of location and colour, the irrelevant non-spatial feature, independently of whether the relevant feature was familiar symbols (Experiment 1A) or simple lines (Experiment 1B).

Second, and even more important in the present context, there are pronounced interactions involving response location. Again, the particular outcome pattern does not suggest a global binding of stimulus and response features, but two different, local bindings, one between the task-relevant feature and response location, and one between the two spatial features stimulus location and response location. There was also some indication of a binding of colour and response location in Experiment 1B, but it was unreliable and clearly on a different scale to the form- and location-related bindings. Therefore,

Experiment 1 provides good evidence for the existence of event files integrating stimulus and response information, but on the stimulus side only task-relevant and spatial features seem to be involved.

One interpretation of the binding of stimulus form and response location is in terms of rule verification. Another way of putting this is that it represents a benefit of repeating the valid stimulus–response mapping rule. Consider, for instance, the case when an X (S2) is responded to by pressing a left key (R2). Based on the interaction obtained, this response was faster when it was preceded by a left keypress (R1) to an X (S1) or a right keypress to an O, than when it was preceded by a left keypress to an O or a right keypress to an X. In other words, although the stimulus–response relationship was completely unimportant for R1, R2 was faster if it followed a stimulus–response combination that obeyed the stimulus–response mapping rules valid for R2 than if it followed a mapping-rule "violation". That is, following a mapping rule is easier if it has been "confirmed" by the preceding stimulus–response combination, although this combination did not result from *applying* the mapping rule. This again suggests that rule-governed behaviour (i.e. S2–R2 performance) can be affected by the retrieval of traces of previous combinations of the present stimulus and a response. Logan (1988) has argued that performing a task leads to the formation of such traces. Once formed and stored, a trace or instance will be automatically retrieved whenever the corresponding stimulus or response occurs again. Thus, if the S1–R1 combination X→right key is followed by the S2–R2 combination X→left key, automatic trace retrieval and intentional rule application will yield conflicting outcomes, which again should prolong the initiation of the correct response. Under the plausible assumption that stored traces comprise relevant stimulus and response information only, the present interaction of stimulus-form and response-location repetition is consistent with such an interpretation.

However, it was not only relevant stimulus information that was integrated with response information, but stimulus location too. The presence of this second local response-related interaction points to a strong, intra-domain coupling of spatial stimulus and response codes. Such a tight coupling has already been postulated by Henderson (1996) on the basis of results from eye-movement studies. However, Henderson's idea was that spatial stimulus coding facilitates motor action *towards* the stimulus, just as maintained by proponents of the premotor theory or attention (Rizzolatti, Riggio, & Sheliga, 1994), or by theories of stimulus–response compatibility (see Hommel & Prinz, 1997). Yet, the present interaction has nothing to do with stimulus–response *correspondence*, but represents a benefit of (repeating) the spatial *relationship* between stimulus and response.

Interestingly, virtually identical results were obtained for the response-alternation and single-response conditions, which implies that the latter does not represent a truly neutral condition. Obviously, from the perspective of our subjects, omitting R1 was as different from performing a particular R2 as pressing the alternate key. Although this is an interesting observation, we will see in Experiment 2 that it is not always obtained and must thus be treated with caution. In Experiment 3, the role of the single-response condition will be investigated further.

Taken together, the results of Experiment 1 support the assumption that stimulus and response information is not integrated separately but bound together, thus forming a common event file, or several of them. Yet, the indication that colour information is not integrated with information about stimulus or response location suggests that feature binding is selective. Moreover, although the basic result of previous preview studies—interacting effects of stimulus-form repetition and stimulus-location repetition—was successfully replicated, the absence of three- or four-way interactions suggests that the responsible bindings were local, not global. These observations are inconsistent with the original object-file conception of Kahneman and Treisman (1984; Treisman, 1988), or any response-related extension, and with the uniform-event-file hypothesis described in the Introduction. They rather suggest that integration takes place at multiple levels, and is modulated by task relevance, just as implied by a structured-event-file approach.

EXPERIMENT 2

In Experiment 1, information about stimulus form, stimulus location and response location was found to be involved in mutual interactions, whereas colour information only interacted with stimulus form. What is the reason for this negligible part played by the colour dimension? An obvious interpretation points to the importance of task relevance, or behavioural goals, as Tipper et al. (1994) have put it: Because colour was irrelevant to the task, it may have been considered only in object-related bindings proper (i.e. form and colour), but not integrated with response location, the relevant response feature, or stimulus location, a dimension that may be functional in cross-referencing stimulus and response information. Yet, on the basis of Experiment 1 alone, we cannot firmly conclude that task irrelevance was responsible for the limited "binding willingness" of colour—maybe it was the poor saliency of this dimension or some other factor. An obvious way to test the task-relevance interpretation is to exchange the roles of form and colour, as in Experiment 2. If task relevance is really the decisive factor, we would expect the same outcome as in Experiment 1, but with form- and colour-related effects interchanged; hence, interactions between colour and form, colour and stimulus location, colour and response location, and stimulus and response location.

Method

Subjects. Eight paid volunteers (5 females and 3 males, aged 20–36 years) participated. They reported having normal or corrected-to-normal vision, and were not familiar with the purpose of the experiment.

Apparatus, Stimuli, Procedure and Design. These were as in Experiment 1A, with the following exceptions: The response-relevant stimulus feature of S2 was colour. Half of the subjects responded to a green-coloured stimulus by pressing the left key and to a red one by pressing the right key, while the other half received the opposite mapping. A sessions consisted of two experimental blocks of 192 trials each (composed as in Experiment 1A), preceded by 40 randomly drawn practice trials.

Results

R1 responses were missing, incorrect or anticipated in 1.3, 0.8 and 1.6% of the trials, respectively. Correct R1 responses were given in 371 msec on average. After excluding missing (0.2%) or anticipated (1.8%) R2 responses, the R2 data were treated as in Experiment 1 (see Table 3 for means).

Reaction Times. Figure 3 shows the repetition benefits for each stimulus dimension as a function of the relationship between R1 and R2. As in Experiment 1, repeating stimulus form or location produced a benefit with response repetitions but not with response alternations, where repetition costs were obtained, or with single responses, which were associated with modest costs only. This time, however, there was also a benefit of colour repetition that

TABLE 3
Means of Mean Reaction Times (RT; in msec) and Percentages of Errors (PE) for R2 in Experiment 2 as a Function of the Relationship Between S1 and S2 and Between R1 and R2 (R2 Repeated, Alternated or Single)

	Response					
	Repeated		*Alternated*		*Single*	
Stimulus Feature Repeated	*RT*	*PE*	*RT*	*PE*	*RT*	*PE*
Neither	541	11.9	466	0.8	487	0.7
L(ocation)	516	7.5	504	2.3	500	4.6
F(orm)	540	5.7	451	1.5	516	4.2
C(olour)	523	2.1	519	5.7	520	2.8
LF	520	7.6	495	2.9	532	2.9
LC	469	0.7	528	11.0	512	1.5
FC	482	2.3	510	8.2	512	2.9
LFC	447	0.7	530	9.3	532	2.7

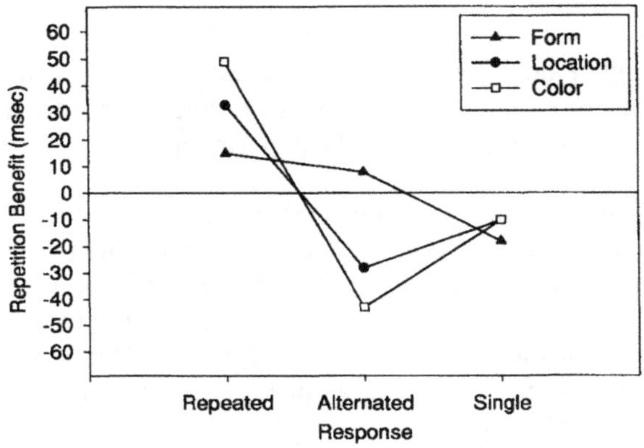

FIG. 3. Stimulus (S1–S2) repetition benefits ($RT_{alternation}–RT_{repetition}$) for stimulus form, colour and location in Experiment 2 as a function of response relation (R1–R2 repetition or alternation, or single).

depended on the inter-response relationship. All three interactions were clearly significant: response by form, $F(2,14) = 6.24$, $p < .05$, response by location, $F(2,14) = 5.40$, $p < .05$, and response by colour, $F(2,14) = 27.43$, $p < .001$. In a separate ANOVA including alternation and single-response trials only, response relation interacted with colour, $F(1,7) = 5.43$, $p < .06$, and with form, $F(1,7) = 6.48$, $p < .05$, but not with stimulus location ($p < .4$). That is, in contrast to Experiment 1, the single-response condition played a more neutral role than the alternation condition.

Single comparisons confirmed that colour and location, but not form, produced significant repetition benefits with response repetition. With response alternation, all three stimulus dimensions produced an effect: The colour cost was significant and the location cost nearly so ($p < .08$), while form yielded a small but significant repetition benefit. In the single-response condition, however, not one effect reached the significance criterion ($.14 < p < .45$).

Apart from a marginally significant interaction between form and colour ($p < .09$ showing the same pattern as in Experiment 1, no further effect reached or approached significance.

Errors. There were only two significant effects on error rates: The main effect of response relation, $F(2,14) = 3.76$, $p < .05$, was a result of error rates being lower with single responses (2.8%) than with response repetitions (4.8%) or alternations (5.2%). The interaction between response relation and stimulus colour, $F(2,14) = 17.45$, $p < .001$, indicated that colour repetition decreased the error rates with response repetitions (1.5 and 8.2% for colour repetition and alternation, respectively), hardly affected them with single responses (2.5 and 3.1%, respectively), but increased them with response alternations (8.5 and 1.8%, respectively). Both effects were also obtained in a separate ANOVA on alternation and single-response trials only, which showed that, in contrast to Experiment 1A, the latter condition was less effective than the former.

Discussion

As expected, exchanging the task relevance of form and colour yielded a partial reversal at least of the results obtained in Experiment 1. In Experiment 1, the response factor interacted most strongly with form, modestly with stimulus location, and not at all with colour. In Experiment 2, this order was completely reversed, with the strongest interaction between response and colour and the weakest between response and form. This dependence of effect-size order on task relevance points to an important role of the latter in the binding of stimulus and response features. Interestingly, however, even the irrelevant form feature produced a reliable interaction with response repetition. This suggests that task relevance only modifies the strengths of stimulus–response bindings, but does not preclude task-irrelevant couplings.

As far as bindings between stimulus features are concerned, the exchange of the roles played by colour and form did not yield an exact reversal of the results. Apart from the marginal form × colour interaction, replicating the corresponding effect in Experiment 1, there were no further interactions between stimulus dimensions. While the absence of the interaction between stimulus location and the now irrelevant form was expected, the absence of an interaction between stimulus location and the now relevant colour was not. Although there is no obvious explanation for this latter outcome, it should be pointed out that the overall pattern suggests a numerical reversal at least in the expected direction (see General Discussion). So, there is reason to assume that the asymmetry between colour- and form-related effects observed in Experimen 1 did not result from any particularities associated with the colour dimension, but was due to the task relevance of form.

EXPERIMENT 3

Experiment 3 was conducted to investigate further the role of the single-response condition used in Experiments 1A and 2. In Experiment 1A, this condition was comparable to the response-alternation condition in interacting in the same way with effects of stimulus-feature repetition. In Experiment 2, however, it rather behaved like the neutral condition it originally was supposed to be. The main aim of the present experiment was to assess whether the non-neutral behaviour of the single condition observed in Experiment 1 was a chance finding, or whether the different outcomes in Experiments 1 and 2 were due to the exchange of form and colour as relevant stimulus dimensions. Therefore, Experiment 3 comprised a replication of Experiment 1, with form as the relevant feature. The critical question was whether the equivalence between alternation and the single condition observed in Experiment 1 could be repeated.

A second aim of Experiment 3 was to investigate the differences between the present findings and those obtained with the preview design used in other studies. With a preview design, significant effects of stimulus-feature repetition (i.e. type priming) are sometimes observed (e.g. Henderson, 1994; Henderson & Anes, 1994) but not always (Kahneman et al., 1992). Although the single-response condition used here is not too different from the typical preview design, there was no indication of any repetition benefit in this condition. On the one hand, investigating and obtaining these effects was not the main objective of the present study, and there are a number of methodological differences, such as the number of previewed stimuli or the timing of preview and probe display, that may well account for the diverging outcomes. On the other hand, however, the observation that the single-response condition in Experiment 1A produced virtually the same results as the alternation condition aroused the suspicion that a different factor may have been responsible —and for a critical assessment of the present task, it seemed crucial to test whether this factor actually played a role.

One possible reason for the absence of non-specific priming with single responses is that not responding to a stimulus may be coded differently if the stimulus is never responded to, compared to when a response also represents a viable alternative. In priming or preview tasks, the prime is never responded to (or, as in the case of prime-signalled saccades, is always responded to, but differently than the probe), so that no decision needs to be made whether or not to respond. In the present design, however, S1 was sometimes responded to and sometimes not, so that such a decision was necessary. Consequently, our subjects may have coded the fact that no response is required explicitly. If so, this no-response code may have been integrated together with stimulus information into an event file just like codes for left- and right-key responses. Consequently, an event file including a no-response code would mismatch with S2 and R2 or the S2–R2 relationship just like event files including alternate responses do, thus leading to comparable performance in the response-alternation and single-response conditions. In contrast, priming or preview designs do not require any response to the prime, so that no response decision is to be made and no no-response code is to be formed, this precluding the integration of this code into an event file. If the event file does not include response information, not even no-response information, its match or mismatch with that in the probe trial cannot depend on the response relationship, hence response-independent type priming is possible.

If these considerations hold, a dependence of stimulus-feature repetition effects in single-response conditions on the response-related task context should be observed. To test for this possibility, Experiment 3 consisted of two sections. In one section (the "mixed" section), Experiment 1A was partially replicated (i.e. without the colour manipulation): S2 form was relevant, stimulus location was irrelevant, and response repetitions, alternations and single-response conditions were presented in random order. The second section (the "blocked" section) consisted of single-response trials only, thus replicating the standard preview experiments. Response decisions associated with S1, the preview part of the trial, were necessary in the mixed section, but not in the blocked section. Consequently, if effects of type priming (i.e. main effects of stimulus-feature repetition) are really dependent on whether or not response decisions are to be made before or during prime presentation, these effects should show up in the blocked section, but not in the single-response trials of the mixed section.

Method

Subjects. Sixteen paid volunteers (8 females and 8 males, aged 19–39 years) participated. They reported having normal or corrected-to-normal vision, and were not familiar with the purpose of the experiment.

Apparatus, Stimuli, Procedure and Design. These were as in Experiment 1A, with the following exceptions: The stimuli (S1 and S2) were always presented in green, hence colour did not vary. The session comprised two sections, the order of which was balanced across subjects. In Section A, the type of R1 varied randomly, just like in the preceding experiments. This section consisted of one practice block and four experimental blocks. Each block was composed of 48 trials, corresponding to the factorial combination of S2 form (O *vs* X) and location (top *vs* bottom), the possible S1–S2 relationships regarding form and location, and the three possible R1–R2 relationships (repetition, alternation or single response). In Section B, only single responses (i.e. R2) were required. The remaining task was in Section A, including the corresponding single-response precues, but subjects were informed that conditions involving R1 responses would never occur in this section. Section B also consisted of one practice block and four experimental blocks, but each block was now composed of 16 trials only, due to the exclusion of response-repetition and response-alternation conditions. Subjects were given the opportunity to rest between the two sections.

Results

R1 responses were missing, incorrect or anticipated in 1.3, 0.8 and 1.6% of the trials, respectively. Correct R1 responses were given in 371 msec on average. After excluding missing (0.2%) or anticipated (1.8%) R2 responses, the R2 data was treated as in Experiment 1 (see Table 4 means). Reaction times and percentages of errors were subjected to $2 \times 2 \times 4$ ANOVAs with S1/S2-form relation, S1/S2-location relation, and R1–R2 relation (repetition, alternation, mixed single, blocked single) as within-subject factors. Control analyses that

TABLE 4
Means of Mean Reaction Times (RT; in msec) and Percentages of Errors (PE) for R2 in Experiment 1A as a Function of the Relationship Between S1 and S2 and Between R1 and R2 (R2 Repeated, Alternated or Single)

	Response							
	Repeated		*Alternated*		*Single (Random)*		*Single (Blocked)*	
Stimulus Feature Repeated	*RT*	*PE*	*RT*	*PE*	*RT*	*PE*	*RT*	*PE*
Neither	537	11.1	487	1.8	509	4.8	507	2.8
L(ocation)	535	7.1	508	5.8	521	2.8	534	3.2
F(orm)	490	1.9	509	6.6	525	3.4	511	2.2
LF)	453	0.4	511	12.1	506	4.2	514	0.7

included the order of sections (mixed first *vs* blocked first) as a between-subjects variable did not reveal any interaction of the variable in question; there was only an interaction of order and response relation in RTs, indicating that performance in the blocked single section was better if that section followed rather than preceded the other section.

Reaction Times. Among the repetition main effects, only the form effect approached significance ($p < .052$). Form and stimulus location interacted significantly, $F(1,15) = 5.63$, $p < .05$. Figure 4 shows the relative repetition benefits for each stimulus dimension as a function of the relationship between R1 and R2. As in Experiment 1, repeating stimulus form or location produced

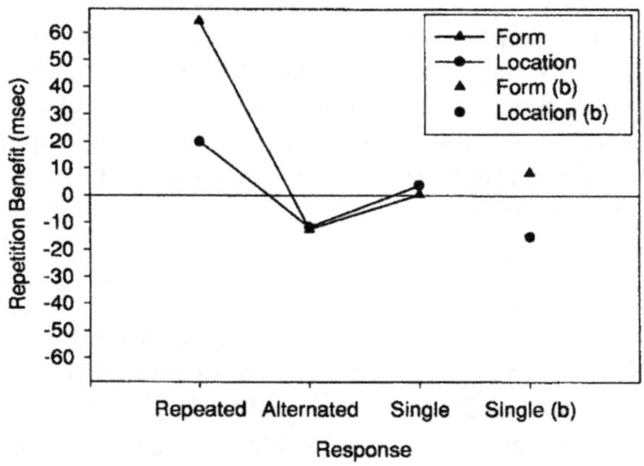

FIG. 4. Stimulus (S1–S2) repetition benefits ($RT_{alternation}–RT_{repetition}$) for stimulus form and location in Experiment 3 as a function of response relation (R1–R2 repetition or alternation, single random, single blocked).

a benefit with response repetition but not with response alternation or without a preceding R1. The corresponding interactions were clearly significant—response × form, $F(3,45) = 13.83$, $p < .001$, and response × location, $F(3,45) = 4.50$, $p < .01$. The fact that both of these interactions disappeared in a separate ANOVA of alternation and single-response trials only (taken from the random section) shows that response repetition was the crucial factor here. Correspondingly, in single comparisons, only the form-repetition benefit and the location-repetition benefit under response repetition were significant or nearly so ($p < .05$ and $p < .08$, respectively). As a specific test of the role of blocked versus random presentation of single-response trials, a separate ANOVA was performed on these trials. Apart from the interaction of form and stimulus-location repetition, no other effect even approached significance.

Errors. There was a main effect of response relation, $F(3,45) = 5.78$, $p < .005$, mainly because fewer errors were made in the single-response conditions (3.8% for mixed and 2.2% for blocked condition) than with response repetitions (5.1%) or alternations (6.6%). The interaction between response relation and stimulus form, $F(3,45) = 15.13$, $p < .001$, was produced by form repetition producing fewer errors then form alternation with response repetitions (1.1 *vs* 9.1%), while the reverse was true for response alternations (9.4 *vs* 3.8%); with single responses, form repetition and alternation yielded much more similar results, whether response relation was mixed (3.8 *vs* 3.8%) or blocked (1.5 *vs* 3.0%). Finally, there was an interaction between response relation and stimulus location, $F(3,45) = 5.75$, $p < .005$, that was of the same type as the form × response interaction: Repetition of stimulus location produced fewer errors than location alternation when the response was also repeated (3.8 *vs* 6.5%), but more errors when the response was alternated (8.8 *vs* 4.2%); again, the different between stimulus-location repetition and alternation was much less pronounced with mixed (3.5 *vs* 4.1%) and blocked (1.2 *vs* 2.5%) single responses. All these effects were also obtained in a separate ANOVA on alternation and single-response trials from the random section only.

Discussion

The main aim of Experiment 3 concerned the relationship between the alternate-response and the single-response conditions. In Experiment 1A, the single-response condition showed interactions with the repetition of stimulus dimensions comparable to those of the alternation condition, whereas in Experiment 2, single responses were not associated with repetition benefits or costs. The results of Experiment 3 do not really clarify matters. On the one hand, the alternate-response and single-response conditions during random presentation interacted similarly with the repetition of stimulus features, thus replicating the findings of Experiment 1A. On the other hand, this was not associated with similar repetition costs, as it was in Experiment 1A, but with an absence of any reliable stimulus–repetition effect in both conditions. Together with the observation that the single-response condition did not produce any perceptible numerical cost or benefit, this suggests that the similarity was more likely due to a floor effect than to some theoretically important special role of form stimuli (relevant in Experiments 1A and 3) compared to colour stimuli (relevant in Experiment 2). Based on the present results all one can say is that the single-response condition does not seem to represent a reliable neutral condition that could serve as a referent for comparing effects of response repetition and response alternation on stimulus-repetition effects. Therefore, the General Discussion focuses mainly on the effects of, and the relationship between, response repetition and alternation.

The second aim of Experiment 3 was to investigate whether dimensional, non-specific priming effects depend on the task context or, more precisely, on whether pure preview trials (i.e. single-response trials) occur in isolation or in the context of trials that require some kind of response decision before or during prime presentation. Although a brief look at Fig. 4 might suggest that something different happened in the blocked and random trials, there was nothing in the results to support this. Moreover, the absence of an interaction involving section order rules out carry-over effects from random to blocked presentation being responsible for the similarity between the two single-response conditions. All this suggests that reliable effects of non-specific, dimensional priming, as reported by Henderson (1994; Henderson & Anes, 1994), cannot be obtained with the particular task used in the present study. One reason for this may be that the prime display always consisted of a single object only, while displays in preview studies usually consist of two or more objects. Possibly, type priming only occurs if feature binding is difficult, hence with several objects. Another reason concerns the temporal lag between prime and probe display, which was very short in the experiments of Henderson (the latency of a saccade), longer in most conditions of Kahneman and co-workers' (1992) study, and consistently very long in the present study. Interestingly, Kahneman et al. obtained the numerically largest non-specific effects for the small (two symbol), static displays with very short preview-probe intervals (100 msec, study 1), and the effect shrank with increasing interval length (see 250 msec condition in study 1 and the longer intervals in study 2). Thus, type priming may be a rather short-lived phenomenon which explains, in view of the 1000 msec intervals used here, why we were unable to find such effects. But most important for assessing the present task, whatever the underlying reason for the lack of dimensional priming was, it seems clear that task context was not responsible.

GENERAL DISCUSSION

The main objective of the present study was to test the hypothesis that response-related information is integrated with stimulus information into event files; that is, episodic memory structures representing both stimulus and response aspects of events. All four experiments reported here provide evidence in favour of this hypothesis, allowing some conclusions to be drawn as to how event files may be internally structured. However, before I discuss the relevant findings and their implications in detail, I will first address two further outcome patterns that are more related to previous studies of object-file formation in perception.

The first interesting outcome concerns dimensional or type priming; that is, the object-unspecific effects of repeating versus alternating particular stimulus features. Figure 5 provides an overview of such repetition effects in Experiments 1A, 1B, 2 and 3. Effects were not only rare, but also very unsystematic. This suggests that the absence of repetition main effects cannot be attributed to the small size of the effects or the limited power of the present experiments to detect them. A reasonable explanation for their absence would be the rather long interval between S1 and S2, during which the activation of primed type nodes may have decayed. As already pointed out, such an interpretation would fit with the unreliable priming effects of Kanheman et al. (1992), who often used rather long intervals, and the large effects reported by Henderson (1994; Henderson & Anes, 1994), who used very short intervals only. In fact, preliminary results from pilot work in our laboratory suggest that non-specific effects decay over time.

The second interesting outcome concerns conjunction priming or object-file formation, as indicated by interactions between stimulus-feature repetition effects. The upper panel of Fig. 6 gives an overview of the degree of interaction for each of the two or three stimulus-feature combinations (see figure legend for computational details). There are two very systematic patterns. One is that stimulus location always interacts with the relevant stimulus feature, be it form, as in Experiments 1A, 1B and 3, or colour, as in Experiment 2. That is, repeating the relevant stimulus feature produces a benefit only if stimulus location is also repeated; if not, alternation tends to yield better performance (the latter being the case for Experiments 1B and 2). The observed benefit associated with conjunction repetitions replicates the results from preview studies and is consistent with the idea that location information is used to address and select object files for retrieval or updating (Kahneman et al., 1992; Treisman, 1988). Another pattern is that, independent of task relevance, the two non-spatial stimulus features, form and colour, always interact. That is, performance is better if form and colour are repeated—or, as in Experiments 1A and 2, if both alternate—compared to when only one alternates while the other is repeated. From an object-file approach, this result is unexpected. True, it does fit the general idea that perceiving a particular feature combination leads to the

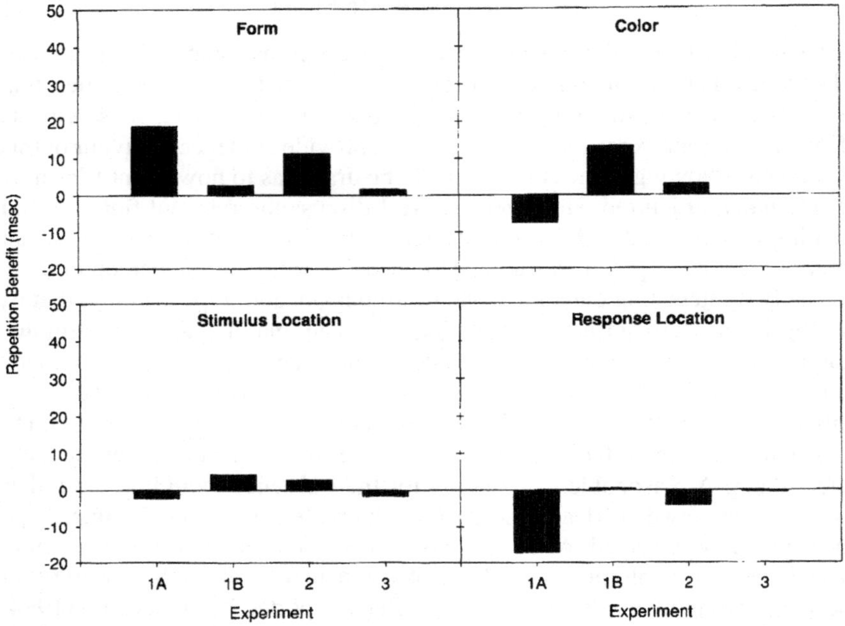

FIG. 5. Repetition benefits ($RT_{alternation}$–$RT_{repetition}$) for stimulus form (F), colour (C) and location (L), and response location in Experiments 1–3. For stimulus features, $RT_{alternation}$ corresponds to the mean of all conditions involving alternation of the respective feature (e.g. conditions Neither, L, C and LC, collapsed across response repetition and response alternation, for stimulus form), while $RT_{repetition}$ corresponds to the mean of all conditions involving repetition of that feature (e.g. conditions, F, LF, FC and LFC). Analogously, for response location, $RT_{alternation}$ corresponds to the mean of all conditions involving response alternation (collapsed across all stimulus repetition or alternation conditions), while $RT_{repetition}$ corresponds to the mean of all conditions involving response repetition. For optimal comparability between experiments, all computations are based on response–repetition and response–alternation conditions only, while single-response conditions were not considered.

formation of an object file: The features are not (or not only) registered independently, but integrated into a common episodic memory structure. If the same combination is then perceived again, it is not necessary to create a new file, but just update the old file. However, if object files are really addressed by location, the benefit of repeating a form-colour combination should depend on whether location is also repeated; yet there was no three-way interaction of form-, colour-, and location-repetition in any experiment in this study.

Although the absence of type priming and the presence of two different stimulus-feature bindings are of some theoretical interest, the main focus of this study is on the binding between stimulus and response features. The lower panel of Fig. 6 gives a summary of the degree of interaction observed between response type (only repetition and alternation conditions considered) and each

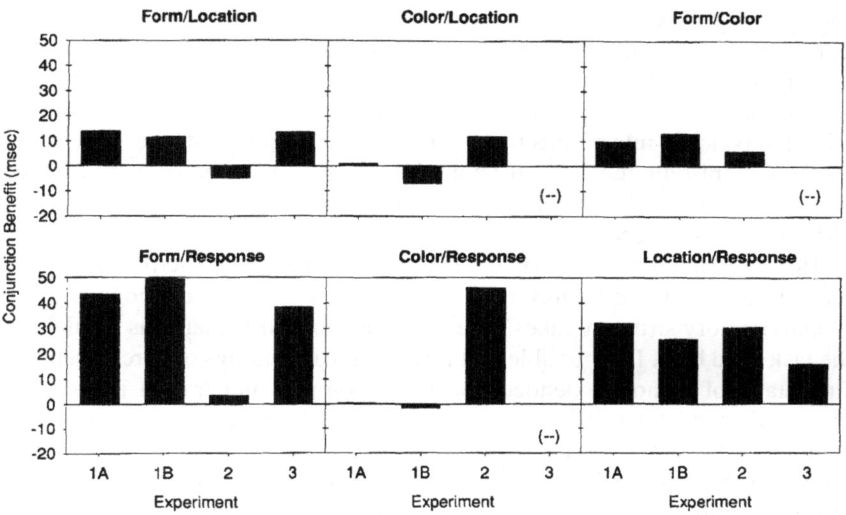

FIG. 6. Conjunction benefits for each combination of stimulus form, colour, and location (upper panel) and for the combination of response location with stimulus form, stimulus colour and stimulus location (lower panel) in Experiments 1–3. Conjunction benefits for the combination of features x and y are computed by taking the signed repetition benefit for x when y is repeated minus the signed repetition benefit for x when y alternates, divided by 2. A value of zero indicates independence between the respective features (i.e. between the effects of repeating versus alternating the features); values above zero indicate a repetition benefit for x if y is also repeated, but a cost if y alternates; values below zero indicate the opposite relationship.

of the three stimulus features. There are again two very systematic patterns. One is that the relevant stimulus feature—colour in Experiment 2 and form in the others—always interacts with the response. That is, repeating the relevant stimulus feature yields a benefit if the response is also repeated; but a repetition cost is observed if the response alternates. This suggests that binding does not only occur between stimulus features, as the object-file concept suggests, but between stimulus and response features as well. True, if such a binding does occur, the relevant stimulus feature and the relevant response feature are the most obvious candidates; yet the fact that stimulus-response binding is observed at all is remarkable. And there is evidence for a further binding: As the right-most graph in the lower panel of Fig. 6 shows, bindings between stimulus location and response location were obtained in all four experiments. This is partly consistent with the general consideration of Henderson (1996) that object files could contain information about both stimulus and response location.

Perhaps the most surprising outcome of this study is the absence of any three- or four-way interaction. The presence of such interactions would have suggested that all the stimulus and response features are integrated into one single structure, as both the extended-object-file hypothesis and the uniform-event-file hypothesis would lead us to expect. The absence of higher-order interactions, however, strongly suggests the formation of many local bindings instead of a unitary whole. That is, the present results point to a distributed and differentiated multi-layered network of stimulus- and response-feature codes with many local interconnections, rather than to the existence of a single, integrated episodic memory structure. Hence, it seems that an event file does not so much resemble a bundle of sheets put into one folder, but rather a system of hyperlinks connecting information stored at distant locations.

However, it must be emphasised that we should not overinterpret the present indications for local bindings only. It may be that the construction of a unitary global memory structure takes time, perhaps more time than was available in the task used here. It is possible that forming local bindings only represents the first stage of a more extended and more complex integration process that eventually results in a fully integrated episodic memory trace. If so, the present findings only represent a single snapshop of a dynamic consolidation process. And there is evidence that this is more than mere speculation: In further studies in our laboratory, we manipulated the stimulus-onset asynchrony between S1 and S2, thus varying the time available for consolidating the S1–R1 memory trace. Although much remains to be done to systematically track the consolidation process, it seems clear that the type of binding, as indicated by interactions between repetition effects, changes over time. So, the absence of more global bindings (i.e. bindings involving more than two features) in the present study does not mean that such bindings are not formed at all—it only shows that there is some point in time where they are only local, not global, bindings.

With these reservations in mind, it is still worthwhile considering the implications of local bindings. Let us begin with the bindings between stimulus features. Interestingly, there was systematic evidence across all four experiments for the binding of form and colour, independent of location. This finding is not consistent with the original object-file concept as proposed by Kahneman and Treisman (1984; Kahneman et al., 1992), where location information was assumed to be the most important ingredient of object files. It also suggests that the crucial binding does not take place on, has direct access to, or used information from, spatiotopically organised feature maps, such as in V1. More plausible sites would be higher areas, where (precise) location information is lost. It is possible that temporary chunks, at least, are formed at the type level, the non-spatial part of which can be roughly localised at V4/IT (Schneider, 1995). This does not necessarily exclude some role of location information, and thus, representations from other areas, in the process of forming form–colour conjunctions. It may be that, as Treisman (1988, 1993) has maintained, spatial codes are functional in sampling to-be-integrated information from lower-level colour and form maps. However, the present results suggest that, once integration has taken place, location is no longer represented.

The second stimulus-related binding observed here, that between stimulus location and the relevant stimulus feature, is much less critical for the object-file approach. It is true that the original approach does not draw a distinction between task-relevant and -irrelevant features that would allow for relevance-modulated binding: If "spatial attention" highlights a particular area of the location map, information from all corresponding feature-map locations is sampled and put into an object file (e.g. Treisman, 1988, 1993). However, this does not necessarily exclude the existence of a mechanism that attenuates information from maps coding task-irrelevant information, so that irrelevant information is less likely to be integrated or integrated only weakly, and thus decays quickly over time. That is, the observation of selective stimulus-feature bindings may indicate that the object-file approach is insufficient, but it does not stand in opposition to it.

Let us now turn to the bindings involving response location. As already pointed out, the consistent findings of bindings between the relevant stimulus feature and response location may be explained along the lines of Logan's (1988; Logan & Etherton, 1994) instance theory of automatisation. The basic idea is that each stimulus–response episode is stored and retrieved automatically if the same stimulus or response occurs again. If we further assume that this only applies to task-relevant stimulus and response features, which seems to be consistent with Logan's proposal that instance storage requires attention, the present interaction can be easily understood. However, another implication, which does not seem to be fully consistent with Logan's approach, arises from the fact that S1–R1 instances were stored even though the pair of S1 and R1 was only accidental. In other words, the mapping rule between S2 and R2 was "learned" by performing R1 to S1, although the latter did not result from applying the rule. How could this happen if, as Logan assumes, attention to co-occurrence is required to store an instance?

A possible answer could be that our subjects may have (more often than not) failed to distinguish between the S1–R1 task and the S2–R2 task. Although the former was a simple reaction task and the identity of S1 was not important, subjects may have been unable to simply "forget" the S2–R2 mapping rule and thus may have tended to apply this rule in the S1–R2 task as well. Some support for this comes from the reaction times in the first task, which ranged from 342 to 376 msec. For a simple reaction, this is actually very slow, although the dual-task context must also be taken into account. Therefore, could subjects have reacted to, or at least have been influenced by, S1 identity? If so, there should have been an interaction between the relevant stimulus feature and response in the RTs or R1, that is, R1 should have been quicker if it was combined with an S1 that obeyed the S2–R2 mapping rule. However, although this interaction approached significance in Experiment 1B ($p = .055$), it was far from significant in Experiments 1A ($p = .95$), 2 ($p = .50$) and 3 ($p = .43$). That renders an account in terms of inadequate rule application untenable and suggests that attention to co-occurrence is not necessary to store stimulus–response relationships.

Response location did not only interact with the relevant stimulus feature, it also interacted in a very consistent fashion with stimulus location. Therefore, even though stimulus location was not involved in as many interactions as the original object-file approach suggests, it did play a major role. Interactions between spatial stimulus and response codes are a common finding: Not only are spatial stimulus cues know to facilitate spatially corresponding actions (e.g. Fitts & Seeger, 1953; for general overviews see Hommel & Prinz, 1997; Protor & Reeve, 1990), even if stimulus location is completely irrelevant to the task (e.g. Simon & Rudell, 1967), spatial action can also be shown to facilitate (Deubel & Schneider, 1996; Hommel & Schneider, submitted) or to impair (Müsseler & Hommel, 1997) the processing of corresponding stimuli, depending on the particular temporal conditions. As already mentioned, these findings are consistent with Henderson (1996) and the basic tenet of the premotor theory of attention (Rizzolatti et al., 1994), that spatial stimulus and response codes may be coupled in some way. However, the particular type of interaction obtained here is not really predicted by this view, because the observed coupling between stimulus and response location did not depend on correspondence. This suggests that correspondence and relationship-repetition effects are produced by two different processes or mechanisms: On the one hand, there seem to be direct spatial interactions during a trial that foster the processing of spatially corresponding stimuli and responses. A plausible candidate for this to happen would be the dorsal "where" pathway, especially the posterior parietal cortex (Rizzolatti et al., 1994; Schneider, 1995), although at least with eye movements the superior colliculus also seems to be heavily involved (Wurtz, Goldberg, & Robinson, 1980). On the other hand, there seems to be a mechanism that monitors the spatial stimulus- and response-coding processes occurring in these areas, or at least registers their outcome, and binds the resulting codes together, whether they correspond or not.

To summarize, the present findings clearly suggest that binding effects, as indicated by mutually interacting repetition effects, are not restricted to stimulus features, but can also be shown to occur between stimulus and response features. This again demonstrates that object files, if they really exist, are only part of the binding story, and thus may be though of as only one component of more complex, and possible widely distributed, event files. One interpretation of the observation of several local, but not global, bindings would be that event files are multi-layered structures comprising bindings that serve different functions: Bindings between stimulus form and location may be a product of a (pre-attentive?) object-construction process; binding stimulus location and the relevant stimulus feature may serve to spatially index the relevant information; binding response location and the relevant stimulus feature may reflect a mechanism subserving the automatisation of mapping rules; and spatial stimulus–response bindings may serve to coordinate visual attention with spatial motor action. However, according to another, not necessarily exclusive interpretation, the formation of local bindings represents only some intermediate stage of a temporally extended event-file construction process that ultimately will produce a single, fully integrated trace connecting all aspects of the experienced stimulus–response episode. Which of these interpretations is correct, and whether they represent theoretical alternative at all, should not be too difficult to determine.

REFERENCES

Allport, D.A. (1987). Selection for action: Some behavioral and neurophysiological considerations of attention and action. In H. Heuer & A.F. Sanders (Eds), *Perspectives on perception and action* (pp. 395–419). Hillsdale, NJ: Lawrence Erlbaum Associates Inc.

Allport, D.A., Tipper, S.P., & Chmiel, N.R.J. (1985). Perceptual integration and postcategorical filtering. In M.I. Posner & O.S.M. Marin (Eds), *Attention and performance XI* (pp. 107–132). Hillsdale, NJ: Lawrence Erlbaum Associates Inc.

Cowey, A. (1985). Aspects of cortical organization related to selective attention and selective impairments of visual perception: A tutorial review. In M.I. Posner & O.S.M. Marin (Eds), *Attention and Performance XI* (pp. 41–62). Hillsdale, NJ: Lawrence Erlbaum Associates Inc.

Danzinger, S., & Robertson, L.C. (1994). Repetition effects of response irrelevant features. Poster presented at the *35th Annual Meeting of the Psychonomic Society*, November, St. Louis, MO.

Deubel, H., & Schneider, W.X. (1996). Saccade target selection and object recognition: Evidence for a common attentional mechanism. *Vision Research, 36*, 1827–1837.

DeYoe, E.A., & Van Essen, D.C. (1988). Concurrent processing streams in monkey visual cortex. *Trends in Neurosciences, 11*, 219–226.

Fitts, P.M., & Seeger, C.M. (1953). S–R compatibility: Spatial characteristics of stimulus and response codes. *Journal of Experimental Psychology, 46*, 199–210.

Fox, E. (1995). Negative priming from ignored distractors in visual selection: A review. *Psychonomic Bulletin and Review, 2*, 145–173.

Henderson, J.M. (1994). Two representational systems in dynamic visual identification. *Journal of Experimental Psychology: General, 123*, 410–426.

Henderson, J.M. (1996). Visual attention and the attention–action interface. In K. Akins (Ed), *Perception* (pp. 290–316). New York: Oxford University Press.

Henderson, J.M., & Anes, M.D. (1994). Roles of object-file review and type priming in visual identification within and across eye-fixations. *Journal of Experimental Psychology: Human Perception and Performance, 20*, 826–839.

Hommel, B., & Prinz, W. (Eds) (1997). *Theoretical issues in stimulus–response compatibility*. Amsterdam: North-Holland.

Hommel, B., & Schneider, W.X. (submitted). Visual attention and the selection of manual responses.

Kahnemann, D., & Treisman, A. (1984). Changing views of attention and automaticity. In R. Parasuraman & D.R. Davies (Eds), *Varieties of attention* (pp. 29–61). Orlando, FL: Academic Press.

Kahnemann, D., & Treisman, A., & Gibbs, B.J. (1992). The reviewing of object files: Object-specific integration of information. *Cognitive Psychology, 24*, 175–219.

Logan, D.L. (1988). Toward an instance theory of automatization. *Psychological Review, 95*, 492–527.

Logan, G.D., & Etherton, J.L. (1994). What is learned during automatization? The role of attention in constructing an instance. *Journal of Experimental Psychology: Learning, Memory and Cognition, 20*, 1022–1050.

May, C.P., Kane, M.J., & Hasher, L. (1995). Determinants of negative priming. *Psychological Bulletin, 118*, 35–54.

Milliken, B., Tipper, S.P., & Weaver, B. (1994). Negative priming in a spatial localization task: Feature mismatching and distractor inhibition. *Journal of Experimental Psychology: Human Perception and Performance, 20*, 624–646.

Müsseler, J., & Hommel, B. (1997). Blindness to response-compatible stimuli. *Journal of Experimental Psychology: Human Perception and Performance, 23*, 861–872.

Neumann, O. (1990). Visual attention and action. In O. Neumann & W. Prinz (Eds), *Relationships between perception and action* (pp. 227–267). Berlin: Springer-Verlag.

Park, J., & Kanwisher, N. (1994). Negative priming for spatial locations: Identity mismatching, not distractor inhibition. *Journal of Experimental Psychology: Human Perception and Performance, 20*, 613–623.

Proctor, R.W., & Reeve, T.G. (Eds) (1990). *Stimulus–response compatibility: An integrated perspective*. Amsterdam: North-Holland.

Rizzolatti, G., Riggio, L., & Sheliga, B.M. (1994). Space and selective attention. In C. Umiltà & M. Moscovitch (Eds), *Attention and performance XV* (pp. 231–265). Cambridge, MA: MIT Press.

Schneider, W.X. (1995). VAM: A neuro-cognitive model for visual attention control of segmentation, object recognition and space-based motor action. *Visual Cognition, 2*, 331–376.

Simon, J.R., & Rudell, A.P. (1967). Auditory S–R compatibility: The effect of an irrelevant cue on information processing. *Journal of Applied Psychology, 51*, 300–304.

Tipper, S.P., Weaver, B., & Houghton, G. (1994). Behavioural goals determine inhibitory mechanisms of selective attention. *Quarterly Journal of Experimental Psychology, 47A*, 809–840.

Treisman, A. (1988). Features and objects: The Fourteenth Bartlett Memorial Lecture. *Quarterly Journal of Experimental Psychology, 40A*, 201–237.

Treisman, A. (1992). Perceiving and re-perceiving objects. *American Psychologist, 47*, 862–875.

Treisman, A. (1993). The perception of features and objects. In A. Baddeley & L. Weiskrantz (Eds), *Attention: Selection, awareness, and control* (pp. 5–35). Oxford: Clarendon Press.

Treisman, A., & Gelade, G. (1980). A feature-integration theory of attention. *Cognitive Psychology, 12*, 97–136.

Ungerleider, L.G., & Mishkin, M. (1982). Two cortical visual systems. In D.J. Ingle, M.A. Goodale, & R.J.W. Mansfield (Eds), *Analysis of visual behaviour* (pp. 549–586). Cambridge, MA: MIT Press.

Van der Heijden, A.H.C. (1992). *Selective attention in vision*. London: Routledge.

Wurtz, R.H., Goldberg, M.E., & Robinson, D.L. (1980). Behavioural modulation of visual responses in the monkey: Stimulus selection for attention and movement. *Progress in Psychobiology and Physiological Psychology, 9*, 43–83.

VISUAL COGNITION, 1998, *5* (1/2), 217–256

Further Evidence for the Division of Attention Among Non-contiguous Locations

Sowon Hahn and Arthur F. Kramer

Beckman Institute and Department of Psychology, University of Illinois at Urbana-Champaign, USA

Models of visual attention have, with few exceptions, suggested that attention is deployed to unitary regions of visual space. Kramer and Hahn (1995) recently reported that attention is considerably more flexible than previously believed, such that under some conditions attention may be focused on multiple non-contiguous areas of the visual field. In the five studies reported here, we examined the boundary conditions on the ability to divide attention among different locations in visual space. In each of the studies, subjects performed a same–different matching task with target letters that were presented on opposite sides of a set of distractor letters. Experiments 1, 2 and 3 provide further support for our proposal that subjects can concurrently attend to non-contiguous locations as long as new objects do not appear between the attended areas. Experiment 4 examined whether the disruption of multiple attentional foci was the result of the capture of attention by new objects *per se*, or by task-irrelevant objects. Multiple attentional foci could be maintained as long as new distractor objects did not appear between target locations. Experiment 5 examined whether attention can be divided among non-contiguous locations within as well as between hemifields. Hemifield boundaries did not constrain subjects' ability to divide attention among different areas of visual space. The results of these studies are discussed in terms of the nature of attentional flexibility and putative neuroanatomical mechanisms which support our ability to split attention among different regions of the visual field.

Requests for reprints should be addressed to Arthur F. Kramer, Beckmam Institute, University of Illinois, 405 North Matthews Avenue, Urbana, IL 61801, USA.

This research was supported by a cooperative research agreement with the Army Research Laboratory (DAAL0196-2-0003) and a by a grant from the Office of Naval Research (N00014-93-1-0253). We would like to thank Bernhard Hommel, Sabbine Maasen, Werner Schneider and Lex van der Heijden for their helpful suggestions on an earlier draft of the manuscript.

INTRODUCTION

A number of different metaphors have been used to describe the manner in which attention is distributed in visual space. One such metaphor is a spotlight in which it is assumed that attention is directed in the visual field much in the same way as a spotlight might be used to illuminate actors on a stage (Broadbent, 1982; Posner, Snyder, & Davidson, 1980). All events within the spotlight are processed, whereas events that fall outside of the beam are ignored. The spotlight is assumed to be of limited spatial extent, and it is shifted from one location to another to process large portions of visual space.

Metaphors which suggest more flexibility in attentional distribution have also been suggested. For example, Eriksen and his colleagues (Eriksen & St. James, 1986; Eriksen & Yeh, 1985) have suggested that visual attention operates like a zoom lens on a camera. Thus, attention can either be focused on a small region of visual space, with a high resolving power, or alternately focused on a large region of space, with a lower resolving power. Gradient metaphors have also been suggested in an effort to accommodate data which suggest that attention can be flexibly deployed in visual space. In these models, the efficiency of processing is considered to fall off from the expected target location, establishing an attentional gradient (Andersen & Kramer, 1993; Cheal, Lyon, & Gottlob, 1994; Downing & Pinker, 1985; LaBerge & Brown, 1989).

It is interesting to note that, with few exceptions (see, for example, LaBerge & Brown, 1989; LaBerge, 1995), models which employ these metaphors assume that attention cannot be simultaneously allocated to non-contiguous areas of the visual field. That is, most visual attention models assume that, although the breadth of attention can be narrow or wide, as suggested by the zoom lens or gradient metaphors, attention can only be directed to a single unitary region at any particular time (Crick, 1984; Treisman & Sato, 1990; Van Essen, Olshausen, Anderson, & Gallant, 1991; Wolfe, 1994). This assumption of a unitary focus places an important constraint on the flexibility of visual spatial attention.

The question of whether attention can be distributed in non-contiguous space was raised by Posner et al. (1980) and further explored by Eriksen and Yeh (1985). Posner et al. (1980) used a simple reaction time (RT) task and found RTs for the second most likely position to be faster than those for the uncued locations when it was adjacent to the most likely position but not when it was separated from it. On the basis of these results, Posner et al. (1980) concluded that, for luminance detection, subjects were unable to divide their attention over non-contiguous areas of the visual field. However, it is not clear what incentive there was for subjects in Posner and co-workers' study to focus attention on multiple locations, since the imperative stimulus usually occurred in the primary location. The faster response to the stimulus in the secondary location close to the primary location could be the result of an imprecise focus of attention on the primary location.

Eriksen and Yeh (1985) required subjects to perform a letter identification task in which either single or multiple locations were precued. Performance benefits were found only for the primary spatial location when two different locations were precued, suggesting a single focus of attention. Other researchers have confirmed the importance of spatial contiguity in classification tasks, demonstrating that it is easier to discriminate whether a probe dot is on or off a particular subregion when that subregion is compact and homogeneous (Crassini, 1986; Podgorny & Shepard, 1983).

Recently, by recording event-related brain potentials (ERPs), Heinze et al. (1994) concluded that attention forms a unitary zone that may expand to encompass multiple relevant locations but must also include the area between them. Subjects performed a same–different matching task and ERPs were recorded to task-irrelevant probes that were presented at different locations in the visual field. The P100 component of the ERP was the same amplitude when elicited by probes presented at target locations and at locations interposed between the targets. However, reduced amplitude P100s were obtained for probes that appeared adjacent to, but not between, the target locations. On the basis of their results, Heinze et al. concluded that subjects were unable to divide attention between non-contiguous areas of the visual field and instead employed a unitary attentional focus.

Despite these failures to find evidence for the allocation of attention in non-contiguous regions of space, other researchers have obtained data which suggest that it may be possible, under some conditions, to divide attention among non-contiguous regions of the visual field. For example, Shaw and Shaw (1977) found that stimulus detection performance varied as a function of the probability with which a target could occur at several different non-contiguous display locations. However, as pointed out by Posner et al. (1980), these results could be due to probability matching across trials rather than the differential allocation of attention among spatially separated display locations within a trial.

On the basis of a theoretical proposal by Hughes and Zimba (1985) that attention can be subdivided between, but not within, hemifields, Castiello and Umiltà (1992) instructed subjects to attend to two locations, one in each hemifield, which were demarcated by boxes. Subjects were required to respond as quickly and accurately as possible when a light was briefly illuminated in one of the two boxes. Three different box sizes were presented to indicate the position of the impending stimulus. Castiello and Umiltà (1992) argued that an inverse relation between box size and RT would suggest that subjects were capable of dividing attention between locations in two hemifields. This follows from the assumption that processing rate will increase if attention is allocated over a small as compared to a large area of space (i.e. predictions of the zoom-lens model). The results were consistent with these predictions and suggest that, at least for simple luminance detection tasks, attention may be divisible among two non-contiguous locations even though these locations are not strongly grouped.

Other research which has used split-brain patients has also obtained findings which have been interpreted as evidence for independent hemispheric attentional systems. Luck, Hillyard, Mangun Gazzaniga (1989) compared the visual search performance of normal and split-brain patients. They found that bilateral stimulus arrays were scanned at a faster rate by "split-brain" subjects than by normal control subjects. These results were interpreted as evidence that each hemisphere in the split-brain patient seems to control its own attentional spotlight and can scan its respective hemifield independently. Presumably, intact hemispheric communication should force normal subjects to maintain a single focus of attention for both unilateral and bilateral arrays.

However, other studies (Holtzman et al., 1981) have found that split-brain patients cannot divide attention in tasks that use symbolic cues to manipulate the direction of attention. Other studies (Kreuter, Kinsbourn, & Trevarthen, 1972; Teng & Sperry, 1973) have indicated that attentional processes may be shared by the separated hemispheres through intact subcortical pathways. In an effort to explain the discrepancies in findings for the split-brain studies, Luck et al. (1989) suggested that, while independently functioning attentional systems are available for visual search, attention can only be focused in a unitary area when oriented on the basis of external cues.

In a recent series of studies performed in our laboratory (Kramer & Hahn, 1995), we found that, under some conditions, subjects were able to allocate attention to multiple non-contiguous locations on the basis of external cues. Subjects performed a task in which they were asked to determine if two target letters matched or mismatched. The positions of the target letters were pre-cued with two boxes which were located in different hemifields on an imaginary circle. An important manipulation was the presentation of two distractors between the two target locations. Furthermore, the distractors were selected such that, on some trials, they would prime the match response [e.g. targets A and A (match), distractors A and A (prime match response); targets A and B (mismatch), distractors A and A (prime match response)], while on other trials the distractors would prime a mismatch response [e.g. targets A and A (match), distractors C and D (prime mismatch response); targets A and B (mismatch), distractors C and D (prime mismatch response)]. Thus, in essence, we incorporated a response compatibility manipulation (Eriksen & Eriksen, 1974; Pan & Eriksen, 1993) into a same–different matching task. If subjects were unable to selectively process the two non-contiguous targets and ignore the distractors, we would expect an interaction between response type (match or mismatch) and distractor type (prime match or mismatch response). The response incompatible distractors would be expected to increase RT and decrease accuracy of responding. If, on the other hand, subjects were able to selectively process the two non-contiguous targets, we would expect that the distractors would have no effect on the target responses (i.e. no interaction between response type and distractor type).

There was one additional aspect of the studies which is critical to the story. On some trials the targets and distractors were present as onset stimuli (i.e. the targets and distractors were presented simultaneously as sudden onsets), while on other trials the target and distractor letters were formed by removing segments of figure eight pre-masks (i.e. non-onset stimuli). We believed that such a distinction may, in fact, be a crucial determinant of whether subjects would be capable of dividing attention between non-contiguous locations. Yantis and colleagues (Yantis, 1993; Yantis & Jonides, 1984, 1990; see also Muller & Rabbitt, 1989; Theeuwes, 1991, 1992) have performed an extensive series of studies in which they have shown that sudden onset stimuli capture attention in a stimulus-driven fashion. That is, onset stimuli (e.g. new objects) receive preferential treatment in terms of attention and processing when they occur in a field of non-onset stimuli (i.e. old objects which have changed in some characteristic, such as shape or colour), even when the onset stimuli do not predict the identity or location of a target.

We reasoned on the basis of this sudden onset attentional capture effect that the failure to find evidence in favour of the division of attention in non-contiguous space in previous studies might have been due to the capture of attention by distractor stimuli. Thus, in previous studies (e.g. Heinze et al., 1994; Pan & Eriksen, 1993), subjects may have been able to allocate attention to non-contiguous locations of the basis of precues, but the occurrence of sudden onset targets and distractors may have reoriented attention, in a stimulus-driven fashion, to the distractors on a subset of trials. If this speculation is correct, we would expect to find an interaction between response type and distractor type, indicating active processing of the distractors, only on the onset trials. This is the pattern of results that we obtained. Young adult subjects were able to ignore the distractors on the non-onset but not on the onset trials.

In the studies reported here, we examined further the division of attention effect reported by Kramer and Hahn (1995). Experiment 1 examined whether subjects were actually dividing attention between non-contiguous locations on non-onset trials, or were rapidly switching attention between the two target locations. The results suggested that subjects were indeed capable of dividing attention among non-contiguous locations. Experiments 2 and 3 examined whether subjects selectively attended the targets within a spatiotopic representation, or within an abstract, spatially invariant representation. The results of the two studies argue strongly that subjects deployed attention to the locations of the targets within a spatiotopic representation of the visual field. In Experiment 4, we investigated whether sudden onsets *per se* disrupted the focus of attention on non-contiguous locations, or whether the sudden appearance of onset distractors, between the two targets, was responsible for subjects' inability to maintain multiple foci of attention on target locations on the onset trials. The results suggested that the appearance of sudden onset distractors were responsible for the disruption of multiple foci of attention on the onset trials. Finally, in Experiment 5, we examined whether attention could be divided within, as well as between, hemifields. Attentional flexibility, in the form of the division of attention among non-contiguous locations, was not constrained by hemifield boundaries.

EXPERIMENT 1

Although the results obtained in our previous studies (Kramer & Hahn, 1995) suggest that people can distribute attention among non-contiguous regions of the visual field, what was actually measured was interference from the irrelevant distractor items. Therefore, even though the subjects' matching task performance on the non-onset trials was not affected by the nature of the distractors, this result, in and of itself, does not conclusively indicate that the two non-contiguous locations were selected simultaneously. We assumed that the 60 msec stimulus duration used in our studies was short enough to preclude either eye movements or attention switching between the two target locations. Previous researchers have estimated that it takes from 150 to 250 msec (Eriksen & Yeh, 1985; Krose & Julesz, 1989; Madden, 1992; Sperling, 1984), or even as much as 500 msec (Ward, Duncan, & Shapiro, 1996), to identify a stimulus at a precued location and switch attention to a second location. However, research performed in visual search paradigms has found that subjects can search through large displays quite rapidly, suggesting that attention may be switched among locations in less than 30 msec, at least with well-practised subjects (Czerwinski, Lightfoot, & Shiffrin, 1992). Although the visual search task would appear to lend itself to faster shifts of attention than the matching task, given that in search the target is known in advance and is often unchanged across many experimental trials (i.e. targets are consistently mapped to responses), a more direct examination of the attention switching hypothesis would be a prudent course of action.

Egeth and Dagenbach (1991) proposed a diagnostic to distinguish between parallel and serial processing in visual search. This method entails manipulating the processing speed of elements in a visual display by varying within-trial visual quality. This diagnostic was developed for a simple case in which there are two elements per display in a search task. In this case, some straightforward predictions can be made for reaction times on target-absent trials in which processing should be exhaustive. Three kinds of displays can be constructed when visual quality is manipulated: pairing two high visual quality letters (HH pair), pairing two low visual quality letters (LL pair), or pairing one high and one low visual quality letter (HL pair). Assuming that the processing times required to identify a high-quality and a low-quality stimulus are T and $T + Dt$, respectively, we would expect a different pattern of reaction times for serial and parallel modes of processing. The parallel model predicts subadditivity of visual quality effects; that is, RT for the LL trials should be approximately equal to the RT for the HL trials, which in turn should both be slower than the RT for the HH trials. This follows from the fact that the low-quality stimulus is the limiting factor in parallel and exhaustive processing. In contrast, the serial model predicts additivity of visual quality effects. The decrement in RT between LL and HL should be equal to the decrement between HL and HH trials. These predictions are illustrated in Table 1.

However, even with parallel processing, processing time may not be equally slow in the HL and LL trials, because of the race effect or statistical considerations concerned with the degree of overlap between distributions of processing times (Egeth & Dagenbach, 1991; Miller, 1982). If two channels that contain a target are being sampled, one might expect statistical facilitation (race gain) for response time because the response can be made as soon as a target is detected in either channel. This means that the overall mean response time is slightly faster than the mean response time for either channel. However, when the processing is exhaustive, such as on target-absent trials in visual search or in same–different matching tasks, the race effect works in the opposite direction. The subjects must wait for the slower channel before responding, and hence one might obtain statistical inhibition (race loss). This effect works against getting subadditivity; the race loss with LL trials should be larger than race loss with HL trials because the sampling distributions overlap more in the LL trials. Because of this statistical consideration, the diagnostic of Egeth and Dagenbach works in such a way that, if the RT difference between the HL and LL trial is substantially smaller than the difference between the HL and HH trial, it is likely that the stimulus items were processed in parallel.

TABLE 1
Predictions of the Time Required to Process Pairs of Low- and High-quality Visual Stimuli for Serial and Parallel Models of Information Processing

	Processing Mode	
Visual Quality	*Serial*	*Parallel*
LL	$2^* (T + Dt)$	$T + Dt$
HL	$T + (T + Dt)$	$T + Dt$
HH	$2T$	T

Note: T = the amount of time required to process a single high-quality stimulus; Dt = the extra time required to process a low-quality stimulus.

In this experiment, we used Egeth and Dagenbach's (1991) diagnostic to determine if the two targets in the non-onset version of our same–different matching task can be selected in parallel. If processing of the two targets occurs in parallel, processing time for the HL trials should be similar to that of the LL trials, since the low-quality stimulus is the limiting factor. In contrast, if two target letters are processed in series, RT on the HL trials should be intermediate to those obtained on the HH and LL trials. If we find the data consistent with parallel processing of two targets, it will support our claim that people can attend to multiple non-contiguous locations simultaneously. Predictions for the onset trials are less critical, since it appears that subjects cannot divide attention between non-contiguous locations in the presence of onset distractors. However, if attention is distracted from the target locations by the onset distractors, and is then subsequently reoriented to the target locations, serial processing[1] would appear to be a likely outcome. Thus, in this case, we would expect an ordering of RT from the LL to the HL and, finally, to the HH trials.

Method

Subjects. Forty young adults participated in the experiment. They were recruited via a sign-up sheet and paid $5 an hour for their participation. Each subject performed one 50 min session. Twenty subjects participated in the non-onset condition and the other 20 subjects participated in the onset condition. For the non-onset condition, the subjects (9 females, 11 males) were aged 19–29 years. For the onset condition, the subjects (14 females, 6 males) were aged 19–33 years. The subjects had at least 20/25 corrected/normal visual acuity as tested with a Snellen chart.

Apparatus and Stimuli. Stimulus letters were displayed by a Zeos 486-DX33 computer with a 15 inch Amdek SVGA monitor. Subjects made all responses with a standard IBM PC keyboard. The stimulus letters were displayed in white against a black background. The brightness contrast of letters was manipulated to control visual quality. High-quality stimuli were presented in white and low-visual quality stimuli were presented in light-grey to manipulate brightness contrast. Also, high-quality stimuli were displayed three times thicker than low-quality stimuli to maximize the difference in visual quality. Luminance values of the high- and low-quality stimuli were 27.5 ft lambert (94 cd/m^2) and 12.8 ft lambert (44 cd/m^2), respectively. The luminance value of distractors, precues and pre-masks was the same as the high-quality stimuli.

---

[1]It is important to point out that Egeth and Dagenbach's (1991) procedure is asymmetrically diagnostic. Although a subadditive visual quality effect suggests parallel processing of the two objects, additivity does not necessarily imply serial processing of the objects. As previously suggested (Townsend, 1971), additive patterns of RTs can either result from serial processing or limited capacity parallel processing of multiple objects.

The upper-case letters E, H, P, S and U served as targets and distractors. In the onset condition, the targets and distractors were presented simultaneously; in the non-onset condition, the targets and distractors were presented by removing two of seven segments of a pre-mask. Each letter subtended a visual angle of 0.4° in width and 0.6° in height from a viewing distance of 60 cm. Each stimulus was presented on an imaginary circle with a radius of 8.5° of visual angle. The two target letters appeared at either the 10:30 and 1:30 clock positions or at the 4:30 and 7:30 clock positions. The two distractors were interspersed between the two target letters. The location of the two target letters was precued with two square boxes. The precue boxes subtended a visual angle of 2° in width and height.

Design. Three within-subject factors were manipulated in this study: visual quality (HH, LL, HL), response type (match *vs* mismatch) and distractor type (same *vs* different). Three levels of visual quality were manipulated by pairing two high visual quality letters for targets (HH pair), two low visual quality letters for targets (LL pair), or one high and one low visual quality letter for targets (HL pair). For response type, two target letters either matched or mismatched. On the target match trials, two distractors were either the same as the target and the same as each other (same distractors), or different from the target and different from each other (different distractors). On the target mismatch trials, distractors were either the same as one of the targets and the same as each other (same distractors), or different from either of the targets and different from each other (different distractors). Thus, same distractors were designed to prime match responses and different distractors were designed to prime mismatch responses. All three factors were randomized within trial blocks. Display type, either onset or non-onset, was a between-subjects factor. The "L" and "D" keys on the computer keyboard were used for match and mismatch responses. The keys were counterbalanced across subjects. Each subject performed 10 blocks of 80 trials. The first block was treated as practice and was not analysed.

Procedure. Each trial started with a fixation cross presented in the centre of the display. Once the subjects fixated the cross, they pressed the space bar to initiate the trial. For the non-onset condition, two precue boxes appeared along with four pre-masks, two in the target positions and two in the distractor positions. After 150 msec, two segments were removed from each of the pre-masks to reveal two targets and two distractors. For the onset condition, two precue boxes appeared when subjects pressed the space bar. After 150 msec, two targets and two distractors were presented. The targets and distractors remained on the display for 70 msec. A blank screen was then presented until the subjects responded. The task was to decide whether the two target letters matched or mismatched by pressing the specified keys. Immediately after they responded, the fixation cross for the next trail was presented. The subjects were presented with feedback after each block of 80 trials, which included their average response speed and accuracy.

Results and Discussion

The mean RT and accuracy data for each of the visual quality conditions are presented in Fig. 1. As can be seen in Fig. 1, the RT results would appear to suggest that subjects did indeed process the two targets in parallel on the non-onset but not on the onset trials. This follows from the large RT difference between the HH and HL trials, and the relatively small RT difference between the HL and LL trials, in the non-onset condition.

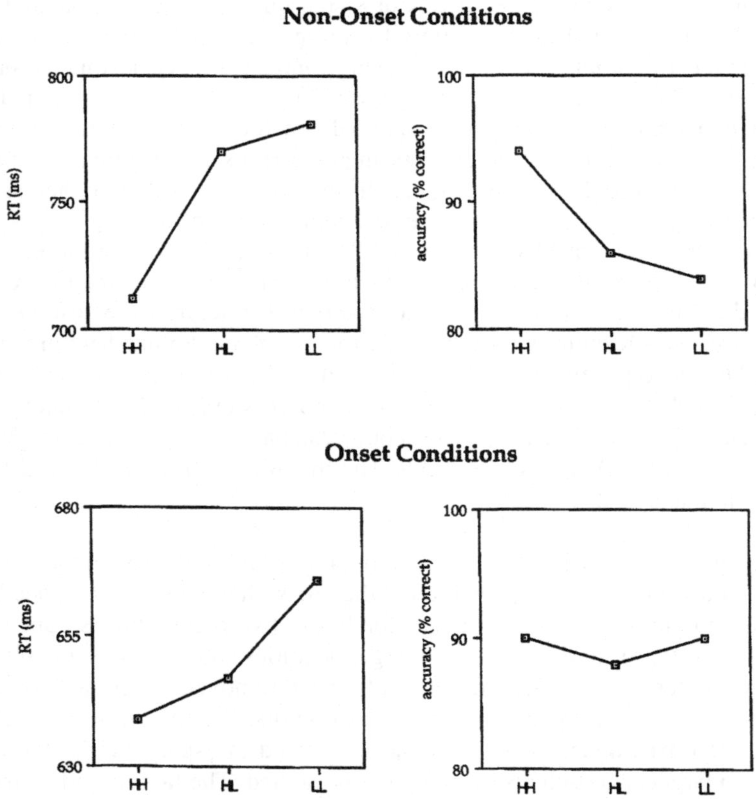

FIG. 1. The mean RT and accuracy data for each of the visual quality conditions and the onset (bottom panels) and non-onset (top panels) trials in Experiment 1. Note that the RT scales differ for the onset and non-onset figures.

The mean RTs and accuracies were submitted to four-way analysis of variance, with display type as a between-subjects factor and visual quality, response type and distractor type as within-subject factors. A main effect was obtained for the visual quality factor [for RT: $F(2,39) = 22.2$, $p < .001$; for accuracy: $F(2,39) = 36.6$, $p < .001$]. The LL trials were slower and less accurate than the HH and HL trials. More importantly, a significant interaction was obtained between visual quality and display type [for RT: $F(2,39) = 6.3$, $p < .01$; for accuracy: $F(2,39) = 26.4$, $p < .001$]. *Post-hoc* analyses with Duncan's multiple range test were conducted separately for the onset and non-onset display conditions. For the non-onset display condition, RTs for the HH trials were significantly faster than RTs for the HL or LL trials, while the RTs for the HL and LL trials were not significantly different. As predicted, it would appear that subjects are capable of processing the two targets in parallel, and of selectively ignoring the distractors, on the non-onset trials. For the onset display condition, RTs for HH and HL were not significantly different, while the RTs for the LL trials were significantly slower than in both the HH and HL trials. This result is not suggestive of parallel processing on the onset trials.

Thus far, the analyses have suggested that subjects can process targets appearing in two non-contiguous locations in parallel as long as the targets and distractors appear as non-onsets. However, although previous studies have suggested that the two non-onset targets can be selectively attended (Kramer & Hahn, 1995), we have yet to demonstrate this selectivity in the present study. To that end, we have presented the mean RT and accuracies for the response type, distractor type and display type conditions in Fig. 2. As can be seen in Fig. 2 it would appear that subjects were indeed able to attend selectively to the non-contiguous target locations on the onset but not on the non-onset trials. This conclusion follows from the significant three-way interaction among the display type, response type and distractor type factors [for RT: $F(1,39) = 13.0$, $p < .001$; for accuracy: $F(1,39) = 8.6$, $p < .01$]. The physically interspersed distractors influenced target responses only when all of the letters were presented as onsets. When the targets and distractors were presented as non-onsets, subjects' performance was not influenced by the nature of the distractors.

The interactions obtained between response type and distractor type for the onset but not for the non-onset trials (see Fig. 2), together with the subadditive visual quality effects obtained for RT on the non-onset trials, are consistent with our suggestion that people are capable of splitting attention among non-contiguous locations as long as new objects do not appear among the attended locations. However, although we have, thus far, interpreted our results in terms of the division of attention among locations within a retino- or spatiotopic representation, the results are also consistent with an alternative interpretation. It could be argued that, since the target but not the distractors were demarcated by box precues, attention was not selectively directed to the target locations but to high-level representations of the letters which appeared

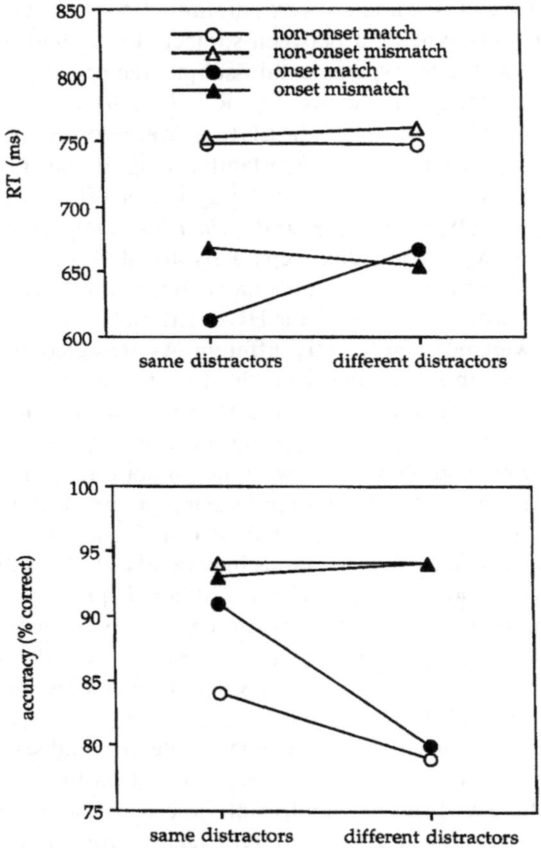

FIG. 2. The mean RT and accuracy data collapsed across the visual quality levels for the response type, distractor type and trial type conditions in Experiment 1.

within boxes. Indeed, such an interpretation is consistent with proposals that objects can be selected from abstract, spatially invariant representations (Humphreys, Olson, Romani, & Riddoch, 1996; Vecera & Farah, 1994), or that selection can be achieved solely on the basis of categorical distinctions between stimuli (Duncan & Humphreys, 1989).

EXPERIMENT 2

In an effort to determine whether subjects were selectively attending to target locations, as we have speculated, or selectively attending to highly processed abstract representations of letters inside of boxes, we modified our precueing procedures. As illustrated in Fig. 3, precue boxes were now used to mark both distractor and target locations.

If subjects had been attending to the locations of the targets within a retino- or spatiotopic representation, then we would expect the same pattern of RT and accuracy results obtained in previous studies (Kramer & Hahn, 1995) and illustrated in Fig. 2. That is, we would expect an interaction between response type and distractor type for RT and accuracy for the onset but not for the non-onset trials. Thus, if selection was mediated by location, we would expect that subjects would still be capable of selectively attending to the non-contiguous target locations as long as new objects did not appear in the display. However, if subjects had been selectively attending to the targets in an abstract, spatially invariant representation (i.e. given that the targets could be distinguished from the distractors by the surrounding boxes), then we would expect an interaction between response type and distractor type for both the onset and non-onset trials when boxes surrounded both targets and distractors. Thus, in this case, we would expect distractor interference with target processing, even on the non-onset trials, given the increased similarity of the target and distractor representations.

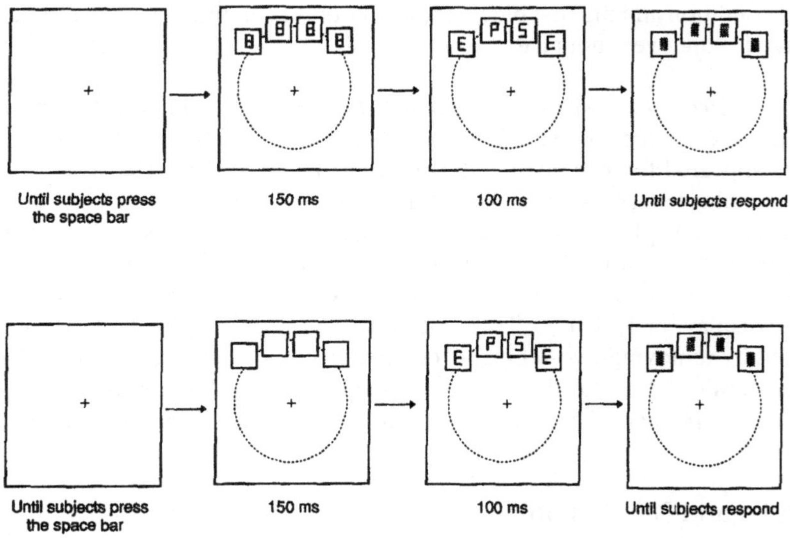

FIG. 3. A schematic illustration of the displays presented in Experiment 2. Displays for the non-onset trials are presented in the top set of panels, displays for the onset trials are presented in the bottom set of panels.

Method

Subjects. Eight students (4 females, 4 males) aged 19–26 years participated in this experiment. They were recruited via a sign-up sheet and were paid $5 an hour for their participation. All subjects had at least 20/25 visual acuity as tested by a Snellen chart.

Apparatus and Stimuli. The stimuli and apparatus were equivalent to those used in Experiment 1 with the following exceptions. First, all stimuli were presented at the high luminance level used in the first study. Second, rather than just precueing the target locations, both target and distractor locations were precued in the present experiment by white boxes. Third, following the brief presentation of the target and distractors, masks were presented at each stimulus location until the subjects responded.

Design. There were three within-subject factors: display type (onset *vs* non-onset), response type (match *vs* mismatch) and distractor type (same *vs* different). Trials were blocked by display type (onset and non-onset). Response type and distractor type were randomized within trial blocks. For 20% of the trials, target letters were presented without distractors to serve as a control for the presence of distractors. The "L" and "D" keys were used for match and mismatch responses. The response keys were counterbalanced between subjects. Each subject performed 10 blocks of 120 trials. The first block of the onset condition and the first block of the non-onset condition were each treated as practice and were not analysed.

Procedure. After subjects fixated the cross, they initiated a trial by pressing the space bar on the computer keyboard. In the onset condition, the four precue boxes appeared for 150 msec and were immediately followed by a display of four stimulus letters inside each box for 100 msec. Each letter was then masked and the mask display stayed on until the subjects responded. The subjects could start the next trial whenever they were ready. In the non-onset condition, when subjects began each trial, the four precue boxes and four pre-masks appeared on the display for 150 msec. Then, the target and distractor display, which was created by removing two segments of each pre-mask, appeared for 100 msec. Each stimulus letter was then masked and the mask display stayed on until the subjects responded. The subjects could start the next trial following their response.

Results and Discussion

The mean RT and accuracy data are presented in Fig. 4 for each of the experimental conditions. The RTs and accuracies were submitted to repeated measures three-way analysis of variance, with response type, distractor type

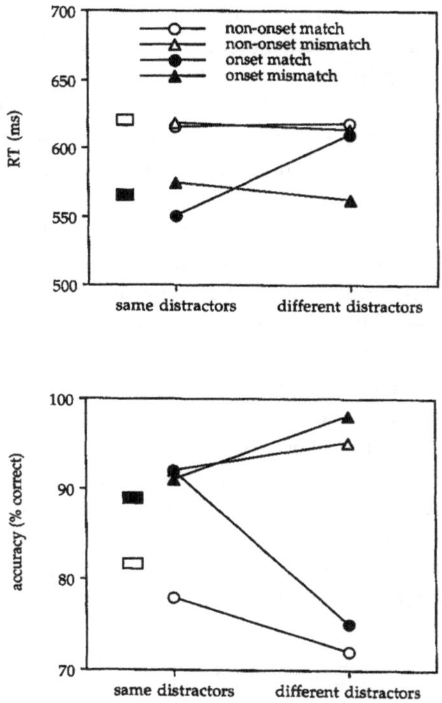

FIG. 4. The mean RT and accuracy data for each of the conditions in Experiment 2. The empty and solid boxes presented on the left of the two panels represent the control conditions in which the onset and non-onset targets were presented without the distractors.

and display type as within-subject factors. A main effect was obtained for the display type for RT, $F(1,7) = 5.8$, $p < .05$, indicating that onset trials were responded to more quickly than non-onset trials. A significant interaction was obtained for the response type and distractor type factors for both RT, $F(1,7) = 21.9$, $p < .01$, and accuracy, $F(1,7) = 24.3$, $p < .01$. Most importantly, however, we obtained a significant three-way interaction among the display type, response type and distractor type factors [for RT: $F(1,7) = 17.7$, $p < .01$; for accuracy: $F(1,7) = 15.8$, $p < .01$], indicating that subjects were able to ignore the distractors when the targets and distractors were presented as non-onset stimuli.

These results suggest that subjects were indeed attending to the locations of the targets rather than selecting the targets from a high-level abstract representation on the basis of their surrounding precue boxes. The results also suggest that subjects are capable of directing attention to non-contiguous locations in a goal-directed fashion, since unique physical cues were not available for the target locations.

We also included two control conditions in which onset and non-onset targets were presented in the absence of distractors (see the filled and unfilled boxes in Fig. 3). These conditions were included to examine whether the faster responses found in previous studies (Kramer & Hahn, 1995) and in Experiment 1 (see Figure 2) for the onset than for the non-onset trials were due to distractor interference or, alternatively, to differential effectiveness of the onset and non-onset stimuli to cue the appearance of the targets, In other words, it might be suggested that the slower RTs obtained on the non-onset trials belie our claim that subjects are capable of selectively attending to the targets on these trials. However, if the overall difference in RT between the non-onset and onset trials is due to the differential effectiveness of these stimuli to alert the subjects to the appearance of the targets, due to the larger luminance change on the onset than on the non-onset trials, then we would expect the same magnitude of RT difference between the onset and non-onset trials in the absence of distractors. This is exactly what we found. The difference in RT and accuracies between the onset and non-onset trials was equivalent for the control and experimental trials (all $p > .35$). Therefore, the overall RT difference between onset and non-onset trials would appear to be the result of the differential effectiveness of these stimuli to alert subjects to the appearance of the targets rather than distractor interference on the non-onset trials.

EXPERIMENT 3

The results of Experiments 1 and 2 suggest that subjects are able to divide attention between non-contiguous locations as long as new objects do not appear between the attended locations. Our finding in Experiment 2 of a lack of distractor interference with target processing on non-onset trials, even when both targets and distractors were surrounded by precue boxes, was interpreted as evidence against the suggestion that the targets were selected from a high-level abstract representation. The logic underlying this interpretation is that, with boxes surrounding the targets and distractors, it would not longer be possible for subjects to select the targets from representations which coded them as appearing in boxes, independently of their positions. Thus, we have argued, by default, that subjects would be required to focus attention on the locations in which the targets would subsequently appear.

There is, however, another possible interpretation of the results obtained in Experiment 2. That is, that spatial relations among objects (e.g. above–below, left–right, top–bottom, etc.) are coded in an abstract propositional representation and it is within such a representation that selective attention operates. Indeed, Logan (1995) has proposed a propositional theory of attention in which attention maps objects between two representations, a perceptual representation containing objects and surfaces, and a conceptual representation containing propositions about objects and surfaces. Within Logan's model, the perceptual representation is created automatically via bottom-up processing as one scans the environment. Although not explicitly stated by Logan, it seems plausible that the perceptual representation would take the form of a spatiotopic layout of objects. The conceptual representation is the result of goal-directed processing and codes objects in terms of propositions which express spatial (e.g. the motorcycle is in front of the lorry) and conceptual (e.g. the lorry is an International Harvester) relations.

Within the context of our same–different matching task, it is conceivable that, even with the lack of distinguishing cues for the targets and distractors (Experiment 2), subjects selectively attend to the targets in a conceptual representation on the basis of their spatial relations (i.e. the targets are always in the leftmost and rightmost positions in the display). Thus, in this case, attention would not be selectively directed to specific locations in a spatiotopic representation (e.g. Logan's perceptual representation), but instead would be directed to the propositional representations of the targets (e.g. Logan's conceptual representations).

In the present study, we contrasted the spatiotopic and propositional accounts of our data by employing a post-display probe technique to index the extent to which attention was directed to different spatial locations on onset and non-onset trials. The logic of this technique is as follows: If selection is based on location, then the benefits of attention should be obtained for any stimulus which occurs in the selected location(s).

Kim and Cave (1995) used the post-display probe technique to investigate spatial attention in visual search (see also Luck, Fan, & Hillyard, 1993). In their primary task, subjects were instructed to attend to a digit that appeared in a particular colour and to report its value. Digits that appeared in other colours in the same display were to be ignored. Subjects responded, by naming the appropriately coloured digit, when prompted 2 sec after the disappearance of the digits. The secondary task, which occurred on 25% of the trials, required subjects to make a speeded response to the occurrence of a small black rectangle that appeared at a location which was previously occupied by either a target or distractor digit. Consistent with the logic outlined above, Kim and Cave found that probes which occurred at the location previously occupied by a target digit were responded to more quickly than probes which appeared at a location previously occupied by a distractor digit. Other researchers have used similar probe procedures to index the breadth of spatial attention (Hoffman, Nelson, & Houck, 1983; LaBerge, 1983), to determine whether attention to colour is mediated by location (Tsal & Lavie, 1993), and to determine the role of spatial attention in selecting separated and superimposed objects (Kramer, Weber, & Miller, 1997a; Kramer, Weber, & Watson, 1997b).

In the present study, we employed the post-display probe technique, together with the same–different matching task, to examine spatial attention to target and distractor locations on onset and non-onset trials. If subjects direct attention to the locations of the stimuli in our task, as suggested by the spatiotopic hypothesis, then we would expect fast RTs when the probe appears at locations previously occupied by the targets and slow RTs when the probe appears at locations previously occupied by the distractors on the non-onset trials. This follows because we assume that attention is selectively focused and maintained on the target locations as long as new objects do not appear between the target locations. Furthermore, if attention is directed to stimulus locations in our task, we would expect similar RTs on the onset trials when the probe appears at locations formerly occupied by the targets and distractors. Such a prediction is consistent with our speculation that attention is directed to all of the onset stimuli, for at least a brief period of time, on the onset trials.

The proposition representation hypothesis makes a different set of predictions.[2] Since in this context attention is presumed to be directed to abstract propositional representations rather than specific spatial locations of the stimuli, there is no expectation of differential probe RTs for the target and distractor locations on onset or non-onset trials. That is, the RTs obtained for the infrequent post-display probes should be independent of their location, given that all of the probes appear at the same retinal eccentricity.

Method

Subjects. Eleven students (6 females, 5 males) aged 18–24 years were paid for their participation in the experiment. The subjects had at least 20/30 visual acuity as tested by the Snellen chart.

Apparatus and Stimuli. The primary task stimuli were the same as those used in the previous study with one exception: Precue boxes were only presented at the target locations. A small white rectangle appeared immediately after the primary probe on probe trials. The probe extended 0.2° in height and 0.2° in width. The probe occurred at the four letter locations equiprobably. On half of the probe trials the probe appeared at a target location, and on the other half it appeared at a distractor location.

Design. For the primary matching task, there were three within-subject factors: display type (onset *vs* non-onset), response type (match *vs* mismatch), and distractor type (same *vs* different). Display type served as the blocking factor. Response type and distractor type were randomized within trial blocks.

[2]The propositional representation hypothesis can also be considered to be a version of early parallel processing/late serial processing hypotheses (Van der Heijden, 1992). That is, under the propositional representation hypothesis, it is assumed that a perceptual representation is created in parallel across the visual field, while selection of particular objects and events occurs from a conceptual representation which codes objects in terms of propositions concerning spatial and conceptual relations.

For the probe detection task, there were two within-subjects factors, the location of probe and the display type of the primary task. The probe location was randomized within trial blocks. Each subject received 800 trials, presented in 10 blocks of 80 trials each. The probe occurred on 25% of the primary task trials. Thus, subjects performed 200 trials of the probe detection task.

Procedure. The sequence of displays is illustrated in Fig. 5. Each trial began with the presentation of a fixation cross at the centre of the screen. This was the subjects' cue to fixate the cross and prepare for the trial. For the non-onset condition, after subjects pressed the space bar, four figure eight pre-masks and two square box precues were displayed. For the onset condition, after subjects pressed the bar, two square box precues were displayed. After 100 msec, four letters were presented and remained on the screen for 100 msec. On each trial, a blank screen appeared for 2 sec, followed by the statement, "Please respond match or mismatch". Subjects responded by pressing a designated key on the keyboard. Subjects were instructed that speed was not important in making their response to the matching task. If the response was incorrect, a tone sounded.

Twenty-five percent of the trials included a probe. The procedure was similar to that in the non-probe trials, except that a probe appeared immediately after the letters and remained visible for 100 msec. Subjects were instructed to respond as quickly as they could after detecting the probe. After 2 sec, subjects were asked to respond to the matching task (i.e. match or mismatch).

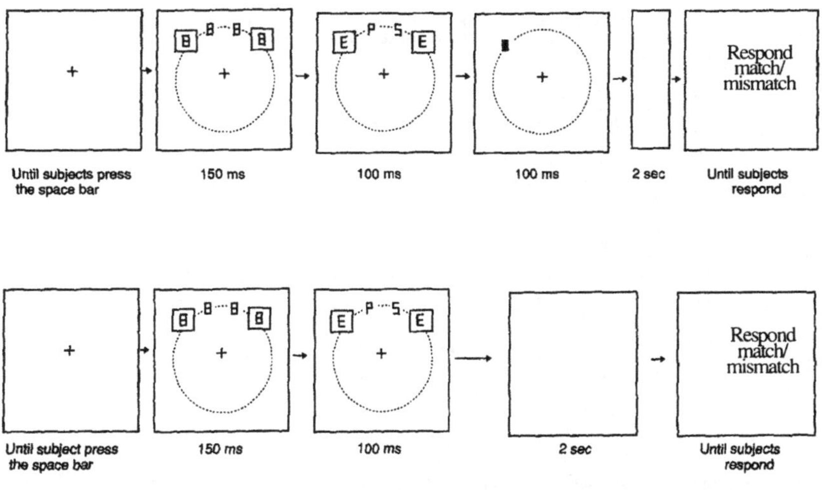

FIG. 5. A schematic illustration of the displays presented for the non-onset trials with (top panels) and without (bottom panels) the post-display probes in Experiment 3.

Results and Discussion

The mean RT and accuracy data for the probe trials are presented in Fig. 6. As can be seen in Fig. 6, the data patterns are quite dissimilar for the onset and the non-onset trials. These data were submitted to two-way analysis of variance with probe location (target location *vs* distractor location) and display type (onset *vs* non-onset) as within-subjects factors. A main effect was obtained for probe location, $F(1,10) = 26.3, p < .01$. Probes were responded to more quickly when they occurred at locations that had previously been occupied by a target than when occupied by a distractor. More importantly, however, was the significant two-way interaction between probe location and display type, $F(1,10) = 7.8$, $p < .01$. *Post-hoc* comparisons indicated that the interaction could be attributed to faster probe RTs on the target than on the distractor trials for the non-onset trials, but statistically equivalent probe RTs for target and distractor trials on the onset trials. The same tendency was found for the accuracy data, although it was not statistically significant.

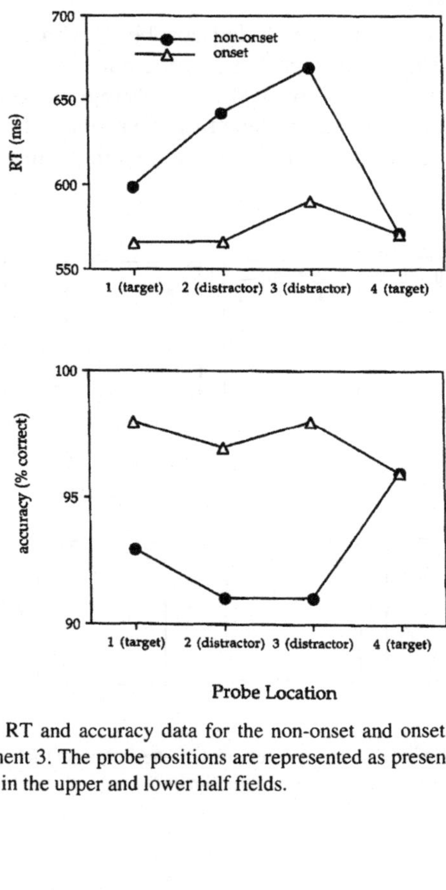

FIG. 6. The mean RT and accuracy data for the non-onset and onset trials for each of the probe positions in Experiment 3. The probe positions are represented as presented on the display, collapsed across presentations in the upper and lower half fields.

These data are consistent with the spatiotopic hypothesis, thereby suggesting that subjects' attention was directed towards the locations of targets and distractors rather than to abstract, spatially invariant representations of the targets and distractors. Therefore, within the context of Logan's (1995) proposition theory of attention, it would appear that, on the non-onset trials, subjects directed and maintained attention on the non-contiguous target locations in the perceptual representation. Attention would also appear to be directed within the spatiotopically organized perceptual representation on the onset trials. However, in this case, it would appear that both target and distractor locations were attended, for at least some period of time, on the onset trials.

EXPERIMENT 4

In the studies reported thus far in this paper, as well as those described in Kramer and Hahn (1995), subjects appear unable to maintain multiple foci of attention on non-contiguous locations when onset distractors appear among the target locations. This conclusion follows from several results obtained on onset trials, including additive visual quality effects (Experiment 1), an interaction between response type and distractor type for RT and accuracy (Experiment 2), and equivalent post-display probe RTs at target and distractor locations (Experiment 3). We have interpreted each of these effects in terms of the capture of attention by the onset distractors, thereby disrupting the foci of attention on target locations.

However, it is important to note that, in each of our studies, targets and distractors have either all appeared as onset or as non-onset stimuli. Given that display type (i.e. onset *vs* non-onset stimuli) was not manipulated within trials, it is conceivable that the disruption of the multiple foci of attention on onset trials was not the result of capture of attention by the onset distractors *per se* but instead by the inability of subjects to maintain attention on non-contiguous locations during the appearance of multiple onsets or new objects. That is, the appearance of multiple onsets, whether these objects are relevant or irrelevant to the task at hand, may result in a forced seriality of processing, as suggested by the visual quality effects obtained in Experiment 1. This could occur if an attentional interrupt generated on the basis of high-priority onsets or new objects can only be directed to one object at a time (Yantis & Johnston, 1990; Yantis and Jones, 1991). In such cases, subjects' attention may be misdirected to a distractor, on some proportion of trials, during the course of shifting attention from one target to the other.

Such a hypothesis predicts that it will be difficult to maintain attention on onset target locations even if the distractors are non-onset stimuli. This follows because it is the appearance of multiple onsets and not just onset distractors that renders it difficult or impossible to maintain attention on two or more non-contiguous locations. Henceforth, we will refer to this possible explanation as the "multiple onset hypothesis". Alternatively, it could be the case that, as we have implicitly assumed thus far, multiple foci of attention are disrupted when irrelevant but high-priority objects, such as onsets or new objects, appear in the visual field. In the absence of such high-priority distractors, goal-directed processing based on the intention to extract information at the target locations suffices to establish and maintain attention at multiple non-contiguous locations. Henceforth, we will refer to this possible explanation as the "onset distractor capture hypothesis".

These two hypotheses were examined in the present study by presenting target onset trials, in which the distractors appeared as non-onsets but the targets appeared as onsets, and distractor onset trials, in which the distractors appeared as onsets but the targets appeared as non-onsets. Both hypotheses predict that it will be difficult for subjects to maintain attention on the target locations on the distractor onset trials. However, the two hypotheses can be distinguished on the basis of performance on the target onset trials. The multiple onset hypothesis predicts distractor interference on the target onset trials, since the appearance of the onset targets will disrupt the multiple foci of attention. On the other hand, the onset distractor capture hypothesis does not predict distractor interference on the target onset trials, since the distractors do not appear as onsets or new objects and hence do not capture attention.

Methods

Subjects. Eight young adults (5 females, 3 males) aged 19–29 years were paid for their participation in this study. All subjects had at least 20/25 corrected visual acuity as tested by a Snelen chart.

Apparatus and Stimuli. The apparatus and stimuli were identical to those employed in Experiment 2 with the following exceptions. First, precue boxes were only presented at the target locations. Second, two onset and two non-onset stimuli were presented on each trial, rather than four onset or four non-onset stimuli as in previous studies.

Design. There were three within-subject factors: display type (onset *vs* non-onset), response type (match *vs* mismatch) and distractor type (same *vs* different). Display type was either distractor onset, in which distractors were sudden onsets but targets were constructed by removing portions of the pre-masks, or target onset, in which distractors were constructed by removing two portions of pre-masks but targets were sudden onsets. Each subject performed 10 blocks of 100 trials each. Display type was blocked by half-session, and response type and distractor type were randomized within blocks. For 20% of the trials, targets were presented without distractors to serve as a baseline against which to evaluate overall differences in RT and accuracy that were observed for the onset and non-onset conditions.

Procedure. The fixation cross was presented prior to each trial at the centre of the screen. When the subjects pressed the space bar, two unfilled precue boxes appeared either above or below fixation. For the distractor onset condition, two figure eight pre-masks appeared at the target locations inside the precue boxes. For the target onset condition, two figure eight pre-masks appeared at the distractor locations. After 150 msec, two target letters and two distractor letters were presented for 100 msec. The subjects judged whether the two target letters matched or mismatched and responded by pressing the "*L*" or the "*D*" key on the computer keyboard.

Results and Discussion

The mean RT and accuracy data are presented for each of the experimental conditions in Fig. 7. These data were submitted to three-way repeated measures

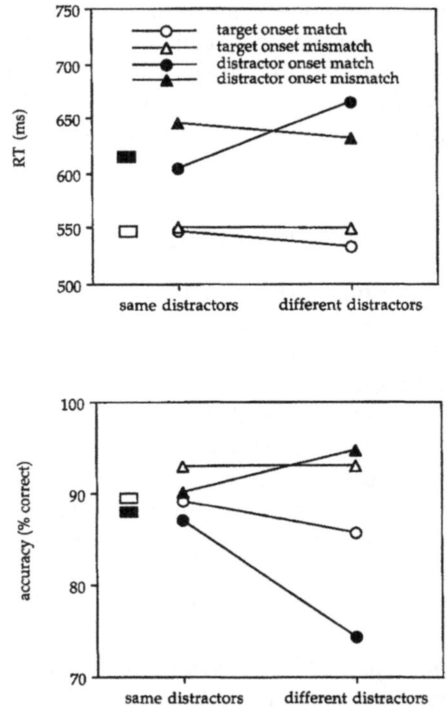

FIG. 7. The mean RT and accuracy data for each of the conditions in Experiment 4. The empty and solid boxes represent the distractor onset (i.e. distractors occur as onsets and targets occur as non-onsets) and target onset (i.e. targets occur as onsets and distractors occur as non-onsets) conditions, respectively.

analysis of variance, with display type, response type and distractor type as within-subjects factors. A significant main effect was obtained for display type with faster RTs, $F(1,7) = 13.2$, $p < .01$, and higher accuracies, $F(1,7) = 4.8$, $p < .06$, for the target onset than for the distractor onset trials. A significant three-way interaction was obtained for the display type, response type and distractor type factors [for RT: $F(1,7) = 49.3$, $p < .01$; for accuracy: $F(1,7) = 15.6$, $p < .01$]. Distractors interfered with target processing on the distractor onset but not on the target onset trials. Consistent with the onset distractor capture hypothesis, distractor interference occurred when the distractors but not the targets appeared as sudden onsets. Thus, it would appear that subjects can maintain attention on multiple non-contiguous locations as long as new distractors do not appear in the visual field.

The data for the control conditions in which the targets appeared without the distractors were consistent with the overall performance differences between the distractor onset and target onset trials. As can be seen in Fig. 7, performance on the control trials in the target onset condition was faster than performance on the control trials in the distractor onset condition. Thus, these results, together with the control conditions included in Experiment 2, suggest that the overall difference in performance between the onset and non-onset trials depends on the effectiveness of the targets, with onset targets being more effective than non-onset targets, presumably due to their greater luminance change, to cue the appearance of the imperative stimuli.

EXPERIMENT 5

The studies that we have reported thus far have provided evidence for the division of attention between non-contiguous locations when the two target locations appeared in different hemifields. Interestingly, a number of investigators (Castiello & Umiltà, 1992; Hughes and Zimba, 1985; but see Hughes & Zimba, 1987) have suggested that spatial attention is directed to hemifields such that, when a particular location is cued, attentional benefits are obtained for any stimulus presented in the cued hemifield.

A number of electrophysiological findings are also consistent with this proposal. For example, it has long been known that the parietal cortex plays a role in directing visual spatial attention (Wurtz, Goldberg, & Robinson, 1980; Yin & Mountcastle, 1977) and that lesions in the parietal lobe reduce the ability of patients to orient to the contralesional hemifield (Posner, Walker, Frances, & Rafal, 1984). The neuropsychological syndrome of hemi-neglect also shows attentional lateralization across the hemifields (Heilman & Valenstein, 1979; Mesulam, 1981). Patients with unilateral parietal lobe damage often have difficulty detecting stimuli in the contralesional field despite intact visual sensory function. This attentional deficit often covers most of the contralesional field. Other studies with split-brain patients have shown independent control of attention in the right and left hemifields (Luck et al., 1989).

Given these data, it would appear conceivable that, although subjects might be capable of dividing attention between non-contiguous locations in the two hemifields, as demonstrated in our previous studies, it might not be possible to split attention in the same fashion between non-contiguous areas in the same hemifield. The present experiment examined the issue of attention division within hemifields by presenting the two target letters and two distractor letters in a single hemifield.

Method

Subjects. Eight students (5 females, 3 males) aged 19–29 years were paid for their participation in the study. All of the students had at least 20/30 corrected visual acuity as tested with a Snellen chart. The subjects served in two experimental sessions.

Apparatus and Stimuli. The stimuli and apparatus were the same as in Experiment 2 with the following exceptions. First, precue boxes were only presented at the target locations. Second, the two targets appeared at either the 1:30 and 4:30, or at the 10:30 and 7:30, clock positions, with the distractors interspersed between the targets.

Design. Three within-subject factors—display type (onset vs non-onset), response type (match *vs* mismatch) and distractor type (same *vs* different)—were employed. Display type served as the blocking factor. Response type and distractor type were randomized within trial blocks. The "L" and the "D" keys were used for responses. The keys were counterbalanced for the match and mismatch responses across subjects. The subjects performed 10 blocks of 80 trials for each session. The first blocks of the onset and non-onset conditions were treated as practice blocks and were not analysed.

Procedure. After subjects fixated the centrally located cross, they initiated the trial by pressing the space bar on the computer keyboard. In the onset condition, the precue boxes appeared for 150 msec and were immediately followed by a display of four stimulus letters for 100 msec and then erased immediately. Each stimulus letter was then masked and the mask display remained on until the subjects responded. The next trial could be started immediately after the subject responded.

In the non-onset condition, when subjects began each trial, the precue boxes and four pre-masks appeared on the display for 150 msec. Then, the target and distractor displays, which were created by removing two segments of each pre-mask, appeared for 100 msec and were immediately erased. The target and distractor locations were then masked until subjects responded. The next trial could be started immediately after the subjects responded.

Results and Discussion

The mean RT and accuracy data are presented for each of the experimental conditions in Fig. 8. Consistent with previous studies, RTs and accuracies display an interaction between response type and distractor type for the onset but not for the non-onset trials.

These data were submitted to three-way repeated measures analysis of variance, with response type, distractor type and display type as factors. A significant two-way interaction between response type and distractor type was found for both RT, $F(1,7) = 68.1, p < .01$, and accuracy, $F(1,7) = 5.3, p < .05$. More importantly, however, we found a significant three-way interaction among the display type, response type and distractor type factors [for RT: $F(1,7) = 15.3, p < .01$; for accuracy: $F(1,7) = 10.2, p < .01$. As in previous studies, in which the target locations were located in different hemifields, subjects were able to focus and maintain attention on two non-contiguous locations as long

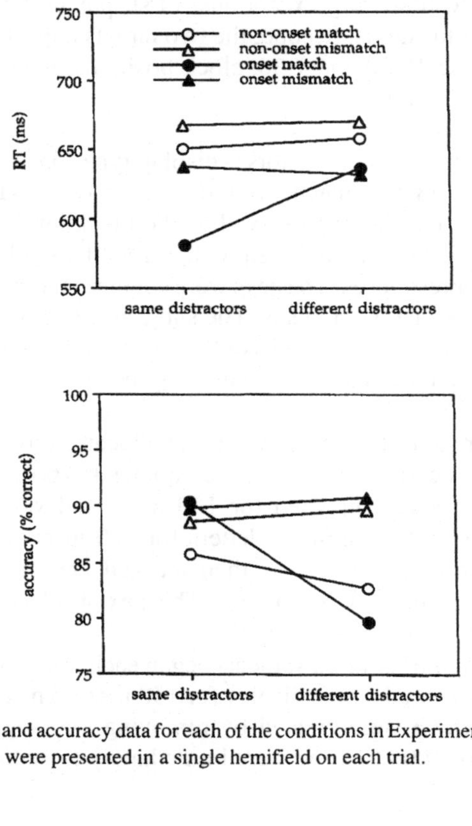

FIG. 8. Mean RT and accuracy data for each of the conditions in Experiment 5 in which the two targets and two distractors were presented in a single hemifield on each trial.

as onset distractors did not appear between the target locations.[3] Thus, these results, when taken together with our previous results, suggest that there is a good deal of flexibility in the deployment of spatial attention both between and within visual hemifields.

GENERAL DISCUSSION

The results obtained in the five studies reported here provide additional support for our proposal (Kramer & Hahn, 1995) that attention can be divided among non-contiguous locations as long as onsets or new objects do not appear among target locations. Experiment 1, which used Egeth and Dagenbach's (1991) diagnostic for parallel/serial processing, found evidence for parallel processing, in the form of subadditive effects of visual quality, for the non-onset trials. Therefore, it appears that subjects are indeed able to attend to information in non-contiguous locations.

Experiments 2 and 3 were designed to determine whether attention was deployed to non-contiguous locations within a spatiotopic representation or within an abstract, spatially invariant representation. In the latter case, attention would not need to be split between non-contiguous locations but instead selectively focused on the two targets defined by their unique surrounding box cues or by propositional representations that code their spatial relations (i.e. the targets were always the rightmost and leftmost objects). The results of both experiments were consistent with the deployment of attention within a spatiotopic representation.

---

[3]Given the relationship between targets and distractors in our studies, it might be argued that other strategies (other than attempting to divide attention between non-contiguous locations)—in particular, strategies that involve the intentional processing of both the targets and distractors—might have been used by subjects to perform the same–different matching task. For instance, the four experimental conditions represented by the orthogonal manipulation of target type (match *vs* mismatch) and distractor type (same *vs* different) are amenable to a strategy in which subjects enumerate the number of dissimilar letters and respond on the basis of this figure. That is, there were no dissimilar letters (across targets and distractors) in the target match/distractor same condition, two dissimilar letters in the target match/distractor different condition, one dissimilar letter in the target mismatch/distractor same condition, and four dissimilar letters in the target mismatch/distractor different conditions. Thus, the target match (i.e. detecting either no or two dissimilar letters in the target/distractor letter string) or mismatch (i.e. detecting either one or four dissimilar letters in the target/distractor letter string) response could potentially be made on the basis of the number of dissimilar letters in the target/distractor letter string. However, if we make the reasonable assumption that RT (and perhaps accuracy) varies in a systematic fashion with the number of dissimilar letters detected in the target/distractor letter string, then we would expect RTs to be slowest in the target mismatch/distractor different condition. Clearly, this was not the case. Furthermore, the pattern of response times to the location probes in Experiment 2 is inconsistent with a strategy in which responses are based on both targets and distractors. Therefore, it is reasonable to conclude that subjects performed the same–different matching task on the basis of target and not target/distractor information.

In Experiment 2, subjects were able to avoid distractor interference on the non-onset trails even in the absence of unique box cues at target locations. In Experiment 3, post-display probe RTs were faster, on the non-onset trials, when they occurred at a target location than when they appeared at a distractor location. When viewed together, the results of Experiments 2 and 3 strongly suggest that attentional selection and, in the case of the non-onset trials, selection from non-contiguous locations, was spatially mediated. Therefore, these results suggest the need for the modification of many current models of visual attention (Eriksen & St. James, 1986; Treisman & Sato, 1990; Van Essen et al., 1991; Wolfe, 1994) to allow for more flexible deployment of attention in the visual field.[4]

Experiment 4 was conducted to examine whether multiple onsets, regardless of their role as targets or distractors, were responsible for the disruption of the non-contiguous foci of attention on the onset trials. Indeed, Yantis and colleagues (Yantis & Johnston, 1990; Yantis & Jones, 1991) have argued that, when several new objects or sudden onsets appear in the visual field, these objects generate attentional interrupts which, in turn, result in their being assigned high-priority tags. The items with high-priority tags are processed, in a sequential fashion, prior to all untagged items (e.g. non-onset items). This notion of a priority hierarchy or queue implies that the presence of two onset targets may be sufficient to disrupt multiple attentional foci. That is, in the context of the same–different matching task, it may be difficult or impossible to selectively attend to the target locations when the targets occur as onsets but the distractors are non-onset items.

---

[4]It might be suggested, however, that subjects did not divide attention between two non-contiguous locations in our studies but instead focused attention on a single, albeit rectangularly shaped, area. As illustrated in Fig. 3, the distractors were actually located slightly above (when the targets were presented in the upper half field) or slightly below (when the targets were located in the lower half field) the targets. Although this was done to ensure equivalent retinal eccentricity for the targets and distractors, it is conceivable that this stimulus arrangement might have led to the deployment of attention in a highly elliptical or rectangular region which enclosed both of the targets but neither of the distractors. Indeed, a number of investigators have suggested that attention can be employed in a ring-like fashion centred on fixation (Egly & Homa, 1984; Juola, Bouwhuis, Cooper, & Warner, 1991). In our studies, a ring of attention centred peripheral to the stimuli could selectively enclose the targets without the need for proposing non-contiguous deployment of attention. To examine this alternative explanation, we performed a study (Hahn & Kramer, in prep.) in which distractors were presented above, below, to the left and right of each of the targets. We reasoned that, in such a case, it would be quite unlikely that a single unitary focus of attention could enclose the targets but not the distractors. The results of this study were equivalent to those obtained in our other studies. We found no evidence of distractor interference on the non-onset trials. Therefore, it does indeed appear that subjects are capable of selectively attending to non-contiguous locations in the visual field.

Alternatively, it might be the case that top-down factors, such as knowledge that targets will appear in particular locations on the display, may be sufficient to override the disruption of the attentional foci by the occurrence of multiple targets. However, top-down guidance of attention to non-contiguous target locations may not be sufficient to override attentional capture by non-target onset objects, particularly when these objects appear between the attended locations. The lack of distractor interference when targets appeared as onsets but distractors appeared as non-onsets (i.e. target onset trials), but the presence of distractor interference when distractors appeared as onsets but targets appeared as non-onset objects (i.e. distractor onset trials), suggests that it is the nature of the distractors and not the targets that determines whether attention can be maintained at multiple non-contiguous locations. That is, the simultaneous appearance of several targets does not appear to disrupt the maintenance of attention at non-contiguous display locations. Thus, it is not the appearance of onsets *per se* that disrupts spatial attention, but the occurrence of new objects at unattended locations.

These results are particularly interesting when viewed in the context of previous studies, which suggested that the capture of attention by new objects or sudden onsets can be overridden under some conditions. For example, Yantis and Jonides (1990) found that, if subjects are given a sufficient amount of time to focus their attention on a potential target location, sudden onsets that occur elsewhere in the visual field do not disrupt performance (see also Koshino, Warner, & Juola, 1992; Theeuwes, 1991). In fact, Yantis and Jonides (1990) found that a location precue–target stimulus onset asynchrony (SOA) of 200 msec was sufficient to override the influence of a sudden-onset distractor.

In our studies, a precue–target SOA of 150 msec was ineffective in eliminating the influence of sudden-onset distractors on the processing of the two targets. As suggested by the results of Yantis and Jonides (1990), 150 msec may be an insufficient amount of time to focus attention on target locations, thereby precluding the capture of attention by onset distractors. However, when we extended the precue–target SOA to 600 msec (Kramer & Hahn, 1995), subjects were still unable to ignore onset distractors effectively. Therefore, it would appear unlikely that interference by onset distractors in our studies can be attributed to an insufficient amount of time to focus attention on the target locations.

Another possible factor that may be responsible for attentional capture by onset distractors in our studies is the spatial relationship between targets and distractors. In each of our studies, distractors occurred between target locations. Given that it appears that subjects often direct attention, either overtly (Coeffe & O'Regan, 1987; Findlay, 1987) or covertly (Grabowecky, Robertson, & Treisman, 1994), to the centre of mass of groups of closely packed objects, it is conceivable that onset distractors may disrupt the focus of attention on target locations only when they appear situated between the targets. On the other hand, distractors may have considerably less influence on target processing when they appear at equivalent retinal eccentricities as the targets, but at positions other than between target locations. In an effort to examine this distractor position hypothesis, we contrasted conditions in which (a) onset distractors appeared between the target locations, as in our previous studies, (b) distractors appeared directly adjacent to the targets on an imaginary circle, but not between the target locations, and (c) distractors appeared on the opposite side of the imaginary circle from the targets. Onset distractors interfered with target processing only when they appeared between the target locations. Therefore, it would appear that attention can be focused on multiple non-contiguous locations even in the presence of task-irrelevant onsets or new objects, as long as these objects do not appear between locations in which targets will appear.

Modelling the Division of Attention Among Non-contiguous Locations. As discussed previously, the vast majority of visual attention models suggest that attention is deployed in contiguous regions of visual space. A notable exception to this modal view has been offered by LaBerge and Brown (1989, p.109), who suggested that, "Under circumstances in which targets are highly likely to appear at two different locations, the gradient could form two modes or peaks, with the locations of the peaks corresponding to the locations of the target locations". Such a proposal appears to provide a reasonable account of our finding of a lack of distractor interference on target processing in non-onset trials.

In an effort to examine, in more detail, the utility of the LaBerge model (LaBerge & Brown, 1989; LaBerge, 1995) in characterizing the data obtained in our investigation of attentional flexibility, we attempted to represent processing on the onset and non-onset trials within the context of the model that LaBerge initially designed to explain search for a single target. Since this model includes both cognitive and neuroscience descriptions of attentional processes, we describe the time course of processing, on onset and non-onset trials, in terms of changes in activation levels in different neuroanatomical modules that constitute a neural circuit for the control and expression of visual attention.[5]

A representation of the time course of attentional processes during the presentation of the precues and premasks, and the presentation of the targets and distractors on the non-onset trials, is presented in Fig. 9a and 9b, respectively. Representations of the time course of attentional processes during the presentation of precues, the intial presentation of the targets and distractors, and

[5]Although we consider the representation of processing on the onset and non-onset trials in our same/different matching task in the context of LaBerge's (1995) model to be a useful exercise we want to make clear that other neurophysiologically plausible attentional models (Schneider, 1995; Olshausen, Anderson, & Van Essen, 1993) may also be capable of predicting our data. Contrasting the predictions of these models will be a useful endeavour for future studies.

(a)

(b)

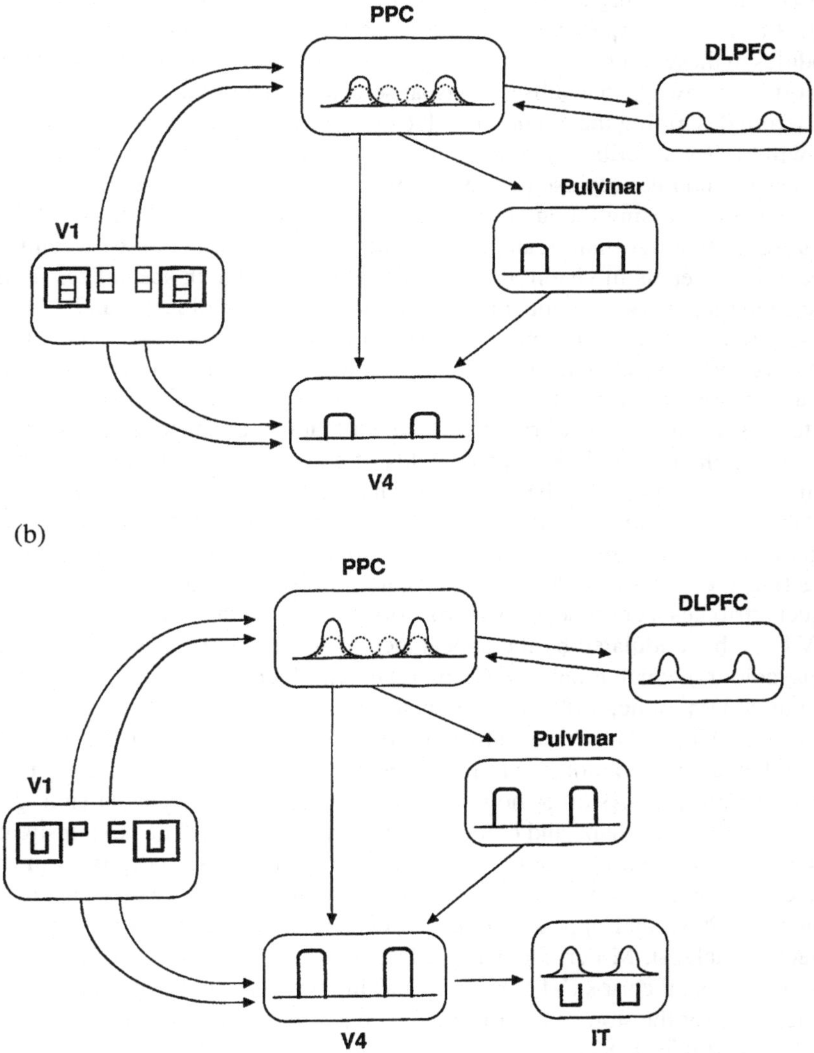

FIG. 9. (a) The activation levels in attentional modules at the time of presentation of the precues and pre-masks on the non-onset trials. (b) Activation levels in attentional modules at the time of presentation of the targets and distractors on the non-onset trials. PPC = posterior parietal cortex; DLPFC = dorso-lateral prefrontal cortex.

subsequent processing of the targets on the onset trials, are presented in Figs 10a, 10b and 10c, respectively. The connections illustrated between processing modules in these figures are not meant to be exhaustive, but instead to represent important pathways that subserve visual selective attention.

Before describing the manner in which our task is represented in the model, we will briefly describe the functional significance of the different attentional processing modules represented in Figs 9 and 10 (for a more detailed description of the processing modules and their role in attention, see LaBerge, 1995; Maunsell, 1995). A main feature of the model is the distinction between two processing streams in vision: (1) The ventral stream, which specializes in the discrimination between, and identification of, specific objects; and (2) the dorsal stream, which specializes in the spatial localization of objects, which subserves both object identification and goal-directed eye and limb movements. Visual information for both streams arrives via V1, an initial region of visual cortex responsible for discerning component features of shapes such as orientation, length and width. Receptive fields of cells in V1 are quite small, from 1° in the fovea to 4–5° in the periphery, and are topographically organized.

Within the ventral stream, area V4—in which cells are topographically organized but with large receptive fields—appears to play an important role in selective attention by modulating information flow corresponding to particular object attributes. A number of investigators have found that the activity of cells in V4 can be modulated by the appearance of specific attributes (e.g. orientations, colours) which monkeys (Connor, Gallant, Preddie, & Van Essen, 1996; Moran & Desimone, 1985) are instructed to attend and match to previously presented objects. These same attributes elicit much less activation in V4 cells when they are to be ignored. Similar types of effects have been reported in V4 during positron emission tomography (PET) studies of humans attending to objects defined by shape and colour (Corbetta et al., 1991). The next upstream module in the ventral system, inferotemporal (IT) cortex, specializes in the processing of complex shapes and objects, including body parts and faces (Tanaka, 1993), and appears to be involved in visual search for predefined objects (Chalazzi, Miller, Duncan, & Desimone, 1993). Finally, the ventral–lateral prefrontal cortex (VLPFC) is a working memory area that appears to be responsible for the storage of information concerning object shape and identity (Goldman-Rakic, 1987).

Within the dorsal stream, cells in the posterior parietal cortex (PPC) provide a coarse-coding of space within a head-centred coordinate system. Cells in the PPC have also been found to be modulated by visual attention such that they exhibit an enhanced firing rate in spatial attention tasks (Goldberg, Colby, & Duhamel, 1990), and PET studies indicate activation of PPC as human subjects shift attention among different locations in the visual field (Corbetta, Miezin, Shulman, & Petersen, 1993). The dorsal–lateral prefrontal cortex (DLPFC) appears to serve as the working memory module for spatial locations of

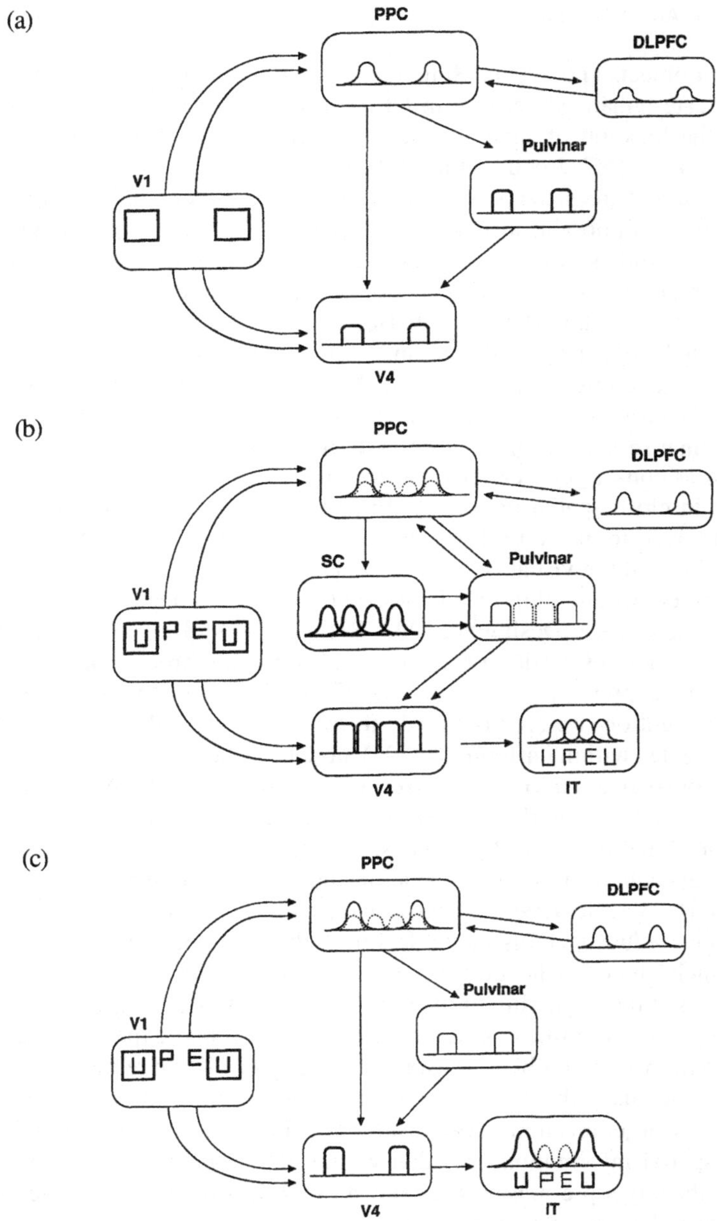

FIG. 10. (a) Activation levels in the attentional modules at the time of presentation of the precues on the onset trials. (b) Activation levels of the attentional modules during the initial appearance of the targets and distractors on the onset trials. (c) Activation levels in the attentional models once attention has been reoriented to the targets on the onset trials.

task-relevant objects and events. Single unit monkey studies and human PET studies indicate enhanced activity in DLPFC when subjects are required to remember the location of several objects in delayed match to sample tests (Goldman-Rakic, 1987; Jonides et al., 1993).

Two subcortical areas, the pulvinar nucleus of the thalamus and the superior colliculus in the midbrain, also appear to play an important role in visual attention. PET studies have found increased activation in the pulvinar when subjects are required to selectively process a target surrounded by a number of closely spaced distractors (LaBerge & Buschbaum, 1990). Rafal and Posner (1987) reported that patients with pulvinar lesions were greatly impaired when required to engage attention in areas of the visual field contralateral to the lesions. On the basis of these results and others, LaBerge (1995) has suggested that the pulvinar serves to enhance information at target locations and suppress information at non-target locations, particularly when targets and distractors are located in close spatial proximity. Finally, the superior colliculus (SC), which is involved in the control of oculomotor function, receives inputs both from the retina and the visual cortex (i.e. area V1) and appears to be involved in the movement of attention to salient events, such as sudden-onsets, in the environment (Gattass & Desimone, 1992; Rafal et al. 1998).

Given this brief description of a number of important processing modules involved in the expression (e.g. PPC, V4, SC, pulvinar) and control (DLPFC, VLPFC) of attention, we are now ready to proceed to describe how our task can be represented within LaBerge's (1995) model. We begin with a description of the time course of attentional processes on the non-onset trials. As illustrated in Fig. 9a, activation from the pre-masks and precues flows from V1 towards both the dorsal and the ventral pathways. In PPC, some activation is initially represented at each of the stimulus locations based upon the sensory information provided by V1. However, information is rapidly enhanced in PPC at target locations and reduced at distractor locations based upon inputs from the DLPFC, which has coded the locations of the targets from instructions provided to the subjects at the beginning of the experiment (i.e. targets will only appear in the leftmost and rightmost locations in the display) and experience in the task. Spatial information is both transmitted directly to V4 and relayed through the pulvinar nucleus of the thalamus, which serves to further sharpen the focus of attention on target locations. As a result of the information from V1 and the additional spatial information provided via the dorsal pathway, information concerning the target pre-masks is enhanced in V4. It is important to note that, in this figure and others, there is an absence of support from the VLPFC (which would be connected to IT which, in turn, would be connected to V4). This follows because in the same–different matching task, subjects cannot pre-store the identities of the targets, since the targets change across trials.

Figure 9b represents activation in the attentional modules soon after the pre-masks have been changed into the target and distractor letters. As can be seen, activations at target locations in PPC, pulvinar and V4, represented by the heights of the solid distributions, have further increased relative to preparatory attention represented in Fig. 9a. This occurs as a result of further development of the location-specific attentional distributions during the precue–target SOA. As a result of attentional enhancements in V4, there is little interference of the distractor identities during the processing and identification of the target, which are now represented in IT.[6]

As represented in Fig. 10a, attentional effects unfold similarly during the presentation of the precues on the onset trials. In fact, there is no activation of distractor locations in PPC given the lack of sensory input for these locations from V1. However, the representations of the targets and distractors are quite dissimilar during the initial appearance of the stimuli on the onset and non-onset trials. As can be seen in Fig. 10b, the sudden appearance of the four stimuli results in an enhancement of activation at both the target and distractor locations. This occurs both as a result of activation from V1 to V4 due to the appearance of the four new objects, as well as amplification of attentional distributions that result from the SC's sensitivity to sudden onsets or new objects. Thus, as a result of the lack of differential target/distractor activation, representations of all stimuli begin to develop in IT. Of course, if this process remained unchecked, subjects would be unable to discern targets from distractors, and accuracy would be no better than chance. However, as illustrated in Fig. 10c, selective enhancement of target locations is rapidly reasserted as a result of decay of the locational representations in SC and additional activation of target locations provided via the spatial working memory system in DLPFC. As illustrated by the differential line thickness, this results in a relative enhancement of the target compared to the distractor letter identities in IT.

In summary, the description of activation in the attentional modules in our instantiation of LaBerge's (1995) model provides a good account of the lack of interference from distractors on the non-onset trials as well as the interference observed from distractors on onset trials. Furthermore, the visual quality effects obtained in Experiment 1 are consistent with the simultaneity of processing assumed in the model, as are the post-display probe effects obtained in Experiment 3.

The model, along with the supporting literature, also prompts a number of interesting questions. For example, if additional priming of the targets had been available from the VLPFC, would subjects be able to reduce distractor inter-

[6]It is important to note that the attentional distributions, represented by the solid and dashed curves in Figs 9 and 10, indicate both relative locations of activation in a topographic coordinate system (for all modules but IT) as well as the magnitude of activation (i.e. indicated by the thickness and height of the curves). For IT, the distributions indicate the magnitude of activation of the letter forms but not their relative locations, because of the very large receptive field sizes of cells in IT.

ference even on the onset trials? This could be examined by providing subjects with target identities prior to each trial. Another question prompted by the literature which supports the model is the role of both facilitation and inhibition in selectively attending to non-contiguous locations. Our results only permit us to suggest that attention is deployed differentially to target and distractors but not to discern the mechanisms which underlie these attentional processes. Neuroscience (Moran & Desimone, 1985; Desimone, Spitzer, & Moran, 1988) and behavioural (Neill & Valdes, 1996) findings suggest that the differential enhancement of target stimuli at non-contiguous locations could be the result of some combination of target activation and distractor inhibition. Finally, the model suggests that attentional flexibility is dependent upon the effective utilization of prefrontal regions to prime task-relevant locations (i.e. DLPFC) and shapes (i.e. VLPFC), particularly in the presence of onset distractors. This suggests that subjects with reduced spatial and shape working memory may be expected to be particularly disadvantaged when irrelevant objects appear in the visual field.

REFERENCES

Andersen, G.J., & Kramer, A.F. (1993) Limits of focused attention in three-dimensional space. *Perception and Psychophysics, 53*, 658–667.

Broadbent, D.E. (1982). Task combination and selective intake of information. *Acta Psychologica, 50*, 253–290.

Castiello, U., & Umiltà, C. (1992). Splitting focal attention. *Journal of Experimental Psychology: Human Perception and Performance, 18*, 837–848.

Cheal, M., Lyon, D.R., & Gottlob, L.R. (1994). A framework for understanding the allocation of attention in location-precued discrimination. *Quarterly Journal of Experimental Psychology, 47*, 699–739.

Chelazzi, L., Miller, E., Duncan, J., & Desimone, R. (1993). A neural basis for visual search in inferior temporal cortex. *Nature, 363*, 345–347.

Coeffe, C., & O'Regan, K. (1987). Reducing the influence of non-target stimuli on saccade accuracy: Predictability and latency effects. *Vision Research, 27*, 227–240.

Connor, C., Gallant, J., Preddie, D., & Van Essen, D. (1996). Responses in area V4 depend on the spatial relationship between stimulus and attention. *Journal of Neurophysiology, 75*, 1306–1308.

Corbetta, M., Miezin, F., Dobmeyer, S., Shulman, G., & Petersen, S. (1991). Selective and divided attention during visual discriminations of shape, color, and speed: Functional anatomy by positron emission tomography. *Journal of Neuroscience, 11*, 2383—2402.

Corbetta, M., Miezin, F., Shulman, G., & Petersen, S. (1993). A PET study of visual spatial attention. *Journal of Neuroscience, 13*, 1202–1226.

Crassini, B. (1986). On the spatial distribution of visual attention. *Journal of Experimental Psychology: Human Perception and Performance, 12*, 380–382.

Crick, F. (1984). Function of the thalamic reticular complex: The searchlight hypothesis. *Proceedings of the National Academy of Sciences, 81*, 4586–4590.

Czerwinski, M., Lightfoot, N., & Shiffrin, R.M. (1992). Automatization and training in visual search. *American Journal of Psychology, 105*, 271–315.

Duncan, J., & Humphreys, G.W. (1989). Visual search and stimulus similarity. *Psychological Review, 96*, 433–458.

Downing, C.J., & Pinker, S. (1985). The spatial structure of visual attention. In M.I. Posner & O.S.M. Marin (Eds), *Attention and performance XI* (pp. 171–187). Hillsdale, NJ: Lawrence Erlbaum Associates Inc.

Egeth, H.E., & Dagenbach, D. (1991). Parallel versus serial processing in visual search: Further evidence for subadditive effects of visual quality. *Journal of Experimental Psychology: Human Perception and Performance, 17*, 550–559.

Egly, R., & Homa, D. (1984). Sensitization of the visual field. *Journal of Experimental Psychology: Human Perception and Performance, 10*, 778–793.

Eriksen, B.A., & Eriksen, C.W. (1974). Effects of noise letters on the identification of a target letter in the nonsearch task. *Perception and Psychophysics, 16*, 143–149.

Eriksen, C.W., & St. James, J.D. (1986). Visual attention within and around the field of focal attention: A zoom lens model. *Perception and Psychophysics, 40*, 225–240.

Eriksen, C.W., & Yeh, Y.Y. (1985). Allocation of attention in the visual field. *Journal of Experimental Psychology: Human Perception and Performance, 11*, 583–597.

Findlay, J. (1987). Visual cognition and saccadic eye movements: A computational perspective. *Spatial Vision, 2*, 175–189.

Gattass, R., & Desimone, R. (1992). Stimulation of the superior colliculus (SC) shifts the focus of attention in the macaque. *Society for Neuroscience Abstracts, 18*, 703.

Goldberg, M., Colby, C., & Duhamel, J., (1990). Representation of visuomotor space in the parietal lobe of the monkey. *Cold Spring Harbor Symposia on Quantitative Biology, 55*, 729–739.

Goldman-Rakic, P. (1987). Circuitry of primate prefrontal cortex and regulation of behavior by representational memory. In F. Plum (Ed.), *Handbook of physiology: The nervous system* (pp. 373–417). Bethesda, MD: American Physiological Society.

Grabowecky, M., Robertson, L. & Treisman, A. (1994). The center of mass influences normal attentional orienting. Paper presented at the *35th Annual Meeting of the Psychonomic Society*. St. Louis, MO.

Heilman, K.M. & Valenstein, E. (1979). Mechanisms underlying hemispatial neglect. *Annals of Neurology, 5*, 166–170.

Heinze, H., Luck, S.J. Muente, T.F., Goes, A., Mangun, G.R., & Hillyard, S.A. (1994). Attention to adjacent and separate positions in space: An electrophysiological analysis. *Perception & Psychophysics, 56*, 42–52.

Hoffman, J.E., Nelson, B. & Houck, M.R. (1983). The role of attentional resources in automatic detection. *Cognitive Psychology, 15*, 379–410.

Holtzman, J.D., & Gazzaniga, M.S. (1983). Enhanced dual task performance following corpus commissurotomy in humans. *Neuropsychologica, 23*, 315–321.

Holtzman, J.D., Sidtis, J.J. Volpe, B.T., Wilson, D.H., & Gazzaniga, M. (1981). Dissociation of spatial information for stimulus localization and the control of attention. *Brain*, 104, 861–871.

Hughes, H.C., & Zimba, L.D. (1985). Spatial maps of directed visual attention. *Journal of Experimental Psychology: Human Perception and Performance*, 11, 409–430.

Humphreys, G.W., Olson, A., Romani, C., & Riddoch, M. (1996). Competitive mechanisms of selection by object and space: A neuropsychological approach (pp. 365–394). In A.F. Kramer, M.G.H. Coles, & G.D. Logan (Eds.), *Converging operations in the study of visual selective attention*. Washington, D.C.: APA Press.

Jonides, J., Smith, E., Koeppe, R., Awh, E., Minoshima, S., & Mintun, M. (1993). Spatial working memory in humans as revealed by PET. *Nature, 363*, 623–625.

Juola, J., Bouwhuis, D., Cooper, E., & Warner, C. (1991). Control of attention around the fovea. *Journal of Experimental Psychology: Human Perception and Performance, 17*, 125–141.

Kim, M., & Cave, K. (1995). Spatial attention in visual search for features and feature conjunctions. *Psychological Science, 6*, 376–380.

Koshino, H., Warner, C., & Juola, J. (1992). Relative effectiveness of central, peripheral, and abrupt-onset cues in visual attention. *Quarterly Journal of Experimental Psychology, 45*, 609–631.

Kramer, A.F., & Hahn, S. (1995). Splitting the beam: Distribution of attention over noncontiguous regions of the visual field. *Psychological Science, 6*, 381–386.

Kramer, A.F., Tham, M., & Yeh, Y. (1991). Movement and focused attention: A failure to replicate. *Perception and Psychophysics, 50*, 537–546.

Kramer, A.F., Weber, T.A., & Miller, G.A. (1997a). Selective processing of superimposed objects: An electrophysiological analysis of object-based attentional selection. *Biological Psychology, 45*, 159–182.

Kramer, A.F., Weber, T.A., & Watson, S.E. (1997b). Object-based attentional selection: Grouped-arrays or spatially-invariant representations? *Journal of Experimental Psychology: General, 126*, 3–13.

Kreuter, C., Kinsbourne, M., & Trevarthen, C. (1972). Are disconnected cerebral hemispheres independent channels? A preliminary study of the effect of unilateral loading on bilateral finger tapping. *Neuropsychologica, 10*, 453–461.

Krose, B., & Julesz, B. (1989). The control and speed of shifts in attention. *Vision Research, 29*, 1607–1619.

LaBerge, D. (1983). Spatial extent of attention to letters and words. *Journal of Experimental Psychology: Human Perception and Performance, 9*, 371–379.

LaBerge, D. (1995). *Attentional processing*. Cambridge, MA: Harvard University Press.

LaBerge, D., & Brown, V. (1989). Theory of attentional operation in shape identification. *Psychological Review, 96*, 101–124.

LaBerge, D., & Buchsbaum, M. (1990). Positron emission tomographic measurements of pulvinar activity during an attention task. *Journal of Neuroscience, 10*, 613–619.

Logan, G.D. (1995). Linguistic and conceptual control of visual spatial attention. *Cognitive Psychology, 28*, 103–174.

Luck, S.J., Hillyard, S.A., Mangun, G.R., & Gazzaniga, M.S. (1989). Independent hemispheric attentional systems mediate visual search in split-brain patients. *Nature, 342*, 544–545.

Luck, S., Fan, S., & Hillyard, S. (1993). Attention related modulation of sensory-evoked brain activity in a visual search task. *Journal of Cognitive Neuroscience, 5*, 188–195.

Madden, D. (1992). Selective attention and visual search: Revision of an allocation model and application to age differences. *Journal of Experimental Psychology: Human Perception and Psychophysics, 18*, 821–836.

Maunsell, J. (1995). The brain's visual world: Representation of visual targets in cerebral cortex. *Science, 270*, 764–768.

Mesulam, M.M. (1981). A cortical network for directed attention and unilateral neglect. *Annals of Neurology, 10*, 309–325.

Miller, J. (1982). Divided attention: Evidence for coactivation with redundant signals. *Cognitive Psychology, 14*, 247–279.

Moran, J., & Desimone, R. (1985). Selective attention gates visual processing in the extrastriate cortex. *Science, 229*, 782–784.

Muller, H., & Rabbitt, P. (1989). Reflexive and voluntary orienting of attention: Time course of activation and resistance to disruption. *Journal of Experimental Psychology: Human Perception and Performance, 15*, 315–330.

Neill, T., & Valdes, L. (1996). Facilitatory and inhibitory aspects of attention. In A.F. Kramer, M.G.H. Coles, & G.D. Logan (Eds), *Converging operations in the study of visual selective attention* (pp. 77–106). Washington, DC: APA Press.

Olshausen, B., Anderson, C., & Van Essen, D. (1993). A neurobiological model of visual attention and invariant pattern recognition based on dynamic routing of information. *Journal of Neuroscience, 13*, 4700–4719.

Pan, K., & Eriksen, C. (1993). Attentional distribution in the visual field during same–different judgments as assessed by response competition. *Perception and Psychophysics, 53*, 134–144.

Podgorny, P., & Shepard, R.N. (1983). Distribution of visual attention over space. *Journal of Experimental Psychology: Human Perception and Performance, 9*, 380–393.

Posner, M.I., Snyder, C.R.R., & Davidson, B.J. (1980). Attention and the detection of signals. *Journal of Experimental Psychology: General, 109*, 160–174.

Posner, M.I., Walker, J.A., Frances, J.F., & Rafal, R.D. (1984). Effects of parietal injury on covert orienting of attention. *Journal of Neuroscience, 4*, 1864–1874.

Rafal, R., & Posner, M. (1987). Deficits in human visual spatial attention following thalamic lesions. *Proceedings of the National Academy of Sciences, 84*, 7349–7353.

Rafal, R., Posner, M., Freidman, J., Inhoff, A., & Bernstein, E. (1988). Orienting of visual attention in progressive supranuclear palsy. *Brain, 111*, 267–280.

Schneider, W. (1995). VAM: A neuro-cognitive model for visual attention, control of segmentation, object recognition and space-based motor action. *Visual Cognition, 2*, 331–375.

Shaw, M., & Shaw, P. (1977). Optimal allocation of cognitive resources to spatial location. *Journal of Experimental Psychology: Human Perception and Performance, 3*, 201–211.

Sperling, G. (1984). A unified theory of attention and signal detection. In R. Parasuraman & D. Davies (Eds), *Varieties of attention* (pp. 103–182). New York: Academic Press.

Spitzer, H., Desimone, R., & Moran, J. (1988). Increased attention enhances both behavioral and neuronal performance. *Science, 240*, 338–340.

Tanaka, K. (1993). Neuronal mechanisms of object recognition. *Science, 262*, 685–688.

Teng, E.L., & Sperry, R.W. (1973). Interhemispheric interaction during simultaneous bilateral presentation of letters or digits in commisurotomized patients. *Neuropsychologica, 11*, 131–140.

Theeuwes, J. (1991). Cross-dimensional perceptual selectivity. *Perception and Psychophysics, 50*, 184–193.

Theeuwes, J. (1992). Perceptual selectivity for color and form. *Perception and Psychophysics, 51*, 599–606.

Townsend, J.T. (1971). A note on the identifiability of parallel and serial processes. *Perception and Psychophisics, 10*, 161–163.

Treisman, A., & Sato, S. (1990). Conjunction search revisited. *Journal of Experimental Psychology: Human Perception and Performance, 16*, 459–478.

Tsal, Y., & Lavie, N. (1993). Location dominance in attending to colour and shape. *Journal of Experimental Psychology: Human Perception and Performance, 19*, 131–139.

Van der Heijden, A.H.C. (1992). *Selective attention in vision.* London: Routledge.

Van Essen, D.C., Olshausen, B., Anderson, C.H., & Gallant, J.L. (1991). Pattern recognition, attention, and information processing bottlenecks in the primate visual system. *SPIE Visual Information Processing from Neurons to Chips, 1473*, 17–28.

Vecera, S. (1994). Grouped locations and object-based attention: Comment on Egly, Driver and Rafal (1994). *Journal of Experimental Psychology: General, 123*, 316–320.

Vecera, S., & Farah, M. (1994). Does visual attention select objects or locations? *Journal of Experimental Psychology: General, 123*, 146–160.

Ward, R., Duncan, J., & Shapiro, K. (1996). The slow time course of visual attention. *Cognitive Psychology, 30*, 79–109.

Wolfe, J.M. (1984). Guided Search 2.0. A revised model of visual search. *Psychonomic Bulletin and Review, 1*(2), 202–238.

Wurtz, R.H., Goldberg, M.E., & Robinson, D.L. (1980). Behavioral modulation of visual responses in monkeys. In J.M. Sprague & A.N. Epstein (Eds), *Progress in psychobiology and physiological psychology* (Vol. 9, pp 43–83). New York: Academic Press.

Yantis, S. (1993). Stimulus-driven attentional capture. *Current Directions in Psychological Science, 2*, 156–161.

Yantis, S., & Johnston, D.N. (1990). Mechanisms of attentional priority. *Journal of Experimental Psychology: Human Perception and Performance*, *16*, 812–825.

Yantis, S., & Jones, E. (1991). Mechanisms of attentional selection: Temporally modulated priority tags. *Perception and Psychophysics*, *50*, 166–178.

Yantis, S., & Jonides, J. (1984). Abrupt visual onsets and selective attention: Evidence from visual search. *Journal of Experimental Psychology: Human Perception and Performance*, *10*, 601–621.

Yantis, S., & Jonides, J. (1990). Abrupt visual onsets and selective attention: Voluntary versus automatic allocation. *Journal of Experimental Psychology: Human Perception and Performance*, *16*, 121–134.

Yin, T.C.T., & Mountcastle, V.B. (1997). Visual input to the visuomotor mechanisms of the monkey's parietal lobe. *Science*, *197*, 1381–1383.

VISUAL COGNITION, 1998, *5* (1/2), 257–286

Mechanisms of Visuospatial Attention: Evidence from Event-related Brain Potentials

Martin Eimer

Department of Experimental Psychology, University of Cambridge, Cambridge, UK

A series of experiments are reviewed that studied mechanisms underlying visuospatial attention by measuring the influence of attentional selectivity on event-related brain potentials (ERPs). The results are interpreted within a theoretical framework developed by LaBerge (1995) and LaBerge and Brown (1989). Spatial attention can have an effect on occipital P1 and N1 components in trial-by-trial cueing situations, which indicate a spatially selective modulation of processing in the VI–IT pathway. However, this effect is strongly attenuated when unattended locations are potentially relevant, suggesting that early attentional modulations within the ventral stream are optional rather than obligatory. A distinct parietal negativity (Nd1) that is elicited in cued attention tasks is assumed to reflect the existence of a transient location expectation gradient within the posterior parietal cortex (PPC). This effect is not present in sustained attention situations. The fact that this effect is also observed with auditory stimuli suggests that this spatially selective PPC activity is modality-unspecific. Attentional selectivity in multi-stimulus arrays is reflected by the N2pc component, which may indicate location-specific processing modulations in the ventral pathway that are contingent upon an initial feature analysis.

INTRODUCTION

Selective attention serves an important function in regulating the impact of external stimulation on behaviour. Attentional mechanisms are responsible for selecting which environmental objects and events come to control the discriminative performance of organisms when they are confronted with multiple

---

Requests for reprints should be addressed to Martin Eimer, Department of Experimental Psychology, University of Cambridge, Downing Street, Cambridge CB2 3EB, UK. E-mail: me209@cam.ac.uk

This research was supported by the Max-Planck-Institute for Psychological Research, Munich, Germany, and by a grant from the Deutsche Forschungsgemeinschaft (Ei 266/4-1). I would like to thank Erich Schröger and two anonymous reviewers for valuable comments on an earlier draft of the manuscript.

potentially relevant stimuli. Attentional selectivity has often been interpreted to result from the fact that processing capacity is limited and that objects and events therefore have to compete for perceptual processing, identification and control of performance. Mechanisms of selective attention are thought to bias this competition in favour of information that is currently most important for adaptive behaviour (Desimone & Duncan, 1995).

Given this interpretation, selective attention may have several different functions, depending on the locus of competitive processes that are influenced by attention. Attention may serve to ensure that relevant sensory information is adequately processed (Broadbent, 1958), but may also be necessary for the selection and execution of specific responses (Allport, 1980). Because of this multiplicity of attentional functions, it is unlikely that the search for unitary mechanisms underlying selective attention will be successful. A more fruitful research strategy is to specify, as precisely as possible, different attentional functions and mechanisms and to relate these in turn to evidence from behavioural as well as neurobiological studies (Allport, 1993). This approach may eventually show that some of the controversial issues in the study of selective attention—including the debate over "early" versus "late" selection and the discussion about the special status of selection by spatial location—were based on simplified assumptions about general properties of attentional mechanisms that will come to be replaced by more specific characterizations of single attentional functions.

Studies of brain anatomy and function have played an increasingly important role in the investigation of selective attention, and the last decade has seen numerous studies in which attentional modulations on brain activity and effects of brain lesions on attentional functions were investigated. These studies have begun to reveal some of the mechanisms responsible for attentional selectivity by directly relating behavioural effects with underlying brain processes.

The focus of the present paper is the study of selective spatial attention with event-related brain potentials (ERPs). First, some general issues related to mechanisms underlying attentional selectivity will be discussed, focusing on a model originally proposed by LaBerge and Brown (1989) and further developed by LaBerge (1995), as this model will later serve as a conceptual framework for the interpretation of the ERP data. Then, a brief introduction to the methodology of ERP recordings will be given, and it will be argued that ERPs are a particularly suitable tool for investigating attentional functions and mechanisms. In the following sections, several ERP studies will be reported that investigated mechanisms of attentional selection by location in single-stimulus and multiple-stimulus arrays. The aim of this paper is to illustrate that ERP measures may provide a valuable source of information about the functional organization of attentional mechanisms.

MECHANISMS OF ATTENTIONAL SELECTIVITY

One particularly prominent issue in the debate about the nature of attentional mechanisms concerns the locus of selectivity: Does attention operate at an early stage of perceptual processing—that is, before object identification and categorization—or at post-perceptual stages that follow the identification of objects? While initial studies of attention seemed to support the early selection view (Broadbent, 1958), late selection theories came to dominate the field inspired by numerous studies that found evidence of an automatic processing of unattended stimuli (Shiffrin & Schneider, 1977). Kahneman and Treisman (1984) suggested that this paradigm shift was due to the fact that the experimental situations investigated in the earlier studies ("filtering paradigms") were typically more complex than the "selective set paradigms" employed in more recent research. They warned against direct inferences from the results obtained in studies of selective set to the nature of attentional mechanisms that operate in filtering situations. Early and late selection accounts are no longer viewed as mutually exclusive, and a number of theories have been put forward that combine assumptions from both the early and the late selection approach (Bundesen, 1990; Kahneman & Treisman, 1984; Lavie, 1995). Instead of searching for a single "locus of attentional selectivity", it is now generally assumed that selection may occur at multiple loci within the information processing stream, and that the processes underlying these different selective processes may also differ from each other. Selection may proceed through a modulation of the activity of sensory neurons, can involve the selective facilitation or inhibition of neuronal responses in parietal or temporal cortex mediated by competitive processes, may affect the entry of specific information into a limited-capacity, short-term memory store, or could gate the admission of information to an executive control system (Allport, 1993).

Related to the issue of early versus late selection is the question of whether spatial location plays a unique role in attentional selectivity, so that the selection of other stimulus attributes is contingent on the correct detection of their location (Nissen 1985; Tsal & Lavie, 1993). Evidence for a specific role of location arises from the fact that spatial cues are more effective in directing attention than non-spatial cues (Johnston & Dark, 1986). In fact, the superior selectivity when relevant and irrelevant objects are spatially separated has often been interpreted as evidence in favour of an early selection account (see Allport, 1993, for a critique of this assumption). While some theorists explicitly assume that spatial location plays a unique role in selective attention (LaBerge & Brown, 1989; Treisman & Gelade, 1980; Van der Heijden, 1993), others hold that there is no qualitative difference between location and other, non-spatial selection attributes (Bundesen, 1990; Desimone & Duncan, 1995; Duncan & Humphreys, 1989).

Given that there are multiple loci of attentional selectivity, and different mechanisms underlying these selective processes, it is crucial for models of selective attention developed by cognitive psychologists to take into account the functional architecture of the primate cortex and, more specifically, results from neurobiological studies investigating the impact of attentional factors on cortical activity. One such model has been proposed by LaBerge and Brown (1989; see also LaBerge, 1995). It was originally designed to describe attentional mechanisms underlying the identification of objects in multi-stimulus arrays, but can also be applied to single-stimulus events. The main aspects of this model will now be described in some detail, since they are employed in later sections to interpret several findings from event-related brain potential studies of selective attention.

According to this model, attentional selectivity is the result of an interaction between the two main visual processing pathways—the dorsal stream and the ventral stream (Ungerleider & Mishkin, 1982)—that is mediated by subcortical structures (the thalamus and the superior colliculus). The ventral pathway connects visual areas V1 and V2 with V3, V4 and the posterior and anterior areas of the inferotemporal (IT) cortex (areas TEO and TE). Its main function is the discrimination and identification of objects. The dorsal stream connects areas V1 and V2 to the posterior parietal cortex (PPC) and deals mainly with the spatial aspects of object perception. In the ventral stream, visual information is initially received and processed by areas V1 and V2, and is then sent via V4 to the IT cortex, where object identification takes place. Attentional selectivity is assumed to modulate the information flow in the pathways connecting V1 with IT. This modulation is mediated by thalamic circuits that are under the control of spatial information originating from the dorsal stream. When the location of a relevant object is precued, an attentional location expectation gradient is set up in the posterior parietal cortex. If the object is then presented at the expected location, this attentional gradient acts either directly or through the thalamus to increase the flow of information from this location in the pathways connecting V1 with IT, while simultaneously suppressing the information flow from other locations. As a result of this filtering operation, the IT cortex only receives and operates on feature information originating from a selected location. When the target object is presented at an uncued location, the expectation gradient set up by the cue will initially be in competition with the activation elicited by the target within the posterior parietal cortex, thus delaying the attentional selection of relevant information in the ventral processing stream.

In addition to these mechanisms, processing within the dorsal and ventral streams is also assumed to be controlled by prefrontal structures. The dorsolateral prefrontal cortex (DLPFC) is involved in spatial memory and serves an important role in eliciting voluntary shifts of attention (e.g. in response to the task instructions "attend to objects presented in the leftmost position"). Accordingly, the DLPFC has direct projections to the PPC, where prefrontal signals may set up an attentional gradient, which in turn influences processing in the ventral stream. The ventrol-lateral prefrontal cortex (VLPFC) is involved in memory for object features and may thus be important when attention is directed to non-spatial features (e.g. in response to the task instructions "attend to all squares regardless of their position"). The VLPFC is assumed to exert a modulatory influence on processing within the IT cortex.

The model developed by LaBerge and Brown (1989) and LaBerge (1995) explicitly assumes that location plays a unique role in attentional selectivity: The modulation of the pathways connecting V1 to IT is under the control of location information represented in PPC or DLPFC. Moreover, it can be viewed as an early- selection theory, since it assumes that attentional selectivity, as instantiated by a filtering process, operates before stimulus identification: that is, before objects are processed within IT cortex. It should be noted, however, that our present knowledge of functional architecture of the ventral stream does not allow a clear distinction between "early", pre-categorical perceptual processing and processes related to the identification of an object. It is not obvious that there is a unique place within the V1–V2–V4–TEO–TE pathway where elementary feature analysis is terminated and object identification begins. Instead of trying to determine if the modulatory influence of spatial information on visual processing is "early" or "late", a more fruitful research strategy would be to localize specific areas within the ventral pathway where neuronal activity is affected by attention.

In later sections, several ERP studies are reported that studied the impact of selective spatial attention on information processing as indicated by a differential modulation of ERP waveforms elicited by stimuli at attended and unattended locations. The results of these studies will be discussed within the theoretical framework developed by LaBerge and Brown (1989) and LaBerge (1995), focusing on two central issues: (1) Is there evidence for an attentional modulation of information processing in the ventral stream and, if there is, does this modulation take place within the V1–IT pathway? (2) Can ERP measures provide information with respect to the presence of attentional location expectation gradients in the PPC cortex that are assumed to be set up in response to spatial precues? Before these experiments are discussed, the next section provides some general considerations about the ERP method and its utility for studying mechanisms of selective attention.

ERP STUDIES OF VISUOSPATIAL ATTENTION

Event-related brain potentials (ERPs) reflect phasic modulations of brain activity that are time-locked to the onset of external or internal events. ERPs can be obtained by averaging the EEG activity measured in response to such events over a number of recording epochs. The result ERP waveforms consist of positive- and negative-going deflections that are assumed to be generated at least partially by synchronous post-synaptic activities at the apical dendrites of pyramidal cells in cortical layer IV. These ERP deflections are labelled with respect to their polarity (positive or negative) and latency. In contrast to other measures of brain activity, such as single-cell recordings, ERPs provide a non-invasive method of monitoring brain events that take place during cognitive processing. They can thus be obtained with normal voluntary subjects under standard experimental conditions. Since ERPs provide a continuous on-line measure of cerebral activities, they can, in principle, be used as markers for specific stages of human information processing. To do this, the functional significance of ERP components has to be determined by studying how various experimental manipulations affect these components. Thus, one of the major aims in ERP research is to describe the relationship between ERP components and cognitive processes (see Coles, Gratton, & Fabiani, 1990, for a further discussion of this issue). Moreover, by localizing the cortical generators of ERP components that are markers for specific cognitive functions, ERPs can also provide information with respect to the functional architecture of the brain. It should be noted, however, that it is not possible to determine unequivocally the cerebral generators of ERP components exclusively on the basis of ERP scalp distributions. To discover which brain processes are responsible for ERP components, the ERP methodology has to be combined with other electrophysiological or neuroimaging techniques.

As a non-invasive continuous measure of the time course of cognitive processing that can also be obtained in the absence of overt response requirements, ERPs seem particularly suited for the study of attentional processes. In typical ERP studies of selective spatial attention, stimuli are presented at attended or at unattended locations, and ERP waveforms are computed for these different conditions. By comparing the ERPs elicited by attended-location and unattended-location stimuli, it is possible to determine when, and in what way, spatial attention comes to influence processing as reflected by the ERP waveforms. If specific ERP components are related to different cognitive operations, the presence or absence of systematic effects of selective attention on these components in different experimental circumstances may provide important information about the mechanisms underlying attentional selectivity. And by localizing the cerebral origin of the ERP components found to be sensitive to attentional manipulations, it is possible to identify those areas of the brain that subserve specific attentional functions.

ERP EFFECTS OF VISUOSPATIAL ATTENTION IN THE VENTRAL PATHWAY

Visual information is first received by areas V1 and V2, where elementary feature information is represented and is then sent via V4 to IT cortex. In the model described above (LaBerge, 1995), a spatially selective modulation of perceptual processing within the pathway connecting V1 to IT is caused by direct or indirect inputs from posterior parietal cortex, where expectancies about the location of relevant objects are represented by an attentional gradient that is set up in response to spatially informative precues. Such an influence of PPC signals on visual processing stages prior to IT may be responsible for behavioural effects of spatial precueing where single target stimuli are displayed in an otherwise empty field (Posner, Snyder, & Davidson, 1980). If such an influence does exist, one would expect to find evidence for it in the ERP waveforms elicited by stimuli at attended and unattended locations under conditions where the relevant location is specified in advance.

Most ERP studies on visuospatial attention have used a sustained attention paradigm. Instead of using precues, subjects are instructed at the beginning of each block to direct their attention to a specific location to detect target stimuli at that location (Eason 1981; Mangun & Hillyard, 1987). The typical outcome of such an experiment is shown in Fig. 1. In this unpublished study, letter stimuli (M and W) were presented with equal probability 6° to the left or right of the fixation. Subjects were instructed to response to the letter W only when it was presented at the side specified prior to the start of each block (which was changed from left to right and back again between experimental blocks). A comparison of the ERPs elicited by attended- and unattended-location stimuli at occipital electrodes (collapsed over electrodes OL and OR, located halfway

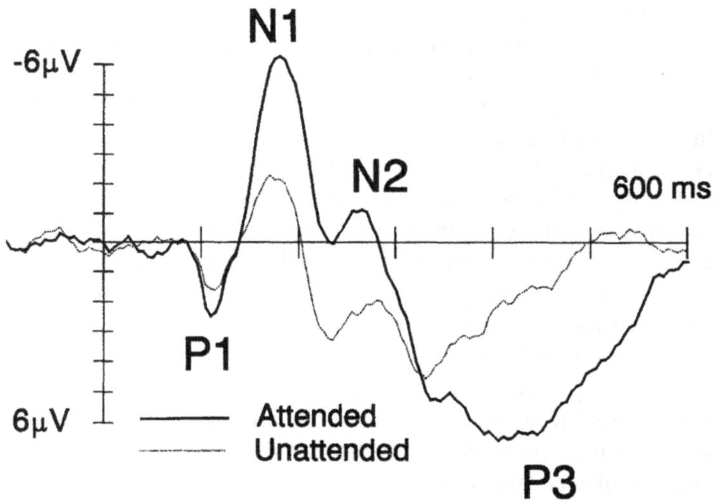

FIG. 1. Grand-averaged event-related brain potentials (ERPs) elicited by stimuli at attended locations (solid line) and unattended locations (dotted line) at lateral occipital sites (collapsed over electrodes OL and OR), in an experiment where subjects were instructed to keep their attention focused on the left or right side for an entire experimental block.

between O1 and T5, and O2 and T6, respectively) revealed systematic differences. Attention was found to modulate the P1, N1, N2 and P3 components, with larger amplitudes elicited by stimuli at attended locations. The earliest attentional effect was the amplitude modulation of the P1 component that started around 100 msec post-stimulus.

What conclusions can be drawn on the basis of this pattern of results? The enhancement of the N2 and P3 amplitudes are probably a result of the fact that 50% of the attended-location stimuli required a response, as N2 and P3 are known to be sensitive to the relevance of a stimulus for overt performance. In contrast, the earlier attentional modulations of the P1 and N1 components may be more directly related to mechanisms of spatial selectivity. The P1 and N1 components are often referred to as exogenous components, since they are triggered by visual stimuli independently of their psychological significance. Moreover, P1 and N1 are assumed to be sensory-specific, because they are elicited within different time windows, and with a different scalp distribution when non-visual stimuli are presented. This makes it likely that these components reflect early stages of visual-perceptual processes. In the context of the model discussed above, their attentional modulation may thus indicate a selective influence on processes that occur before the entry of visual information into IT cortex. Which visual areas within the V1–IT pathway are affected by attention? If it could be shown that the P1 component (where the earliest attentional amplitude modulations can be observed; see Fig. 1) is generated near to, or even within, striate cortex (V1), this would make a strong case in favour of an attentional modulation of elementary feature analysis.

Where is the cortical locus of the generator processes responsible for the P1 component? This was investigated in a study by Mangun, Hillyard, and Luck (1993), who instructed their subjects to attend to one out of four possible stimulus locations to detect infrequently presented targets at that location. To localize the attentional modulation of ERP components more precisely, current source density (CSD) analyses were conducted on the basis of ERP scalp distribution maps. The CSD maps were brought into register with the cortical gyri and sulci that were determined on the basis of each subject's individual MRI scan. With this technique, Mangun et al. (1993) located the P1 component over the ventrolateral prestriate occipital cortex; that is, outside V1, but presumably posterior to IT cortex. If P1 amplitude modulations constitute the earliest effects of visuospatial attention on ERP waveforms, and the P1 is generated in extrastriate areas, this would indicate that attention may not affect processes within the primary visual cortex. That would be in line with evidence from single-cell recordings that failed to find an attentional influence on the electrical activity of cells within striate cortex, but obtained strong modulatory effects for extrastriate cells (Desimone, 1993; but see Motter, 1993, for different results). With the help of ERP measurements, there is a direct way of finding out whether brain processes within striate cortex are modulated by spatial attention. Since the human primary visual cortex is folded within the calcarine fissure, stimuli from the lower and upper visual fields are projected to separate, oppositely oriented cortical areas within the upper and lower banks of the calcarine fissure. An ERP component that is generated within striate cortex should therefore be strongly dependent upon the vertical location of a stimulus within the visual field. It should reverse polarity when ERPs elicited by stimuli from the upper and lower visual fields are compared. If an ERP component that showed this sort of polarity reversal was modulated by spatial attention, this would constitute a strong case in favour of attentional effects on processes within striate cortex.

This was investigated in an experiment (Eimer, 1997) where stimuli were presented in a regular (clockwise or counterclockwise) order in one of the four visual quadrants (see Fig. 2a). Occasionally, stimuli were presented at irregular and, therefore, unexpected locations. The subjects' task was to respond to infrequently presented target stimuli. It was assumed that subjects would direct their attention in accordance with the regular order of stimulus presentation, and that stimuli at irregular positions would therefore be unattended. The reaction time (RT) results confirmed these predictions, with faster RTs to targets at regular (attended) compared with irregular (unattended) positions. ERPs were computed for expected- and unexpected-location stimuli separately for stimuli presented in the upper and lower visual fields. As pointed out before, an ERP component generated within striate cortex should reverse polarity in response to upper versus lower visual field stimuli. When the ERPs elicited by upper and lower visual field stimuli were compared, one component indeed showed a polarity reversal. This component (NP80) was maximal at midline parietal sites (electrode Pz), had a latency of about 70–80 msec (indicated in Fig. 2b by the arrow), and was positive for stimuli in the lower visual field, but negative for stimuli in the upper visual field. These properties are consistent with the assumption that the NP80 is generated within striate cortex. Further analyses revealed that this component was not affected by attention (see Mangun, 1995; for similar observations). At occipital electrodes, visuospatial attention again had a small but significant effect on the amplitudes of the P1 and N1 components, whereas the NP80 was not affected by attention at all (see Fig. 2c, for stimuli in the upper visual field).

Whereas the P1 is likely to be generated in the extrastriate ventro-lateral cortex, the exact location of the generator processes responsible for the occipital N1 component are unknown. One reason for this is that the N1 is rather broadly distributed over posterior as well as anterior regions of the scalp, indicating that it may result from the activity of several, spatially distinct generator regions. Recent evidence (Johannes, Münte, Heinze, & Mangun, 1995) has indicated that there are at least two functionally distinct posterior N1 components. A parietal N1 that is maximal around 170 msec after stimulus onset is followed by another N1 peaking around 200 msec with a distinct occipito-temporal

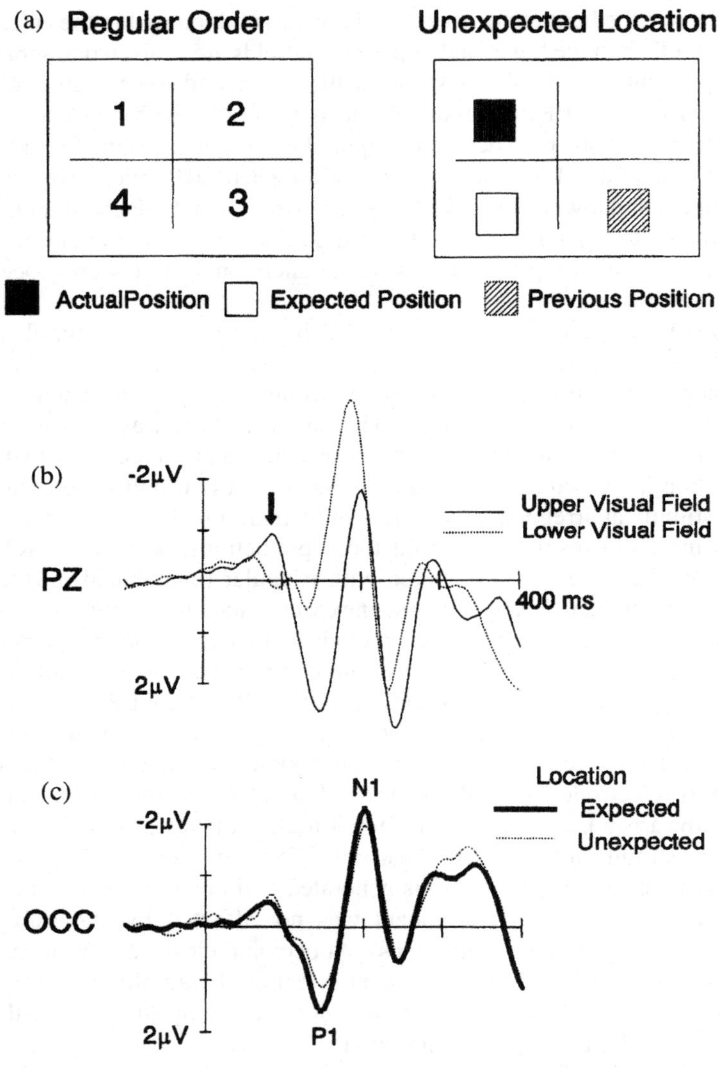

FIG. 2. (a) Illustration of an experiment where most stimuli were presented sequentially at predictable locations (clockwise: 1-2-3-4), and occasional stimuli were presented at unexpected (unattended) locations. (b) Grand-averaged ERPs elicited at electrode Pz by stimuli in the upper half (solid line) and lower half (dotted line) of the visual field. The arrow indicates the presence of a component (NP80) that inverses polarity for upper as compared with lower field stimuli. (c) Grand-averaged ERPs elicited at occipital electrodes (collapsed over OL and OR) by expected-location (solid line) and unexpected-location stimuli (dotted line) in the upper visual field.

distribution. Mangun (1995) has tentatively argued that the occipital P1 and N1 components reflect processing within the ventral pathway, whereas the parietal N1 component is related to processing within the dorsal stream. If the parietal N1 and the occipital N1 components reflect activity within separate pathways, it is likely that attentional modulations of these components indicate functionally different selective processes. This will be discussed further below.

It should be noted that attentional modulations of the occipital P1 component were not found in ERP studies where attention was directed to a non-spatial feature like stimulus colour (Wijers et al., 1989). Non-spatial selective attention usually results in a negative enhancement of the ERPs elicited by stimuli with to-be-attended features that starts more than 150 msec post-stimulus, and therefore does not affect the amplitude of the P1 component. Hillyard and Münte (1984) found that these ERP effects of attention directed to colour were larger for stimuli at attended locations than for stimuli at unattended locations, and argued that the selective processing of colour may even be contingent upon the prior selection of stimuli on the basis of their location. This seems to support the assumption that the location of objects plays a unique role in attentional selectivity (see above). However, in another condition of Hillyard and Münte, (1984) experiment, where both possible stimulus locations were in close proximity, ERP effects of colour selection preceded the effects of spatial selectivity, indicating that the latency of the attentional ERP effects may depend not only on the type of stimulus attribute relevant for attentional selection, but also on the relative discriminabilities of these attributes.

The ERP studies reported so far provide evidence that processes in the primary visual cortex are not modulated by spatial attention, but that attention affects processing in extrastriate visual areas involved in the processing of object features (like orientation, form, colour, and movement direction). These results can thus be interpreted as evidence for the assumption that processes within the pathway linking V1 to IT can be selectively influenced by expectations about the location of relevant stimulus information. In the next section, I discuss whether this sort of influence is an inevitable consequence of spatial precueing or the result of an optional processing strategy.

OPTIONAL AND OBLIGATORY ATTENTIONAL INFLUENCES ON PERCEPTUAL PROCESSING

Most ERP studies on visuospatial attention have employed a sustained attention paradigm where subjects are instructed to keep their attention focused on a specific location for a longer period of time. Experiments in which behavioural parameters (response speed or accuracy) are measured are usually conducted under rather different circumstances. Here, the to-be-attended location is indicated by a precue at the beginning of each trial, and attention has to be shifted between locations in successive trials (Posner et al., 1980). The sustained attention paradigm differs from trial-by-trial cueing studies not only in what may be called "attentional allocation dynamics" (sustained versus transient), but also with respect to the relevance of stimuli presented at unattended locations. In ERP experiments that use a sustained attention paradigm, overt responses are only required to infrequent targets at attended locations, but not to stimuli presented at unattended locations. Trial-by-trial cueing studies are usually conducted to investigate performance differences in response to stimuli at attended and unattended locations, and responses are therefore required to attended as well as to unattended stimuli.

Transient and sustained attentional allocation dynamics may elicit different selective mechanisms, as will be discussed later. However, differences in the response relevance of stimuli presented at unattended locations may also affect attentional processes. When stimuli at unattended locations are always irrelevant and can therefore be completely ignored, enhanced occipital P1 and N1 amplitudes have been observed for stimuli at attended locations (cf. Fig. 1), presumably indicating a spatially selective modulation of processing in the V1–IT pathway. One may ask whether this sort of effect is inevitably elicited whenever specific expectations about the location of relevant stimulation are induced. Biasing the sensory input to IT cortex in favour of information presented at one attended location might be a reasonable strategy when all other locations are irrelevant for response selection, but may actually result in overall performance decrements when relevant information is presented at unexpected locations on a certain percentage of trials. This potential problem could be overcome if such modulatory influences of positional expectancies on visual processing in the V1–IT pathway were optional rather than obligatory.

Although the distinction between obligatory and optional selective influences on information processing may be important for models of attentional mechanisms, it has often been ignored (Allport, 1993). To determine whether the attentional modulation of occipital P1 and N1 components is affected by the response relevance of stimuli at unattended locations, a trial-by-trial cueing experiment was conducted where this factor was varied (see Eimer, 1994b, experiment 2). Each trial started with a 200 msec presentation of a central precue (an arrow pointing to the left or right side). Then, 700 msec after cue offset, a target stimulus (the letter M or W) was presented for 100 msec 6° to the left or right of fixation. Seventy-five percent of the trials were valid; that is, the target was presented at the side indicated by the cue. In the remaining 25% invalid trials, the target was presented contralateral to the cued location. In one part of the experiment, subjects were instructed to respond to all target stimuli (the letter M required a left-hand reaction, and the letter W a right-hand response) irrespective of whether they were presented at cued or uncued locations. In the other part, the task was to respond to validly cued targets only, and to withhold response when a target was presented at the uncued locations.

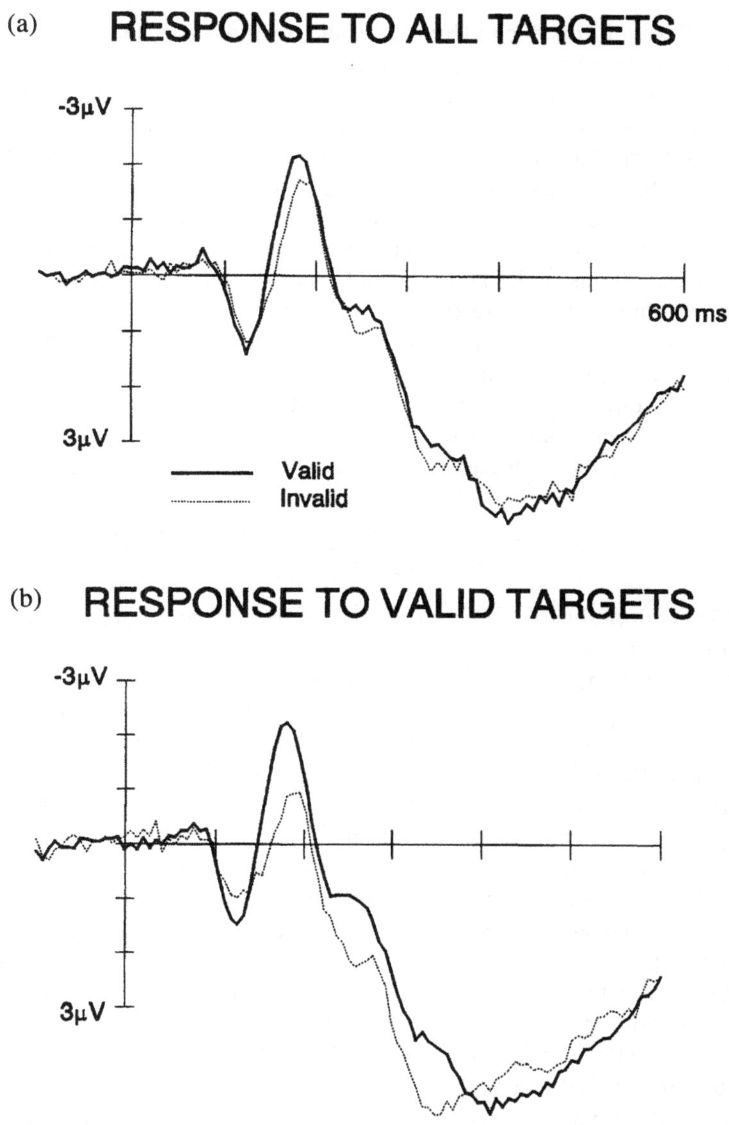

FIG. 3. Grand-averaged ERPs elicited at occipital electrodes ipsilateral to the location of the target stimulus in a trial-by-trial cueing experiment by valid trials (solid lines) and invalid trials (dotted lines). (a) ERPs elicited in a condition where responses were required in valid and in invalid trials. (b) ERPs elicited in a condition where responses were required in valid trials only.

The ERP waveforms elicited by validly and invalidly cued targets at occipital electrodes ipsilateral to the position of the target in these two conditions are shown in Fig. 3. When all targets were relevant, no statistically reliable attentional modulations of P1 and N1 amplitudes were elicited, even though overt performance showed faster RTs in valid than in invalid trials. In contrast, when only validly cued stimuli required a response, the P1 and N1 amplitudes were clearly affected by cue validity (see Fig. 3b). These ERP results suggest that the spatially selective modulation of perceptual processing, as indicated by the attentional effects on P1 and N1 amplitudes, is not completely obligatory, but may be influenced by the response relevance of unattended-location stimuli. A spatially selective bias for processing within the V1–IT pathway is elicited by advance information about stimulus location when stimuli at uncued locations do not require a response and can therefore be completely ignored, but not (or to a lesser degree) when uncued locations are potentially relevant (Eimer, 1993; see also Mangun & Hillyard, 1991).

ATTENTIONAL GRADIENTS IN THE POSTERIOR PARIETAL CORTEX

A notable result of the experiment reported in the last section was the presence of attentional effects on overt performance in the absence of a reliable attentional modulation of exogenous ERP components (Fig. 3a). While the former result indicates that the cue was effective in directing spatial attention, the latter result suggests that perceptual processing in the V1–IT pathway was not significantly affected. In the framework of LaBerge and Brown's (1989) model, one may assume that no location expectation gradient is elicited in PPC in response to cues when uncued locations are potentially relevant, and therefore no modulatory influence on ventral stream processing is exerted by PPC signals. However, such an account cannot explain why overt performance was superior in response to validly cued (attended) stimuli. Alternatively, it is possible that an attentional gradient was set up in PPC areas by the cue but that this gradient affected processing within the ventral stream only at a later stage. Are there any observations to be made in the ERP waveforms obtained in the above experiment with respect to the presence of specific location expectations within posterior parietal cortex?

This was investigated by comparing the ERPs elicited in valid and invalid trials at the midline electrodes Fz, Cz and Pz in the experimental condition described above, where responses were required in both the valid and invalid trials. Figure 4 shows these ERPs together with the difference waves obtained by subtracting the ERPs for invalid trials from the ERPs for valid trials (right side). Valid trials elicited an enlarged negativity compared with invalid trials, with a first peak (Nd1) around 160 msec post-stimulus that was maximal at parietal sites (electrode Pz), and a second, more broadly distributed negativity

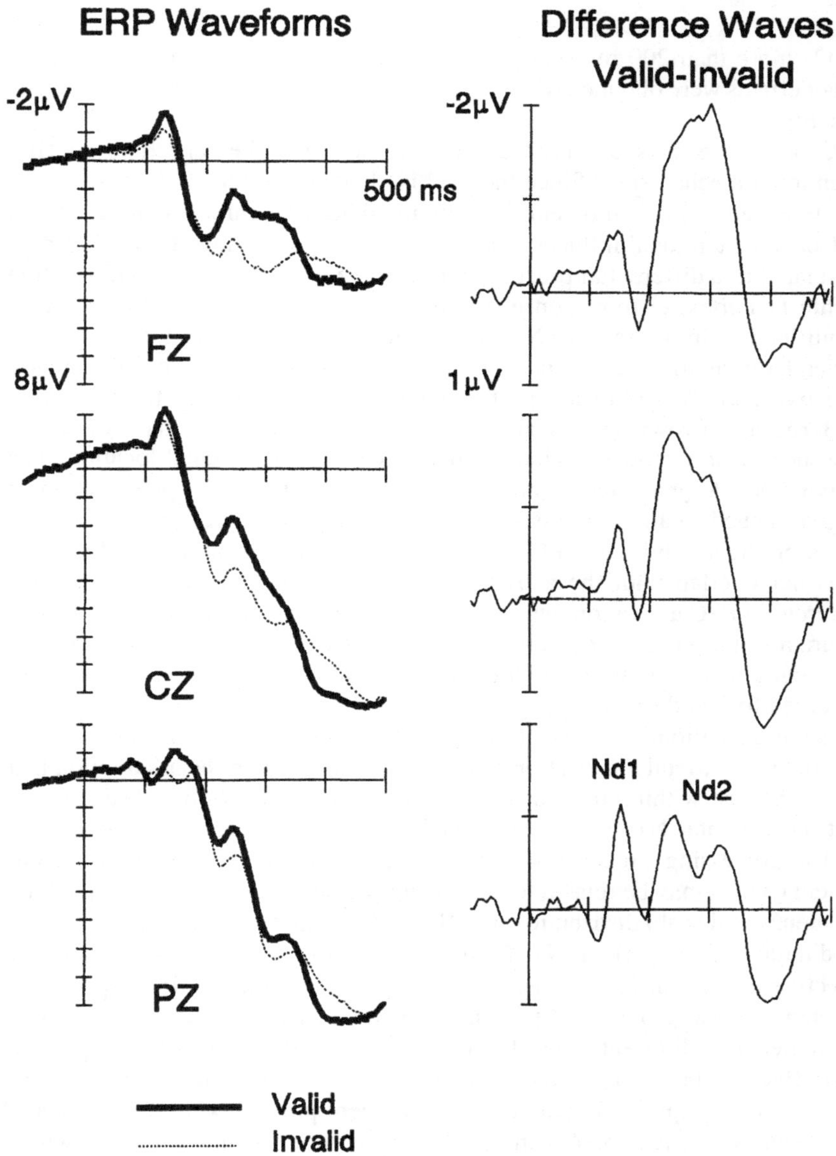

FIG. 4. (Left) Grand-averaged ERPs elicited at midline electrodes Fz, Cz and Pz in a trial-by-trial cueing experiment for valid trials (solid lines) and invalid trials (dotted lines) in a condition where responses were required in valid as well as in invalid trials. (Right) Difference waveforms obtained by subtracting the ERPs recorded in invalid trials from the ERPs recorded in valid trials. Valid trials elicited an enhanced negativity with an initial parietal peak (Nd1) that was followed by a fronto-centrally distributed effect (Nd2).

(Nd2) more than 200 msec post-stimulus. Very similar, although somewhat larger effects were obtained when only validly cued targets required a response. (see Fig. 5).

Can these effects observed at midline electrodes be related to specific attentional mechanisms? Since the Nd2 is elicited more than 200 msec post-stimulus and has a fronto-central scalp distribution, it can be assumed that it reflects an attentional influence at later stages of processing. This effect may be related to a differential processing of attended and unattended information within IT cortex, or to response selection processes that occur after stimulus identification. In contrast, the Nd1 has a latency of about 160 msec and a distinct parietal distribution. It is thus possible that this effect indicates spatially selective activity within the posterior parietal cortex. In the framework of LaBerge and Brown (1989) and LaBerge (1995), the Nd1 may reveal the presence of an attentional gradient that is centred at the cued location. The activity profile generated in posterior parietal cortex by the presentation of targets at cued locations corresponds to the already established location expectation gradient, while the PPC activity elicited by targets at uncued locations does not overlap with the activity related to the attentional gradient. This differential PPC activation, which is assumed to be reflected by the Nd1, may in turn result in an earlier or more effective selective gating of target information from cued locations in the ventral stream (as indicated by the RT advantage observed for valid trials).

Is there additional evidence to support this interpretation of the Nd1 effect? The distinct parietal localization of the Nd1 is in line with the assumption that it is generated within posterior parietal cortex. It has previously been argued that the occipital N1 component (which is presumably generated within the ventral processing stream) has to be distinguished from the parietal N1 component (which may be related to processing within the dorsal pathway). Given its latency and scalp distribution, the Nd1 effect may be considered a selective modulation of the parietal N1. Furthermore, if the Nd1 reflects the spatially selective activity in PPC areas due to the presence of a location expectation gradient that was produced in response to a previously presented precue, it may be elicited with different types of spatial cues. Accordingly, a distinctly parietal Nd1 effect has been observed not only with centrally presented symbolic cues, but also in an experiment (Eimer, 1994a) where precues were presented at a horizontal eccentricity of 6° in the left or right hemifield under conditions where this cue was spatially informative, but also when the cue was not informative with respect to the location of an upcoming target stimulus. Here, the Nd1 effect was present even though no systematic attentional enhancements of occipital P1 and N1 components were observed. This latter finding again suggests that, if the Nd1 reflects the presence of location expectancies within posterior parietal cortex, such expectations do not necessarily result in a spatially selective modulation of processing within the V1–IT pathway. Moreover, the presence of a Nd1 in response to uninformative peripheral onsets indicates that attentional gradients within PPC may be triggered in a rather reflexive way (Jonides, 1981).

If a parietal location expectation gradient that is generated (either voluntarily or reflexively) in response to spatial precues is reflected by the Nd1, it is conceivable that qualitatively similar effects are elicited for targets of different modalities. Schröger and Eimer (1993) did observe a distinct parietal Nd1 in a study where visual cues and auditory target stimuli were used. Figure 5 compares the ERP results of two experiments where visual (Eimer, 1994b, experiment 2b) or auditory (Schröger, 1994) target stimuli were preceded by informative visual arrow precues and only validly cued targets were relevant for the subjects' response. The ERP waveforms obtained from Pz and from lateral parietal sites (electrodes PL and PR, located halfway between Pz and the ear channels) in response to visual and auditory stimuli are shown together with the resulting valid–invalid difference waveforms. The ERP waveforms elicited by visual and by auditory stimuli were quite different. Auditory stimuli elicited a modality-specific N1 component that peaked around 100 msec post-stimulus (Fig. 5b), whereas the visual N1 peaked about 60 msec later (Fig. 5a). In spite of these differences between modalities, the ERP effects of spatial cueing that can be seen in the difference waveforms, obtained by subtracting the ERPs elicited in invalid trials from the ERPs elicited in valid trials, were strikingly similar (Fig. 5c). A distinct Nd1 of comparable amplitude and latency was elicited for visual as well as for auditory stimuli at all three recording sites. Moreover, the modulations observed in the difference waveforms at longer latencies (Nd2) were also quite similar for the two modalities.

Analogous results have been found in a number of other trial-by-trial cueing studies that employed auditory target stimuli, suggesting that, in contrast to the attentional modulations of the occipital P1 and N1 components, the Nd1 effect reflects selective processes that are largely independent of stimulus modality. This is in line with the assumption that the Nd1 indicates the existence of a location expectancy gradient within posterior parietal cortex that is generated in response to precues, which in turn operates upon selective thalamic circuits that gate the sensory input to object identification processes. The fact that different brain areas are involved in the initial analysis of visual and auditory stimuli does not rule out the possibility that the control of spatial selectivity within these two modalities is based on partially overlapping mechanisms within the posterior parietal cortex.

What remains to be answered is why behavioural effects of spatial cueing have been observed in the absence of reliable ERP evidence for a selective modulation of processing within the V1–IT pathway. If the Nd1 is a reflection of an attentional gradient within the PPC areas, the absence of attentional effects on occipital P1 and N1 components in the experiment described above cannot be explained by assuming that no specific positional expectancies at all were

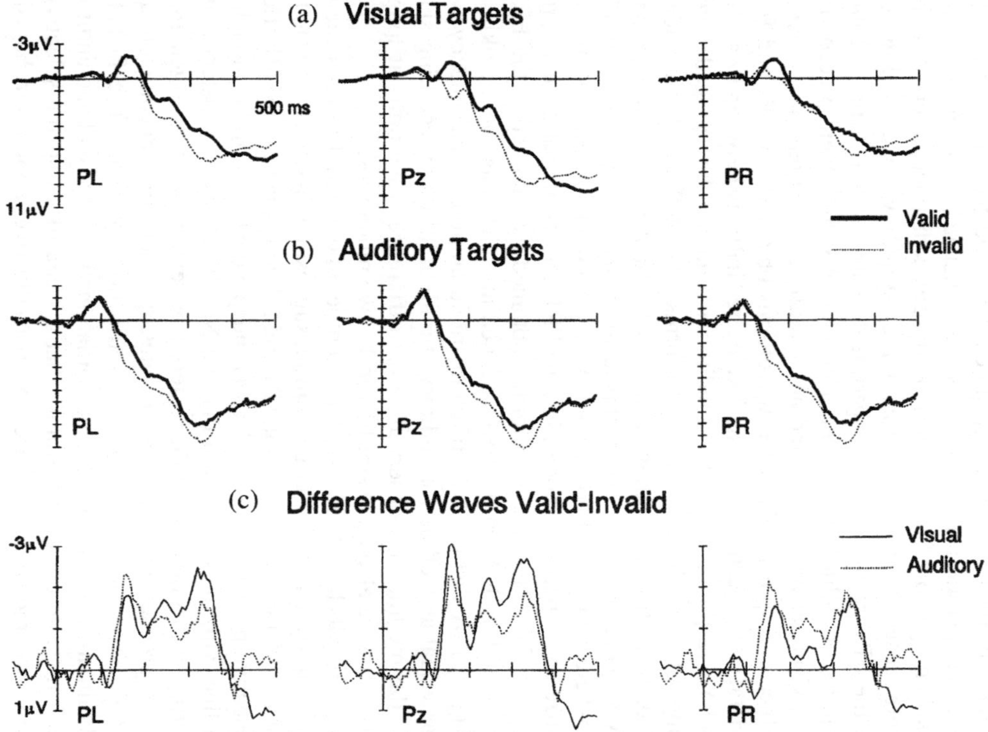

FIG. 5. (a, b) Grand-averaged ERPs elicited at electrodes PL, Pz and PR in trial-by-trial cueing experiments for valid (solid lines) and invalid trials (dotted lines) where visual stimuli (a) or auditory stimuli (b) were preceded by a centrally presented arrow precue. (c) Difference waveforms obtained by subtracting the visual ERPs (solid line) and the auditory ERPs (dotted line) obtained in invalid trails from the visual and auditory ERPs obtained in valid trials.

generated. Alternatively, one may speculate that spatially selective PPC signals influence later stages of visual processing without affecting the V1–IT pathway. Anatomical connections that may subserve this type of influence (e.g. direct link's between areas within PPC and regions in IT cortex) have already been described (Andersen, Asanuma, Essick, & Siegel, 1990).

TRANSIENT AND SUSTAINED MODES OF SELECTIVE SPATIAL ATTENTION

The Nd1 may reflect location expectation gradients within the posterior parietal cortex that are set up in a transient and possibly reflexive way in response to the presentation of cue stimuli. The reflexive nature of this process is suggested by the finding reported above that distinct Nd1 effects were also observed in response to uninformative peripheral cues (Eimer, 1994a). The transient nature of a position expectation gradient has been stressed by LaBerge and Brown (1989), especially under conditions where to-be-attended locations are eccentric to the fovea. The presence of such a gradient may thus critically depend upon the previous presentation of a precue. If this is the case, one may expect to find differences between experimental situations where the to-be-attended location is cued on each trial (transient attention) and a condition where the relevant location is specified by instruction at the beginning of an experimental block and is kept constant throughout this block (sustained attention). If the Nd1 effect reflects transient activity within PPC areas induced by the previous presentation of a precue, this effect should be attenuated or even absent under sustained attention conditions.

This was investigated in a study by Eimer (1996a, experiment 2), in which the ERP effects of transient and sustained spatial attention were directly compared. In the transient attention condition, a centrally presented arrow precue indicated the location of the next target with 75% validity, and 25% of the trials were invalid. In the sustained attention condition, subjects were informed at the beginning of each experimental block at which location (left or right) targets would appear with 75% probability. Because the precues employed in the transient attention condition may exert an unspecific alerting effect, an uninformative plus sign was presented at the beginning of each trial in the sustained attention condition instead of an arrow precue. In both attention conditions, the subjects' task was to respond to the target letters M and W at attended and at unattended locations with a left-hand or right-hand button press.

Do transient and sustained spatial attention have different effects on overt performance and ERP waveforms? The behavioural data showed no difference at all. Response times for valid and invalid trials were 485 and 509 msec in the transient attention condition, and 487 and 509 msec in the sustained attention condition. This finding, that the behavioural effects of transient and sustained attention on RT are virtually identical, differs from that of Posner et al. (1980, experiment 1), who found larger effects in a transient attention condition than in a sustained attention condition.[1] Do the ERP waveforms reveal any differences between transient and sustained attention? In both conditions, a small but significant attentional enhancement of the occipital N1 component was elicited, suggesting a moderate selective influence on processing within the V1–IT pathway. Figure 6 shows the ERPs elicited at electrode Pz in valid and invalid trials for the transient and the sustained attention conditions, together with the corresponding difference waveforms. As can be seen, transient and sustained spatial attention had rather different effects on the ERP waveforms. In the transient attention condition, the Nd1–Nd2 pattern discussed in the previous section was again present (Figure 6c). In contrast, the attentional modulations elicited by sustained attention were of much smaller amplitude. Statistical analyses revealed that the Nd1 was virtually absent, and only the Nd2 effect approached significance.

Although the attentional effects on performance were identical, transient and sustained spatial attention resulted in rather different ERP modulations. The absence of the Nd1 effect under sustained attention conditions is in line with the assumptions that the Nd1 reflects transient activity within PPC areas that is critically dependent upon the previous presentation of a cue. If no transient attentional gradient is set up in the sustained attention condition, as suggested by the absence of a Nd1 effect, how can the RT advantage for attended target stimuli observed in this condition be explained? One may speculate that, under sustained attention instructions, a representation of the relevant stimulus location was activated in spatial working memory (possibly within dorso-lateral prefrontal cortex), but that this information does not elicit an attentional gradient within PPC in the same way that such a gradient is set up in response to single precues. With sustained attention, stored spatial expectations may influence object identification processes directly, possibly through links connecting DLPFC with the ventral stream (Felleman & Van Essen, 1991).

The results obtained in this experiment generally illustrate how ERP measures can provide information about functional differences between mechanisms of attentional selectivity operating in different experimental circumstances, which are not available on the basis of behavioural data alone. While the RT data were virtually equivalent for the transient and sustained attention conditions, the ERP waveforms revealed marked differences suggesting important functional differences between the underlying selective processes.

---

[1]It should be noted that four possible stimulus locations were used in the Posner and co-workers' (1980) experiment, and stimulus eccentricity was much larger (24° and 8°) than in the ERP study reported here.

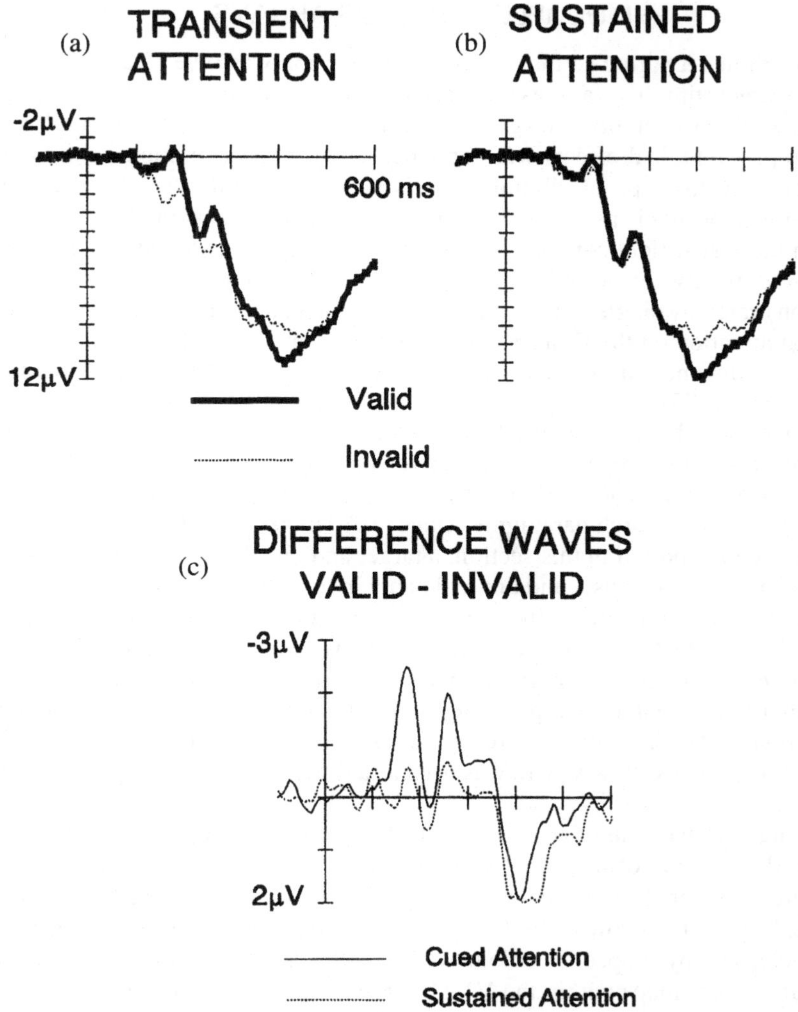

FIG. 6. (a, b) Grand-averaged ERPs elicited at electrode Pz in valid trials (solid lines) and invalid trials (dotted lines) under transient (left) and sustained (middle) attention conditions (see text for details). (c) Difference waveforms obtained by subtracting ERPs obtained in invalid trials from ERPs obtained in valid trials for the transient (solid line) and sustained (dotted line) attention conditions.

VISUOSPATIAL ATTENTION IN MULTIPLE-STIMULUS ARRAYS

In the studies reported so far, visuospatial attention was investigated where a single target stimulus was presented at attended or unattended locations in front of an otherwise empty background. Although systematic behavioural and electrophysiological effects were obtained under these conditions, it may be argued that this type of circumstance is not ideally suited for the study of attentional mechanisms. Attentional selectivity should be maximal in situations when the visual field contains multiple objects that compete with each other. The role of between-stimulus competition for attentional selectivity has been demonstrated by single-cell studies that have found a modulatory influence of spatial attention on the firing rate of single cells only when both attended and unattended stimuli are located within the receptive field of that cell (Moran & Desimone, 1985).

Attention selectivity should therefore also be studied when several stimuli are displayed simultaneously, and the relevant target position is either specified in advanced by precueing (Downing, 1988) or varied randomly from trial to trial as in visual search paradigms (Duncan & Humphreys, 1989). In the ERP experiments reported in this section, a target and one distractor stimulus were presented simultaneously and unpredictably in the left and right visual fields at an eccentricity of about 3°. In a form discrimination task, the letters M and W served as targets (requiring a left-hand and right-hand response, respectively), and an ensemble of two short and two long vertical bars, which was equal in size to the target letters, was presented as a distractor. In a colour discrimination task, blue and green squares were used as targets (again requiring a left or right response), and a yellow square was used as a distractor (Eimer, 1996b, experiment 2).

Which mechanisms of attentional selectivity operate under these conditions? Since the location of the target stimulus (left or right) was unpredictable, no advance positional expectancies can be generated. In the framework described by LaBerge and Brown (1989), instructing subjects to respond to targets characterized by a specific colour (or form) leads to a selective priming of colour or form maps within the V1-IT pathway that may be under the control of feature-specific working memory in ventro-lateral prefrontal areas. This will result in increased activity at the location of stimuli with relevant attributes, which will in turn activate PPC areas and thalamic circuits, finally leading to a selective gating of target information in the ventral stream.

Is there evidence in the ERP waveforms elicited by the target–distractor arrays indicating that this sort of selective processing actually takes place? Figure 7 shows the ERP waveforms recorded at a lateral occipital electrodes ipsilateral and contralateral to the position of the target stimulus in the form and in the colour discrimination task. A systematic influence of target location on

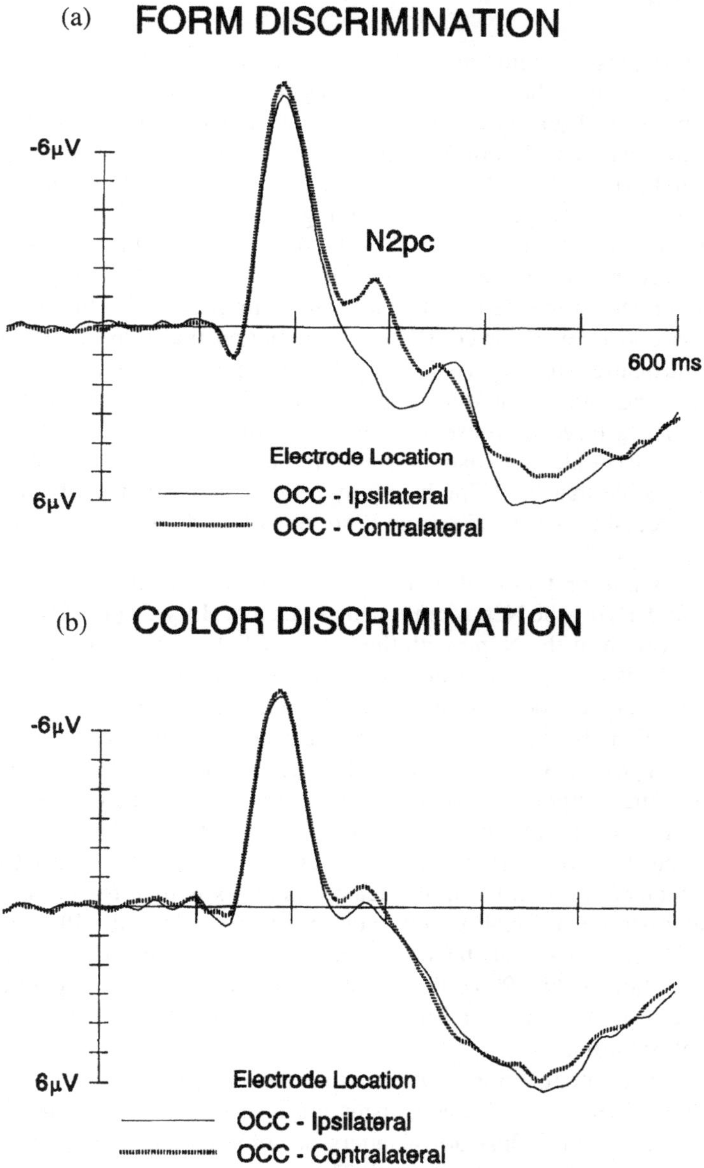

FIG. 7. Grand-averaged ERPs elicited at lateral occipital electrodes ipsilateral (solid lines) and contralateral (dotted lines) to the location of a target stimulus that was presented together with a distractor in the opposite visual hemifield in a form discrimination task (a) and a colour discrimination task (b) (see text for details). An enhanced N2 component was elicited at occipital sites contralateral to the location of the target (N2pc).

the ERPs was present, with enlarged N2 amplitudes elicited at occipital electrodes contralateral to the location of the target. This effect was considerably larger in the form discrimination task (Fig. 7a), but was also present for the colour discrimination task (Fig. 7b). Analogous ERP effects have been reported by Luck and Hillyard (1994) in visual search tasks where one target was presented together with numerous distracting stimuli. The enhanced N2 component at occipital sites contralateral to the position of the target was termed N2pc (N2 posterior-contralateral). Luck and Hillyard (1994) argued that the N2pc may reflect both the selection of relevant stimuli as well as the attentional suppression of irrelevant or conflicting information that may interfere with target identification during visual search. As shown in Fig. 7, the N2pc component is not only elicited in visual search tasks with multiple distractors, but also when a target is presented together with just one distractor in the opposite visual field, and distractor interference should be minimal. It is therefore possible that the N2pc primarily reflects the selective enhancement of target processing that results from a previous localization of task-relevant features.

Given this interpretation, it would be important to localize the generator processes underlying the N2pc component. Luck and Hillyard (1994) estimated the cortical origin of the N2pc with the help of CSD analyses, and found that the focus of this effect was located about the ventro-lateral occipital cortex, close to the estimated locus of the visual P1 component (see above). Although the N2pc is elicited about 150 msec later than the P1 component (see Fig. 7), this result suggests that it is probably also generated in extrastriate occipital areas. The N2pc component may thus be interpreted to reflect a selective gating of information processing in the ventral pathway that is contingent upon the previous detection of task-relevant features. The information about target location obtained through the initial feature analysis is then re-entrantly sent back to extrastriate occipital cortex, possibly mediated by the PPC and the thalamus. Re-entrant signals have been assumed to play an important role in visual integration (Zeki, 1993). The N2pc component might directly reflect the consequences of such re-entrant connections for the selective processing of relevant information.

Another experiment (Eimer, 1996b, experiment 3) was conducted to investigate if these hypothesized mechanisms are also sensitive to more abstract target-defining features. Instead of letters or coloured squares, word strings were used as targets and distractors. The target words differed from the distractors with respect to their meaning, as location words (the German words for "left" and "right") were used as targets, and colour words (the German words for "white" or "brown") as distractors. Subjects were instructed to respond to the target words, either by pressing the button indicated by their meaning (left *vs* right), or by pressing the button spatially corresponding to the target location. Figure 8 shows the ERP waveforms elicited by target words in

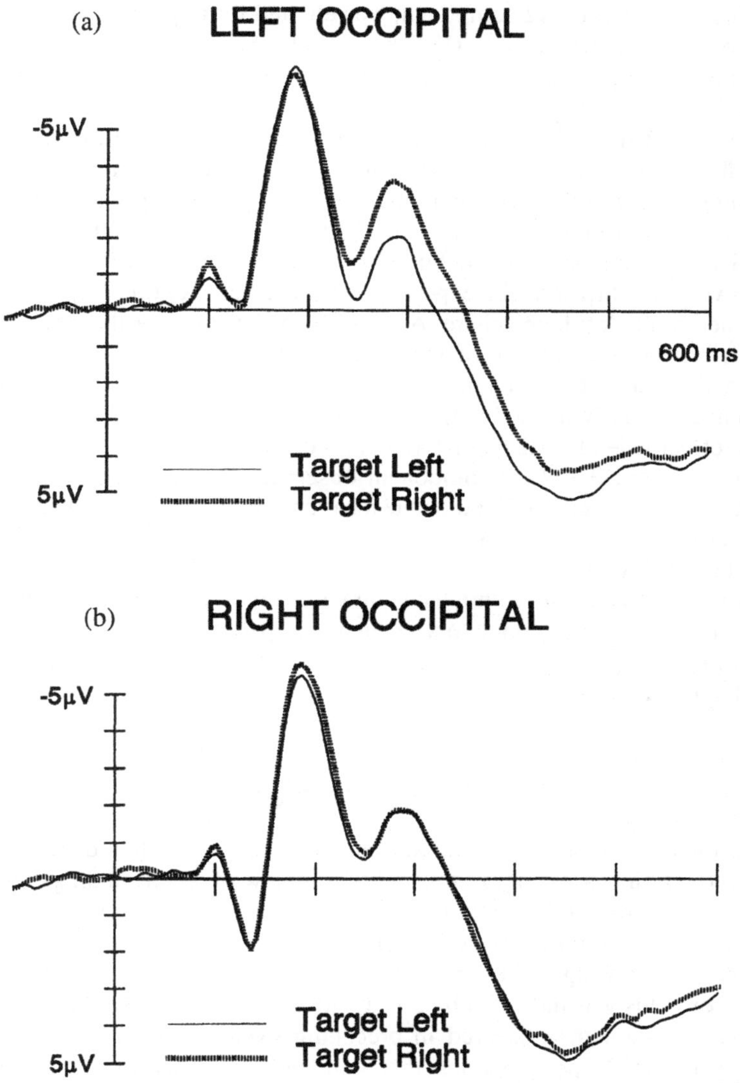

FIG. 8. Grand-averaged ERPs elicited at left occipital (a) and right occipital (b) electrodes by stimulus arrays that contained a target word in the left (solid lines) or right (dotted lines) visual field. An N2pc was elicited at left occipital electrodes (a) but not over the right hemisphere (b).

the left and right visual fields at left and right occipital electrodes. Over the left hemisphere, a larger N2 component was elicited for target words presented at the contralateral (right) side (Fig. 8a). While this is in line with the results obtained before, no N2pc was elicited at all over the right occipital hemisphere (Fig. 8b).

The fact that an N2pc was observed over left occipital cortex when targets and distractors were words that had to be distinguished on the basis of their meaning, suggests that the attentional gating of processing within the ventral stream is controlled by selective mechanisms that are sensitive not only to physical stimulus properties, but also to more abstract semantic features. However, in contrast to the experiment reported above, this N2pc effect was confined to the left hemisphere. A possible explanation for this asymmetry is that it reflects the activity of the language-dominant left hemisphere when between-word discriminations are required. However, additional empirical evidence is clearly needed with respect to the hemispheric asymmetry of the N2pc effect when linguistic material is used.

In summary, the N2pc component observed in experiments where target stimuli are presented at unpredictable locations simultaneously with at least one distractor could serve as an important tool in further investigations of attentional selectivity, because it may reflect the gating of information from potentially relevant locations within the ventral stream in search-like situations, thus possibly indicating a modulatory influence of parietal signals that are not due to positional expectancies, but are generated on the basis of an initial pre-attentive feature analysis.

CONCLUSIONS

Attentional processes serve various functions and may affect different stages of information processing. In this paper, a review of recent findings regarding effects of visuospatial attention on ERP waveforms was presented, suggesting that there are different cortical loci of spatial selectivity. Spatial attention may influence processing in the ventral stream within the pathways linking V1 with IT cortex. This was indicated by the attentional modulation of the occipital P1 and N1 components observed in precueing experiments, as well as by the existence of the N2pc component that is elicited in response to targets presented simultaneously with distracting stimuli. However, these two effects are likely to be under the control of rather different attentional mechanisms. While the attentional effects on exogenous components in precueing contexts are likely to result from positional expectancies within parietal areas that gate the flow of information within the V1–IT pathway, either directly or through the thalamus, the N2pc is assumed to be contingent upon a previous detection of task-relevant features within the ventral stream.

Additional evidence was collected with respect to the spatially selective attentional gradient postulated by LaBerge and Brown (1989), which is assumed to be located within posterior parietal areas. A distinct ERP effect (Nd1) that was maximal over parietal cortex was interpreted to reflect the presence of such a location expectation gradient. It was assumed to indicate the differential activation of PPC areas in response to targets at cued and uncued location, which may in turn influence processing in the ventral stream. The fact that similar Nd1 effects were elicited in response to centrally presented symbolic precues and peripheral precues (even when these are uninformative with respect to the location of the target) suggests that spatially selective parietal activation patterns might be relevant for voluntary as well as for reflective spatial attention. Very similar Nd1 effects have also been observed in studies where either visual or auditory targets were preceded by visual cues. This is interpreted as evidence for the assumption that spatially selective parietal processes underlying the Nd1 effect are not entirely modality-specific. Moreover, the Nd1 was found to be virtually absent in a sustained attention condition. This may indicate that location expectation gradients within PPC areas, as evidenced by the Nd1, are transient in nature and thus critically depend upon the previous presentation of cue stimuli.

Some preliminary evidence has also been obtained with respect to the relation between spatially selective processes within posterior parietal cortex (indexed by the Nd1) and location-specific modulations of processing in the V1–IT pathway (indexed by the attentional effects on occipital P1 and N1 amplitude). The selective modulation of processing within the ventral stream seems to be optional rather than obligatory, as it was found to be markedly reduced when uncued locations were potentially relevant. However, a distinct Nd1 was elicited in this condition, indicating the presence of an attentional gradient within PPC. These location expectancies may have selectively influenced later stages in the ventral stream (like stimulus identification) even in the absence of modulatory effects within the V1–IT pathway, possibly via direct or indirect links from PPC to IT cortex. Attentional modulations of exogenous components may even be found in the absence of corresponding parietal Nd1 effects, as in the sustained attention experiment described above. In the present framework, this would suggest a spatially selective gating of information within the V1–IT pathway without corresponding transient positional expectancies generated in PPC areas. Such an influence could possibly be mediated by direct links from the dorso-lateral prefrontal cortex (one potential site for spatial short-term memory) to the ventral stream.

In conclusion, it has to be stressed that the above interpretations of specific ERP modulations, observed in experiments on selective spatial attention that were guided by the model of attentional selectivity depended by LaBerge and Brown (1989) and LaBerge (1995), are highly speculative at the present time, and further research is required to confirm them. Measuring attentional effects on event-related brain potentials is just one way of investigating the nature of selective processes, and ERP waveforms reflect only a fraction of the activities within the brain that may be modulated by attention. The aim of the present paper was to illustrate that ERP studies may provide one valuable source of information about the nature of the mechanisms underlying selective attention. Uncovering these mechanisms requires the joint activity of researchers that employ different, but complementary, techniques.

REFERENCES

Allport, A. (1980). Attention and performance. In G. Claxton (Ed.), *Cognitive psychology: New directions* (pp. 112–153). London: Routledge.

Allport, A. (1993). Attention and control: Have we been asking the wrong questions? A critical review of twenty-five years. In D.E. Meyer & S. Kornblum (Eds), *Attention and performance XIV* (pp. 183–218). Cambridge, MA: MIT Press.

Anderson, R.A., Asanuma, C., Essick, G., & Siegel, R.M. (1990). Corticocortical connections of anatomically and physiologically defined subdivisions within the inferior parietal lobule. *Journal of Comparative Neurology, 296*, 65–113.

Broadbent, D.E. (158). *Perception and communication*. London: Pergamon Press.

Bundesen, C. (1990). A theory of visual attention. *Psychological Review, 97*, 523–547.

Coles, M.G.H., Gratton, G., & Fabiani, M. (1990). Event-related potentials. In J.T. Cacioppo & L.G. Tassinary (Eds), *Principles of psychophysiology: Physical, social, and inferential elements* (pp. 413–455). New York: Cambridge University Press.

Desimone, R. (1993). Neural circuits for visual attention in the primate brain. In G.A. Carpenter & S. Grossberg (Eds), *Neural networks for vision and image processing* (pp. 343–364). Cambridge, MA: MIT Press.

Desimone, R., & Duncan, J. (1995). Neural mechanisms of selective visual attention. *Annual Review of Neuroscience, 18*, 193–222.

Downing, C.J. (1988). Expectancy and visual-spatial attention: Effects on perceptual quality. *Journal of Experimental Psychology: Human Perception and Performance, 14*, 188–202.

Duncan, J., & Humphreys, G.W. (1989). Visual search and stimulus activity. *Psychological Review, 96*, 433–458.

Eason, R.G. (1981). Visual evoked potential correlates of early neural filtering during selective attention. *Bulletin of the Psychonomic Society, 18*, 203–206.

Eimer, M. (1993). Spatial cueing, sensory gating and selective response preparation: An ERP study on visuo-spatial orienting. *Electroencephalography and Clinical Neurophysiology, 88*, 408–420.

Eimer, M. (1994a). An ERP study on visual-spatial priming with peripheral onsets. *Psychophysiology, 31*, 154–163.

Eimer, M. (1994b). "Sensory gating" as a mechanism for visual-spatial orienting: Electrophysiological evidence from trial-by-trial cueing experiments. *Perception and Psychophysics, 5*, 667–675.

Eimer, M. (1996). ERP modulations indicate the selective processing of visual stimuli as a result of transient and sustained spatial attention. *Psychophysiology, 33*, 13–21.

Eimer, M. (1996b). The N2pc component as an indicator of attentional selectivity. *Electroencephalography and Clinical Neurophysiology, 99*, 225–234.

Eimer, M. (1997). Attentional selection and attentional gradients: An alternative method for studying transient visual-spatial attention. *Psychophysiology, 34*, 365–376.

Felleman, D.J., & Van Essen, D.C. (1991). Distributed hierarchical processing in the primate cerebral cortex. *Cerebral Cortex, 1*, 1–47.

Hillyard, S.A., & Münte, T.F. (1984). Selective attention to color and location: An analysis with event-related brain potentials. *Perception and Psychophysics, 36*, 185–198.

Johannes, S., Münte, T.F., Heinze, H.J., & Mangun, G.R. (1995). Luminance and spatial attention effects on early visual processing. *Cognitive Brain Research, 2*, 189–205.

Johnston, W.A., & Dark, V.J. (1986). Selective attention. *Annual Review of Psychology, 37*, 43–75.

Jonides, J. (1981). Voluntary versus automatic control over the mind's eye's movement. In J.B. Long, & A.D. Baddeley (Eds), *Attention and performance IX* (pp. 18–203). Hillsdale, NJ: Lawrence Erlbaum Associates Inc.

Kahneman, D., & Treisman, A. (1984). Changing views of attention and automaticity. In. R. Parasuraman & D.R. Davies (Eds), *Varieties of attention* (pp. 29–61). New York: Academic Press.

LaBerge, D. (1995). *Attentional processing: The brain's art of mindfulness.* Cambridge, MA: Harvard University Press.

LaBerge, D., & Brown, V. (1989). Theory of attentional operations in shape identification. *Psychological Review, 96*, 101–124.

Lavie, N. (1995). Perceptual load as a necessary condition for selective attention. *Journal of Experimental Psychology: Human Perception and Performance, 21*, 451–468.

Luck, S.J., & Hillyard, S.A. (1994). Spatial filtering during visual search: Evidence from human electrophysiology. *Journal of Experimental Psychology: Human Perception and Performance, 20*, 1000–1014.

Mangun, G.R. (1995). Neural mechanisms of visual selective attention. *Psychophysiology, 32*, 4–18.

Mangun, G.R., & Hillyard, S.A. (1987). The spatial allocation of visual attention as indexed by event-related brain potentials. *Human Factors, 29*, 195–211.

Mangun, G.R., & Hillyard, S.A. (1991). Modulations of sensory-evoked brain potentials indicated changes in perceptual processing during visual-spatial priming. *Journal of Experimental Psychology: Human Perception and Performance, 17*, 1057–1074.

Mangun, G.R., Hillyard, S.A., Luck, S.J. (1993). Electrocortical substrates of visual selective attention. In D.E. Meyer & S. Kornblum (Eds), *Attention and performance XIV* (pp. 219–243), Cambridge, MA: MIT Press.

Moran, J., Desimone, R. (1985). Selective attention gates visual processing in the extrastriate cortex. *Science, 229*, 782–784.

Motter, B.C. (1993). Focal attention produces spatially selective processing in visual cortical areas V1, V2, and V4 in the presence of competing stimuli. *Journal of Neurophysiology, 70*, 909–919.

Nissen, M.J. (1985). Accessing features and objects: Is location special? in M.I. Posner & O.S.M. Marin (Eds), *Attention and performance XI* (pp. 205–219). Hillsdale, NJ: Lawrence Erlbaum Associates Inc.

Posner, M.I., Snyder, C.R.R., & Davidson, B.J. (1980). Attention and the detection of signals. *Journal of Experimental Psychology: General, 109*, 160–174.

Schröger, E. (1994). Human brain potential signs of selection by location and frequency in an auditory transient attention situation. *Neuroscience Letters, 173*, 163–166.

Schröger, E., & Eimer, M. (1993). Effects of transient spatial attention on auditory event-related potentials. *Neuroreport, 4*, 588–590.

Shiffrin, R.M., & Schneider, W. (1977). Controlled and automatic human information processing: II. Perceptual learning, automatic attending and a general theory. *Psychological Review, 84*, 127–190.

Treisman, A.M., & Gelade, G. (1980). A feature-integration theory of attention. *Cognitive Psychology, 12*, 97–136.

Tsal, Y., & Lavie, N. (1993). Location dominance in attending to color and shape. *Journal of Experimental Psychology: Human Perception and Performance, 19*, 131–139.

Ungerleider, L.G., & Mishkin, M. (1982). Two cortical visual systems. In D.J. Ingle, M.A. Goodale, & R.J.W. Mansfield (Eds), *Analysis of visual behaviour* (pp. 549–586). Cambridge, MA: MIT Press.

Van der Heijden, A.H.C. (1993). The role of position in object selection in vision. *Psychological Research, 56*, 44–58.

Wijers, A.A., Mulder, G., Okita, T., Mulder, L.J., & Scheffers, M.K. (1989). Attention to color: An analysis of selection, controlled search, and motor activation, using event-related potentials. *Psychophysiology, 26*, 89–109.

Zeki, S. (1993). *A vision of the brain*. Oxford: Blackwell.

VISUAL COGNITION, 1998, *5* (1/2), 287–309

Visual Selective Attention: Outlines of a Choice Model, a Race Model and a Computational Theory

Claus Bundesen
Centre for Visual Cognition, University of Copenhagen, Copenhagen, Denmark

A computational theory of visual selective attention is presented. The theory developed out of a choice and a race model for visual selection from multi-element displays. The choice model (Bundesen, Pedersen, & Larsen, 1984) provides a rule for computation of selection probabilities, which accounts for effects of the selection criterion and the numbers of targets and distractors in the stimulus. The race model (Shibuya & Bundesen, 1988) provides a process interpretation of the choice model and accounts for effects of the exposure duration of the stimulus. The computational theory (TVA; Bundesen, 1990) was constructed by integrating the race model with a biased-choice model for single-stimulus recognition (Luce, 1963). TVA describes two mechanisms (filtering and pigeonholing) by which selection is assumed to be carried out, and it organizes a large body of empirical data on human performance in visual recognition and attention tasks. A recent theoretical development (CTVA; Logan, 1996; Logan & Bundesen, 1996) combines TVA with a theory of perceptual grouping by proximity. CTVA explains effects of spatial separation between items in multi-element displays. The neural localization of the operations described in TVA is considered in the final section.

INTRODUCTION

This paper describes the development of a computational theory of visual selective attention. The theory was originally published under the title "A theory of visual attention" (TVA; Bundesen, 1990). TVA was developed from earlier models of visual selection in particular experimental tasks. The first of these models was a "choice model" for visual selection from multi-element displays (Bundesen, Pedersen, & Larsen, 1984). The choice model provides a

Requests for reprints should be addressed to Claus Bundesen, Centre for Visual Cognition, Psychological Laboratory, University of Copenhagen, Njalsgade 90, DK-2300 Copenhagen S, Denmark. E-mail: bundesen@axp.psl.ku.dk

This research was supported by grants from the Danish Ministry of Education and Research and the International Human Frontier Science Program Organization. Thanks are due to Werner Schneider and anonymous reviewers for helpful comments on an earlier draft of the manuscript.

rule for computation of selection probabilities, and it accounts for effects of both the selection criterion and the numbers of targets and distractors in the stimulus. The choice model is simple, and it is described in the first section of this paper.

The second section describes a "race model" for selection from multi-element displays (Bundesen, 1987; Shibuya & Bundesen, 1988). The choice model can be derived from the race model, so the race model explains all that the choice model explains. The race model also provides a picture of the temporal course of processing. The choice model is only a descriptive model, but the race model is a process model.

The third section outlines the more general theory, TVA. The race model can be derived from TVA, so TVA explains all that the race model explains. TVA also provides a picture of the mechanisms by which selection is assumed to be carried out. The race model is only a process model, but TVA is a computational theory of selective attention in vision.

The third section describes further a recent development of TVA, the "CODE theory of visual attention" (CTVA; Logan, 1996; Logan & Bundesen, 1996). TVA organizes a large body of empirical data on human performance in visual recognition and attention tasks, but TVA has been criticized for neglecting spatial effects in visual attention (e.g. van der Heijden, 1993). CTVA combines TVA with a theory of perceptual grouping by proximity (van Oeffelen & Vos, 1982). The resulting theory explains a wide range of spatial effects in visual attention.

The final section considers the neural localization of the operations described in TVA. Pattern recognition and categorization are assumed to occur in a ventral visual pathway, but the ventral stream of processing is modified by attentional weighting. It is suggested that the weighting is done by a system in the posterior parietal cortex that takes input from the ventral pathway and feeds back to the ventral pathway.

CHOICE MODEL

The choice model for visual selection was developed to describe the results of a series of "partial-report" experiments (cf. Sperling, 1960) performed in our laboratory. In a partial-report experiment, the subjects are presented with a briefly exposed visual display showing a number of different elements. The task is to report as many of those elements as possible that satisfy a particular selection criterion (targets) and ignore any other elements (distractors). For example, the display may show a mixture of red and black letters, and the task may be to name as many of the red letters as possible and ignore the black ones (selection by colour). Or the display may show a mixture of letters and digits, and the task may be to report the digits and ignore the letters (selection by alphanumeric class). Usually, the exposure duration is shorter than the reaction time for eye movements so that information from the display must be extracted from a single fixation.

In our early partial-report experiments (Bundesen et al., 1984; Bundesen, Shibuya, & Larsen, 1985), the exposure duration was kept constant at a value of approximately 100 msec. Before and after the presentation of a stimulus display, the field was dark. The selection criterion varied between experiments. We investigated selection by brightness, selection by colour, selection by shape and selection by alphanumeric class. In each experiment with a given selection criterion, we systematically varied both the number of targets and the number of distractors in the displays.

The results showed that the number of correctly reported targets depended on the selection criterion, the number of targets and the number of distractors in the display. The joint effects of the three factors could be described by a simple model, the choice model.

In the choice model for visual selection, subjects can report a given display element if, and only if, they succeed in encoding the element into a short-term memory store with very limited capacity.[1] The capacity is limited to K elements, and K is one of two basic parameters in the model. In the experimental conditions I have described, subjects are assumed to have enough time to encode K elements from the stimulus display; that is, enough time to fill up the short-term store with elements from the display. In these conditions, the number of correctly reported targets depends on the ability of subjects to encode targets rather than distractors into the short-term store.

Read-in to the short-term store is conceived as selective sampling of elements from the stimulus display. Each element in the display has a certain attentional weight. Until the short-term store has been filled up with elements, the probability that any not-yet-encoded element is the next one to be encoded equals the weight of that element divided by the sum of the weights of all those elements that have not yet been encoded (cf. Luce, 1959).

In our experiments, the elements were alphanumeric characters, and it was plausible to assume that targets had higher weights than distractors, but any two targets within the same display had the same weight, and any two distractors within the same display had the same weight. Without loss of generality, then, the weight of a target could be set to 1 and the weight of a distractor to α. Parameter α is the second of the two basic parameters in the model.

Parameter α is a measure of the efficiency of selection. If α equals 0 (i.e. if the weight of a distractor is 0), then the probability that a distractor is encoded into the short-term store also equals 0. Thus, selection is perfect; only targets are encoded. If α equals 1 (i.e. if the weight of a distractor equals the weight of

[1]In some applications of the model, this assumption has been relaxed. Bundesen et al. (1985) assumed that each target that entered the short-term store was correctly reported with probability θ. Our estimate for θ was .92

a target), then the probability that an element is encoded into the short-term store is independent of whether the element is a target or a distractor. Thus, encoding is non-selective.

Figure 1 shows a maximum likelihood fit of the model to results from an experiment on partial report by colour (blue *vs* green; Bundesen et al., 1985). The mean number of correctly reported targets is plotted as a function of the number of distractors (D) in the display with the number of targets in the display as the parameter. The observed data points are marked by squares, circles and a diamond. The curves show predictions from the choice model with short-term storage capacity K at a value of 3.5 elements and parameter α at .06. (Non-integral values of K were treated as probability mixtures. For example, a value of 3.53 for K was treated as a mixture of the values 3 and 4 such that, on any trial, $K = 4$ with a probability of .53).

Figure 2 shows a maximum likelihood fit of the model to results from a similar experiment on partial report by alphanumeric class (letters *vs* digits; Bundesen et al., 1985). The fit was obtained with parameter K at 3.5 elements and parameter α at .42. It is reassuring that the estimate for K was the same for selection by alphanumeric class and for selection by colour; the capacity of the

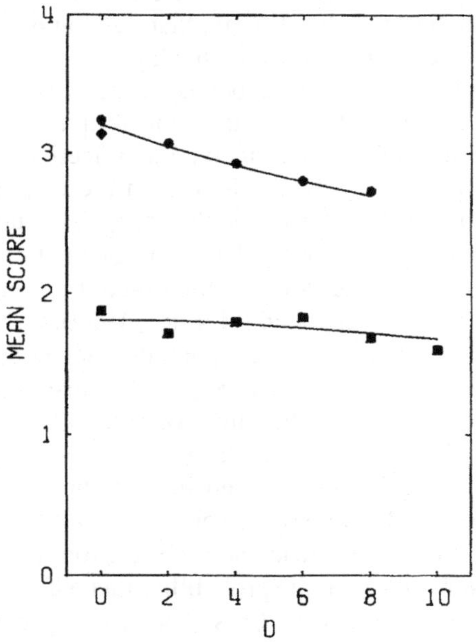

FIG. 1. Number of correctly reported targets (mean score) for subject HS as a function of the number of distractors (D) with the number of targets as a parameter for selection by colour. The number of targets was 2 (squares), 4 (circles) or 12 (diamond). Unmarked points connected by straight lines represent a theoretical fit to the data by the choice model. Reproduced with permission from Bundesen et al. (1985). ©1985 by The International Association for the Study of Attention and Performance.

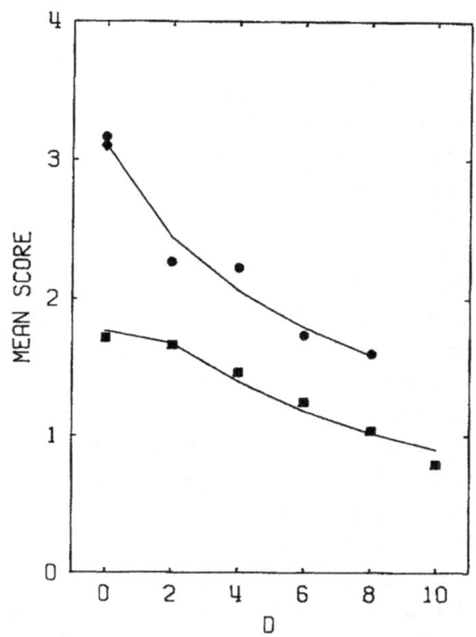

FIG. 2. Number of correctly reported targets (mean score) for subject HS as a function of the number of distractors (D) with the number of targets as a parameter for selection by alphanumeric class. The number of targets was 2 (squares), 4 (circles) of 12 (diamond). Unmarked points connected by straight lines represent a theoretical fit to the data by the choice model. Reproduced with permission from Bundesen et al. (1985). © Copyright 1985 by The International Association for the Study of Attention and Performance.

short-term store should not depend on the selection criterion. The effect of the selection criterion was completely accounted for by variation in parameter α; α was much higher for selection by alphanumeric class than for selection by colour.

RACE MODEL

The choice model is easily understood and readily applied, and it has helped to provide a good description of many experimental results. But the choice model is lacking in depth. It provides a rule for calculating selection probabilities, but it provides no explanation for the rule.

Bundesen et al. (1985) noted that the choice model can be derived from a simple race model of the underlying processes. The race model describes the selection process as a race between the elements in the visual field: The presentation of a stimulus display releases an encoding process for each of the elements in the display, and the elements that are selected are those elements that get encoded into the short-term store before the stimulus presentation terminates and before the short-term store has been filled up. If the encoding times for different elements are stochastically independent and exponentially distributed, the choice model must hold. That is, the choice model can be derived mathematically from the general race model if one assumes that the encoding times are mutually independent, exponentially distributed random variables (Bundesen et al., 1985; also see Bundesen, 1993b).

Shibuya and Bundesen (1988) developed a particular race model called FIRM, which stands for "Fixed-capacity independent race model" (see also Shibuya, 1991). FIRM describes the processing of a stimulus display as a two-stage process. During the first stage of processing, a weight is computed for each element in the display. The weight is a measure of the strength of the sensory evidence that the element is a target.

During the second stage of processing, a fixed amount of processing capacity (C elements per second) is distributed among the elements in the display, and the race between the elements takes place. The amount of processing capacity that is allocated to an element determines how fast the element can be encoded into the short-term store. The total processing capacity of C elements per second is distributed across the elements in proportion to their weights. Thus, every element x is allocated a processing capacity equal to C times the weight of x divided by the sum of weights across all elements.

The time taken to encode an element x is assumed to be exponentially distributed, with probability density function $\mu_x \exp(-\mu_x t)$, where the rate parameter μ_x equals the amount of processing capacity that is allocated to the element. Encoding times for different elements are stochastically independent. The elements actually selected are those elements whose encoding processes are completed before the stimulus presentation terminates and before the short-term store has been filled up.

Because the choice model for visual selection can be derived from FIRM, FIRM explains all that the choice model explains. In addition, FIRM predicts effects of variations in the exposure duration of a stimulus display. Shibuya and Bundesen (1988) tested such predictions in a comprehensive partial-report experiment. The stimulus displays showed mixtures of letters and digits, and the task was to report as many of the digits as possible while ignoring the letters. Exposure durations ranged from 10 to 200 msec, and each display was terminated by a pattern mask.

Figure 3 shows the probability distribution of the number of correctly reported targets as a function of the exposure duration, the number of targets (T) and the number of distractors (D) in the display for one representative subject. For example, the panel in the lower right-hand corner shows the results for displays with six targets and four distractors. The top curve represents the probability that the subject reported at least one element correctly as a function of exposure duration; the curve below shows the probability that the subject reported at least two elements correctly, and so on. The observed data points

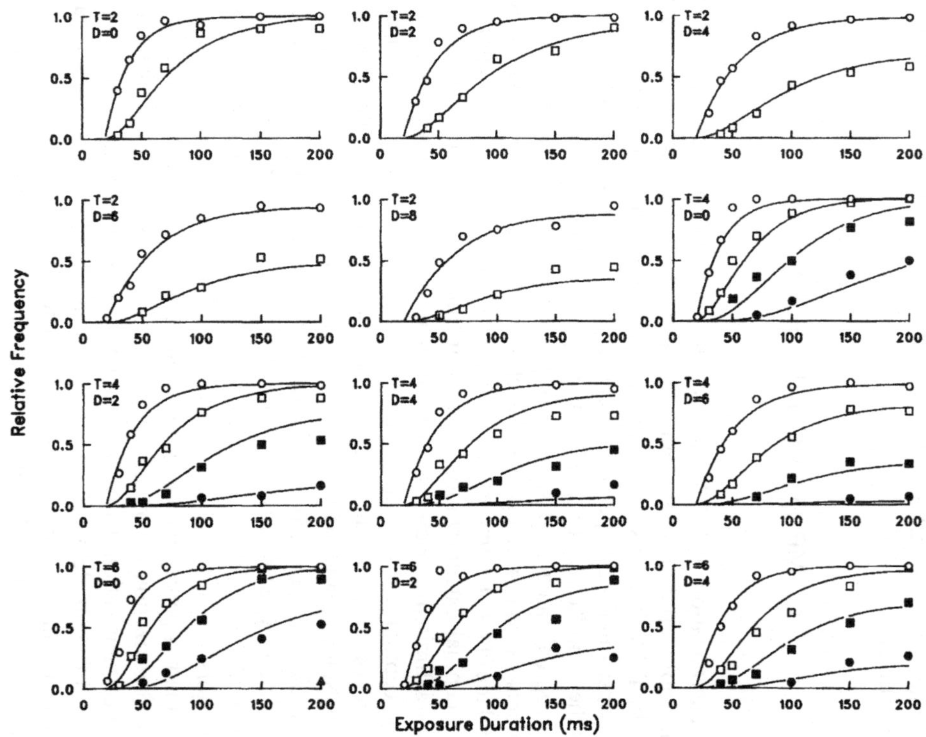

FIG. 3. Relative frequency of scores of *j* or more correctly reported targets as a function of exposure duration, with *j*, number of targets (*T*), and number of distractors (*D*) as parameters in the experiment of Shibuya and Bundesen (1988). Data are shown for subject MP. Parameter *j* varies within panels; *j* is 1 (open circles), 2 (open squares), 3 (solid squares), 4 (solid circles) or 5 (triangle). *T* and *D* vary among panels. Smooth curves represent a theoretical fit to the data by the race model. For clarity, observed frequencies less than 0.02 were omitted from the figure. Reproduced with permission from Shibuya and Bundesen (1988). © 1988 by the American Psychological Association.

are marked by circles and squares. The smooth curves show predictions from FIRM with short-term storage capacity K at a value of 3.7 elements, total processing capacity C at 49 elements per second, and parameter α (the weight ratio of a distractor to a target) at .40. As can be seen, the results agreed well with the predictions.

COMPUTATIONAL THEORY

TVA

TVA is a generalization of FIRM. It integrates findings on single-stimulus recognition, whole report, partial report, detection, and search in a race model framework. In TVA, both visual recognition and selection of elements in the visual field consist in making perceptual categorizations. A perceptual categorization has the form "x belongs to i", where x is an element in the visual field and i is a perceptual category. Examples of perceptual categories are the class of red elements (a colour category), the class of letters of type A (a shape category) and the class of elements in the right visual field (a location category).

That a perceptual categorization is made means that the categorization is encoded into a limited-capacity short-term memory store. If and when one makes the perceptual categorization that x belongs to i (i.e. if and when the perceptual categorization is encoded into the short-term store), element x is said both to be selected and to be recognized as a member of category i. Thus, an element is said to be selected if, and only if, it is recognized as a member of one or other category. Similarly, an element is said to be represented in the short-term store if, and only if, some categorization of the element is represented in the store.

At the moment a perceptual categorization of an element completes processing, the categorization enters the short-term store, provided that memory space for the categorization is available in the store. The capacity of the store is limited to K different elements, and space is available for a new categorization of element x if element x is already represented in the store (with another categorization) or if less than K elements are represented in the store. There is no room for a categorization of element x if the short-term store has been filled up with other elements.

Consider the event that a particular perceptual categorization, "x belongs to i", completes processing at time t. The hazard function of this event has a certain value which I call the v value of the perceptual categorization.[2] Thus the v value is a measure of speed of processing, a measure of the speed at which

[2]The hazard function of the event is the conditional probability that the event occurs at time t, given that the event has not occurred before time t.

the perceptual categorization is processed. In TVA, the v value is determined by two basic equations. By equation 1,

$$v(x, i) = \eta(x, i)\beta_i \frac{w_x}{\sum_{z \in S} w_z} \quad (1)$$

where $\eta(x, i)$ is the instantaneous strength of the sensory evidence that element x belongs to category i; β_i is a perceptual bias associated with category i; S is the set of all elements in the visual field; and w_x and w_z are attentional weights of elements x and z, respectively.

The attentional weights are derived from pertinence values. Every perceptual category is assumed to have a certain pertinence value. The pertinence of a category is a measure of the current importance of attending to elements that belong to the category. The weight of an element x in the visual field is given by equation 2:

$$w_x = \sum_{j \in R} \eta(x, j)\pi_j \quad (2)$$

where R is the set of all perceptual categories; $\eta(x, j)$ is the instantaneous strength of the sensory evidence that element x belongs to category j; and π_j is the pertinence value of category j. By equation 2, the attentional weight of an element is a weighted sum of pertinence values. The pertinence of a given category enters the sum with a weight equal to the strength of the sensory evidence that the element belongs to the category.

By equations 1 and 2, v values can be expressed as functions of eta, beta and pi values. When eta, beta and pi values are given, processing times for different perceptual categorizations are assumed to be stochastically independent.

In most applications of the theory to the analysis of experimental data, eta, beta and pi values are assumed to be constant during the presentation of a stimulus display. When eta, beta and pi values are constant, v values are also constant. The v values were defined as hazard functions, and when v values are kept constant, processing times become exponentially distributed. The v value of the perceptual categorization that element x belongs to category i becomes the exponential rate parameter for the processing time of this perceptual categorization.

Mechanisms of selection

The theory embraces two mechanisms of selection (cf. Broadbent, 1970, 1971): a mechanism for selection of elements (filtering) and a mechanism for selection of categories (pigeonholing). The filtering mechanism is represented by attentional weights, which are derived from pertinence values. As an example, if selection of red elements is required the pertinence of "red" should be high. Equation 2 implies that when "red" has a high pertinence, red elements get high attentional weights. Accordingly, by equation 1, processing of red elements is fast, so red elements are likely to win the processing race and be encoded into the short-term memory store.

The pigeonholing mechanism is represented by perceptual bias parameters. Pertinence values determine which elements are selected, but perceptual bias parameters determine how the elements are categorized. If particular types of categorizations are desired, bias parameters of the relevant categories should be high. By equation 1, then, the desired types of categorizations are likely to be made.

Applications

TVA has been applied to the results of a broad range of paradigms concerned with single-stimulus recognition and selection from multi-element displays (see Bundesen, 1990, 1996). For single-stimulus recognition, the theory provides a simple derivation of a successful model of effects of visual discriminability and bias—the biased-choice model of Luce (1963; see Bundesen, 1990, p. 527).

Parallel Processing. For selection from multi-element displays, the fixed-capacity independent race model, FIRM, can be derived as a special case of TVA. FIRM describes the selection process as a race between the elements in the visual field. TVA describes the selection process as a race between perceptual categorizations of elements in the visual field. The correspondence between FIRM and TVA is established by identifying the encoding of an element in the short-term store with the encoding of a perceptual categorization of the element. The K parameter of FIRM corresponds to the K parameter of TVA, and the attentional weights of FIRM correspond to the attentional weights of TVA, the w parameters.

Consider the C parameter of FIRM and the associated assumption that the total processing capacity is constant. In TVA, the total processing capacity C can be defined as the sum of v values across all perceptual categorizations of all elements in the visual field:

$$C = \sum_{x \in S} \sum_{i \in R} v(x, i) \tag{3}$$

By equation 1 of TVA, C can often be treated as a constant. For example, suppose we are dealing with stimuli that are equal in discriminability, etc., so that there is a constant k such that

$$\sum_{i \in R} \eta(x, i)\beta_i = k$$

for every element x. Equations 1 and 3 then imply that

$$C = \sum_{x \in S} \sum_{i \in R} \eta(x, i) \beta_i w_x / \sum_{z \in S} w_z = k$$

To put this into words, for the stimulus material in question, the total processing capacity C is a constant.

Serial Processing. Serial processing is assumed to occur when the time cost of shifting attention is outweighed by gain in speed of processing once attention has been shifted. For example, suppose targets and distractors are equal in attentional weights, and consider search through a set of two display items. If the items are processed in parallel with a total capacity of C, the mean time to the first completion of an item is $1/C$, but the mean time from the first to the second completion is twice as high, $2/C$. If processing is serial with a capacity of C, the mean time to the first completion is again $1/C$. The mean time from the first to the second completion equals the time taken to shift attention between items plus $1/C$. Therefore, to optimize performance, processing should be serial if, and only if, the time taken to shift attention is less than $1/C$. For example, if $1/C$ is 100 msec per item, processing should be serial if a shift of attention takes less than 100 msec.

Bundesen (1990) extended this line of reasoning and considered the time cost of shifting attention to a group of n items and then processing the n items in parallel. The time cost per member of the group is found to be shortest if group size n is about the same as the product of the processing capacity (C) and the time taken to shift attention. Numerical calculations suggest that typical data on slow feature (Treisman & Gormican, 1988) and conjunction (Treisman & Gelade, 1980) search can be explained by attention shifting among groups of display items, so that processing is parallel within groups but serial between groups (see Bundesen, 1990, p. 537).

CTVA

Logan has recently proposed a theory—the "CODE theory of visual attention" (CTVA)—that integrates space-based and object-based approaches to visual attention (Logan, 1996; see also Logan & Bundesen, 1996). The theory combines TVA with van Oeffelen and Vos' (1982, 1983) "COntour DEtector" (CODE) theory of perceptual grouping by proximity. In the theory of van Oeffelen and Vos, locations of items in visual displays are represented as distributions in one- or two-dimensional space. Van Oeffelen and Vos originally used normal distributions, but Compton and Logan (1993) found that Laplace distributions worked just as well, and they are easier to work with.

Grouping by proximity is modelled as follows (see Fig. 4). First, each stimulus item is represented by a distribution centred on the position that the object occupies in one- or two-dimensional space. In the one-dimensional case

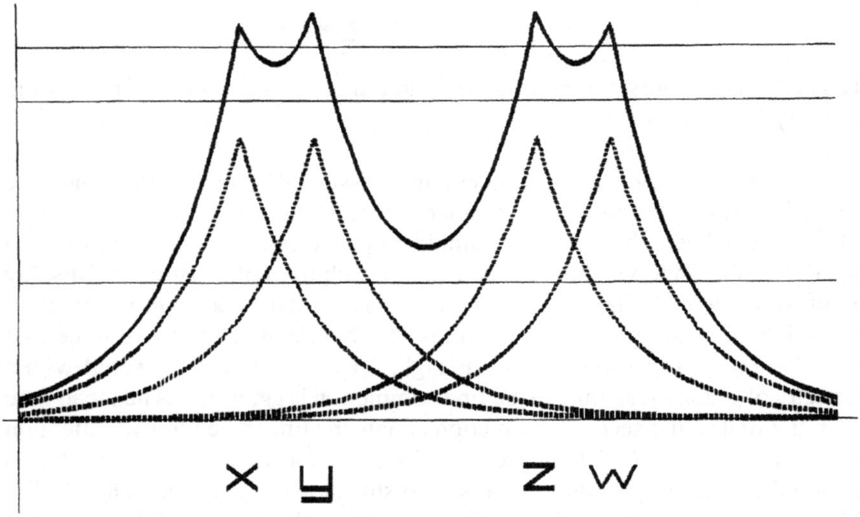

FIG. 4. Perceptual grouping by proximity. Laplace distributions (broken curves) and a CODE surface (solid curve) are shown for four items (x, y, z and w) arrayed in one dimension. Thresholds applied to the CODE surface are shown by horizontal lines. The low threshold includes all four items in one group. The middle threshold generates two groups with two items each. The high threshold separates all four items.

(e.g. a linear array of items positioned along a u-axis), item y may be represented by the Laplace distribution:

$$f_y(u) = \tfrac{1}{2}\lambda_y \exp\left(-\lambda_y \mid u - \theta_y \mid\right) \tag{4}$$

with scale parameter λ_y and position parameter θ_y. Second, a CODE *surface* is constructed by summing the distributions for different items over space. Third, a threshold is applied to the CODE surface, cutting off one or more "above-threshold regions." A perceptual group is defined as an above-threshold region of space; that is, a region for which the code surface is above the threshold.

Groups of different sizes are formed by raising and lowering the threshold. A low threshold produces a small number of groups with many items in each group; a high threshold produces a large number of groups with few items in each. Grouping is hierarchical, so that the smaller groups are nested within the larger groups.

To link CODE to TVA, Logan (1996) assumed that the distribution for an item is a distribution of information about the features of the item. Thus, in equation 4, $f_y(u)$ is the density of information about features of y at spatial position u. Logan further assumed that TVA samples information from one or more above-threshold regions of the CODE surface. An above-threshold region of the CODE surface is the same as an element in the visual field. At any point in time, the set of regions (elements) from which information is being sampled by TVA is called the "field of spatial attention, A" (Logan & Bundesen, 1996). The field of spatial attention can be a single element such as a particular letter in a multi-letter display. The field of spatial attention can also be a set of elements that make up a single higher-level element. One example is the set of all individual letters in a multi-element display. Another example is a set of letters that form a smaller perceptual group within a multi-letter display.

The amount of information in a given above-threshold region of the CODE surface about a feature from a particular stimulus item is called the "feature catch" from that item in the given above-threshold region (see Fig. 5). It equals the area or volume of the distribution for the item that falls within the limits of the above-threshold region. The amount of information is greatest for items that fall within the above-threshold region, in the sense that the points that represent the centres of their distributions fall within the region. The amount of information is positive for all items in the display, but it decreases as the spatial distance of the item from the given region is increased. Accordingly, in CTVA, "location is special" (cf. Bundesen, 1991, 1993a; Nissen, 1985; van der Heijden, 1993; van der Velde & van der Heijden, 1993).

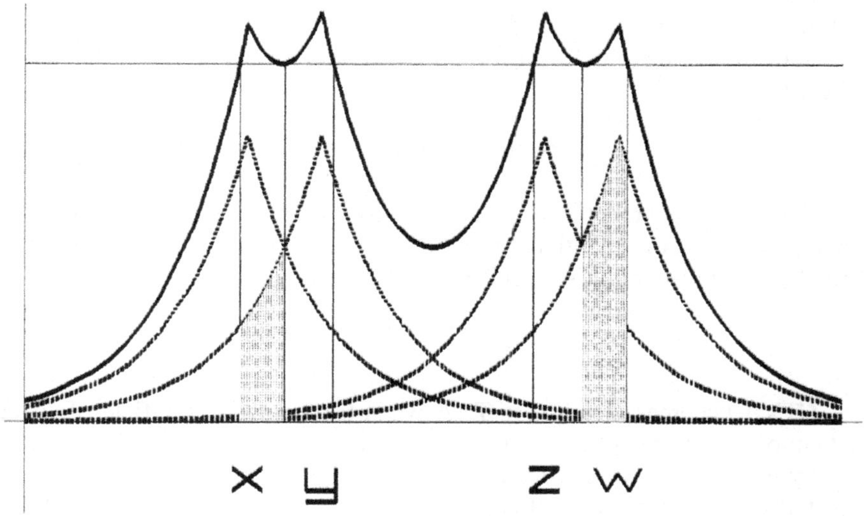

FIG. 5. Feature catch. Laplace distributions (broken curves) and a CODE surface (solid curve) are shown for items *x*, *y*, *z* and *w*. A threshold (horizontal line) applied to the CODE surface generates four above-threshold regions (separated by vertical lines). The feature catch from item *y* in the above-threshold region formed by item *x* [i.e. $c(x, y)$] equals the shaded area to the left. The feature catch from item *w* in the above-threshold region formed by item *w* [i.e. $c(w, w)$] equals the shaded area to the right.

Suppose a threshold is applied to the CODE surface for a multi-element display so that each item in the display forms a separate above-threshold region.[3] Let x and y be items in the display; that is, above-threshold regions of the CODE surface. The catch in the x region of features extracted from the y region, $c(x, y)$, is a measure of the likelihood of sampling features stemming from item y in the processing of item x. In the one-dimensional case,

$$c(x, y) = \int_{\text{region } x} f_y(u)\,du \tag{5}$$

where $f_y(u)$ is given by equation 4, and the integration is done over the above-threshold region formed by item x (cf. Fig. 5).

The feature catch modulates the information input to TVA. Formally, this is represented by replacing eta values $\eta(x, i)$ by "effective" eta values $\eta_e(x, i)$ in equations 1 and 2 of TVA. The effective eta value for the categorization that item x is a member of category i (i.e. x has feature i) is given by:

$$\eta_e(x, i) = \sum_{y \in S} c(x, y)\eta(y, i) \tag{6}$$

where S is the set of all items in the display. By equation 6, the effective evidence that item x has feature i depends upon the evidence that item y has feature i to the extent that features stemming from item y are caught in the above-threshold region formed by item x.

Substituting $\eta_e(x, i)$ for $\eta(x, i)$ in equation 1 of TVA yields the CTVA equation:

$$v(x, i) = \eta_e(x, i)\beta_i \frac{w_x}{\Sigma_{z \in S} w_z} \tag{7}$$

Substituting $\eta_e(x, i)$ for $\eta(x, i)$ in equation 2 of TVA, and incorporating the assumption that the attentional weight of an item is 0 if the item is outside the field of spatial attention A, yields the CTVA equation

$$w_x = \begin{cases} \Sigma_{j \in R}\, \eta_e(x, j)\pi_j & \text{if } x \in A \\ 0 & \text{if } x \notin A \end{cases} \tag{8}$$

CTVA becomes identical to TVA when (a) $A = S$ (i.e. the field of spatial attention coincides with the set of items in the display) and (b) $c(x, x) = 1$ for every item x, but $c(x, y) = 0$ when x is different from y. For example, in many partial-report experiments, it is plausible that (a) the field of spatial attention encompasses all items in the display, and (b) inter-item distances are so long

[3] The condition that each item in the display forms a separate above-threshold region allows feature catch factors to be written as functions of ordered pairs of items, $c(x, y)$. This makes the present formalization more simple than the formalizations in Logan (1996) and Logan and Bundesen (1996)

that feature catches from adjacent items can be neglected. In such cases, an analysis based on CTVA reduces to an analysis based on TVA (e.g. an analysis in terms of the fixed-capacity independent race model of Shibuya & Bundesen, 1988). Thus, CTVA can be viewed as a generalization of TVA, and TVA can be viewed as a special case of CTVA.

Parallel Processing and Feature Integration. Implicit in the account of CTVA by Logan and Bundesen (1996) is a distinction between two types of parallel processing of a multi-element display. The first type of parallel processing is used when a low threshold is applied to the CODE surface, so that the whole stimulus display is processed as a single unit. In this case, feature catch factors are close to 1, so processing is fast, but all features that are extracted are bound to the display as a whole, rather than being bound to the individual elements in the display. Being bound to the display as a whole, the features may be thought of as "free-floating" within the display (c.f. Treisman & Gelade, 1980; Treisman & Schmidt, 1982).

The second type of parallel processing requires that a high threshold is applied to the CODE surface, so that each element in the display is represented by a separate above-threshold region of the CODE surface. In this case, feature catch factors are well below 1, so processing is not so fast, but features are bound to individual elements and not to the display as a whole.

To illustrate the distinction between the two types of parallel processing, consider some recent results reported by Cave (1994; see also Kim & Cave, 1995). In one experiment, subjects searched for the letter *F* in a display of eight letters. The search display was occasionally followed by a probe, which was a small square at one of the eight letter locations. Responses to probes at the target's location were faster than responses to probes at distractor locations, and the size of this difference was greater when the distractor set included letters that were highly confusible with the target (e.g. *E* and *P*). Cave concluded that effects of selective attention were stronger when the distractors were physically more similar to the target.

A possible explanation of the findings of Cave (1994) is as follows. Performance reflected a mixture of the two types of parallel processing. When target–distractor similarity was low, parallel processing with a low threshold predominated. In this case, search was undertaken by testing for the presence of a particular feature in the stimulus display (c.f. the account of "feature search" in the theory of Treisman & Gelade, 1980). The whole display was processed as a single unit and the subject tested whether the unit (the display) had a particular (target-specific) feature. Because the display was processed as a single unit, all features that were extracted were bound to the display as a whole, rather than being bound to units at the level of individual letters. With only one unit in the visual field, that unit received all of the available processing capacity. There was no attenuation of processing due to spatial attention, so processing was fast. When this mode of processing was used, reaction times to probe dots were the same for dots presented at target locations as for dots presented at distractor locations.

When target–distractor similarity was high, parallel processing with a high threshold predominated. Performance could not be based on whether a particular visual feature was present or absent in the display, and search was undertaken by processing target and distractors in parallel as individual units. Thus, spatial attention was directed to the individual letters, so that the attended part of the visual field was restricted to a set of spatial regions, one for each letter; rates of processing were then attenuated, but features were bound to individual letters and not to the display as a whole. In this mode of processing, the target and distractors competed for processing capacity, but the target had a higher attentional weight than the distractors, so the target attracted more processing capacity than the distractors (cf. equation 7). By spatial and temporal proximity, the probe dot tended to be included in the same perceptual unit as the (target or distractor) letter it replaced, so the probe dot received more processing capacity when it replaced a target than a distractor. Hence, when this mode of processing was used, processing of the probe dot was faster for dots presented at target locations than for dots presented at distractor locations.

Other Applications. Logan (1996) applied CTVA to the results of a number of studies on the effects of perceptual grouping and spatial distance between items on reaction times and error rates in visual attention tasks. The studies included effects of grouping (Prinzmetal, 1981) and effects of distance between items (Cohen & Ivry, 1989) on occurrence of illusory conjunctions, effects of grouping (Banks & Prinzmetal, 1976) and effects of distance between items (Cohen & Ivry, 1991) in visual search, and effects of distance between target and distractors in the flankers task (Eriksen & Eriksen, 1974). Logan and Bundesen (1996) applied CTVA to a variety of spatial effects in partial report (e.g. Mewhort, Campbell, Marchetti, & Campbell, 1981). Providing quantitative accounts for such phenomena seems an important step forward.

NEURAL LOCALIZATION

Figure 6 is a flowchart of the algebraic operations of equations 1 and 2 of TVA.[4] Figure 6 can also be viewed as a flowchart of the corresponding operations in CTVA (equations 7 and 8). The latter view presupposes that (a) the eta values

---

[4]In Fig. 6, equation 1 of TVA is implemented by first multiplying $\eta(x, i)$ by β_i and then multiplying the product of $\eta(x, i)$ and β_i by $w_x/\Sigma_{z \in S} w_z$. Alternatively, the equation could be implemented by first multiplying $\eta(x, i)$ by $w_x/\Sigma_{z \in S} w_z$ and then multiplying by β_i.

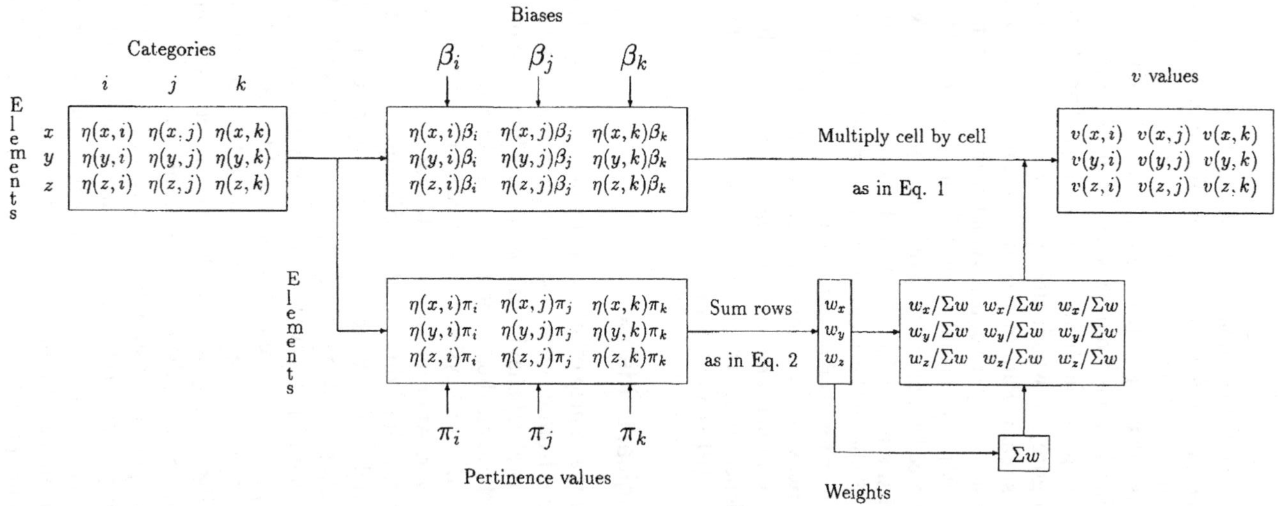

FIG. 6. Flowchart of the algebraic operations of equations 1 and 2 of TVA.

in the figure are interpreted as effective eta values [e.g. $\eta(x, i)$ is interpreted as $\eta_e(x, i)$], and (b) the set of items shown in the figure is the set of items in the field of spatial attention (i.e. $A = \{x, y, z\}$).

Figure 6 suggests a distinction between two streams of processing—a main stream of processing leading from sensory input to pattern recognition and categorization (the upper route from left to right), and an attentional loop (the lower part of the figure), in which attentional weights are computed and fed back to the main stream. Pattern recognition and categorization are often assumed to be subserved by a ventral visual pathway running from primary visual cortex (area V1) via visual areas V2 and V4 to infero-temporal (IT) cortex (see Goodale & Milner, 1992; Mishkin, Ungerleider, & Macko, 1983; Ungerleider & Mishkin, 1982). On this hypothesis, the main stream of processing in Fig. 6 should be located in the ventral pathway. The loop for attentional weighting should take input from the ventral pathway and feed back to the ventral pathway, but intermediate computations in the loop may be undertaken in dorsal rather than ventral areas of the brain. Indeed, as argued below, extant evidence suggests that the attentional weights are represented in the posterior parietal (PP) cortex (for related suggestions, see Schneider, 1995).

Electrophysiological Evidence

Results suggesting that a map of attentional weights is located in the posterior parietal cortex come from electrophysiological studies of visual responses of parietal neurons in awake, behaving monkeys. Bushnell, Goldberg and Robinson (1981) trained the same rhesus monkeys on several visual tasks. In one task (the fixation task), the monkeys were required to fixate a spot of light turned on by pressing a lever. After an unpredictable interval (1–4 sec), the fixation point dimmed and remained dim for about 500 msec. If the monkey released the lever while the light was dim, he was rewarded by receiving a drop of water. A second spot of light presented in the periphery of the visual field shortly after the onset of the fixation point was behaviourally irrelevant to the monkey. Another task (the peripheral attention task) was like the fixation task, except that on 50% of the trials the peripheral stimulus dimmed but not the fixation point. In this task, the monkey should release the lever in response to dimming of either the fixation point or the peripheral stimulus.

Responses to the peripheral stimulus were recorded from single neurons in area 7 of posterior parietal cortex. About half of the studied cells showed a significantly stronger response (i.e. greater increase in the rate of firing) to the peripheral stimulus in the peripheral attention task than in the fixation task. A similar enhancement of the visual response to the peripheral stimulus (relative to the response to the peripheral stimulus in the fixation task) was found in tasks in which the monkeys were required to make a saccadic eye movement to the peripheral stimulus or to reach out and touch the stimulus. The fact that the enhancement occurred when the monkeys behaved differently when attending to the stimulus suggested that the enhancement was involved in a general process of visual selective attention. In particular, the results seem consistent with the hypothesis that the rate of firing in a neuron with the peripheral stimulus in its receptive field represented the attentional weight of the peripheral stimulus.

Bushnell et al. (1981) noted that area 7 receives rich inputs from the limbic system (substantia innominata, claustrum and cingulate gyrus). They suggested that, whereas the activity in the limbic neurons depends on the way in which the stimulus is pertinent to the animal (the quality of the motivation involved), "area 7 may serve to integrate motivation-specific information into a general attentional mechanism" (p. 769). More specifically, the summation described in equation 2 of TVA may be done in area 7.

Neuropsychological Evidence

Posner, Walker, Friedrich and Rafal (1984) investigated effects of parietal injury on allocation of attention. Patients with unilateral damage to the parietal lobe were tested using the cost–benefit cueing paradigm developed by Posner and his associates (e.g. Posner, Nissen, & Ogden, 1978). The patients were instructed to fixate the centre of a screen where the outline of a small box was presented. Each trial began with a cue event, which was a brief brightening of one of two peripheral boxes located at 8° to the left and 8° to the right of the fixation box, respectively. At intervals varying from 0 to 1000 msec after cue onset, a bright asterisk (target) was presented in one of the peripheral boxes. On 80% of the trials, the target appeared in the cued box, so that the cue was valid. On the remaining 20% of the trials, the target appeared in the uncued peripheral box, so that the cue was invalid. In either case, the subject's task was to press a single key as quickly as possible whenever the target appeared.

The main findings of Posner et al. (1984) are illustrated in Table 1. The data in the table are mean reaction times for the group of six patients with right-hemisphere lesions on trials with a cue–target interval of 1000 msec. When the cue was valid, there was only a modest advantage of targets on the side ipsilateral to the lesion. When the cue was invalid, reaction times were longer, and there was a greater advantage of targets on the side ipsilateral to the lesion. Thus, very long reaction times were noted when the cue indicated that the target would appear on the same side as the lesion, but the target in fact appeared on the opposite side. Posner et al. (1984) explained this "extinction-like" reaction time pattern by assuming that the parietal patients had problems in "disengaging" attention from stimuli on the side ipsilateral to their lesion.

The parietal patients of Posner et al. (1984) showed no general deficit in disengaging attention. Posner et al. proposed that the patients showed a deficit in disengaging attention from particular spatial locations (viz., locations on the

TABLE 1
Observed and Predicted Mean Reaction Times for Right Parietal Patients in the Main Experiment of Posner et al. (1984)

	Side Relative to Lesion			
	Contralateral		*Ipsilateral*	
Cue Validity	*Observed*	*Predicted*	*Observed*	*Predicted*
Invalid	906	910	629	625
Valid	564	548	461	477

Note: The observed data are mean reaction times (msec) for the group of six patients with right parietal lesions on trials with a cue-target interval of 1000 msec. The means are calculated from the data presented in Table 3 of Posner et al. (1984). The predictions assume that attentional weights were reduced by 36% in the contralesional visual field

side ipsilateral to the lesion). Later work with parietal patients by Posner, Walker, Friedrich and Rafal (1987) indicated that, when both the cue and the target appeared on the side ipsilateral to the lesion, but the target was displaced from the cued location, reactions were slower when the direction of the displacement was contralesional rather than ipsilesional. Posner et al. (1987) tentatively concluded that the patients showed a deficit in disengaging attention from a spatial location when the disengagement operation should be followed by a movement of attention in the contralesional direction.

A simpler explanation of the extinction-like reaction time pattern found in parietal patients by Posner et al. (1984, 1987) is based on the assumption that the attentional weight of an element was lower, the farther the element was moved in the contralesional direction. This is illustrated by the predicted values in Table 1.

The predictions in Table 1 were based on TVA and the assumption that attentional weights of elements (target or noise) at the ipsilesional stimulus location were normal, but weights of elements at the contralesional location were reduced to a certain proportion, m, of their normal value. Following Bundesen (1990, p. 532), the ratio of the normal value of the weight of an element (target or noise) on the cued side to the normal value of the weight of an element on the uncued side was assumed to be 2:1. For the patients, therefore, the ratio of the attentional weight of a cued target on the contralesional side (*valid, contra*) to noise on the ipsilesional side should be $2m$:1. The weight ratio of an uncued target on the ipsilesional side (*invalid, ipsi*) to contralesional noise should be 1:$2m$. The weight ratio of a cued target on the ipsilesional side (*valid, ipsi*) to contralesional noise should be 2:m, and the weight ratio of an uncued target on the contralesional side (*invalid, contra*) to ipsilesional noise should be m:2. The predicted mean reaction times are given by:

$$E(\mathrm{RT} \mid \text{valid, contra}) = [C \times 2m/(2m + 1)]^{-1} + b$$
$$E(\mathrm{RT} \mid \text{invalid, ipsi}) = [C \times 1/(2m + 1)]^{-1} + b$$
$$E(\mathrm{RT} \mid \text{valid, ipsi}) = [C \times 2/(2 + m)]^{-1} + b$$
$$E(\mathrm{RT} \mid \text{invalid, contra}) = [C \times m/(2 + m)]^{-1} + b$$

where C is the overall rate of processing and b is a base reaction time.

The fit shown in Table 1 was obtained with processing rate C at 6.48 elements per second, base reaction time b at 273 msec, and parameter m at 0.64. Note that b and C act only as translation and scaling parameters. What captures the observed extinction-like reaction time pattern is the hypothesis that weights at the contralesional stimulus location were reduced by a fixed proportion. The estimated value of 0.64 for m means that attentional weights were reduced by 36% at the location contralateral to the lesion.

CONCLUSION

Results from both electrophysiological and neuropsychological studies seem to suggest that attentional weights are represented in posterior parietal cortex. The evidence seems to suggest that the attentional loop in Fig. 6 takes input from the ventral pathway and feeds back to the ventral pathway, but the loop goes through the posterior parietal cortex. As suggested by Posner and Petersen (1990), transfer of information between the ventral system and the posterior parietal cortex may occur through the thalamus (cf. Petersen, Robinson, & Morris, 1987). A rough sketch of the anatomical localization of the information flows shown in Fig. 6 is thus available. I am currently working on more detailed models of the way in which the operations described in TVA and CTVA may be implemented in the brain.

REFERENCES

Banks, W.P., & Prinzmetal, W. (1976). Configurational effects in visual information processing. *Perception and Psychophysics, 19*, 361–367.

Broadbent, D.E. (1970). Stimulus set and response set: Two kinds of selective attention. In D.I. Mostofsky (Ed.), *Attention: Contemporary theory and analysis* (pp. 51–60). New York: Appleton-Century-Crofts.

Broadbent, D.E. (1971). *Decision and stress*. London: Academic Press.

Bundesen, C. (1987). Visual attention: Race models for selection from multielement displays. *Psychological Research, 49*, 113–121.

Bundesen, C. (1990). A theory of visual attention. *Psychological Review, 97*, 523–547.

Bundesen, C. (1991). Visual selection of features and objects: Is location special? A reinterpretation of Nissen's (1985) findings. *Perception and Psychophysics, 50*, 87–89.

Bundesen, C. (1993a). The notion of elements in the visual field in a theory of visual attention: A reply to van der Velde and van der Heijden (1993). *Perception and Psychophysics, 53*, 350–352.

Bundesen, C. (1993b). The relationship between independent race models and Luce's choice axiom. *Journal of Mathematical Psychology, 37*, 446–471.

Bundesen, C. (1996). Formal models of visual attention: A tutorial review. In A.F. Kramer, M.G.H. Coles, & G.D. Logan (Eds), *Converging operations in the study of visual selective attention* (pp. 1–43). Washington, DC: American Psychological Association.

Bundesen, C., Pedersen, L.F., & Larsen, A. (1984). Measuring efficiency of selection from briefly exposed visual displays: A model for partial report. *Journal of Experimental Psychology: Human Perception and Performance, 10*, 329–339.

Bundesen, C., Shibuya, H., & Larsen, A. (1985). Visual selection from multielement displays: A model for partial report. In M.I. Posner & O.S.M. Marin (Eds), *Attention and performance XI* (pp. 631–649). Hillsdale, NJ: Lawrence Erlbaum Associates Inc.

Bushnell, M.C., Goldberg, M.E., & Robinson, D.L. (1981). Behavioral enhancement of visual responses in monkey cerebral cortex. I. Modulation in posterior parietal cortex related to selective visual attention. *Journal of Neurophysiology, 46*, 755–772.

Cave, K.R. (1994). Changes in the strength of spatial attention. Poster session presented at the conference on *Converging Operations in the Study of Visual Selective Attention*, University of Illinois at Urbana-Champaign, May.

Cohen, A., & Ivry, R. (1989). Illusory conjunctions inside and outside the focus of attention. *Journal of Experimental Psychology: Human Perception and Performance, 15*, 650–663.

Cohen, A., & Ivry, R.B. (1991). Density effects in conjunction search: Evidence for a coarse location mechanism of feature integration. *Journal of Experimental Psychology: Human Perception and Performance, 17*, 891–901.

Compton, B.J., & Logan, G.D. (1993). Evaluating a computational model of perceptual grouping by proximity. *Perception and Psychophysics, 53*, 403–421.

Eriksen, B.A., & Eriksen, C.W. (1974). Effects of noise letters upon the identification of a target letter in a nonsearch task. *Perception and Psychophysics, 16*, 143–149.

Goodale, M.A., & Milner, A.D. (1992). Separate visual pathways for perception and action. *Trends in Neurosciences, 15*, 20–25.

Kim, M.-S., & Cave, K.R. (1995). Spatial attention in visual search for features and feature conjunctions. *Psychological Science, 6*, 376–380.

Logan, G.D. (1996). The CODE theory of visual attention: An integration of space-based and object-based attention. *Psychological Review, 103*, 603–649.

Logan, G.D., & Bundesen, C. (1996). Spatial effects in the partial report paradigm: A challenge for theories of visual spatial attention. In D.L. Medin (Ed.), *The psychology of learning and motivation* (Vol. 35, pp. 243–282). San Diego, CA: Academic Press.

Luce, R.D. (1959). *Individual choice behavior*. New York: Wiley.

Luce, R.D. (1963). Detection and recognition. In R.D. Luce, R.R. Bush, & E. Galanter (Eds), *Handbook of mathematical psychology* (Vol. 1, pp. 103–189). New York: Wiley.

Mewhort, D.J.K., Campbell, A.J., Marchetti, F.M., & Campbell, J.I.D. (1981). Identification, localization, and "iconic memory": An evaluation of the bar probe task. *Memory and Cognition, 9*, 50–67.

Mishkin, M., Ungerleider, L.G., & Macko, K.A. (1983). Object vision and spatial vision: Two cortical pathways. *Trends in Neurosciences, 6*, 414–417.

Nissen, M.J. (1985). Accessing features and objects: Is location special? In M.I. Posner & O.S.M. Marin (Eds), *Attention and performance XI* (pp. 205–219). Hillsdale, NJ: Lawrence Erlbaum Associates Inc.

Petersen, S.E., Robinson, D.L., & Morris, J.D. (1987). Contributions of the pulvinar to visual spatial attention. *Neuropsychologia, 25*, 97–105..

Posner, M.I., Nissen, M.J., & Ogden, W.C. (1978). Attended and unattended processing modes: The role of set for spatial location. In H.L. Pick & E. Saltzman (Eds), *Modes of perceiving and processing information* (pp. 137–157). Hillsdale, NJ: Lawrence Erlbaum Associates Inc.

Posner, M.I., & Petersen, S.E. (1990). The attention system of the human brain. *Annual Review of Neuroscience, 13*, 25–42.

Posner, M.I., Walker, J.A., Friedrich, F.J., & Rafal, R.D. (1984). Effects of parietal injury on covert orienting of attention. *Journal of Neuroscience, 4*, 1863–1874.

Posner, M.I., Walker, J.A., Friedrich, F.J., & Rafal, R.D. (1987). How do the parietal lobes direct covert attention? *Neuropsychologia, 25*, 135–145.

Prinzmetal, W. (1981). Principles of feature integration in visual perception. *Perception and Psychophysics, 30*, 330–340.

Schneider, W.X. (1995). VAM: A neuro-cognitive model for visual attention control of segmentation, object recognition, and space-based motor action. *Visual Cognition, 2*, 331–375.

Shibuya, H. (1991). Comparison between stochastic models for visual selection. In J.-P. Doignon & J.-C. Falmagne (Eds), *Mathematical psychology: Current developments* (pp. 337–356). New York: Springer-Verlag.

Shibuya, H., & Bundesen, C. (1988). Visual selection from multielement displays: Measuring and modeling effects of exposure duration. *Journal of Experimental Psychology: Human Perception and Performance, 14*, 591–600.

Sperling, G. (1960). The information available in brief visual presentations. *Psychological Monographs, 74*(11, Whole No. 498).

Treisman, A.M., & Gelade, G. (1980). A feature-integration theory of attention. *Cognitive Psychology, 12*, 97–136.

Treisman, A.M., & Gormican, S. (1988). Feature analysis in early vision: Evidence from search asymmetries. *Psychological Review, 95*, 15–48.

Treisman, A., & Schmidt, H. (1982). Illusory conjunctions in the perception of objects. *Cognitive Psychology, 14*, 107–141.

Ungerleider, L.G., & Mishkin, M. (1982). Two cortical visual systems. In D.J. Ingle, M.A. Goodale, & R.J.W. Mansfield (Eds), *Analysis of visual behavior* (pp. 549–586). Cambridge, MA: MIT Press.

van der Heijden, A.H.C. (1993). The role of position in object selection in vision. *Psychological Research, 56*, 44–58.

van der Velde, F., & van der Heijden, A.H.C. (1993). An element in the visual field is just a conjunction of attributes: A critique of Bundesen (1991). *Perception and Psychophysics, 53*, 345–349.

van Oeffelen, M.P., & Vos, P.G. (1982). Configurational effects on the enumeration of dots: Counting by groups. Memory and Cognition, 10, 396–404.

van Oeffelen, M.P., & Vos, P.G. (1983). An algorithm for pattern description on the level of relative proximity. Pattern Recognition, 16, 341–348.

Subject index